Eyewitness

Eyewitness
A Filmmaker's Memoir
of the Chicano Movement

Jesús Salvador Treviño

Arte Público Press
Houston, Texas

This volume is made possible through grants from the Charles Stewart Mott Foundation, the Ewing Marion Kauffman Foundation, the Rockefeller Foundation, and the City of Houston through The Cultural Arts Council of Houston, Harris County.

Recovering the past, creating the future

Arte Público Press
University of Houston
Houston, Texas 77204-2174

Cover design by James Brisson
Cover photos courtesy of George Rodríguez

Treviño, Jesús Salvador.
    Eyewitness: a filmmaker's memoir of the Chicano Movement / by Jesús Salvador Treviño.
    p. cm.
    ISBN 1-55885-349-9 (trade pbk. : alk. paper)
    1. Mexican Americans—Civil rights—History—20th century. 2. Civil rights movements—United States—History—20th century. 3. United States—Ethnic relations 4. Treviño, Jesús Salvador. 5. Mexican Americans—Biography. 6. Motion picture producers and directors—United States—Biography. 7. Civil rights workers—United States—Biography. I. Title.
    2001
    813'.54—dc21
                                         2001035545
                                               CIP

1 2 3 4 5 6 7 8 9 0   10 9 8 7 6 5 4 3 2 1

Table of Contents

Foreword

The 1960s and 1970s were critical years for Latino community organizing and advocacy across the United States. Spanish-speaking peoples from New York to San Antonio and from Chicago to California's Central Valley were engaged in groundbreaking civil rights efforts during these years. These efforts, which built on earlier decades of struggle by Latino and Latina activists, established the national Hispanic population as an important new factor in U.S. society and race relations. But the gains achieved through this work were particularly hard fought.

The most volatile and probably the most challenging region of Latino activism during this era was southern California. In Los Angeles, levels of discrimination and institutional racism targeted to Mexican Americans were especially pronounced. Not surprisingly, therefore, some of the most important events in Chicano community development occurred in Los Angeles during the late 1960s and early 1970s. The Chicano student blowouts, the Chicano moratorium, and the killing of *Los Angeles Times* correspondent Rubén Salazar at the Silver Dollar Cafe in East Los Angeles were all sources of fuel for a national movement that would forever change the face of Latino identity and politics in America.

During these years, more so than now even, Latino presence in the national media was extremely muted, almost non-existent. Television was an especially vacant space for Chicano and other Latino reporters and commentators. The absence of Latino perspectives on the news and events shaping the times, in turn, mitigated public attention to the compelling case of disaffected Spanish-speaking communities relative to the need for national reforms in education, employment, political representation, and access to essential public goods. The net effect of this relative absence in the public sphere was continuing institutional disregard for Latino rights and opportunities nationwide.

One of the foremost exceptions to the general invisibility of Latino voices during the movement years was Jesús Salvador Treviño. From his base at KCET-TV in Los Angeles, Treviño, a young recent college graduate, found himself cast as one of the only Latino media professionals to produce and host public affair talk shows and documentaries on the Public Broadcasting System during the early 1970s. Treviño, himself a product of the Mexican American experience in Los Angeles, gave unprecedented perspective and authenticity to public reporting on the major events of the Chicano Movement.

Being a Los Angeles native and a product of the barrio, Treviño was personally affected by the events of the era. His younger sister had been one of the students involved in the walkouts at Woodrow Wilson High School that began more aggressive Chicano community protest efforts to reform the Los Angeles Unified School System. He and his then wife, Gayla, were at the scene of the Los Angeles Sheriff's Department assault on peaceful Chicano protesters against the Vietnam War in East L.A.'s Belvedere Park, where, nearby, only a few hours later, Los Angeles County Sheriffs' fire would kill Rubén Salazar.

Because of his personal appreciation of the significance of these developments, Treviño subsequently pursued historic filmmaking efforts to capture the national Chicano/Latino Movement. This engagement involved him with the major protest leaders of the day, including Rodolfo "Corky" Gonzales in Denver, José Angel Gutiérrez in Texas, and Reies López Tijerina in New Mexico. Treviño's coverage of these leaders' work and ideas would help to document pivotal moments in the Movement.

Significantly, Treviño's contributions to expanding public understanding of the issues were not limited to reporting in established mainstream venues and ways. Treviño was a trailblazer in the development of important new, Latino-produced and Latino-directed news reporting, documentary film production, and public television programming. This work included decidedly political and public interest content. *Ahora!*, *Requiem 29, América Tropical*, and *Yo Soy Chicano* were among the many important shows and documentaries Treviño helped to birth during the early 1970s. (Later on, during the 1990s, Treviño was also one of the leading producers of the landmark PBS series: *Chicano! The History of the Mexican American Civil Rights Movement.* Treviño's programs helped to put Mexican Americans on the map, often for the first time, in Anglo homes across the nation.

In addition to these important accomplishments, Treviño's work engaged him with some of the great figures of modern Mexican and Chicano cultural expression, including the painter David Alfaro Siqueiros and theater director and film producer Luis Valdez. His important interviews and interactions with these key individuals add weight to Treviño as an "eyewitness" to history.

Treviño's body of work throughout the Movement years, and his colorful, yet balanced recollections of the times that shaped that work, are vividly captured in the pages that follow. "History is as the media tells us it is," writes Treviño in his Preface to *Eyewitness: A Filmmaker's Memoir of the Chicano Movement.* "The converse is also true," he goes on to add: "If mass media ignores an event, it simply didn't happen." But the struggle for justice by Chicano and other Latino Americans has been a real and longstanding one, full of important events and contributions that have compelled America to become a more inclusive and culturally expansive society. As Treviño reminds us:

Americans might be surprised to learn that Mexican Americans championed equal education under the law long before the historic *Brown v. Topeka Board of Education* Supreme Court decision or that the success of the Brown ruling was based, in part, upon the precedent set down in the Mexican American case of *Méndez v. Westminster Board of Education.* Americans are unlikely to know that Mexican Americans were key protagonists in challenging the system by which minority voters were gerrymandered in voting districts, or that Mexican Americans were involved in labor actions that have benefited all Americans such as securing an eight-hour workday.

Why are most Americans not familiar with these facts?

The answer is simple. Yesterday, when the events occurred, these events were simply not reported or their importance was downplayed. Mexican Americans were not the minority of record. They were, as so often described, the "invisible minority."

Today, as Hispanics are projected to comprise fully one-quarter of the U.S. population by 2050, it is more imperative than ever that Americans of all backgrounds learn about the important historical experiences and contributions of Spanish-speaking peoples in American society. The University of Houston, Arte Público Press Hispanic Civil Rights Series is intended to help expand public understanding of these experiences and contributions. With major support from funders, including the Charles Stewart Mott Foundation, the Ewing Marion Kauffman Foundation, and the Rockefeller Foundation, Arte Público will produce more than twenty works over the coming years, chronicling the leaders, the organizations, and the events that have shaped U.S. civil rights and social justice from a Latino perspective. These works will seek, especially, to educate younger readers, many of whom were not yet born before the 1980s, as well as general readers interested in the field, about this critical, yet heretofore largely overlooked aspect of American history. The series will add new perspective on what it means to be an American at a time when expanding diversity and multiculturalism make it essential for all of us to expand our notions of the American experience and community.

Arte Público Press is pleased and proud to include Jesús Salvador Treviño's reflections on key moments in post-war Hispanic civil rights as one of the leading works in our series. His recount of the Chicano Movement's most active years, and of the media's role both in resisting and advancing the Movement's aims, are as important and informative today as they were then. Like the other works in our series, *Eyewitness: A Filmmaker's Memoir of the Chicano Movement* will contribute mightily to the public record and establish itself as a staple of study curricula, library collections, and community discourse across the United States for years to come.

Henry A. J. Ramos
Executive Editor
Arte Público Press Hispanic Civil Rights Series

Preface

In his autobiography *My Last Sigh*, the Spanish director Luis Buñuel writes about the relationship between memory and personal identity: "Our memory is our coherence, our reason, our feeling, even our action. Without it, we are nothing."

In George Orwell's prophetic novel *1984*, memory is linked to the *collective* identity of society. When his protagonist Winston Smith, encounters Big Brother's propaganda about the immediate past, he realizes that history is being constantly altered around him. Here, the very essence of a society, the truth of its existence, is being changed. Winston's individual memory is the only witness, the only link to society's real history:

> But where did that knowledge exist? Only in his own consciousness, which in any case must soon be annihilated. And if all others accepted the lie that the Party imposed—if all records told the same lie—then the lie passed into history and became the truth.

While we may not have a malevolent Big Brother monitoring us and daily altering yesterday's fact, we do have omnipresent mass media that in many ways serve a similar function. The evening news, documentaries, primetime television, radio, movies, and other forms of popular culture establish the facts of record, set the tone and parameters for their acceptance, endorse what will be remembered as historically important, and sanction what is valid in society.

From time to time, these facts of record are passed on to posterity through remembrance ceremonies such as anniversaries, revivals, sequels, and rediscoveries of events and individuals. They soon become incontrovertible history. It is the collective voice of mass media that can manipulate and alter our history—at times into a semblance virtually unrecognizable by the individuals who experienced it. *History is as the media tell us it is.*

The converse is also true. If mass media ignore an event, it simply didn't happen. Although individuals may remember the importance of a given event, unless validated by media, its significance for society may be forever lost in a black hole of cultural forgetfulness.

Mexican Americans know this only too well. The images remembered from television and print coverage of the 1960s, for example, featured white anti-war protesters at the Chicago Democratic National Convention, police dogs attacking black civil rights demonstrators in Alabama, or hippies smoking pot in San Francisco's Golden Gate Park. Yet, during the 1960s, an important movement for civil rights and for self-affirmation and identity was under way in the urban barrios and rural *campos* of America.

Americans might be surprised to learn that Mexican Americans championed equal education under the law long before the historic Brown vs. Topeka Board of Education Supreme Court decision or that the success of the Brown ruling was based, in part, upon the precedent set down in the Mexican-American case of Méndez vs. Westminister Board of Education. Americans are unlikely to know that Mexican Americans were key protagonists in challenging the system by which minority voters were gerrymandered in voting districts, or that Mexican Americans were involved in labor actions that have benefitted all Americans—such as securing an eight-hour work day.

Why are most Americans not familiar with these facts?

The answer is simple. Yesterday, when the events occurred, these events were simply not reported or their importance was downplayed. Mexican Americans were not the minority of record. They were, as so often described, the "invisible minority." Since that time, the importance of those Mexican-American events that were recorded have diminished in comparison to the importance of other events and people sanctioned by mass media.

Thus, names such as Malcolm X, Rev. Martín Luther King, Jr., Eldrige Cleaver, Huey Newton, the Berrigan brothers, Abbie Hoffman, Tom Hayden, and Jerry Rubin may sound familiar, but few Americans will recognize names such as Dolores Huerta, Reies López Tijerina, José Angel Gutiérrez, or Rodolfo "Corky" Gonzales. César Chávez is perhaps the only Mexican-American leader whose exploits caught the media's attention enough to make his a recognizable name at the time. Today it is doubtful that many Americans know who he was or what he represented.

This is the case with many of the events I write about in this book. I was an eyewitness, but, like Winston Smith, I find that history has been altered around me. The events I saw somehow never found their way into American history texts or the popular culture's understanding of this period.

I was reminded of this fact on August 29, 1990, during the twenty-year commemoration march of the East Los Angeles police riot that is better known in the Chicano community as the Chicano Moratorium. This moratorium—the largest civil disturbance involving Latinos this nation has ever known—is largely unknown to mainstream American society. As I watched on television, young news reporters, for whom the events of 1970 were ancient history, fumbled live broadcasts from the commemorative march, trying to get at the "news" of the initial event in 1970. I was not surprised when many of the reporters got the story wrong. Their ignorance is understandable. The films and news reports about the Vietnam War rarely mention the extraordinary number of Mexican-American casualties. And news accounts of the anti-war movement seldom mention the participation of Mexican Americans. It is as if many of these events never occurred.

I wrote this book because we need it. My purpose was the same reason that I and several other Chicano filmmakers spent six years of our lives developing the historic PBS documentary series *CHICANO! History of the Mexican American Civil Rights Movement.* Hector Galán, Sylvia Morales, Myléne Moreno, Susan Racho, José Luis Ruiz, Luis R. Torres, and I simply wanted to tell of the contributions of a large segment of American society that has been historically ignored in the grander scheme of American history, politics, and popular culture. We wanted to bring the important issues, events, and personalities of our history out in the open, to validate that legacy, and make it a worthy topic of discussion, debate, and reflection, not just for Mexican Americans but for all Americans.

It was the revolt of a "nation within a nation," more than fifteen million Mexican Americans who, in the 1960s, waged an important struggle for their civil and human rights and for their cultural identity. We called ourselves "Chicanos," politically empowered and socially conscious Americans of Mexican descent. In this volume I will use "Chicano" interchangeably with Mexican American and will use the term "Latino" when referring to Spanish-surnamed people of all origins living in the United States.

The Chicano Movement, also known as *la lucha* (the struggle), *la causa* (the cause), or simply *el movimiento* (the movement), was a social uprising led, primarily, by the first generation of Mexican-American youth who rejected an American identity of inferiority that labeled them "socially disadvantaged." Instead, they reached far back in their collective history to redefine themselves as citizens of "Aztlán," a mythic Indian homeland, which, as we shall see, empowered their quest for social justice. By their actions, they wrote another chapter in the story of what it means to be American. They transformed the nature of political, economic, and social participation of Latinos in this country, and left a profound legacy whose fruits are still enjoyed today—not just by Latinos, but by all Americans.

The writing of this recollection of our Chicano group history also has a deep personal meaning for me. It traverses an arc of personal growth covering the many facets of my identity: filmmaker, writer, director, Chicano militant, social activist, American citizen. I was fortunate to be at key events in the history of the Mexican-American people, as a chronicler and filmmaker, and to undergo a personal evolution that mirrored the ideological developments taking place in the Chicano Movement.

At the conclusion of this personal and public trajectory, I have come to terms with my identity as an American citizen. The result has been a continued commitment to achieve the goals of social justice and equality inspired by the Chicano Movement more than thirty years ago.

The realizations I came to during the experiences I describe in this book are personal, but I hope that they will offer insight into the issues and obstacles facing Latinos in the twenty-first century and suggest new avenues for activism.

Ours was a youthful generation, impatient with the discrimination and abuse to which our people had been subjected for decades. At a given moment in history, we rose to our feet to declare *Ya Basta!* (Enough!) and to proclaim proudly *I Am Chicano!* This is a personal story of that affirmation.

Acknowledgments

I wish to thank the many people chronicled in this book who reviewed various drafts of the manuscript and who reminded me of events, incidents, and conversations that took place between us. These include Chuck Allen, Terri Francis Butler, Erik Butler, Francisco and Lorenza Camplís, Claude Fischer, José Angel Gutiérrez, Henry Gutiérrez, Shifra Goldman, Gilbert "Magú" Luján, Elizabeth "Betita" Martínez, Jim Miller, Sylvia Morales, Carlos Muñoz, Jr., Martín Quiroz, Dan Rubin, Adele and Sam Rubin, José Luis Ruiz, David Sandoval, Jim Tartan, Thandeaka, Luis R. Torres, David Treviño, and Rudy Vargas. I wish to especially thank Gayla Treviño, my ex-wife, who lived through the Chicano years with me and who was extraordinarily supportive throughout the writing of this memoir, reviewing chapters, reminding me of incidents and people, filling in details when my memory failed me, and keeping me honest to the events as they happened. My thanks also to my sister, Olinda Farley, and my mother, María Pipan, for their remembrances, insights, and support. I also wish to thank my friend Carl Mumm, who helped edit the manuscript, and who helped clarify my thinking, refine my storytelling, improve my writing style, and forced me to make the events portrayed accessible to a wide readership. Thanks also to Ana Rosa Ramos for transcribing portions of this manuscript. I thank Nicolás Kanellos for his encouragement and for hounding me to get the manuscript finished, and for editing the final draft. Lastly, I wish to thank my wife, Bobbi Murray, for her constant inspiration, encouragement, humor, and love, all of which sustained me throughout the writing of this work.

Chapter One

Walkout!

Call it peace or call it treason, call it love or call it reason,
but I ain't a marchin' anymore.

—*Phil Ochs*

On Friday, March 1, 1968, I turned on my twelve-inch black-and-white Sony TV to the evening news as I prepared dinner for my roommate, Jim Miller, and myself in the cramped kitchen of our apartment at 1582 Munson Street. The apartment was located across from Occidental College, a small liberal arts institution we both attended in the Los Angeles suburb of Eagle Rock.

As I went about preparing the hamburger-rice hash that had become a staple of our student diet, the lead story froze me in place. Several hundred Mexican-American students had walked out of a high school on the Eastside. What captivated my attention was not only the fact that it was Mexican-American students that had walked out—a first in Los Angeles history—but that the school in the news footage was none other than my alma mater, Woodrow Wilson High.

Immediately after the news report, still clutching at the pan of hamburger-rice hash, I called my sister, Olinda, at our family home in the Los Angeles neighborhood of El Sereno. A junior at Woodrow Wilson High, she filled me in on what had happened. The school principal, Donald Skinner, had decided to cancel the production of a school play already in rehearsal. Skinner thought the play, *Barefoot in the Park*, was too risqué for the Mexican-American parents who would come to see it. Student leaders at Wilson considered his actions

1

unfair and, that morning, several hundred students walked out. My sister, Olinda, was among them.

"Students were just fed up with school," she told me. "And when someone started shouting 'walkout!' we all just went out." The following Monday, there were more Mexican-American student walkouts. In the week that followed, more than 4,000 high school students walked out of the four predominantly Mexican-American high schools in East Los Angeles—Garfield, Roosevelt, Lincoln, and Wilson. At Garfield and Roosevelt, students were beaten by police and arrested. Citywide, sympathy walkouts by Mexican Americans at other schools reached a total of 15,000 students. What my sister did not know at the time was that the Wilson walkout, though spontaneous, was part of a larger civic protest that had been in the offing for months and that had been planned to coincide at all four Eastside high schools in late March.

At the root of these walkouts were the deplorable conditions in the four predominantly Mexican-American high schools of the Eastside. Student leaders from the four schools had met for several months and had concluded that the only way to bring public attention to their plight was to coordinate a massive walkout of all the schools on the same day. The cancellation of the Wilson High School play provoked walkout leaders at Wilson to jump the gun. But the other schools quickly followed suit. Olinda told me of a community meeting called by parents and students to debate the walkout issue and the "21 Demands" that the student leaders had drafted. I surprised myself by telling her I would try to attend.

Flower Power and Vietnam

At the time, my mind-set could not have been further from the walkouts being reported on the evening news. I was in my senior year in college, majoring in philosophy, minoring in religion. My greatest concern at that moment was the completion of a term paper on the British philosopher Ludwig Wittgenstein. I was also spending much of my time with my future wife, Gayla Beauchamp.

Like many of our generation, in 1968, Gayla and I dabbled in the "flower power" counterculture of the time. The summer before, we had explored San Francisco's Haight-Ashbury district, where we enjoyed foreign movies, bookstores, and Bohemian cafes. The sounds of Jefferson Airplane, the Doors, The Lovin' Spoonful, the Beatles, Ian and Sylvia, and Joan Baez filled our ears, and flower shirts, jeans, and sandals filled our closets. I painted large oil canvasses depicting other-worldly, phantasmagoric scenes when I wasn't exploring the works of Sartre, Kafka, and Gertrude Stein.

Gayla was petite, alluring, and beautiful, with straight hair that descended halfway down her back. She made sand candles and experimented with silk-screen posters in the style of Sister Corita Kent. During daylight hours, we took long strolls and speculated about the future. At night we studied and occasionally spoke at length about the recent trauma in her life, the suicide of her father a year earlier.

Hanging over this otherwise untroubled student lifestyle was a rumbling thunderhead—the military draft for the war in Vietnam.

During the first three and a half years at Occidental College, the loss of my student deferment seemed to be an interminable distance away. As graduation neared, however, the conflict snowballed. What had once been just a vague possibility for me began to take on a horrifying tangibility too insidious to ignore.

Helping to bring the issue into high relief were the regular letters I received from my close high school friend Dan Rubin. Tall, curly-haired with a perennial smirk on his face, Dan was attending Reed College in Portland, Oregon, and had become actively involved in the anti-draft movement there. Dan's opinions were particularly important to me since we had been fast friends throughout high school and college and had, over the years, helped to shape one another's sensibilities.

Recently, he had written that the impending loss of his student deferment had impelled him to petition his draft board for exemption from the Vietnam War as a conscientious objector. To be reclassified as a conscientious objector to war, you had to convince your draft board that you held deep religious beliefs that prevented you from participating. Because so many young men were applying for this exemption, however, obtaining it was a rarity. The determination was made by the local draft board, and many draft boards had decided out of hand not to grant C.O. status at all. Uncertain as to the outcome of his petition, Dan was seriously considering the other option that existed for our generation of anti-war American youth: moving to Canada to avoid the draft.

Dan was following through on a mutual understanding that the two of us would leave the United States and move to Canada rather than fight in a senseless, immoral war. We knew one could cross the border as a tourist and then request immigrant status. Dan was already involved as a volunteer on the Portland leg of an "underground railroad" that moved American youth through California, Oregon, and Washington in a series of safe-houses leading to Canada. Escape was the easy part. It was the aftermath upon which Dan focused most in his letters: Once in Canada, could we enroll in graduate school? What kind of jobs might we find? What was our risk of arrest if we returned to the States? Was our possible expatriation to be as final and definitive as it seemed? The gloom of our uncertain futures weighed heavily upon us.

Another person with whom I discussed the war and resistance to the draft, was my roommate, who was also considering applying for conscientious objector status. In Jim Miller's case, however, the decision-making was doubly hard because his father was a retired army colonel, a career man, who expected his son to be patriotic and do his duty for his country. While we both agreed that we would resist the draft, Jim didn't feel that Canada was an option for him. He felt that the war was morally wrong. If he was denied C.O. status, he intended to fight the war effort by going to jail rather than flee to Canada. "I feel like history is running up on us," he told me in his typically poetic fashion, "and it's going to leave us bloody and fallen to the ground."

All of this prodded me into working on a first draft of my conscientious objector argument. With only a few months to go before graduation, and already having received notice to appear for my pre-induction physical at the end of April, my stomach became increasingly knotted with anxiety.

The Shaping of Dissident Ideas

My opposition to the war was nothing new. I had first voiced my opposition to the war in high school when, along with Dan Rubin and another friend, Chuck Villalobos, we had articulated our views about the futility of war. At this time, in the early 1960s, we spoke of war in the abstract—this was before Vietnam had become a household name.

As three young minds coming to terms with the world about us, we spent many an afternoon debating war and the issues of justice, equality, and human progress raised by the emergent civil rights movement. It was an explosive time, as television images of police dogs attacking civil rights demonstrators in the South demonstrated in graphic detail. Like so many others our age, we were in a time of intellectual growth and philosophic questioning.

For me, personally, it was also a time for challenging beliefs and precepts that had been instilled in me as a child. I had begun to see many of these notions as limited, flawed, or, in some cases, completely ludicrous.

I read voraciously, particularly on topics related to history, politics, philosophy, science, and the civil rights movement. Although I was neither intellectually nor emotionally prepared to discard the religious beliefs at the core of my being, my readings raised questions about these convictions, and I anxiously sought answers. I battled with myself on issues that troubled me deeply but which I did not discuss with anyone.

The bulk of these questions concerned the existence of God. If God existed and was, by all accounts, a good and loving God, why then was there injustice and poverty in the world? The arguments posed at the Emmanuel Baptist Church, the Spanish-language church my family attended, was that the injustice we saw in the world had a purpose that only God understood. This rang hollow to me. I saw reports on the evening news of a civil rights movement that sought to free Negroes from years of discrimination. If I were a true Christian, shouldn't I be part of that struggle? And if this was the role of a true Christian, then why were so many Christians I saw at church apparently oblivious to the civil rights movement?

These were questions that I could not properly raise in the traditional environment of my home. As luck would have it, however, my intellectual and philosophic musings found another outlet: in the home of my best friend, Dan Rubin.

Dan's parents, Sam and Adele, had come to Los Angeles from Chicago in the early 1950s. Sam was an accomplished artist with a rebellious spirit and a caustic wit. His independence melded with innovative artistic techniques to produce highly original works of art. Adele was a working mother who set high goals for her children and supported the family as a credit manager for a wholesale floor covering firm. Although they lacked material wealth, the Rubins led an immensely rich intellectual and cultural life. They fostered in their two children, Dan and Helen, an appreciation for nature, the arts, and intellectual reasoning that stemmed from exposure to literature, great painters, and classical composers. The two-story Rubin home, perched on Pyrites Street in the Rose Hills neighborhood of Los Angeles, reflected this lifestyle. Musical instruments populated their home: a piano, a violin, a guitar, a banjo, a mandolin, and several flutes and recorders. Their walls and furniture were adorned with Sam's projects: crayograph prints (a technique he pioneered), clay sculpture, and beautiful oil landscapes.

Weekends at the house were events full of excitement and intellectual ferment. Often this would include a jam session where adults and children were encouraged to play music together. At other times, the afternoon barbecue might include a poetry reading, a discussion of current affairs, a book someone had read, or the unveiling of one of Sam Rubin's latest creations. I gradually adopted the Rubins as surrogate parents. In their open support for questions I raised, their accepting attitude toward new ideas, and their enthusiasm for artistic creativity, I found an environment for intellectual growth that was missing in the more traditional working-class background in which I had been raised.

In contrast to the Rubins, the outlook of my parents was traditional and conservative. My mother, María Evangelina Mercado Armendariz Farley, who had been born in Ciudad Juárez, Mexico, in 1922, was a devout Christian whose formal education had ended at the fifth grade. As a teenager, she worked at a department store in El Paso, Texas, to help support her family across the border. She had gotten the job without being able to speak a word of English, but quickly taught herself with the help of other clerks by memorizing the names of all the items in the store inventory. Dark-haired, vivacious, with striking Indian features, my mother had a portrait of the world construed by deeply felt fundamentalist religious beliefs—though her reality was confined by the pragmatic struggle to maintain a subsistence income for herself and her children. She worked in a variety of low-paying jobs that included working in a sweatshop, packaging noodles at a spaghetti factory, decorating pastries at a bakery, and, in later years, tending to the elderly in their homes. All of this she did willingly, at great sacrifice to herself, in order to help provide my two younger sisters, Olinda and Rosalba, and me with clothing, school supplies, and other essentials.

Edward Shelton Farley, my Anglo-American stepfather, was the primary breadwinner of the family. My biological father had abandoned my mother and me when I was two years old, and Eddie was the only father I knew as I grew up. He was tall, ruggedly handsome, and had a quiet, easygoing disposition. But his job as a steam fitter's assistant for the County of Los Angeles brought in only a modest salary. Because of this my mother worked and, as soon as I was of age, I also took on part-time jobs.

My stepfather had been raised in a mountain community on the outskirts of Hinton, West Virginia. A warm, generous, and honest person, he was also a romantic born out of his time. I learned this when I was fifteen years old, when he took our family back East to visit his birthplace.

As we walked through the waist-tall grass that had overgrown the dirt road leading to the homestead, I recalled the many stories he had told my sisters and me about his rustic childhood. He always spoke of his childhood fondly. To hear him tell it, his home had been a mansion. It was here that his family had weathered winter storms huddled by the warm fireplace. It was in the surrounding hills that he had spent warm summers scampering down hillsides with his brothers as they made their way to the local swimming hole.

When we finally reached the site, we found a tiny, rotting log cabin that resembled a shack more than a home. The stone fireplace had crumbled. A few rotting boards were all that was left of the floor, and the walls looked like they would cave in with the slightest breeze. As I read the disappointment in his face, I suddenly understood why my father felt so out of place, so estranged, in the modern world. He longed for the simpler, bucolic past of his childhood—at least as he remembered it—where he had few responsibilities and time to himself. As an adult, all of this was gone. It was all that he could do to face the daily challenges of contemporary life—Los Angeles traffic, a low-paying job, nightly calls from irate bill collectors, and trying to be a father to three children.

As we made our way back to the car, I realized why my stepfather's favorite escape was plucking Carter Family songs on the guitar we shared (the first song I learned to play was *The Wildwood Flower*) and watching his favorite television westerns. My stepfather would have been happier as a cowboy in the West of a bygone era than battling freeway traffic and smog in urban Los Angeles.

Not surprisingly, he was a fervent traditionalist and a political conservative. He labored at a job that got him to work early and returned him home late. This left him with little time or energy to engage in political debates or to indulge my intellectual questioning. The few times that he did comment on political issues, his words echoed with stone-graven concepts acquired long ago.

Once, when I was seventeen years old, I wrote to the Congress of Racial Equality (CORE) for information about their goals and philosophy. The Congress of Racial Equality was a middle-of-the-road organization that sought gains in civil rights articulated by the Rev. Martín Luther King Jr. During the 1960s, it was one of the civil rights organizations to which non-Negroes were allowed to join, and I was eager to do so. As luck would have it, on the day the CORE material arrived, my stepfather intercepted the mail, and when he saw what it was, he tore the information to pieces and threw it into the trash.

When I found out what he had done, I confronted him. I was outraged. "How dare you open and throw out mail addressed to me!"

He replied with neither malice nor anger. "No boy of mine is going to belong to a Communist organization," he said. "The Negro movement is influenced by Communists and you'll have no part of it."

My response to my father's actions was to place another mailbox next to the one on our front porch. At the time we lived at 4803 Carnegie Street. I labeled the second mailbox "4803½" and from then on received my mail at this address.

By my junior year in high school, Dan, Chuck, and I had forged an intellectual alliance By challenging each other's arguments and beliefs, we eventually developed a mutual position against war and in support of the civil rights movement. Fueled by the music of Bob Dylan, Phil Ochs, and others of the folk era, Dan Rubin and I performed as a folk duo. Dan played banjo, and I played guitar. We founded the high school folk music club and performed at school and at private functions.

Our repertoire included anti-war songs such as *Two Brothers*, *Blowin' in the Wind*, and *Masters of War*. We even composed our own anti-war song, *And the North Winds Blow*, in which we compared humanity to the lemmings of the arctic tundra:

And, are we not like the lemmings?
Running to our suicide?
Building our bombs, to an end in vain?

It was not until college, however, that my anti-war sentiments consolidated into an integrated world view. In my freshman year, I became friends with a professor of English named Phillip Allen. Before coming to Occidental, Allen had spent two years as a military advisor in Vietnam. My philosophic and (what would eventually become) religious reasons for opposing the war combined with Allen's grisly descriptions of what he had seen, to cement my views. By my senior year in college, I knew one thing for certain: No matter what, I was not going to go to Vietnam.

A Community Meeting

A few days following the walkouts, I prepared to attend the Eastside meeting of walkout students and parents. Gayla voiced the question that I had been asking myself since I had heard about the walk-outs. "Since when are you interested in politics?"

She was right. This interest *was* a bit unusual for me. My earlier interest in civil rights had led me to join the Occidental chapter of CORE in my freshman year. But by my senior year at Oxy I had grown politically inactive. I no longer participated in CORE nor in anti-war activities. My apathy had grown in response to the estrangement I felt at school for being a Mexican American in a school that was predominantly white. Given my lack of political activism, and our laid-back "flower child" lifestyle of pot, rock-and-roll, and art, it was not surprising that Gayla's response to my abrupt interest in the high school walkouts was one of astonishment.

"What do you think you'll find?" she pressed.

"I don't know," I replied. The truth was that I *didn't* know. I only knew that this was something that I had to do. That evening I attended the first of what would eventually come to be weekly meetings of the Educational Issues Coordinating Committee (EICC)—the *ad hoc* group of parents, students, and teachers that was created in the wake of the walkouts.

The meeting of the EICC was convened at the auditorium of the Plaza Community Center, a square, brick structure off Indiana Street in East Los Angeles. I had gotten directions to the place from a Mexican-American sophomore at Occidental, Henry Gutiérrez. He had attended Garfield High School before attending Oxy and had been present as a college monitor at the Garfield walkout the week before. Although we did not know each other very well, the fact that we were two of perhaps a dozen Mexican-American students on a campus of two thousand students connected us in a special way.

When I arrived, the meeting was already in progress. As I looked across the room, I saw a crowd of about a hundred and fifty strangers. A few of these people would later become intimate friends. But at this first meeting, I was awed by them, intimidated by their articulate, passionate speeches. They seemed so certain of their beliefs, which only underscored my own ignorance of the issues. I was there to learn, but, at the same time, I felt inadequate. I fought a powerful urge to leave, but nevertheless made my way to a seat.

As I sat down, a charismatic, hawk-nosed man of diminutive build addressed the large assembly. The Reverend Vahac Mardirosian, I would later learn, was torn of Armenian parents, but had been raised in Mexico. He had come to the United States as a youth and had responded to a calling to the clergy. At the time of the walkouts, he was pastor of the First Baptist Church of East Los Angeles.

Like so many of the parents of the walkout students, Mardirosian had grown up within the Mexican tradition of education. In Mexico, the teacher was a revered mentor, someone to be respected and trusted—above all, someone who regarded the education of the child as his paramount duty. Mardirosian had assumed that the schools of the Eastside were doing a good job of educating children, and that the teachers and administrators had only the best interests of Mexican children in mind.

As with so many parents, he was caught off guard by the walkouts. It was only after he began to inquire into the working of the Los Angeles Unified School District that he began to uncover cases of child abuse, discrimination, ridicule, and a dropout rate of more than 50 percent among the Mexican students attending Eastside schools. These facts infuriated him into action. Soon he became chair of the EICC.

The issue being discussed at this meeting was what to do now that the walkouts were over. With many of the walkout leaders facing expulsion from school and other students clamoring for more walkouts, administrators were threatening retribution by calling in police. Parents were alarmed. They recalled the brutal beatings of student activists by police and wanted no more of it. It was a volatile time, one that called for clear heads. Mardirosian spoke in a fiery voice that night, pacing in front of the audience, emphasizing his points with emphatic gesticulations and punctuating his harangue with an occasional joke. It was a powerful secular sermon that took hold of the audience by the throat. He spoke of the courage the students had demonstrated by their walkout action.

"But now it is up to the adults to take over," he said. "We are not going to allow this situation to continue. We are not going to allow young people below the age of eighteen to do the work that belongs to us." This was not to be a "children's crusade," he stressed. "This must be an organized effort by all of us—parents, teachers, and students—working together."

As the evening progressed, other people got up to speak. In each case I was struck by how well-spoken these people were. I did not know it at the time, but these were the community leaders who, in the years that followed, would make up the backbone of the urban Chicano movement of Los Angeles.

There was the Baptist minister Reverend Horacio Quiñonez, the Presbyterian minister Antonio Hernández, and the Episcopalian priest Father John Luce. There were committed Mexican-American high school teachers like Sal Castro, Federico Sánchez, and Frank Cruz, university instructor Rodolfo Acuña, and labor activist Esteban Torres. There were outspoken parents like Julia and George Mount, Ben Carmona, Ben and Kay Gurulé, Sara and Tom McPherson, and Eva Romero. The high school walkout leaders were there as well: Freddy Reséndez, Paula Crisóstomo, and Margarita Cuarón. University leaders also attended: María Baeza, Pat Borjón, Phil Castruíta, Moctesuma Esparza, Raquel Galán, Henry Gutiérrez, Carlos Muñoz, Monty Pérez, Susan Racho, Raúl Ruiz, and Juan Gómez-Quiñonez. And ever menacing with their dark glasses, khaki uniforms, crossed arms, and grim expressions were members of the paramilitary group known as the Brown Berets that included the likes of David Sánchez, Carlos Montes, and Ralph Ramírez.

I had never witnessed such eloquent oratory by Mexican Americans before, and much less Mexican Americans as young as I was. The nearest thing in my memory was the time I had heard Dr. Martín Luther King, Jr. speak at a church in South Central Los Angeles in my senior year of high school. Now, as I listened to the speakers, unfamiliar feelings stirred within: sorrow at the plight of my people, joy at the sight of this vehement assembly, and, most of all, pride.

But beneath this satisfaction lurked pangs of jealousy. I suddenly wanted to be like them—to believe in a cause with this much passion. I yearned to belong to a group of people who were fighting for justice and human decency, for these people championed the same conduct I had been taught during my religious upbringing, supported the beliefs that had shaped me in high school, promoted the values of the Rubins, and reaffirmed my own personal world view. On a more pragmatic level, the discrimination and abuse to which the students and adults referred brought back a cascade of unpleasant memories.

I knew what it was like to be called a "dirty Mexican," to be singled out in class for speaking Spanish, to feel like a social outcast, a pariah, a misfit, a failure. I had experienced all of this, time and again, as a child. Yet, before that meeting, I was ashamed of those episodes and I had accepted such derision as truth. Now I saw these abuses from a different perspective: it was all unjust and it was something that we could change.

I returned home that night exhilarated. This had been a truly mesmerizing night. Now I was part of something. I had been initiated into the incipient Chicano Movement. I scanned the familiar clutter of my apartment. Jake, the still operable 1949 Wurlizer jukebox, was the centerpiece. Opposite it was a porcelain bathroom commode I had picked up at a yard sale. I had painted it purple and installed a round mirror inside so that when you lifted the seat, you saw yourself—one of my recent *objets d'art*. Art and philosophy books were scattered about. A partially completed sand candle stood on the coffee table. And my *requinto* guitar sat in a corner. When Gayla came to the living room to greet me, I let loose a torrent of enthusiasm in her direction.

"Henry Gutiérrez gave a wonderful speech," I said. "I met his girlfriend, Raquel Galán. They want to meet you. They're fine people. And there are many other Mexican Americans involved. People our age. There's going to be a revolution! You wait and see!"

Gayla listened patiently, but it was like trying to experience the thrill of a roller-coaster secondhand. Although Gayla would soon become a committed movement activist in her own right, on this evening of my first Chicano meeting, she was at a loss to understand my ebullience.

"I'm glad it was a nice meeting," she said cautiously.

"It was a GREAT meeting!"

How could I expect her to comprehend what I hardly understood myself? I had played a role for years—that of the "ideal" Mexican American—the model student who behaved as he should, the young man who wanted so desperately to be liked that he would do anything to fit into American society, to be a "good American." That evening something that had laid dormant in my life for many years was awakened: a sense of purpose emerging from the feeble stirring of self-worth. While I had shaped for myself a philosophic world view that dealt with matters of God, humanity, and the universe, I had completely buried my deep psychological issues of self-deprecation and ethnic self-hatred. Accustomed to living in a world of shadows, my eyes were suddenly cleared of the psychological cataracts that had afflicted me for so long. I could see. The feelings of inferiority that I began to shake loose had been firmly established long ago as a child growing up in East Los Angeles.

Beginnings

Jesús Vásquez Treviño, whose ancestors had settled in the Northern Mexican territory known as Tejas in the 1700s—before there was a United States—went off to war in 1942. He returned to the United States in 1945 and took up residence at the Fort Bliss medical facility in El Paso, Texas. He had left a portion of his right foot in a field in Germany during the Battle of the Bulge. While convalescing at Fort Bliss, he met an attractive volunteer nurse, Evangelina Mercado. They fell in love, were married, and a year after that Jesús Salvador Treviño entered into the world.

Shortly after my birth, my father took my mother and me to live with the extended Treviño family clan in Crystal City, Texas, a small agricultural community a hundred miles south of San Antonio, Texas. The Treviños—five brothers and two sisters—had expanded the elder Treviño's produce business and were making regular deliveries to the produce mart in downtown San Antonio.

For my mother, life with the extended Treviño family soon became unbearable. The matriarch of the Treviño clan was a forceful woman who pampered her boisterous sons and demanded of their wives and her daughters total allegiance to the family. My mother soon found out that there was little patience for an upstart wife with attitudes of self-reliance and independence.

After only a few months, matters came to a head when my mother demanded that my father choose between his extended family and his new wife and child. She wanted him to move us out of the cramped Treviño household on Piedras Street and to our own apartment. Torn between the only family he had ever known and the new family he was starting, he finally agreed to return to El Paso. On the way back, we hit a blizzard during the course of which I caught pneumonia. I survived the illness, as I would later survive a house fire that completely consumed our apartment home and even a shoot-out between rival *pachuco* gangs in the streets of El Paso's *segundo* barrio neighborhood, where we lived.

In El Paso, my father had replaced his military uniform with the "reet pleats" of the uniform worn by Mexican-American youth of the time, the *pachuco* "zoot suit." He would dress his two-and-a-half-year-old son as a *pachuquito* (little *pachuco*), to my mother's dismay, but to the approval of his *palomilla* (gang of friends). I frequently accompanied him when he went partying with the boys, clinging to my father's pant leg as he frequented El Paso bars. My mother, who had crossed the border from nearby Juárez, Mexico, in hopes of improving her life, found my father's carefree lifestyle insufferable. By the time I was three, relations between them had gone from bad to worse. My father decided to return to the comfort offered by the extended Treviño clan in Crystal City. My mother was left to fend for herself and her baby son.

Armed with the characteristic tenacity with which she faced any misfortune, my mother quickly found herself a job waiting tables at a downtown cafe, moved us into an nearby hotel, and filed for divorce. Within a short time she met an affable, mild-mannered G.I. stationed at Fort Bliss, who courted her in his quiet, methodical manner by coming each evening to have dinner at the cafe where my mother worked. Eventually, this country boy from the hills of West Virginia, Edward Shelton Farley, built up enough courage to ask my mother for a date. Within a few months they were married and made plans to move from El Paso to Los Angeles.

We made the move in 1949, when I was three years old. In 1951, a fourth member, my sister Olinda, was added to our family. By the fall of 1951, the four of us were living in a two-room apartment of a two-story Victorian house (turned apartment complex) on Pleasant Avenue in the Boyle Heights section of Los Angeles. One room was the bedroom, the other the kitchen, dining and living room. The apartment included a small closet-sized bathroom.

The community of Boyle Heights had originally been populated by Jews from New York during the 1930s and 1940s, but was now quickly being transformed into a Mexican-American barrio. Edward Farley raised me as his own. What few memories I had of my namesake were soon forgotten.

Neither my stepfather, Eddie, nor my mother had been educated beyond the fifth grade, and survival in their new home was not easy. Eddie managed to eke out a hand-to-mouth existence by working at the concession stand of the Floral Drive-In Theater in East Los Angeles, and by taking on odd jobs. With a family to support, he was thankful for having an income at all in a city so vastly different from the small town of Hinton, West Virginia, where he had been raised.

My stepfather's job was a delight for me. Although he worked late hours, he would often take me with him. One of my earliest childhood memories is of sitting alone in a car that my father borrowed nightly from a generous neighbor, watching first-run movies until I fell asleep. This was how I got to see many of my first American movies: *The Wolf Man, Dracula, Dr. Jekyll and Mr. Hyde,* and *The Wax Museum.*

By age five, I was ready to enroll at Bridge Street Elementary School. My first day of kindergarten, like that of many Spanish-only or bilingual speakers, was traumatic. My mother walked me to school and left me in the strange classroom. An Anglo woman spoke to me in English, but it was not the soft, kind English I often heard from my stepfather. It was loud and menacing. I comprehended the words well enough, but could not fathom the brusque, indifferent, and demanding tone that accompanied them. Suddenly, I was frightened beyond my young understanding. How could my mother leave me with this mean woman who used the same words my father used but in such a brutal fashion? I ran after my mother, catching up with her in front of the school yard. I cried forgiveness, thinking that perhaps I had done something wrong, and begged for her to take me home. But she refused. With tears in her eyes, she returned me to the classroom, where I spent the next several hours sitting alone in a corner. My remembrance is that I cried for hours, but it was probably only a matter of minutes. Still, they were horrible, asphyxiating, air-sucking minutes.

My mother tried to compensate for the trauma of school by speaking only Spanish to me at home. Since my stepfather was a quiet person by nature, rarely speaking at all, the only extended dialogue I had as a child was with my mother. As a result, it took several years before I would feel comfortable with English. English was the language of school, of the outside world. I associated it with strangers, danger, and suffering. As for Spanish, it was the language of warmth, security, and love.

The dominant condition that overshadowed my childhood was that of constant deprivation. Though from different ethnic backgrounds, my mother and stepfather found a commonality in poverty. The earliest Christmas I remember was at the two-room apartment on Pleasant Avenue. I received only one gift—a silver plastic gun without a holster. It probably cost my parents all of ten cents, but at that time in their lives, this was all they could afford. In later years, when I wanted a new bike, I received a second-hand bike that my father rode to and from work during the week to save on bus fare. Though it was, technically, my bike, the only time I could ride it was on weekends and in the evenings after my stepfather returned home.

After he lost his job at the Floral Drive-In, my father was employed as a grounds keeper for the County Parks and Recreation Department. His jobs always seemed temporary and paid very little. We stayed ahead of the bill collectors by moving often: from Pleasant Avenue to Echandia Street to Townsend Avenue and then to Michigan Avenue. Relocation was easy because we had little furniture and few personal possessions. The apartments were invariably semi-furnished or fully furnished. After the birth of my sister Olinda, the struggle to sustain a family became even greater, more than one man could bear.

One day, Eddie did not come home. He was gone for two weeks, leaving my mother with two children and no means of support. The church we attended delivered bags of groceries to us each week. My mother would say that the food "came from God." Later, Olinda told me that when she heard this as a four-year-old, she imagined the ceiling of the house opening up at night and God's hands descending through the kitchen ceiling as he laid the bags of groceries on the table.

When my father returned, he was exhausted and remorseful with blisters on his feet. I later learned that he had been fired for speaking out on behalf of a Mexican worker. He had spent the two weeks looking for work, eating at the homeless mission by day, and sleeping at a nearby church by night. In his mind, not having a job was so unbearably shameful, that he thought it better to abandon his family until he could secure work rather than go home and suffer the ignominy of unemployment. Once he was back and armed with another menial job, however, he was willing to give family life another try. We never spoke of this incident again.

In the spring of 1955, I began to complain of aches and pains in my elbow and knee joints. At first, my parents assumed I was feigning injury to avoid work around the house. One afternoon, however, my mother sent me to the local market for groceries. The pain became so intense that I could hardly walk. I managed to get to the store and purchase the groceries, but I couldn't make it home. They found me an hour later, lying on the sidewalk.

I was rushed by taxi to the Children's Hospital. After a cursory examination, one of the attending doctors blanched in horror. "This child is dying," he said. I was diagnosed with rheumatic fever. For the next several days it was uncertain if I would live. But after several days of intravenous feeding, I regained my strength, and the doctors informed my parents that I would live, although the disease would leave me with a heart murmur.

For the next eleven months of my life, I lived in the sprawling one-story convalescent home of the Children's Hospital located on Westmoreland Avenue in Hollywood. I spent all my waking and sleeping hours with perhaps fifty other children suffering from a variety of illnesses. Throughout it all, I was not allowed to leave my bed, even to go to the toilet. Despite my excruciating experience, my term at the hospital was the best thing that had happened to me in my early life.

Before I went into the hospital, I had been attending Breed Elementary School in Boyle Heights. Although I was in the fourth grade, I could not read past the first-grade level. In the hospital, flat on my back for twenty-four hours a day, at a time before televisions were a common feature in hospital rooms, I was bored to tears. I had no choice. I had to read.

I began with the reading primers that candy striper volunteers brought to my bed. Initially, it was the First Grade Primer, a book that contained reading and writing exercises, grammar rules, and, most important of all, extensive vocabulary lists. After the first-grade book, I plunged straight into the second-grade text, chapter by chapter. Then the third-grade primer, and the fourth. And the fifth. By the time I left the hospital, I had a working vocabulary comparable to that of a seventh-grader, though my grammar skills still lagged. In the end, I returned to the barrio with some powerful tools that would, in the years to come, keep me out of gang life, drugs, and crime, and would open the doors of the world to me: I could read!

When I returned to Boyle Heights, I was still receiving medication and required absolute quiet and rest. I could not go back to public school, but a home tutor, paid for by the hospital, made regular visits, so I could keep up with my education. This helped to consolidate the gains I had made on my own while in the hospital. Since I was confined to the house, I had no opportunity to make friends. It was a lonely time. I found solace the only way I could: I read incessantly. First it was childhood fantasies, Grimm and Anderson fairy tales, and comic books. Later, I consumed countless science fiction and fantasy stories.

I returned to Breed Street for only one semester before my family moved once again, this time to the northeast Los Angeles community of Lincoln Heights. As we relocated within the community, I attended Hillside Elementary, then Griffin Avenue Elementary, then Lincoln Junior High School. In 1959, we moved once again, this time to El Sereno, where I attended Woodrow Wilson Junior High School, and later Woodrow Wilson High School.

Just prior to the move to El Sereno, our economic situation finally took a turn for the better. My father secured a job working for the County of Los Angeles in its metal shop, and this led to an eventual apprenticeship to a journeyman welder in 1959. My mother also worked continuously throughout this period. The move to El Sereno, then a new suburb of Los Angeles already populated with many Mexicans, represented for us a definite step upward.

The Making of a Mexican American

One afternoon towards the end of the eighth grade, I returned home from school with a report card that contained four F's and a D. At that time, my friends were the local Mexican kids in the neighborhood, a poorer section of El Sereno. We spent our time working out at gymnastics and other sports and hanging out listening to rock-and-roll. Neither my friends nor I concerned ourselves much with school.

But when I received this dismal report card, I debated with myself over the direction my life had taken. My options seemed clear. If I continued to hang out with my Mexican-American friends, I would continue to get F's and would spiral down the abyss of utter failure. I was acutely aware that academic courses at Wilson High School were attended primarily by the Anglo-American and Asian students. Despite the fact that Mexican Americans formed a majority of the school population and of the neighborhood, we were not to be found in large numbers among the ranks of academic or social achievers. We were the dropouts.

If I were to succeed in school and in life, I would have to become part of this clique of super achievers. There was no doubt about it: I had to become "more American."

When I returned to Woodrow Wilson Junior High in the fall of 1959, I was determined to become one of *them*. Because I was Mexican, I believed I could never really become a full-fledged American. So, I reasoned, I would have to settle for second best. I would settle on being just a Mexican American, but an *ideal* Mexican American. In short, I would learn to rise above my disability. Like a snake, I had to shed my skin to be reborn.

I vowed to leave behind as much of my Mexican identity as possible. I asked my friends to call me Jess—a far more suitable name for my new "American" personality than Jesús (heh-SOOS).

My family was surprised, but went along with it. I distanced myself from Mexican friends (though for years, two of them—George and Chuck Villalobos—would remain close friends). Instead, I began to cultivate other, more "American" friends—guys with names like Jess Miller, Bill Eklund, and Jim Comefort, and later Charlie Palmer,

David Polin, Jim Wright, and, of course, my closest friend, Dan Rubin.

I was convinced that I was inferior in intellect, ability, and potential to the white students at school, but I was determined not to let my heritage stand in my way. I adopted an attitude whereby I would try two, three, or four times as hard as ordinary people—white people. By spending more time on my studies, I believed that I might gain entrance into that select group I knew as the "academics"—students who were on their way to college. By this time, my nightly visits to the public library had convinced me that I wanted to go to college and had to do so at whatever cost. Getting ahead meant going to college, and by now I knew that I wanted to make something of my life and not go the route of so many of the young gang members I saw around me.

At the end of the next semester, my new strategy was vindicated. I received four A's and a B+. Friends who knew me from before started calling me "the brain." The next semester, I was moved from the low-achieving track to the "academic" track, and found myself in classes with college-bound students.

But the respect of the Mexican-American students did not bolster my self-esteem. My entry into the academic track brought on intense insecurity. I felt like an ugly duckling masquerading as a swan and believed that my true nature would be revealed at any moment. My skin was brown. I had distinctively Indian features. And my poverty was betrayed by the shoddy clothing I wore to school. This caused me to drive myself even harder. Despite my fears, I felt I had made the right decision. By rejecting my ethnicity, I was excelling in ways that I never had before. For the first time in my life I was being accepted as an "American."

I joined high school organizations and participated in student government. I was even invited to join the Demolays, the junior auxiliary of the Masons, as prestigious an indicator of white privilege as one would find at Wilson High School. I declined, feeling that I didn't belong.

In my junior year, I was accepted to a summer college program for high-ability science students at Arizona State University and spent the summer discovering what college life was like. In my senior year I ran unsuccessfully for student body president, but was elected class vice-president. My acceptance to Occidental College was accompanied by a full scholarship. By the time I arrived on campus, I was convinced from my successes in high school that as long as I presented myself as being more American than the next guy, I would be fine.

Needless to say, the identity I had adopted was rife with contradictions. While Mexican Americans made up more than 75 percent of the student body at Woodrow Wilson High School, at Occidental College I was only one of a handful of Mexican-American students. Of the four hundred members of the Oxy class of '68, only a half dozen of us were Mexican Americans. I tried to adapt to the new college experience in my freshman year, but instead found only estrangement and confusion.

After my freshman year, I began a different kind of quest that remained unfulfilled until the walkouts. It was a quest—at times conscious, but usually unconscious—of finding out more about my Mexican heritage. I retreated from school activities at Occidental and instead devoted myself to searching for something that affirmed who I was. I began by spending hours in downtown Los Angeles record shops collecting Mexican music.

I would return to campus and learn the words and music to *corridos* and *boleros,* which I practiced on my guitar—at times scheduling my practice times to coincide with the classes I considered particularly threatening because of the many rich, white classmates in attendance.

By my senior year at Occidental, I had accustomed myself to being on the fringe and had retreated to a circle of close friends who, like me, eschewed the "preppy" social life at Occidental. I concentrated on my philosophy studies and met my future wife, a kindred iconoclastic spirit who rejected pretense and conformity. Throughout this period, I hid my feelings of inadequacy and inferiority deep within myself.

Kill the Gabacho

On the Friday of the walkout week, a public meeting was convened in the auditorium of Woodrow Wilson High. The open forum was to publicly discuss the "21 Demands" that students had raised and to defuse any further walkout talks. My sister and I were eager to attend, and we were particularly excited about the prospect of sharing the experience with my stepfather, her full-blooded father, Eddie Farley.

Like many parents, my stepfather had reacted negatively to the student walkouts and had chastised my sister for her participation in them. I had sided with Olinda and had tried to convince him of the importance of changing education in East Los Angeles. Olinda and I felt that if we could get our father to attend the public assembly, we might win him over. He agreed to accompany us.

That evening, Eddie, Olinda, and I walked into the auditorium and took seats near the front. On stage were several of the walkout leaders, including Phil Castruíta and Lincoln High School teacher Sal Castro. Opposing them were Wilson High School principal Donald Skinner and a conservative Mexican-American spokesperson, Richard Forte.

The meeting turned into a visceral debate between walkout supporters, who pointed to the inferior educational system in Eastside schools, and more conservative members of the community who defended it— many who spoke from the auditorium floor, denouncing the student "law-breakers" and calling for punishment of the walkout leaders.

At one of the more heated moments in the discussion, the Mexican-American speakers on stage called for "death to the *gabacho!*" Puzzled, my stepfather turned to me.

"What's a *gabacho,* Jesse?"

I was mortified. What could I tell him? How? My mind spun with lies and half-truths, but I knew they wouldn't work. He would learn the true meaning eventually.

"A *gabacho* . . ." I hesitated. There was no easy way to do it, so I decided to just blurt it out. "It's like *gringo.* He's talking about white people."

I watched helplessly as the meaning of the diatribe from the stage sank in: *death to white people.* Color drained from my stepfather's face. Then, wordlessly, he rose with what dignity he could muster and marched straight out of the auditorium.

Olinda and I exchanged a dreadful look and then simultaneously rushed off after him, each of us wondering how to explain the changing world to our father.

At home, a family argument erupted. Eddie questioned how I could repay him for all his years of sacrifice by belonging to a movement that, in his mind, was Communist-inspired and that called for his own death.

I tried to reason with him, but he was, understandably, unwilling to hear me out. After witnessing the call for death to an entire race of people, there was little I could say to make the Chicano Movement appear to be anything but evil incarnate.

I finally gave up trying to convince my stepfather of the righteousness of our cause. This left me with a profound guilt that would never, entirely, fade away, even with the wash of many years.

Despite these feelings, I continued to immerse myself in the Movement. My absolute dedication was expressed by a phrase that was reiterated time and again at public meetings: *Por la raza todo, afuera de la raza, ¡nada!* (For our people, everything! Outside of our people, nothing!) There was no turning back. I had to put both my guilt and my father aside and carry on with the struggle.

A Chicano Handshake

Guadalupe Saavedra de Saavedra—a pockmarked poet with a Zapata mustache and a riveting bass voice—had risen from humble beginnings. His parents had been seasonal Texas farm workers who barely survived from harvest to harvest. Saavedra had worked in the fields since he was a child.

By 1968, he had already gone through a period of movement activism, working with the United Farm Workers' Union—something he let everyone know within five minutes of meeting him. What he did not tell people was that he had also been asked to leave César Chávez's union. After his departure from the farm workers, he made his way to Los Angeles, where he soon incorporated himself into the urban Chicano Movement.

In many ways, Guadalupe personified the movement—brash, outspoken, charismatic, and impulsive. He was an enigma hidden by dark glasses, dressed in jeans and a camouflage army jacket.

He came into the Occidental campus lounge a short time after the walkouts and made his way to me across a roomful of white college students sipping Cokes and coffee. He remembered me from community meetings I had attended and came to where I sat with several classmates from a philosophy class.

When he came to the table, he ignored the others and spoke to me alone. "*¿Quiubo carnal?*" (What's up, brother?) he said and extended his hand to mine. I reached out to shake it and found him manipulating my hand with his strong fingers into what was for him a well-practiced routine: the Raza handshake of the Chicano Movement. It began with the traditional handshake, then a firm thumb clasp, and then back to the traditional handshake. The ritual ended with the touching of the knuckles.

I followed along awkwardly, for although I had seen other Chicanos meet in this way, it was my first such greeting that would, over the years, become second nature to me. We spoke for a moment. He needed directions to get to a classroom where he was to talk about the walkouts. I directed him, and he left. "*Órale,*" he said. "*Ahí te wacho.*"(I'll be seeing you.)

As I settled back into my chair, I noted a dead silence among my college friends. They had never seen me like this, talking one on one with someone so militant-looking and exchanging greetings in Spanish. This wasn't the philosophy nerd they thought they knew.

Suddenly, I *did* feel different. This was a kinship with someone I hardly knew that set me apart from my white friends. For years I hadn't belonged. As an outsider at this expensive, pristine "Princeton of the West Coast," I had grown used to being the loner, the "disadvantaged" student. These feelings had nearly resulted in my dropping out of school in my freshman year. But now, suddenly, with this simple handshake, something had changed. I felt empowered. Yes, I was different from my friends, but for the first time I felt that this difference was a privilege, something of which I could be proud.

In the wake of Guadalupe's departure, conversation resumed around the table. My friends joked about the tough demeanor of the intruder. Someone speculated that he had a gun hidden in his army jacket. Someone else made a crack about me: "Better watch yourself, Jess, you might become a militant!" There was laughter.

But instead of feeling embarrassed or inferior, all I could feel at that moment was intense pride.

On that spring afternoon in the lounge at Occidental College, I awakened to the fact that I did not have to keep up the pretense of being a model "Mexican American" anymore. Now I could be something else—myself. This new knowledge undercut all other relationships and allegiances I had forged up to that time. For the first time in my life, I was at home with who I was. I accepted the poverty in which I had been raised and the years of my denial and self-deprecation. I understood now why I had felt so inferior for so many years. There was nothing to be ashamed of. Like the Eastside high school students who had walked out of school, I had suddenly walked out of life as I knew it and into a new identity. I was brown and proud of it.

I was Chicano.

Chapter Two

Delano

I am convinced that the truest act of courage, the strongest act of humanity, is to sacrifice ourselves for others in a totally nonviolent struggle for justice . . .

—César Chávez

"Do you think anyone will come?" I asked nervously.

"I guess. I hope," Henry replied, scanning the quad area outside Mosher 1 lecture hall.

As my friendship with Henry Gutiérrez grew, we decided that Occidental College needed to continue the legacy set down by Ernesto Galarza, a former Oxy student who had since become a noted scholar, educator, and union activist. The first step would be to form a chapter of the statewide Mexican-American student organization known as UMAS (United Mexican-American Students).

We approached the endeavor methodically. First, we checked for all the surnames in the Occidental College student directory that could even remotely be of Spanish origin. We counted less than twenty-five out of a student population of about two thousand. We put notices in the post office boxes of these students and asked them to attend an organizational meeting. A couple of nights later, Henry and I waited outside one of the college lecture rooms we had reserved.

"Is this the meeting for Mexican Americans?"

We turned to greet our first visitor, an attractive Chicana with long straight hair and a pleasant smile named Anita Contreras.

"This is the place," I replied.

About a dozen students showed up for the Chicano meeting. In this group there were two Italians, an Argentine, a Spaniard, and a native of Mexico City. These individuals, not surprisingly, passed on joining our group, once I explained to them that our organization would be actively working to improve the conditions of Mexican Americans in the United States. About eight of us, all Chicanos, remained.

The meeting went late into the night. Some of the students were, as I had been, removed from their roots, embarrassed about being Chicano. Some even refused to call themselves Chicanos. Yet, in others, our call to action struck home. David Aguayo, Anita Contreras, and David Ramírez, like Henry and myself, welcomed the opportunity to identify and work together for the advancement of our people. At the conclusion of the evening, I was elected chair of the chapter.

The first order of business for our chapter was obvious. Representatives of the farm workers' movement had recently come to speak on campus and were in need of clothing and canned food. For two weeks, we prepared a campus-wide food drive. On April 15, 1968, we set out for Delano, California, in a caravan of cars and trucks to deliver the canned food to the fledgling farm workers' union.

Henry Gutiérrez and I rode in a battered yellow 1955 Ford pickup with "Madre" stenciled on the driver's door. At the wheel was my friend John Nomura, a Japanese American, who had grown up in East Los Angeles and whom I had known since high school. John had acquired the truck when he worked for Amigos Anonymous, a volunteer organization that transported food and clothing to needy families in Mexico. Other members of the chapter rode in separate cars, along with several Protestant ministers, Catholic priests, and a rabbi.

We were running late because coordinating the caravan had taken longer than we had expected, so we did not arrive at the farm workers' headquarters at the "forty acres" in Delano until late afternoon. We expected an audience with César Chávez, but found that he had recently returned from a statewide campaign and was resting from the long trip. We were told that if we wanted to wait, he would be available in perhaps an hour or two. We lingered outside Chávez's modest wooden house in euphoric anticipation.

After an hour, Chávez emerged. The sun had set, and it was now about eight in the evening. He walked among us, making sure to shake everyone's hand. As he approached me, I could see that he was worn-down. His face had the drawn look of someone who had just awakened from an inadequate period of sleep. At his side was a slight woman I first took to be his wife; later I would learn that she was Dolores Huerta, vice-president of the union.

"Thank you for coming. God bless you," he said as he shook my hand.

Chávez indicated for us to sit in the grass. His talk was simple, direct, and brief. He explained the current struggle facing the farm workers. They had recently won a major victory over the Shenley farms, but their struggle to unionize the *campesinos* (farm workers) working for the grape growers of the Delano valley was far from complete. He thanked us for our contributions but stressed the ongoing needs of the farm workers.

His clothing was modest: dark pants and a short-sleeved plaid shirt. I was wearing jeans, one of the multicolored flower shirts that had been my trademark in college, and leather sandals. I felt pretentious compared to this humble man. As he spoke, I became more and more self-conscious of how *agringado*, how Anglo-ized, I had become. Surely, he saw it, too.

I was overcome by the inexplicable charisma of this small, modest person before me. Here was a person to be emulated, a man worth following. His sincere, down-to-earth style radiated a passion for all that is right and just and fair.

As Chávez detailed the struggle being waged by his union, I berated myself for ignoring what had been before my very eyes all along. How could I have been so unaware of the struggle of my own people? Although I had experienced the poverty, discrimination, and abuse that Chávez fought against, I had always accepted the poverty and discrimination into which I was born. Society had trained me to do so. If I was poor, it was because I was inadequate, or perhaps because my parents had passed an inherent inferiority down to me. If I experienced discrimination, it was because Mexicans were innately inferior. Society had convinced me that I was unworthy, that I was "disadvantaged."

Chávez rejected these labels. He began with a simple assumption: all human life was worthwhile. All human beings, even lowly Mexican farm workers, deserved a decent life, respect, and justice. And he had dedicated his life to bringing a decent living to these farm workers.

Those of us in the truck were quiet on the drive back. It was not just that we were physically tired from traveling. After meeting with Chávez, none of us could express the blaze of emotion that the man had sparked. As for me, my mind reeled with troubling thoughts—not thoughts of politics or labor, but with the jumble of unresolved issues I carried around with me.

Then the jumble stopped and fell into place.

My discomfort came from the profound religious atmosphere that had permeated everything I had seen at Delano. In the farm workers' office I had seen the Virgin de Guadalupe, the patron saint of Mexico, displayed prominently. In the course of his talk, Chávez himself had made several religious references. Not just the "God bless you," but the fact that he believed that the Virgen de Guadalupe and that God were on his side.

Rather than seeing Chávez's statement in the context of his social struggle, his comment brought to mind Bob Dylan's lyrics in "With God on Their Side." So often in human history, God had been invoked to justify war, fanaticism, and intolerance. Was Chávez, then, just another religious zealot? An internal conflict was unleashed. At war were deep emotions aroused by meeting Chávez and the carefully thought-out philosophical world view that was the core of my being. The debate between these opposing feelings forced me to examine anew issues that I thought I had settled some time before.

Of Existence, God, and Humanity

At the end of my freshman year in college, I was very close to dropping out. The alienation I felt from the predominantly white Occidental environment and my profound sense of inferiority about being Mexican had been overwhelming during the fall semester.

I attended this privileged educational institution on a full scholarship. At the time, I didn't believe it had been awarded due to merit or talent. I viewed the scholarship as charity to the underqualified and disadvantaged.

The equation that kept me going in high school—that with hard work I could rise above others—was rudely challenged at Oxy. I met classmates who didn't have to study as much as I did, but who still received better grades. Not only were many of them smarter than I was, but they were also more outgoing, involved in sports and a school social life. Topping it all, many of them were handsome or beautiful and came from privileged backgrounds. It was so unfair!

A lot of them had parents who were doctors, lawyers, and businessmen. These were people that wore suits when they visited the campus—not the dirty worn overalls my stepfather wore when he visited. Many students owned expensive cars, had money to burn, and carried themselves with the confidence that they would be important players in that world after they graduated.

All of this hit home during my freshman year. It underscored who I was: "the poor kid," the "disadvantaged" Mexican student, the outcast. I decided to stick out the year because I had nothing to lose. After all, my room, board, and tuition were free. By the spring semester, however, I stopped attending some classes altogether and attended others only sporadically.

This left me with ample free time to pursue other activities. I began to spend much of my time in the school library reading a variety of books that I determined would become my own, self-selected study program. My readings included Sartre, Kierkegaard, Nietzsche, Kafka, and Bertrand Russell. The only class that I did attend, and this with great relish, was the Introduction to Philosophy class taught by a celebrated philosophy professor named Donald Loftsgordon.

I arrived at Occidental when Loftsgorden was already a campus legend. There was standing room only in his classroom, with students auditing not for credit but merely to hear the words of this intellectual *enfante terrible* and critic of the world order as we knew it. I was fortunate enough to find seating.

In Loftsgorden's classroom, I learned that many of the questions I had been asking since high school had been asked before by philosophers and theologians—and that an entire discipline had evolved that addressed these issues. I discovered that there was a history of arguments for the existence of God and a history of refutations against it. Many of the beliefs inculcated in me as a child were not founded on logical deduction, but rather depended on blind acceptance. God was all-powerful and all-knowing because man had defined him that way. These revelations were both devastating and liberating.

I had grown up steeped in traditional religious dogma at my mother's insistence. By the time I was fourteen, I had been baptized three times, once as a Catholic, once as a Presbyterian, and once in the Church of Christ. My religious training instilled positive ideals and values, but the attendant theology and blind acceptance of doctrine also stunted my intellectual, emotional, and creative growth for many years. It wasn't until Oxy that I began to reevaluate my Christian upbringing.

Loftsgordon showed me that something as basic as the word of "God" was applied randomly, depending on which version of the Bible one believed in, and that holy scripture—rather than being set down by a divine power—was created and interpreted by editorial boards at different times in history.

My doubts were supported by the existence of other texts I had never heard about before, such as the Apocrypha and the Dead Sea Scrolls. I was dumbfounded by how depictions of Jesus differed in some of these books, when compared to the Bible, with which I was so familiar. How could anyone believe in the divine inspiration of a book that had been meddled with so often by so many different groups of men?

Then I read the Noble-Prize-winning philosopher Bertrand Russell's book, *Why I Am Not A Christian*. It was this book, more than any other, that did the most to convince me that the ideas I had grown up with were set down by human institutions, not "God." These "sacred" texts had been created by a set of men in order to maintain control and dominion over others for reasons that had more to do with greed than spiritual reverence.

In his book, Russell outlined his own humanistic view of life, one that saw humankind as part of the natural order of the universe, as opposed to the Christian view that man existed on a level above other creatures. I fought every argument Russell put forth against the existence of God and against the value of Christianity. Unlike previous times when these issues had been raised in my mind, however, I could no longer retreat to accepted doctrine or to the reassurances provided by my parents or ministers. Once my questioning began, I could no longer hide from the persistent badgering of my own intellect. Ironically, the value of honesty—something that had been infused in me since childhood and reinforced in church—would not allow me to be intellectually dishonest, no matter what the consequences. I could not counter Russell's logic. Having made short work of several traditional arguments for the existence of God, Bertrand Russell went on to say:

> We want to stand upon our own feet and look fair and square at the world—its good facts, its bad facts, its beauties, and its ugliness; see the world as it is and be not afraid of it. Conquer the world by intelligence and not merely by being slavishly subdued by the terror that comes from it.

What a wonderful notion! The possibility that one might have a sense of morality and human values without the attendant church doctrine that I had for so many years equated with these precepts! For the first time, I seriously considered the notion that it was possible to be a loving and moral human being without believing in God, divine intervention, heaven, or hell.

Not long after reading Bertrand Russell, I encountered the novel *Blood of the Lamb* by Peter De Vries, in which I discovered an outlook that struck me as perfectly sensible:

> We have only our human trinity to see us through: reason, courage, and grace, and the first plus the second equals the third.

This humanistically based philosophy confirmed what was becoming quickly evident to me: the superfluous nature of God.

More evidence came to light in Loftsgordon's philosophy class. I learned about an English Franciscan, William of Ockham (1285–1349), who believed in the principle of economy in thought. Entities, Ockham told us, were not to be multiplied beyond necessity. The shortest and simplest answer to a problem was its solution. This concept had since become known as "Ockham's Razor." When applied to the proposition of the existence of God, one finds that God is simply not necessary to articulate a humanistic philosophy of love for one's fellow man. I sought confirmation in the teachings of Jesus, Buddha, and Mohammed, and saw that their teachings were—when cultural contexts were excised—expressions of similar humanistic beliefs.

This led me to question my own cultural bias. How could I get at truth if my very perceptions and beliefs had been filtered through a set of cultural biases that were the outcome of the arbitrary accident of my birth as a Mexican American? What if I had been born in India, Japan, or Iraq? My view of reality and the universe would be shaped accordingly. I might be as fervent a Hindu or Buddhist or Islamic as my mother was a Christian. How, then, could I ever arrive at an objective reality if I accepted the scriptures passed down to me by a random culture?

By the spring of my freshman year, I had rejected God altogether and had set about to master my life by shaping an integrated world view that would explain all that I knew about the world. This *weltanschauung* would include those human values, ethical precepts, and moral teachings that I had encountered in my readings which I felt were positive and promoted human freedom and happiness. I was determined to eliminate from my world view any beliefs that I held merely because I had been taught them as a child or with that I had been indoctrinated as a function of growing up Mexican American in the United States. But I was also careful not to throw out the baby with the bath water. Some things that I had been taught were not necessarily bad in and of themselves.

With the library at my disposal, I familiarized myself first with the writings of René Descartes and the Rationalists, Hume and the Empiricists, Immanuel Kant, as well as other existential and religious thinkers. I augmented the readings assigned in my philosophy classes with a self-taught mini-course in classic philosophy and religion.

René Descartes (1596–1650) in his *Second Meditation* reasoned that one of the few things he could be certain of in life was his existence. He reasoned that if he thought, the mere process of his thinking implied a thinker, therefore this thinker existed and this thinker was he. I decided to take Descartes dictum, *Cogito ergo sum* (I think, therefore I am), and apply it to my own quest. I reasoned that I should begin my soul-searching as he had with his famous "method of doubt," challenging the very concept of reality and existence itself.

What I set out for myself was nothing less than a systematic evaluation of everything that I believed in. Naturally, to be intellectually honest and thorough, it had to begin with the very basic assumption of them all: my own existence. For three weeks, I wrestled with the question of whether or not I existed at all!

I reviewed variant notions of solipsism (the belief that one is the center of the universe) and examined at length the possibility that the world, as I knew it, did not exist. What if the universe was a fiction of my mind? I examined other possibilities: Was I the figment of someone else's imaginings? Was the universe a dream and I the dreamer? Was believing in myself the only thing that kept me alive?

After several days it dawned on me that such reflection was self-defeating. If mine was a solipsist universe, it would either abide by the laws of physics as I knew them, or it would not. If it did not, then it really didn't matter what I believed, since, by definition, logic and reason did not apply. But if the laws of science did apply, then I would be foolish to walk in front of an oncoming train, say, because I might be killed. The notion of solipsism became subservient to the more important issue of whether I lived in a universe in which knowable laws of science existed. A universe in which the laws of science were operative implied the existence of matter, and this, in turn, implied (though, certainly, did not guarantee) that I existed. It seemed as if every logical presumption, to mean anything, required a suspension of disbelief. Faith. This was my conclusion after three weeks of study and self-reflection: I would believe in my own existence—on faith.

Closely linked to existence was the matter of epistemology. By what standards was I to judge knowledge and therefore proof of my existence? For several days I reviewed this notion. What do we consider valid as an indication of what is knowledge?

After studying ways in which people think, such as rationalism and intuitivism, I came to the conclusion that the only way to truly know something was through empiricism: the theory of knowledge based on the experience of our sensory perceptions as opposed to insight (intuitivism) or by reason alone (rationalism).

But how was I to account for those extraordinary human epiphanies that defined our very being, such as music, art, love, or spiritual experiences? How could epistemology account for these without resorting to something beyond the empirical? I discovered that Immanuel Kant believed that what we experience in the world through our senses is the result of an external source that could not be known on its own terms—the "numenona," or the "thing in itself." For Kant, the world was unknowable and could only be constructed through our sensations and conceptions. He used the concept of "numenona" to explain religious experience, moral duty, and other non-sensate human concerns.

But my modest experiences with drugs, alcohol, and novocaine (during an operation), convinced me that these extraordinary human experiences could be explained without resorting to concepts like "numenona." They could merely be sensory perceptions stimulated by chemical reactions in the human neurological system. I was prepared to accept love and spiritual experience, literally, as a chemical high.

During the course of my self-examination, I tried not to apply value judgments to the process I had undertaken. Once I was liberated from the sense of guilt and obligation associated with a belief in God, I was free to explore all. I had become, at the end of my freshman year, a "free-thinker." Or so I thought.

Of course, I was in terrible anguish. While intellectually I sought to be true to principles I respected and admired, and tried to fashion in my own way the answers to questions I felt needed to be raised, emotionally I was a wreck. I was rejecting years of what had shaped me into the person I was. The old identity of the Mexican American known as Jess Treviño was crumbling, and a new identity was in the process of being born. The first signs of this transformation was the rejection of God and the positing of a new set of moral precepts that elevated humanity over God, reason over ignorance, science over superstition—in short, an ordered universe.

Ultimately, that was what I decided upon: a universe that, at least internally, was ordered and self-reaffirming. In effect, if I were no longer to believe in God, then what I did believe in must be a universe I'd like to live in: one that made sense.

After perhaps two months of this intensive introspection and scrutiny, abetted by many intensive discussions with Loftsgordon and my fellow philosophy students, I finally shaped an approach to life that I labeled "empirical humanism." Simply stated, it held empirical data as the fundamental source of knowledge and the advancement of love of one's fellow human being as the self-justifying moral imperative. Everything else (notions of beauty, love, emotions) were all explainable from this perspective.

This did not necessarily diminish the "meaning" of these human dimensions to me; it only gave them a foundation in something that was scientifically sound and internally consistent. Once thought out and understood, it would be the basic guiding principle on which I would live the rest of my life. All subsequent ideologies, philosophies, and personal views would originate from or be modified by this new mind-set.

One of the first beliefs that clicked into place in my newfound world view was the determination that the war in Vietnam was contrary to the empirical humanism in which I now believed. By April of 1968, then, I had decided that I would apply for conscientious objector status, should I be drafted after graduation. I resolved not go to Vietnam under any circumstances. When the walkouts occurred, I found the emergence of the new Chicano identity emerging within me consistent with this life outlook.

But now, in the quiet of the long drive back to Los Angeles, I was once again confronted by the need to reconcile the role of religion in human affairs. In this case, the question vexing me was simple: how was I to react to the fact that a great man like César Chávez, a leader of my people, was using religious beliefs and icons to advance a just cause?

I had to admit that there was a danger of this religious fervor being used to negative ends—the specter of the Inquisition and the

Crusades loomed once again. Yet, as long as Chávez carried the banner of the Virgin of Guadalupe to fight injustice, as long as he espoused a philosophy of nonviolence, how could I be critical of this? My own empirical humanism required tolerance for the beliefs of others as long as they did not seek to oppress.

I applied "Ockham's Razor" once again. The fight for human justice and equality was empirically valid. To discount others in this struggle merely because they believed in a supreme being was not logical. My own empirical humanism and tolerance for the beliefs of others demanded that I look to the underlying social struggle, a social struggle I was determined to be a part of.

"I'm glad we did this," John Nomura said, interrupting the long silence of the drive. "I mean, bringing them all the food and clothing."

"Yeah, me too. " I replied. "It was about time."

Chapter Three

A Hidden History

All over the country today, La Raza *is in motion . . . Our people are refusing to be filled with shame any longer; they are refusing to be oppressed, they are demanding liberation and a decent life.*

—*Elizabeth "Betita" Martínez*

A gravelly voice shouted above the din of the crowd as I stood with dozens of young men at the pre-induction physical office in downtown Los Angeles. "Hay-SOOS Sol-vador Tre-veeno!" It was two weeks after my trip to Delano, and I stood stripped to my shorts, waiting in line to be examined by one of several doctors whose unenviable assignment was to determine which of us was fit for Uncle Sam's army.

I stepped forward to a bored doctor, who gave me a perfunctory examination, checking mouth, eyes, ears, hammering at my knees with a rubber mallet, and then asking me to pull down my shorts and cough as his gloved hand checked for hernias. Then he nodded for me to move on to the next table, where I was presented with a form that, among other things, inquired if I knew of any reason why I could not be considered for military service.

This is what I had been waiting for.

I checked in the box marked "medical" and proceeded to explain about my childhood bout with death and the damaged condition in which it had left my heart. I was convinced this would make me unsuitable for the draft.

My attention was distracted by shouting. I looked up to see a couple of orderlies dragging away a young man dressed in a flower-patterned dress and high heels. His face was covered with red-and-white paint. The young man was screaming hysterically. "You're trying too hard," I thought to myself as I went back to filling out the form. Insanity was only one of many ploys being used as young men tried desperately to avoid the draft. I finished the form and soon was dressed and on my way home.

The History I Never Knew

The army physical was a wakeup call. I did not know whether or not I would be reclassified as 4-F because of my childhood illness, or listed as 1-A (suitable for military service), but one thing was certain: I really could be drafted. I had already applied to seven graduate schools, but knew that any acceptance, and therefore a decision on where I would spend the fall, would not come until after graduation. In the midst of these uncertainties, I was resolved to restore control back to my life amid the chaos of a war that threatened to consume me.

A week after the physical, I proposed marriage to Gayla. We agreed to wed after graduation. Whatever the future might bring, I felt relieved that I would have a companion to see me through it. I also managed to secure a summer job. In mid-July, I would be teaching Mexican-American history and literature to black and Latino students enrolled in Upward Bound, a federally sponsored program that provided college experience for advanced high school students from minority backgrounds.

As I studied for final exams, I also set out to prepare for the courses I'd be teaching. I soon discovered how very little I knew about either Mexican-American literature or history. The only book available at the time that dealt with the history of the Mexican American in any substantial way was *North from Mexico,* written by the editor of *The Nation* magazine, Carey McWilliams. McWilliams had authored several other works dealing with Southern California life, notably *Brothers Under the Skin* and *Ill Fares the Land.*

As I read the opening chapters of the book, I discovered that there was, indeed, a history of Mexican Americans in the United States. It was one that Carey McWilliams characterized as a "fantasy heritage," established long ago in textbooks and the mainstream press, linking Mexican Americans in an odd way to the legacy of Spaniards who had originally settled in the Southwest. McWilliams described the myth eloquently:

> Long, long ago the borderlands were settled by Spanish grandees and caballeros, a gentle people accustomed to the luxurious softness of fine clothes, to trained servants, to all the amenities of civilized Europeans.

> For the young people it was a life of unrivaled enjoyment, racing their horses over the green rolling hills and mustard fields of Southern California, dancing the contradanzas and jotas, the click of castanets. In the evening, the young rancheros strolled beneath the window of his young boudoir. As the moon rose high over the Sierra Madre, he would sit singing the old love songs of Spain. All in all, this life of Spain away from Spain, in the borderlands of California, was very romantic, idyllic, very beautiful. Indeed, it is really a shame that it never existed.

McWilliams juxtaposed this myth of carefree *Californios* of old with the reality I had seen around me as I grew up: impoverished Mexicans, who were a subclass of migrant *campesinos* and urban factory workers. As I read on, I learned that the Mexican-American experience extended far beyond the borders of East Los Angeles. In Texas we were known as *tejanos*. In New Mexico we called ourselves *manitos*. In each and every region of the Southwest—be it Texas, New Mexico, Arizona, Nevada, Colorado, or California—we were at once separated by our regional differences but united in poverty, exploitation, and discrimination.

I read in fascination about the Mexican-American War of 1848. This war had been provoked when James Polk—exhilarated by a presidential victory based on a platform of westward expansion and knowing that Mexico was ill prepared for war—sent American troops to cross into Mexican lands. I discovered that the war with Mexico was not accidental and had little to do with the United States being pulled into the conflict "by the act of Mexico herself" after Mexican troops had, in the words of President Polk, "shed American blood on American soil." The opposite was true. The Mexican-American War had been a war provoked by a national mission of westward expansion and greed for the natural resources of the West.

In high school I had been taught that gold was first discovered at Sutter's Field in Sacramento by John Marshall in 1849, after the conclusion of the war with Mexico. McWilliams begged to differ. The first gold in California had been discovered much earlier, on March 9, 1842, when Francisco López, a Mexican herdsman, discovered gold in Santa Feliciana Canyon, forty miles from Los Angeles. Years before John James Marshall's famous discovery, Mexicans had mined the coastal range between Los Angeles and Santa Cruz and had found gold in significant quantities. In Arizona, silver, gold, and copper had been recovered since the 1700s.

All of this was common knowledge prior to the Mexican-American War, so much so that the United States at first sent John Slidell to try to purchase part of Texas from Mexico in 1845. When Mexico refused, President Polk devised another way of securing the prized natural resources in the Southwest for the United States. If Mexico would not sell, the United States would acquire it by force. Polk dispatched troops under General Zachary Taylor into Mexican lands to provoke an incident that could justify a declaration of war with Mexico.

McWilliams recounted the painful outcome of the war and the signing of the Treaty of Guadalupe Hidalgo between the United States and Mexico. This treaty guaranteed the Mexicans living in the United States—the first Mexican Americans—all the rights and privileges enjoyed by U.S. citizens, including the right of property, the right to worship as they chose, and the right to speak their own language.

But after the war, Anglo Americans swept into the Southwest, quickly outnumbering the native Mexicans. Through both "legal" and illegal (often violent) means, the Anglos expropriated land and businesses from Mexican Americans. Within two decades after the war, those Mexican-American land owners living in California, New Mexico, and Texas (the gentry class whom McWilliams described as the "gente de razón") lost their land to speculators and others through fraud, coercion, and banditry.

As I read McWilliams's book, a hatred for everything "American" grew within me. Until this time, I had not thought much about patriotism or about any particular allegiance to my country of birth. Like every child, I had pledged my allegiance to the flag of the United States before each day of school without much comprehension of what that pledge meant. Now, as I read about how Mexican Americans had fallen from land owners to peons forced to work on the railroads, in mines, and in fields, I begrudged the fact that I had been forced to recite this pledge as a child. Why should I be loyal to a nation that had robbed my people of their lands in an imperialist war, whose aftermath was evident in the barrio poverty I witnessed daily?

Many Mexicans who remained in the United States after the war had fought back. To me, these were the first courageous "Chicanos." They were people like Juan Nepomuceno Cortina, the Red Robber of the Rio Grande, who formed an army of more than one hundred men to fight against Anglo expropriation of Mexican lands in Texas. Those Mexicans that defended their rights were often branded as Mexican bandits and were hunted down and killed. I began to see that men like Joaquín Murietta, Tiburcio Vásquez and other infamous California "bandits" were freedom fighters, defending their lands and rights from the Anglo incursion into the Southwest. Once the strongest and most defiant freedom fighters had been killed, however, their history was open for reinterpretation by the conquerors.

As a result, Mexican Americans were, in McWilliams's words, "a people whose culture has been under incessant attack for many years and whose character and achievements, as a people, have been consistently disparaged." The conquered became "competitors with the conquerors for land and jobs and power, parties to a constant economic conflict which has found expression in litigation, dispossession, hotly contested elections, and the mutual disparity which inevitably accompanies a situation of this kind."

In addition to the initial defeat of Mexico and Mexicans in 1848, at the conclusion of the Mexican-American War, there had been a "second defeat." This defeat occurred when Spanish-speaking people in the United States were divested of their rights, property, and language, and when the myth of Mexican Americans as docile, subservient, and timorous people was promulgated. Then, during the Mexican Revolution of 1910, more than a million and a half Mexicans fled Mexico and came to settle in the United States. These new immigrants swelled the population of Mexican communities, which provided them with the boldness to improve their lot in the United States.

Early efforts by Mexican Americans included organizing labor unions and assimilating through "Americanization" programs. But many of these early efforts were doomed to failure. During the 1920s and '30s, for example, Mexican Americans sought to organize unions in the agricultural fields. These early union efforts, such as the Cannery and Agricultural Workers' Industrial Union and the *Confederación de Uniones de Campesinos y Obreros Mexicanos,* were crushed by police and sheriffs, who collaborated with growers to keep Mexicans as a powerless work force.

During the Great Depression, Mexican labor was seen as a threat to the American worker, so not only were Mexicans deported in vast numbers, but so, too, were legal United States citizens of Mexican descent. Throughout these years, Mexicans were excluded from any meaningful political representation.

During the 1940s, wartime xenophobia turned Mexicans and Mexican Americans in the Southwest into scapegoats. In the Sleepy Lagoon trial, twenty-one young men were charged with a murder simply because they were *pachucos*, that is, because they wore the stylish "zoot suits" of the time. In 1943, U.S. sailors took to attacking Mexican-American youths dressed in zoot suits and left them lying beaten and naked in the streets, only to be arrested by local police. While these attacks were going on, the older brothers and the fathers of these Mexican Americans were fighting overseas in defense of our country.

The more I read, the more infuriated I became. I had begun reading the book in ignorance, but when I was finished, I had completely identified with the protagonists; it was no longer just "their" history I was reading about, but my own.

When I applied this "new" information about the history of my people to my own life, many things snapped into place. I understood why I had developed such a terrible self-hatred during junior high and high school, and why I had come to believe that Mexicans were an inferior race. Instead of learning of the positive things my people had accomplished, which might have bolstered my self-esteem, I had only been exposed to the Anglo myth of my people—a wretched misrepresentation, at best.

When I was growing up in East Los Angeles, Spanish was banned in the classroom. Poverty ran rampant in my neighborhoods. In high school, I had been advised against applying to a four-year college because I was told I would not be able to handle the heavy work load. I had been given the same advice offered to all Mexican-American graduating seniors: try a trade school, a two-year junior college, or get a job working with your hands. I realized that I had suffered from the prolonged legacy of a national conquest that had taken place a hundred years before I was born!

By the time I finished the book, I was seething with rage. But this vital and devastating information also gave me strength. I was now armed with an arsenal of information with which to tell the world about the terrible crimes that had been committed against my people.

McWilliams had finished his book in 1948. It was incomplete. There was still a vast history that remained untold. Perhaps, some day, I would have the opportunity to add to the saga of my people.

The Groundskeeper

After finishing *North from Mexico*, I wanted to learn even more. But there were no Mexican Americans or African Americans on the faculty—people who might respond to me with some sensitivity. What I desired was a first-hand account of the history in Carey McWilliams's book.

I sought out a man that I had met at one of the early meetings of the Educational Issues Coordinating Committee, Ben Carmona, the groundskeeper of the Occidental College baseball field. I remembered Henry telling me that Ben knew a lot about Chicano history.

I found Ben spreading manure over freshly planted grass in left field.

"Mr. Carmona," I said, "do you have a minute? I don't know if you remember me . . ."

"Sure, you're Jesse, aren't you?" he replied, looking up from his work. I was heartened that he had remembered me. "There are not too many of our people here at Oxy."

Ben was stocky and muscular. His face was creased with wrinkles that came from a lifetime of work in the sun. He was well known on campus because he loved to joke with the track and baseball players as he worked the field.

"I've been meaning to come to you." I felt awkward and nervous. How, exactly would I frame my questions? How do you ask for something when you don't know what it is you need? How does one ask for history, for experience, for truth? "Henry Gutiérrez told me you grew up in East Los Angeles," I finally blurted. "I guess I'd like to know more about how things were back then."

"Sure," he said. "I can tell you anything you wanna know."

"The zoot suit riots," I continued. "Did you experience them?"

He stopped his shoveling and motioned me over to the cement steps that led to the bleachers. We sat down together as he wiped his hands with a worn track towel.

"Yes. I saw the zoot suit riots. That was back in the 1940s. I was a young man then, *era chamaco*, in Lincoln Heights, where I still live now." His eyes were intense with remembrance. "There were these young girls, and there were these sailor boys, who were stationed in Long Beach. They had come to downtown Los Angeles and somehow found their way to Lincoln Heights. They were flirting with these girls. Soon, the boyfriends of the girls got very angry, and they told these guys to stop it. But when they would not stop, and they kept . . . *cómo se dice* . . ." He hesitated, searching his memory for the right word, ". . . *harassing* the girls."

He stopped for a moment, looking out over the baseball field and into the dormitories on the hill behind the track. But I could tell he was seeing straight through the buildings into another time, another place.

"Well, the young Chicanos—the boyfriends—they pushed these

sailors away and beat up one of the sailors.

"You can imagine: young Chicanos beating up an American sailor, a *gringo*. That was not done! Well, the sailors left, but later they came back in taxis, each car with five or six young *americano* sailors. They searched the streets of East Los Angeles, and whenever they saw a Mexican boy, they would jump out of the car and beat him up. *Les quitaron los pantalones*, they took off their clothes—a lot of them wore zoot suits, you see—and they left them naked, right there in the street."

Ben Carmona and I talked all afternoon—first about the infamous zoot suit riots, then about the repatriation of the 1930s. Then he spoke more generally about being Chicano, the poverty of our people, the need for education, and the incessant discrimination dealt out by American society.

He probably didn't get much work done that afternoon, but he did tell me much of what I wanted to know about my own history as a Chicano. I sat there and listened to him as I might a professor telling me what questions were to be asked on a final exam.

As the afternoon waned, I wondered why I had never spoken with this man before. I had seen him almost daily during my four years at Occidental. But I had seen him like everyone else had—as the Mexican gardener cutting the grass on the baseball field, picking up trash after a track meet, or munching a brown bag lunch in the bleachers. I had arrived at Oxy expecting to become educated, to receive the kind of knowledge that transforms a young life. I thought I would get this from learned professors with Ph.D.'s. Instead, the most valuable information—truths that would provide my life with direction—was from a forty-five-year-old gardener.

A Career Challenge

The conversation with Carmona left me unsettled. It raised profound issues that had been nagging at me since the walkouts. My interest had been in philosophy. But now I began to question whether philosophy could lead to the pragmatic changes needed to advance the plight of my people. Philosophy was a copout. I had attempted to grapple with lofty questions of the universe while avoiding questions that confronted me, personally. By running to philosophy, I was also running away from the reality of being Mexican American.

This uncomfortable realization set me on another course. I was outraged about the history I had recently learned, so I vowed to do something about it. I recalled that toward the end of *North from Mexico*, Carey McWilliams pointed out that the events traced in his book could be seen as the latest chapter in the belated discovery of the Southwest and of its people. But his book, he said, was paving the way for something else:

> Of paramount importance to the future is the role that the coming generation of Mexican Americans will play . . . In the past, Mexicans have been a more or less anonymous, voiceless, an expressionless minority . . . There has yet to be written, for example, a novel of southwestern experience by an American-born person of Mexican descent or a significant autobiography by a native-born Mexican. The moment the group begins to achieve this type of expression, a new chapter will be written in the history of the Southwest.

I reexamined the philosophic premises I had undertaken a few years before, and that I had recently reviewed on my trip to Delano, but it didn't help me to see how I could contribute to betterment of my people. What was my role to be? What career would I find myself in? I was still asking myself these questions a few weeks later, on May 22, when I graduated from Occidental College with a B.A. in philosophy.

Gayla and I were married on June 15, 1968, in a small private ceremony on a cliff in the Carmel Highlands overlooking the Pacific Ocean. It was an idyllic ceremony with only a few friends present, far removed from the gritty reality of East Los Angeles. After the serenity of a few days in Carmel, we returned to Los Angeles. Armed with a car Gayla's mother had lent us, and a modest paycheck from Gayla's work teaching children with learning disabilities, we were ready to jump back into the struggle that now consumed our lives.

The East L.A. 13

On June 5, events in the Chicano community took a turn for the worse. Eleven of thirteen individuals indicted by a secret grand jury for leading the high school walkouts in March were arrested by the Los Angeles County Sheriff's Department and the Los Angeles Police Department.

The "East L.A. 13," as they were dubbed, had been charged with "conspiring to disturb the peace." The act of disturbing the peace was only a misdemeanor. If convicted, one might expect a sentence of a few weeks in jail. But since the district attorney added the term "conspiring" to the charge, the East L.A. 13 were facing a felony that carried with it a maximum prison sentence of sixty-six years.

The list of those arrested read like a Who's Who of the people who had participated in the walkouts. Prominent in the list was the charismatic Lincoln High School teacher Sal Castro. Also among the "E.L.A. 13" were members of the Brown Berets organization: Carlos Montes, David Sánchez, Ralph Ramírez, and Cruz Olmeda. Eliseo Riesco and Joe Razo, publishers of the militant *La Raza* magazine, were also arrested, as were college-aged UMAS students Moctezuma Esparza and Carlos Muñoz, and community activists Pat Sánchez, Richard Vigil, Henry Gómez, and Fred López.

Before the indictments, many of us in the EICC thought that a meaningful dialogue with the Los Angeles School Board had, at last, been established. We had hoped that our ongoing meetings with school officials would bring about changes in the deplorable conditions that had provoked the walkouts in March. Now we discovered that, instead of dealing with us in good faith, school officials had been testifying secretly in front of a grand jury to bring about the indictments against leaders of the walkout movement.

The activities of the EICC soon changed in character. We were no longer on the offensive, protesting school abuses, but were now on the defensive, organizing fundraisers and rallies in support of the E.L.A. 13.

Our weekly meetings expanded to two and three sessions a week. I began to devote more and more of my time to working in the EICC. Henry Gutiérrez and I were soon invited into the inner sanctum of the

EICC, the informal steering committee chaired by Rev. Vahac
Mardirosian that also included Rev. Horacio Quiñonez, Joe Ortega,
Raquel Galán, and Ben and Kay Gurulé.

The meetings of the EICC, and interim visits to the board of education, became a major part of my life. Those of us in the inner sanctum became an extended family. We would barbecue together, go to
the beach, always debating the issues that were now the passion of our
lives. At the conclusion of each EICC meeting, we would adjourn to
Googies, a favorite restaurant, to plan future strategies.

It was a heady experience to be twenty-one years old and planning major protests and marches that would bring out hundreds of
people—the antithesis of the armchair philosophy I had been practic-
ing in college. Just as intoxicating was the respect given to my ideas
and suggestions. I was becoming an important player in a movement
for social change. But the energy and joy I experienced was mingled
with anger. For the arrest of the E.L.A. 13, coming on the heels of my
recent introduction to Chicano history, made me grimly aware of
racism against Chicanos.

"Look what they're doing to us," I said in desperation to Gayla
one night, after an E.L.A. 13 protest at the downtown Hall of Justice.

The assembly was remarkable because of the wide range of people that had attended from throughout Los Angeles. There were white
liberals from the Westside, African Americans from South-Central
Los Angeles, as well as Chicanos. The mix included clergy, students,
school officials, and professionals—all marching with placards, all
furious over the trumped-up conspiracy charges.

"They robbed us of our land, turned us into peons, and when we
protest this kind of treatment, they arrest us and throw us in jail! I hate
this country!"

Gayla empathized with my pain. She identified as much as I did
with the Chicano cause. She reveled in her new teaching assignment
with Mexican-American children in Project Head Start, a federally
funded school and daycare program. She was also an active member
of the inner sanctum. We lived and breathed the movement.

Battling My Own Racism

Although the leadership of the EICC had a strong religious base, and though community leaders called for us to embrace all races, the membership of the group included Chicanos of all kinds—many of whom harbored a strong hatred of white people. Often we would attend meetings at which individuals called for "death to the *gabacho*" and "revolution by all means necessary."

At first, I accepted these phrases, and others, as hyperbole and rhetoric—a public outcry after years of injustice. But as my hatred of the United States government and its institutions increased, my intense feelings soon found expression in the anti-white rhetoric of the movement. Before long, I found myself making public comments against *gabachos*. All whites became "the enemy," and I was becoming a racist.

As movement rhetoric accentuated differences between Chicanos and white people, I began to question my loyalty to non-Chicano friends—even those whom I had known for many years. On one occasion, a movement activist was denouncing white people and their oppression of Chicanos. He went on to denounce Jews as a people "who stole from the barrio and oppressed our people."

This comment suddenly brought me to my senses. During my summer at Arizona State University, I had become close friends with a classmate, Claude Fischer, who was in transit from Paterson, New Jersey, to Los Angeles. We shared a love of folk music and discussed philosophy vigorously. Although Claude and I attended different high schools, we often spent weekends together—either hanging out in his largely Jewish Fairfax neighborhood of Los Angeles, or him visiting me in El Sereno. On more than one occasion, I was mistaken for a Jew and was spoken to in Yiddish while visiting Claude. Similarly, he had been mistaken for being Mexican and was addressed in Spanish while he visited me on the Eastside. It was through Claude that I learned of the Holocaust, when, one day, I asked him about the peculiar numbers his parents had tattooed on their arms.

As the militant Chicano continued in his diatribe against Jews, I wondered how I could belong to a movement that was so racist at its core. I thought of my close friends Jim Miller, John Nomura, Claude Fischer, Dan Rubin; I thought of my father, of my wife. How could I be part of a movement that was openly denouncing people who were my closest friends and family, people whom I knew to be honest, kind, and loving? Though I grappled with this issue privately, I was too committed to *el movimiento* to give it up. Instead, I made excuses for the racism I saw and ignored the extent of my participation in it.

My inner turmoil came into sharp relief in my relationship with Gayla. Movement rhetoric was critical of Chicanos who "rapped brown but slept white," a phrase that haunted me whenever Gayla and I appeared together at movement activities. And yet, I loved her. She was the woman whom I had married and to whom I had sworn allegiance.

Compounding the problem was an ideological thrust that praised the very things for which Mexican Americans had been ridiculed for so long: our brown skin and our Indian features. The movement sought to redefine our sensibilities, to reevaluate what was beautiful and what was not. Our brown skin and Indian features were now something in which we could take pride.

One dimension of this newfound ethnic euphoria was the constant extollment of the beauty of Chicana women, praising them as "Aztec goddesses," as "*lindas chicanas*," as "lovely *adelitas*" (revolutionary heroines of the Mexican Revolution of 1910). This kind of rhetoric, and my own willingness to succumb to these ideas, caused an unspoken rift between Gayla and me. Praising the virtues of Chicanas implied a rejection of non-Chicana women. In subtle, mostly unconscious ways, I began to make Gayla feel that she was inadequate. The misunderstandings that are a part of the first year of any marriage became disproportionately intense. It is a tribute to the strength of our love, and our willingness to work things out, that our marriage survived these early years of the movement.

Equally painful was the unresolved relationship with my stepfather, who continued to view my activism in the Chicano Movement as a personal affront and a betrayal of his own values.

Whenever I visited my parents at home, I no longer mentioned the movement or spoke of politics. My mother applauded my involvement in the movement and often participated in rallies but knew that the only way to keep peace in the house was by not mentioning her support of *el movimiento* to my stepfather.

My sister, Olinda, had moved away to school at UCLA and was involved in the movement there. My youngest sister, Rosalba, who had inherited my stepfather's blond hair, sided with the views of our generation and spoke Spanish proudly.

My stepfather could not reconcile what was happening around him. As he saw it, his wife and children were covertly involved in a movement that hated white people, like himself, and that wanted to overthrow the government. He felt betrayed and abandoned by his family. A chasm was developing between him and my mother that would result in his death a few years later.

Rejections

In the meantime, I waited anxiously for my acceptance to graduate schools. Soon the responses began arriving: University of Michigan—rejection. Cal-Berkeley—rejection. Harvard—rejection. UCLA—rejection. University of Edmonton—rejection. By the middle of July, I had been rejected by all seven of the graduate schools to which I had applied. I was devastated. I had an A- average in my major (philosophy) and a B+ average in my minor (religion). I concluded that it must have been my Graduate Record Exam scores that had torpedoed my entry into these programs.

I had thought that acceptance to graduate school would, among other things, keep me out of the draft. Now the draft loomed ominously over my life. What if I were to be certified 1-A? What would I do?

Chapter Four

Adrift

The Mexican can't become a gringo, he can't and he doesn't want to. The Mexican can't become a gringo, he can't and he won't!

—*Chicano Movement* corrido

Shortly after Gayla and I had returned from our wedding in Carmel, Guadalupe Saavaedra de Saavedra—the militant who had taught me the Chicano handshake—stopped me after an EICC meeting in front of the Euclid Center on Whittier Boulevard.

"*Wacha*, Jesse, I have something important for you. I mean, this is really for you." Lupe was dressed in his trademark jeans and army jacket and was wearing dark glasses, though it was well past eleven at night.

Despite his glib tongue and charismatic appearance, Lupe's efforts to integrate himself into the Eastside *movimiento* over the past few weeks had met with failure. Many people knew of his falling out with the United Farm Workers, and some thought of him as unreliable. Others were less kind, and thought he was an unscrupulous opportunist. Undaunted, Lupe had recently founded an Eastside theater company, El Teatro Chicano.

"There's going to be an *escuela de teatro*, a theater school, and it's going to be taught by Luis Valdez, of El Teatro Campesino. *¿Me entiendes? Wacha*, you got to go up to the workshop in Del Rey, *ése*. When you come back, you can join our group here."

54

The thought of theater intrigued me, though I didn't much like the prospect of working with Lupe Saavedra and his fledgling theater company. Still, perhaps this workshop was just what I needed. With the devastating graduate school rejections, it would certainly be wise to explore other options. Theater was not new to me. In my last year at Occidental College, I had taken two courses in theater appreciation and had read numerous plays. After graduation, I wondered whether the arts were the area where I was to make my mark in the world.

Saavedra filled me in. Luis Valdez had recently left the farm workers' movement in Delano and had settled in the San Joaquín Valley town of Del Rey, where he proposed to produce plays dealing with universal Chicano themes. In particular, he wished to address the urban Chicano experience. He had decided to convene a summer workshop in Chicano *teatro* to share his theatrical experience with Chicanos throughout the United States.

When I returned home that night, I told Gayla that I wanted to attend the three-week workshop. Although we were recently married and she preferred that we spend more time together, she went along with my plans.

I hoped to learn important skills from El Teatro Campesino, and perhaps on my return, I would take up acting or even start my own theater company. Why not? With my future so uncertain, I needed a plan to create the illusion that my life was on solid ground.

On the following Monday afternoon, I boarded a Greyhound bus in downtown Los Angeles and left for Del Rey. I arrived at about one o'clock in the afternoon. I hoped this would give me some time to integrate myself into the group before the workshop started.

I stepped down from the air-conditioned bus into the blazing heat—it was well over a hundred degrees. The address I had been given belonged to a storefront with chipped paint, dirty windows, and an ancient screen door.

I peeked through the screen but saw no one. I opened the door and walked inside. The room was spacious and dark. It appeared to be a bar that had been converted into an office. In one corner, a desk and table had been set up. In the middle of the room was a worn couch and chairs.

My eyes adjusted to the darkness. I welcomed the coolness of the room. At the counter, which had been a bar, I called out. After a moment, a Chicana emerged from a back room.

"What do you want?" she asked in a fairly cold voice.

"I'm looking for El Teatro Campesino. I've come to be part of the workshop. Is this the right place?"

"Yeah, this is the *centro*," she said flatly. "The school is going to start in a day or two. Not everyone's arrived yet."

"Is anyone here now?"

"Yeah, they're down at the canal."

"The canal?"

"The canal!" she said to me as if I were an imbecile. "Where the water is." She turned and unceremoniously exited to the back room.

The canal? I didn't get it. I waited until she returned to the main room and asked her again. "Excuse me. Is this 'canal' some place I should be?"

"Oh, yeah," she said, warming to me. "Everyone's down there. That's where we swim in the afternoon, to get away from the heat."

This notion didn't appeal to me. I was here to learn about theater, not practice my backstroke.

"Well, when will they be back?"

"In an hour or two. You can wait. Or you can meet them down there. Did you bring any shorts?"

"I think I'll wait until they get back," I said with a sigh.

I felt stupid killing time waiting for people I didn't even know, but what else was there for me to do? Soon, I grew restless and took a walk through town. Then I came back to the *centro* and waited some more.

At about four o'clock that afternoon, several cars pulled up to the building and people piled out. They were all young men and women, still dripping with canal water. Among them was a short stocky man with a mustache. He was older than the rest, so I presumed that he might know something or be in charge.

"Excuse me," I said. "I'm looking for Luis Valdez."

He hesitated and then inspected me from head to toe. "That's me. Who are you?"

I told him that I was a Chicano from Los Angeles and that I wanted to be part of the theater school.

Valdez explained that he was going to wash up. They would be having dinner in a couple of hours. The school wasn't going to start for another day or two, but I was welcome to stay. When enough people showed up, they'd start the workshops. In the meantime, I was welcome to sleep on the *centro*'s floor.

And off he went.

I was totally taken aback. How could this disorganized group be the great school of Chicano theater?

In a corner, two Chicanos had settled down to play guitars. Being a player myself, I drifted over to watch. I was immediately envious: these guys were good! Soon, several others gathered around. The musicians started a *corrido* that everyone knew, and it didn't take long before the room was alive with singing:

Bueno, pues que'hubo, como le va
Que lindo día para cantar
Noticas que han llegado
De Nuevo México . . .

After a couple of songs, they shifted to instrumentals. One of the young men improvised complex musical riffs while the other played rhythm. I became absorbed in their music. At one point, I asked the person standing next to me who these young men were.

"That's Daniel Valdez, Luis's brother. And that's Augie, Augustine Lira. He's part of the group, too." I was entranced by the improvisational abilities of these two Chicanos, still wet from their swim. As the afternoon disappeared, however, I became impatient and irritated by the haphazard and lackadaisical manner in which everyone conducted themselves. There was no purpose to anything, no order.

In between songs, people began to talk about buying something to drink. Finally, a collection was taken. Before long, a large bottle of cheap wine was being passed around the room.

When Luis Valdez came back, I approached him once again. "Is there a syllabus? Books we should be reading? How should I prepare myself?"

He gave me an amused look and let out a sonorous laugh. He told me there was no syllabus. This was a different kind of school.

"No syllabus?"

"That's right."

I was shocked. How could you teach a course—in anything—without a syllabus? Here I was, a college graduate, having come all the way from Los Angeles to be with a theater instructor who didn't even have it together enough to write up a course syllabus. And the students' only interest seemed to be swimming and drinking. Only a few weeks before, I had organized my own syllabus for my Chicano history and literature classes. I would have been lost without that preparation. How could they possibly be serious about doing theater? What kind of haphazard operation was this?

I questioned several of the members of the group, most of them in their teens, about what I might expect from the workshop. "Oh, we'll probably do some improvs," one of them told me. "Maybe write a one-act play or learn some new songs." Another told me he was going to be a workshop leader. He wasn't more than seventeen years of age. Great, I thought to myself, I'm going to be one of *your* students? What was this, "Romper Room"?

The more I heard about plans for the next few days, the more convinced I was that I had made a mistake. Luis Valdez and the members of his theater company were amateurs. What could they possibly teach me? The thought of spending three weeks with such disorganized people filled me with dread. I didn't have time to waste on this!

I agonized for about an hour. All the while, Daniel Valdez and Augustine Lira played music in the corner and sipped on wine. The others just chatted and drank and acted as though I were invisible. I felt totally out of place. Finally, I called the Greyhound depot and discovered that another bus would leave for Los Angeles in an hour. I made my decision. Two hours later I was on the road back to Los Angeles, fully convinced that El Teatro Campesino was little more than an overly hyped group of lazy dabblers, incapable of teaching me anything.

Deep down inside, of course, I was terribly disappointed. I had talked up the idea of a career in theater with Gayla so much in the past few days, and now I would be returning with dashed hopes. *Teatro* was supposed to provide me the direction I desperately needed in my life. I was in limbo once again.

Hindsight would expose my error. The fault lay not so much in the El Teatro Campesino, but in my own stuffy standards. A few years later, I would become a member of El Teatro Compesino, and would discover that—far from being lazy—Luis Valdez could be a challenging taskmaster that set high goals for *teatro* members. Neither Luis nor Danny Valdez recalled my brief visit with them in 1968, but agreed that the organizational state of the El Teatro Campesino at the time was not likely to inspire confidence in anyone.

July came, and with it Upward Bound. I dedicated myself to the teaching of the history and literature of my people. Like a dry sponge that had suddenly been cast into a pool of water, I absorbed everything I could get my hands on about Chicanos. I became a walking, talking encyclopedia of Chicano history, literature, and art. Gayla and I were settling into married life, and my teaching consumed most of my time. We continued to attend the weekly meetings of the EICC. For the moment, at least, I could avoid thinking about the larger issue of my future career.

A Chance Meeting

As August approached, I become more anxious about what I would do after the Upward Bound job. Gayla's work at Project Headstart would help pay the bills, but that alone was not enough to support us. On top of that, we both knew that I might be called into military service within a few short weeks. Would we have to retreat to Canada? In the meantime, what was I to do with my life?

The answer to my immediate financial worries and to my career problems came from an unexpected source. One night, at a crowded Eastside fundraiser, I accidentally knocked a heavyset Chicano off his feet as Gayla and I were dancing. When I realized what had happened, I helped the man back to his feet.

"I'm awfully sorry!"

"It's no big deal."

I was surprised. Rather than being upset about my clumsiness, the man was downright amicable.

"My name is Frank Sifuentes," he said. He offered to buy me a beer. Soon, he was telling me of the creation of a new minority youth film school for which he was a community advisor.

"A film school?" I asked.

"Government funded," he said.

He went on to explain that a number of socially conscious Hollywood producers had noted the lack of African Americans and Latinos in the motion picture industry and had taken it upon themselves to solicit funds from the federal government for the school. As community advisor, Frank was to help recruit Chicano students for the school, which offered an educational stipend of $100 a week and would last a year. I told him that I would soon be out of a job and that I was interested in applying.

A week later, with Frank's encouragement, I was interviewed by a committee that included Mel Sloan, a cinema professor from U.S.C.; Jack Dunbar, the executive director of the new school; and Mae Churchill, a film producer and chair of the board. I was accepted into the New Communicators program and began my studies in film. My head was spinning. My lack of grace on the dance floor had resulted in a smooth segue from Upward Bound to a year-long film school that would shape the rest of my life.

New Communicators

Jack Dunbar, the executive director, led the orientation session for the New Communicators school on August 22, 1968. Once a bank, the building at 6211 Hollywood Boulevard had recently been converted into New Communicators. On the walls, in bright white, black, and pastels, were images from famous motion pictures that had been painted by the school's instructors.

I found a seat and scanned my fellow students. There were eighteen of us, sixteen men and two women. Of these, there were eight African Americans, seven Mexican Americans, one Native American, and two that I described to myself as "token whites." In the next few weeks, I would learn their names: Sid Baldwin, Alan Edmond, Ron

Edwards, Edna Gibson, Tut Hayes, John Henry, Francisco Martínez, John Parsons, Martín Quiroz, Melvin Ray, Bobby Romero, Alan "Ojenke" Saxon, Bobby Schoeller, Tommy Scott, Ed Trujillo, Esperanza Vásquez, Frank Vega, and me.

"New Communicators Incorporated is a federally funded poverty program," Dunbar began. "It operates on a budget of $283,000, secured from the Office of Economic Opportunity." He stopped for a moment as if to see if we were listening. "Our job is to train you in the craft of filmmaking, which we will do through intensive courses in writing, directing, producing, and editing. We will show you how to operate cameras and sound equipment, and at the end of one year's time, we will help integrate you into Hollywood at an entry-level position."

The orientation session lasted the rest of the morning. We were introduced to one another and to the teaching staff: five instructors who had recently graduated from USC and UCLA film schools: Bill Kerby, Jim O'Neill, Suzanne Opton, Neil Reichline, and Micheal Warren. One by one the instructors spoke to us, explaining what role each would play in our education. I was particularly taken with what Bill Kerby had to say. He was a gruff-voiced hippie with long, flowing blond hair, intense blue eyes, and a fierce kinetic energy.

He raised a Super 8-millimeter film camera high in the air for everyone to see.

"Konica Super 8-millimeter camera. Your weapon of choice!"

He handed the camera to me. "Pass it around."

As I examined the camera in my hand, Kerby continued. "You should be thinking about what kind of groovy little film you would like to make with this," he said. "In the next few weeks we're going to put so much shit in your brains it's going to blow your minds! Your heads will explode with filmmaking facts! You're going to eat, breathe, and live film. Then—here's the cool part—you're going to make your own films, tell your own stories. The sooner you decide what your story will be, the better."

I looked from Kerby down to the camera in my hand. I turned it around and inspected it. It was a sacred moment. I didn't know it then, but I had just been introduced to the instrument that would come to dominate my life. I stared at the camera, lost in a trance. Finally someone whispered to pass the camera on and I did.

I was excited about the prospect of working in film, and I already knew what my first film project might be. In my senior year at Occidental, I had taken a film appreciation class from Dr. Marsha Kindar. The course introduced me to the leading international film directors: Antonioni, Bergman, Fellini, Kurasawa, and others. At the end of the course, rather than do a term paper, I had elected to author an original screenplay I entitled "*Ya Basta!*"(Enough!). Inspired by the high school walkouts, the script involved the story of a young Mexican-American boy who rebels against the irrelevant education he received from the public school system. The principal expels him for his rude behavior, and on the way home the boy is attacked and killed by a gang of Chicanos. I wanted to point out that it was the schools and their insensitive treatment of Chicanos that had "created" the gang kids and had sent my protagonist to his death.

In the next few weeks, I applied myself with diligence to the classes at New Communicators. Our first lessons were both theoretical and practical. In the mornings, we attended classes in film production, learned how to operate cameras and sound equipment, and grappled with film editing. In the afternoons, we worked on our individual assignment: to produce a short silent Super 8 film. To this end, we were each given a Konica Super 8 camera and several rolls of Super-8 film. Within a week, we were at work on our first projects. During these first few weeks, I became friends with several of my classmates—Martín Quiroz and John Parsons, in particular.

Because we were both "*vatos de la Boyle*" (Martín had grown up in Boyle Heights, where I had lived as a child) we felt a strong kinship. John Parsons had grown up as a member of the Alpine gang, whose turf was the downtown area immediately west of Chinatown. Over the years, the neighborhood had lost its Chicano identity as successive influxes of Asians moved in and transformed it into an extension of Chinatown. The once-powerful gang, due to attrition, was in its last days, and John was one of its last members. As one of only two students at New Communicators that had attended college, I soon became a mentor and advisor to some of the Chicanos in the program.

The students at New Communicators were, on the whole,

extremely political. Among these were members of militant groups such as the Sons of Watts, the Student Non-Violent Coordinating Committee (SNCC), and a militant group of Chicano ex-gang members, La Junta. It didn't take long, therefore, before we began to criticize the workings of the school. Most obvious, in our view, was the lack of minority instructors. Although the director of the school and his assistant were black, there were no Latinos on staff. There were also no minorities among the film instructors.

I soon allied myself with the two most outspoken of the African-American students, Tut Hayes and Tommy Scott. The three of us became the unofficial spokesmen for the rest of the students. We compiled a list of changes ("demands") we deemed necessary to improve the school. Chief among our concerns was the fact that there were no students on the board of directors. We petitioned and had the board charter rewritten to include three student representatives with voting privileges on the board. The students would now have a say on matters pertaining to the school and its operation. Not surprisingly, it was Tut Hayes, Tommy Scott, and I who were elected to be the student representatives.

The three of us very quickly became a powerful force within the board. We demanded that the administration seek out qualified minorities to teach at the school. Some of the adult members of the board, mainly minority members, agreed with this idea. But others felt the quality of the training we received was what mattered and that the school should employ only the highest quality instructors, irrespective of race.

Although the board agreed to begin interviews with minority candidates, our demands created divisions within the board that would continue for months. Eventually, destructive in-fighting led to the closure of the New Communicators school.

For the moment, however, I had my hands full finishing my first Super-8 film assignment. I filmed the "*Ya Basta!*" story on location in the back alleys of Boyle Heights, where I had grown up. I managed to get some of my Upward Bound students from Oxy to volunteer as "actors." For the first time in my life, I was setting up scenes, planning camera angles, and directing the actors.

I spent a week editing five rolls of film into a three-minute piece, which I presented to my fellow students at New Communicators. The screening was a success. Not only did they applaud the story, but several Chicano classmates came up to me afterwards to tell me how authentic the film was. I was delighted with the result—I had made a film!

A Conscientious Objector To War

Midway through the Upward Bound summer, on July 23, 1968, I received a notice of reclassification from my draft board. My status had been changed from that of student deferment to 1-A. I had been found "fully acceptable for induction into the United States Armed Forces." I sat on our front steps on Munson Street, staring at the letter. The worst scenario was finally at hand. The letter informed me of my options, should I wish to contest the reclassification, but I already knew them by heart.

Gayla and I had discussed the draft often and had agreed that I should apply for C.O. status. If this did not work, I would carry out the plan that Dan Rubin and I had talked about, and which I had refined in conversations with Jim Miller: Gayla and I would move to Canada.

In the next few days, I carefully fashioned an expression of my beliefs against the war that I hoped would coincide with what the draft board considered necessary for conscientious objector status and that would still be true to my own beliefs. The crux of my position centered on the Supreme Being clause. Conscientious objector status was granted to individuals who professed a "belief in a relation to a Supreme Being involving duties superior to those arising from any human relation." At Gayla's urging, I had recently visited the offices of the American Friends Services Committee in Pasadena and had learned of the "parallel belief" decision of the Supreme Court in 1965. This decision held that one did not have to believe in a traditional God as long as one's belief "occupies in the life of the possessor parallel to that filled by an orthodox belief in God of one who clearly qualifies for the exemption." I was determined not to lie about my beliefs and felt that the philosophical world view I held was well within the guidelines set for C.O. status.

I expressed the view that my humanism took the place in my life that a belief in God did for others. It was a thoughtful, analytical presentation of my beliefs in empirical humanism that I had formulated over the course of my time at Occidental College—all without the trappings of church and God. I based my views of what I referred to as my *agape* (love for humanity) on the writings of Paul Tillich, the German theologian. I wrote:

> My position of conscientious objector to war arises from an earlier commitment of religious belief and training. While my present attitude is often described as humanitarian, for me it is more. It is the basis for evaluating what is and is not meaningful in life. I do not believe in a Supreme Being in the traditional sense. In place of God, I recognize the sacred character of life and dedicate myself to promoting love between myself and my neighbor.

Would my arguments sway the members of my draft board? Would I be permitted to serve out my two years of military service as a conscientious objector? I did not have a clue.

I did know that if my petition were accepted, I would spend two years of my life emptying bedpans in some hospital, or sweeping floors in a welfare office. I was prepared for this. But under no circumstances was I to be a part of the war machine that was laying waste to so many lives in Vietnam. I sent in my C.O. application and requested a personal appearance before my board to argue my case.

The Sal Castro Controversy

Meanwhile, events in the community continued to move at a fast pace. As the beginning of the new school semester neared, Sal Castro, one of the E.L.A 13, was suddenly barred from returning to his teaching job at Lincoln High School because of his felony charge for conspiring to disrupt the schools.

In a special meeting of the EICC, we debated what action to take. Vahac Mardirosian had already placed several calls to sympathetic members of the Los Angeles School Board in hopes of getting them to take Sal Castro back. But even the most sympathetic of board members felt that because of a longstanding rule that barred anyone accused of a felony from teaching, their hands were tied. We discussed our options late into the night. As community members, we felt we had to take a stand. We were also aware of the support that Castro had among students at Lincoln. If we, the parents and community leadership, did nothing, it was likely that the students at Lincoln would stage another walkout. We remembered the police beatings we had witnessed at Roosevelt High. We did not want to put students in jeopardy again.

Late that night, we voted to stage a massive demonstration outside of Lincoln High School on the first day of classes, September 16, which was—conveniently enough—Mexican Independence Day.

As we made plans for the demonstration, it occurred to me that I could contribute in a way I was never able to before. Not only would I help plan and coordinate the demonstration, but I would film it with the Konica Super 8 camera provided by New Communicators. Making my Super 8 version of *"Ya Basta!"* and watching the reaction when I screened it to my fellow students had made me acutely aware of the power of film.

Now I could continue my work in the EICC in a more meaningful way. I carried the idea a step further and decided to make a documentary about the educational neglect of Chicanos in Eastside schools, starting with the protest we were planning at Lincoln High.

It was overcast on the morning of Monday, September 16, 1968. Gayla and I got up early and drove our VW bug to Lincoln High School. Our car was jammed with placards that we and other members of the EICC had painted over the weekend at Ben and Kay Gurulé's house. We gathered at Lincoln Park, a few blocks away from the high school, where we distributed the placards among more than three hundred activists who had gathered to protest.

The morning was exhilarating. The boisterous crowd marched along Eastlake Avenue to the high school, and once there, people marched in an orderly albeit noisy double-file in front of the school. Here were all the activists whom I had come to know on a personal level: parents, students, clergy, community leaders.

I scurried around the line, filming not just the marchers but the reactions of students and teachers attending the first day of the fall semester. Anticipating that I would need sound bytes for my film, I interviewed students and teachers with a tape recorder through the metal fence to get their reactions to the protest. Occasionally, I would also film the undercover police photographers who were quietly taking stills and videotaping the picket line.

The next day, members of the EICC attended the regular Tuesday session of the Board of Education and appealed to the board to reinstate Sal Castro at Lincoln High School. The members of the board reiterated their position that as long as Castro stood accused of a felony, he would not be allowed to teach.

That evening, Gayla and I returned home exhausted. Waiting for me in the mailbox was a letter from my draft board that acknowledged receipt of my C.O. application. It informed me that I was to appear before them on September 19, when I would be allowed to argue my case.

Chapter Five

Sit-In!

In the long run, the indictment will be on the Board Of Education . . . It's not only an indictment of the Los Angeles schools but of all the schools in the Southwest where Chicanos have gone for years and where the schools have failed them.

—Sal Castro

A ruddy-faced man with graying hair, dressed in a light, pin-striped gray suit, sat across the table from me. Next to him were four other men, all white, all in their late forties or early fifties—the members of the review committee of Local Board No. 89 in San Gabriel, California. These were the men who, like it or not, were empowered to determine the course of my life.

"Tell us again, why do you feel you qualify for conscientious objector status?"

"As I said before," I answered, trying not to sound nervous. "I do not believe in a Supreme Being in the traditional sense. In place of God I recognize the sacred character of life. My life is committed to bettering the human condition. To participate in an activity that might require me to maim, cripple, or kill another person would negate all that I consider meaningful in life. I hope you will see my petition in this light."

The men questioned me for more than half an hour. As the counselor at the American Friends Services Committee had anticipated, their questions were designed to elicit inconsistencies, to prove that the applicant was lying about his beliefs. Would you have fought against Nazis in World War Two? Are you against U.S. intervention in Southwest Asia? If someone broke into your house and threatened to kill your mother, would you defend her? If someone struck you in the face, would you defend yourself? Do you believe in abortion? Have you ever gone hunting or fishing? Have you ever killed a fly?

"Thank you, Mr. Treviño. We will notify you of our determination through the mail."

Gayla was waiting in the VW outside. I got into the car and let out a big sigh. For better or worse, the ordeal was over.

"How'd it go?"

"I don't know."

"How did they seem to you?"

"Very businesslike. Not warm, but not overly rude or anything like that. Professional, I guess. I told them the truth. The rest is up to them."

"When will we know?"

"A week or two. Or three."

We sat in unbearable silence for a long while. I had to focus on something else if I was going to retain my sanity.

"Let's go. We should get back to the picket line."

A Sit-In

The protest at Lincoln High School continued, uninterrupted, for ten days straight. A group that varied from a few dozen to as many as two hundred and fifty picketers would arrive at Lincoln every morning at around 8 a.m. We would picket until noon and then break up for the day. The police were always there, watching us and taking photos. By now, the faculty at Lincoln had become polarized. The majority saw the protest as disruptive. The rest felt the picketing was averting another student walkout.

With no progress in sight, we decided at a weekly meeting of the EICC that we would take the battle from Lincoln High to the school board members themselves. It would be a massive community meeting with the school board at which the most distinguished and articulate community representatives would speak on behalf of Sal Castro. On Thursday, September 27, more than three hundred community activists packed the board room at the school district headquarters at 450 North Grand Avenue in downtown Los Angeles.

The Rev. Horacio Quiñones, a heavyset man with dark Indian features who was vice-chair of the EICC, was one of the first people to speak. Sweaty and angry, he stood behind the lectern to face the seven members of the Los Angeles Unified School Board.

"In frustration I am going to address this board," he began. Behind him, an audience made up of Mexican-American parents, teachers, and students sat impatiently. "We have come to say that the Mexican-American community no longer wants the tyranny of a system that would dictate art, culture, and bad education for our children. We want a system where the just rights of the community will be heard."

The crowd rustled about impatiently. "Tell it, Reverend!" someone yelled.

"In front of Lincoln High School last week," the Reverend continued, "the crippled and the blind paraded so that you might have eyes to see and courage to stand on your feet and deal in good faith with the Mexican-American community. Please. You know the issue. If you do not remember, let me repeat it: we want Sal Castro back at his teaching job at Lincoln High School."

Thunderous applause filled the room as Reverend Quiñones returned to his seat. I turned the Konica Super 8 from the speaker to the assembly and swept the brown faces of the audience. I swelled with pride. *Ésta es la raza nueva*, I thought. "These courageous people are rewriting history, and they're beautiful. This protest is beautiful." It struck me as odd to characterize this rowdy assembly as something beautiful, but no other word could describe what I was feeling.

My camera played on placards that proclaimed "We Want Sal Back in School!" "Sal Is for You. Are You for Him?" "Education Not Eradication."

But as my camera captured the audience, I could see that our troops were tired. For ten days we had kept a vigil at Lincoln High.

For more than two weeks we had come regularly to the Tuesday and Thursday meetings of the school board to argue our case. And still the seven members of the Los Angeles School Board were intransigent.

Since Sal Castro had become a *cause célebre*, I had filmed not just the community picket lines and rallies, but the boring school board meetings and the rowdier meetings of the EICC. I hoped all this material would be useful for my documentary that would tell the story of Eastside educational neglect.

Throughout the afternoon, more speakers came to the lectern: student activists, university professors, parents, and community leaders. The board members listened with the indifference of small children in church. Only occasionally, when the audience broke into applause, or hissed and booed, would they stir uncomfortably in their chairs.

The last speaker—Reverend Vahac Mardirosian, our leader— noted the stony faces of the board members and knew they had not been swayed. He turned and surveyed the frustrated audience behind him. What he said surprised us all: "We're not leaving until Sal Castro is reinstated to his teaching job at Lincoln High School."

As I looked around the room at the perplexed faces of the EICC members, I could tell that they were as shocked as I was by Vahac's threat. Were we really prepared to stage a sit-in? No one had ever discussed this before. It seemed rash and impetuous coming from this otherwise moderate minister. Once the idea sank in—and it took only a few seconds—the response from our assemblage was unanimous. A roar of applause left no doubt in anyone's mind that this roomful of Mexican Americans would stay until Sal Castro was reinstated.

The board presumed the threat to be just more community posturing. This was the kind of bravado to which they had become accustomed, and they were now immune to it. The board quickly left the room. Only Julián Nava, the single Mexican-American board member, stayed to try to reason with Vahac Mardirosian. Nava, at least, understood that the community group was dead serious about the sit-in, and he tried, as best he could, to dissuade us from this action.

Immediately following Vahac's announcement, the members of the inner sanctum of the Educational Issues Coordinating Committee held an emergency session right there in the board room. We realized that we had to stay; to do otherwise would erode our credibility and any clout we might have with the school board.

The next issue became one of practicality and logistics. If we were to convene a sit-in, how would we do it? Vahac Mardirosian addressed the group and told everyone that only those people who could afford to stay should stay. Parents should not jeopardize their jobs, nor should teachers set aside their classroom responsibilities. All others that believed in our cause should search their conscience and stay.

Gayla and I looked at each other and knew that we'd be staying. I got on the phone and called the New Communicators office and asked Jack Dunbar to release fifteen more rolls of black-and-white film. My friend John Parsons agreed to deliver it.

It was only a couple of hours before the school offices were scheduled to close. If we were going to get the food and clothing we required for the sit-in, we would have to do so quickly.

Gayla and I agreed that she would go home to get additional clothing, sleeping bags, and our portable TV. I would stay to film the ongoing debate between Julian Nava, the apologist for the board, and Vahac Mardirosian.

I turned my camera on the twosome as they argued back and forth. Nava stated that the sit-in was a bad idea, that we had to follow certain procedures, that he might be able to influence some of his fellow board members to vote for Castro's reinstatement, but only if our group did not press the issue. Nava appealed to Vahac's sense of propriety. Was this any way for a man of the cloth to behave?

Vahac was equally adamant in his replies. For two weeks, the community had peacefully petitioned the board to hear its grievances. Now there was no other option left for the community. We had to take a very significant, decisive step.

"How can we support law and order when the very laws are twisted to incarcerate teachers who stand up for justice? When accusers indict individuals behind closed doors? Before law and order, we must consider justice!"

Others in the board room challenged Nava. Whose side was he on, anyway? Being the only Mexican-American school board member put

Julián Nava in a no-win situation. Community activists considered him a *vendido* (sellout), and fellow board members thought of him as a sympathizer with the community demands. Frustrated and angry, Nava left the room. We were on our own.

As closing time neared, Mardirosian got a concession from the security people at the board of education: after six o'clock, the doors would be locked and only Vahac would be allowed to come and go. The police would not be called in until the matter could be resolved by the board members. At this point, the security staff of the Los Angeles city school system had very little experience with civil disobedience. They hoped we would go home within an hour or two. Our group included several members of the paramilitary Brown Beret organization as well as members of La Junta, an organization made up of hardcore ex-gang members who were working to bring peace to barrio gangs. The school security forces were uncertain about these very tough-looking young men. They did not want to provoke an incident.

Gayla returned to the board room before the head security guard Albert Reddick announced they would be closing the doors to the board room for the evening.

I did a quick count of the people in the room. We were almost a hundred strong. We laid out our sleeping bags in corners of the room. Then, Vahac Mardirosian convened a meeting. It was well past eight.

Our first activity was to elect coordinators for our action. We needed a treasurer and a sergeant-at-arms. Phone, food, and press committees had to be formed. A few hours later, after the official "work" had been done, we occupied the assembly of chairs where the board members normally sat and proclaimed ourselves to be the "Free and Liberated Board of Chicano Education."

We convened a mock meeting of our new board and elected individuals to head the various school committees with which we had become familiar: Raúl Ruiz chaired the Committee of the Whole, Juan Gómez Quiñonez chaired Adult Education, the Budget Committee was chaired by Ben Herrero, Building Committee by Pat Sánchez, College Committee by Raquel Galán, Education Committee by Eva Romero, Law and Rules by Ben Gurulé, and Personnel by Josefa Sánchez.

The first night of the sit-in proved uneventful. We had access to a small bathroom located behind the board offices. We settled down to an evening of discussion and camaraderie. Gayla had brought my guitar, and a group of us gathered in a small circle to sing. Later, one of the activists, Lydia López, and I, wrote *El Corrido de Sal Castro*:

This is the ballad of Sal Castro
And the united Mexican people
On the 26th of September they gathered
To combat disgraceful injustice

Sal Castro, a teacher dedicated
to advance his Mexican people
Had been told by the school
Don't come back,
This is American justice.

And that is why the New People
got together
Justice was the cry of the people
With pride they marched to the test
If not Sal Castro, then no schools.
And no school system!

We were all too excited to sleep much that night. Some played cards. Others read. Most of us were involved in discussing what we might expect the next day.

We knew that the board had purposefully not called the police that night. But questions remained. What action would they take when they returned the next day? Would they permit us to remain there another night? The whole weekend? When would they take action against us?

Other members of our group began to work on getting news out to the community. They drafted a flyer, had it mimeographed, and sent it to community groups throughout East Los Angeles. The heading stated: "A Hundred Protesters Sit In At Board of Education Offices!"

The next morning, Friday, we began to realize how uncomfortable we were going to be during our sit-in. We had to wait in line to get access to the bathroom. Everyone was tired from sleeping on the hard floors. And the food that had been promised by two Mexican restaurants finally arrived late. That morning we dined on tortillas, beans, rice, and *carnitas* (pork meat).

During the course of the day, Vahac Mardirosian, Horacio Quiñones, and Henry Gutiérrez—the leadership of the EICC—met for several hours with Robert Gardner, Julián Nava, and Georgiana Harding—the three board members most sympathetic to our cause. The three board members discussed the options open to us, hoping to get the EICC to leave. But our leadership told them our group would not move until the board changed its decision. The afternoon wore on.

That evening, news came that the Board of Education officials would not press charges if we vacated immediately. Vahac asked the group how we felt. We were committed, and the group unanimously agreed that we had to continue the sit-in. Five o'clock came, and with it, closing time for the board offices. Once again, rather than press the issue, the security guards locked us in. It seemed we would remain for the remainder of the weekend.

Throughout Friday afternoon, we had been visited by print and television journalists. That evening we began to see news reports on television about our sit-in.

Saturday morning, we awoke to find a front-page headline in the *Herald Examiner* reporting the sit-in. A photograph of our group accompanied the article. We had made history. Our fight for Chicano education was now in the public eye.

The weekend passed slowly. Most of the protesters read, watched television, and called their families. Our group represented a spectrum of our community. On the whole, they were young people: high school and college students or recent college grads, plus members of the Brown Berets and La Junta. Also present were the now familiar activists of the EICC: Joe Razo and Raúl Ruiz, editors of *La Raza*, the leading movement magazine; graduate students Juan Gómez Quiñones and Monte Pérez; high school teachers Joe Conway and Sarah McPherson; and parents like Ben and Kay Gurulé, Eva Romero,

Diego Alvarado, and my Oxy gardener friend Ben Carmona. Also present was a man who had become the de facto movement attorney, Oscar Zeta Acosta.

Oscar Zeta Acosta was a special case. Known to movement activists as the "Brown Buffalo," he was destined to gain some notoriety in the years that followed. A highly gifted writer, he balanced his legal practice defending movement activists with the penning of two quasi-biographical novels, *Revolt of the Cockroach People* and *Autobiography of a Brown Buffalo*. He would disappear from the face of the earth under mysterious circumstances in the mid-seventies.

Our excitement mounted as the weekend progressed. We were doing something right. By Saturday afternoon, the school security guards had relaxed the conditions of our stay—we could not leave, but we could have occasional visitors. Thus, Sunday morning, two Episcopalian priests, Father John Luce and Father Roger Wood, came to the boardroom to provide Mass for the protesters. Later, a *mariachi* group came to serenade us.

I wondered what would happen on Monday when the board members returned. By now they had seen the newspaper coverage. From a public relations point of view, they were beginning to appear weak and indecisive. Would they feel compelled to arrest us simply to prove they were in control of the situation?

All weekend long, I filmed the activities of our sit-in: people sleeping, reading, arguing, eating, the creation of the Free and Liberated Board of Chicano Education, the Sunday Mass, the *mariachi*. I tried to ration my film stock as best I could, for I did not know how long the sit-in would last. I didn't want to be caught short in case arrests were made, or some other dramatic event transpired. Meanwhile, I was on the phone every few hours keeping Jack Dunbar advised as to the progress of the sit-in and of my filming.

Dunbar was a political man and sympathetic to our cause. As an African American, he understood the import of our action and fully supported me. Now and then, other New Communicators students would bring me more film or sound stock, or take the footage I had shot away to be processed. I had arranged for this early on, fearful that if the police came in and arrested us, they would confiscate my footage. Once a day I would send it out with my friends Martín Quiroz and John Parsons.

Francisco Martínez, another New Communicators student, was also at the sit-in, but as a participant. Rather than help me in the filming, he spent much of his time arguing for more militant action to be taken. All of the Chicano students at New Communicators understood the importance of the sit-in, and we had put our differences and egos aside to join together in making sure that the event was properly documented. Since I had taken the initiative to begin the documentary, Francisco, Martín, and John agreed that I should be the one to produce, direct, and edit the film.

Monday dawned, and with it, hopes that the Board of Education would come around to our way of thinking. But, once again, it was a day of fruitless exchanges between the Board of Education and members of our group.

That evening I could see that the sit-in was taking its toll. We had not showered since Friday (we would sponge ourselves in the morning using the single wash basin in the cramped bathroom). People were fatigued from sleeping on the floor, and their nerves were frayed. Arguments broke out over petty concerns.

Late that evening, I sat talking with Henry Gutiérrez near the front of the board room, when a commotion erupted.

"*Gabacha!*" someone screamed. I turned and saw that Gayla, who had been seated in one of the board member chairs, was moving quickly away from a young Chicano I did not recognize. Then I saw the gleam of metal in the man's hand. He was chasing my wife with a knife! Gayla was scared, backing away quickly from the man, looking for something with which to defend herself.

I immediately jumped up and moved toward them. The man stopped as soon as he saw me approaching. Even as I intervened, several members of the La Junta group grabbed the Chicano and snatched the knife away. It was all over in a moment. The La Junta members took the man to a far section of the room and tried to calm him down.

"What the hell?" I asked Gayla.

"He said he didn't like *gabachas* . . . and then he came after me." She was shaking with fright and could hardly speak. We agreed she should leave the protest immediately, but Gayla insisted on returning the next day.

Tuesday, the board met again. Many of us had been there for six days now and used the open meeting and the presence of hundreds of community activists as an opportunity to return to our homes, shower, and change clothes. I returned a short time later with Gayla, now calm, expecting the sit-in to continue.

That afternoon, another parade of community speakers addressed the board. Once again, the room was packed. Vahac had gathered a group of highly respected speakers: ministers, community leaders, university professors, educators, and politicians.

But by late afternoon, it was clear that we were at an impasse. The conservative elements on the board, such as J.C. Chambers and Hugh Willett, were dead set against having Castro reinstated. Though less vociferous, Ralph Richardson was also against Castro's return to the classroom. The issue for them was simple. How could they condone having a person charged with a felony teach children? While we agreed, in principle, that felons should be kept from the classroom, the progressive elements of the board represented by Georgiana Harding, Julián Nava, and Arthur Gardner were inclined to make an exception in Sal Castro's case if it meant bringing peace to the community. But they were not going to be stampeded into a decision. They wanted a show of faith from our group, and that show of faith meant our going home.

Rev. James Jones, the only African American on the board, held the deciding vote. Vahac and others of the EICC had been trying to convince him to come around to our side, but he sought to distance himself from our cause and seemed to be using his tie-breaking vote as leverage for his own agenda.

The board adjourned its meeting without resolution by five o'clock Tuesday afternoon. However, in a private conversation with Vahac Mardirosian, the progressive board members let him know that they would lobby Rev. Jones and felt a vote to reinstate Castro was workable if the EICC stopped the sit-in.

We had heard this kind of offer before—promises that the school board was notorious for not keeping. Few people felt that such a compromise would produce fruit. Vahac Mardirosian, on the other hand, felt that this was as close as we were going to get to a resolution. In his mind, any further action would fix board sentiments against us. As the board meeting adjourned, he called an impromptu meeting of our group and tried to get us to agree to call off the sit-in.

A general debate ensued. Mardirosian explained that we already had three board votes on our side. We all knew that J.C. Chambers and Dr. Willett were intractable. Vahac had spoken to Rev. Jones, the wild card, and felt that he would come around to our side if we yielded. Vahac asked the group to leave the board room as a gesture of good faith, to show the board members that they were dealing with honorable people.

Another faction within the Educational Issues Coordinating Committee, led by Raúl Ruiz, Francisco Martínez, and Oscar Zeta Acosta, disagreed. Once again, the board had not responded to our concerns, and they felt that we needed to be arrested to make a point. We had to demonstrate to the board and to the larger Los Angeles community the extent to which we were willing to go in order to have Sal Castro reinstated.

By now our EICC group had dwindled in size to a little over forty people. A vote was taken. Twenty-eight voted in favor and sixteen against leaving the board room the next day, after the board was scheduled to meet with members of a Teachers' Negotiating Council representing Sal Castro. That a majority of EICC members had agreed with Vahac certainly did not guarantee that the sit-in would end the next day, however. Several individuals were determined to be arrested to make a point, regardless of the outcome of the next day's meeting.

The next morning, as a gesture of good faith, we agreed to vacate the room—leaving only thirteen people—for a few hours so that the room could be cleaned up in preparation for the board meeting with Castro's representatives. We welcomed the chance to clean ourselves up, and returned to the board room a short time later.

The Teachers' Negotiating Council of the Teachers' Union, which was representing Sal Castro's interests, presented a plan to the board that would create a board of appeal, to which teachers charged with felonies could turn before being summarily dismissed from the classroom. It further stipulated that only teachers charged with narcotics or morals charges be removed from the classroom. Since Castro had been charged with neither, adoption of the plan would allow for his reinstatement. After a four-hour meeting, the five board members voted unanimously to establish the board of appeals, but against limiting crimes to narcotics and morals charges. Sal Castro was still barred from teaching.

The board adjourned late on Wednesday afternoon, and immediately the debate was renewed among EICC members as to whether or not we should leave the board room. School security informed us that unless we left, they would call in the police. The discussion soon shifted to whether or not we would be arrested if we stayed.

By eight o'clock, several squad cars had surrounded the board room, and an arrest wagon was standing by. An officer came in and told us that they were going to arrest us if we didn't vacate by nine. But when nine o'clock rolled around, we were still actively involved in debating the issue. The police were holding off, hoping that Vahac Mardirosian would be able to coax the rest of us out peaceably.

Like everyone else who had sat in for the seven days, I was grappling with the question of whether or not I should stay and be arrested. The activist part of me wanted to be arrested with the others. I felt we needed to make a dramatic point, and that anything short of this would end in failure to get Castro reinstated. After consulting with my friend Henry Gutiérrez, however, I decided that I would avoid arrest. I knew that filming the events, rather than being dragged away with the others, would provide me with a dramatic ending to my footage. Henry agreed to assist by operating the Sony TC-400 tape recorder while I did the filming.

At nine-thirty, a police officer returned and demanded that we leave. I filmed the voting of the issue: thirty-five hands out of what was now more than a hundred shot up—these were the people who would be arrested.

The others departed, Henry and I among them. We came out the front door and around to the back of the building, where the arrest wagon and several squad cars waited. It was raining lightly, and Henry and I sheltered the equipment as best we could. Gayla and Henry's girlfriend, Raquel Galán, were at hand.

Near the vehicles, a TV crew was preparing to film. This was rather unusual, since during this period many events in the Chicano Movement were not covered by the local news media. They were shooting single-system 16-mm film and had portable lights. Since we lacked lighting equipment, I stuck by the TV crew to steal their illumination of the impending scene.

As we recorded the drama of the arrests, Henry and I became fearful that the police would recognize us as protestors and confiscate our film. Unlike the network crew, we didn't have a press pass, which is legally required before one is allowed to film behind police lines. But since we were near the other film crew, the fact that we lacked press credentials was overlooked entirely.

Afterwards, those people who had not been arrested went to the county jail to secure bail for those who had. Oscar Zeta Acosta, the Chicano attorney who had defended the L.A. 13, was chiefly responsible for arranging bail.

The seven-day sit-in was over. We were exhausted and famished. Henry, Raquel, Gayla, and I decided we needed dinner. Gayla and Raquel took our VW bug to the market to buy food. Henry and I decided to stay to get more footage before meeting up with them at our apartment. Still concerned that the police might confiscate it, I packed all my exposed film into the trunk of our VW before Gayla left.

After talking with some of the EICC members, Henry and I got into his Chevy Nova and drove off. As we descended the sloping driveway of the board parking lot, a young Chicano standing at the street corner looked into our car, saw Henry, and waved at him.

"Someone I knew in elementary school," Henry explained to me. "His name is Albert García. I haven't seen him in years."

Albert came up to driver's window and asked Henry if we could give him a ride. Henry agreed, and Albert climbed into the back. Since we were going to Highland Park—a community adjacent to El Sereno, where Albert lived—it would only be a slight detour.

After a couple of blocks, Henry noticed that we were being followed by a patrol car. "I think they've been with us since the school board," he said nervously.

It was about this time when we realized that Albert was flying high on drugs. He mumbled his words, rambled from one topic to another, and his eyes kept flickering open and closed.

The patrol car was still with us when we headed into El Sereno via Huntington Drive. "We have to get rid of this guy," I said to Henry.

"Albert, we're going to drop you off at Eastern and Huntington. Okay?" Henry asked.

Albert mumbled something unintelligible. As we approached the corner, the police car turned on its lights and siren and pulled us over.

Henry and I got out of the car to speak to the officers in hopes that Albert would be overlooked. To our dismay, however, Henry's friend stumbled out of the car and made a feeble attempt to run away. After a few yards, he collapsed to the ground in a drugged stupor.

One officer ran to him and pulled him to his feet while the other drew his gun and leveled it at me and Henry. He ordered us to spread eagle on the hood of the car.

"Look what we have here!" the officer with Albert shouted. He held up a large plastic bag of red pills for his partner to see. The officer continued to frisk Albert and found two twelve-inch knives that Albert had hidden in his boots.

"Boy, are we going to have fun," the officer said as he let Albert flop to the ground.

The other policeman handcuffed Henry and me and threw us forcefully into the back seat of the patrol car. He inspected the trunk of Henry's car and found a large kitchen knife, part of the cooking supplies from the sit-in. He smiled and held the knife up for his partner to see. Then he closed the trunk and walked over to where his partner stood menacingly over Albert.

The policemen dragged Albert to the shadows of an adjacent wall, away from the street lights. Our hearts sank as we witnessed the violence that followed. Albert was barely conscious, his head nodding on his chest. To make him an easier target, one officer propped Albert up while the other pummeled him with clenched fists. They struck his face repeatedly and kicked him in the groin. When one became fatigued, the officers switched positions, and a surge of fresh blows rained down upon Albert's face.

A strange thought entered my mind: This is the way they beat up people in the movies. One of them holds him while the other works him over. But in the movies, you don't see the terrible carnage. In the movies, flesh is unrealistically resilient to abuse.

The officers took their time, relishing their atrocity. They kept it up for twenty agonizing minutes before both officers were punched out. Now completely unconscious, Albert bled profusely from his nose and mouth. His face was purple and swollen, as if he had been stung by a swarm of angry bees.

They dragged Albert's limp body to the car and threw him in the back seat beside us. Then they grabbed Henry by the collar and began to pull him out of the car.

"Here it comes," I thought. "It's our turn now."

The officer manipulating Henry paused. He inspected Henry's features more closely in the light of the street lamp. "Hey. I know this one."

The other officer drew closer. "Yeah, right. He's the one on TV."

They had recognized Henry from his television appearances as spokesman for the EICC during the sit-in.

"All right, better take them in," one of them said.

The two officers got into the patrol car and drove us to the Highland Park police station located on York Boulevard, where we were booked and thrown into three adjoining jail cells. Even by this time, Albert had not regained consciousness.

During 1968, 1969, and 1970, there were six cases of Mexican-American youths who were alleged to have committed suicide by hanging in their jail cells at the East Los Angeles Sheriff's station. The most infamous of these cases involved a young man named Richard Hernández, who spoke to his mother by phone when he was arrested on January 8, 1970. At the time, he was not intoxicated and in good spirits. Two hours later, police called his mother to tell her that he had hanged himself with his belt in a drunken frenzy. A subsequent coroner's inquest at the request of the family found no indications of hanging and determined that the bruises on his neck were due to a "choke hold" or "arm hold." At the time of my arrest, the first of these suicide cases had already been reported.

After seeing Albert's horrible beating, and recalling these community reports of jail "suicides," I was petrified. Would we survive the night?

Other questions spun through my mind. Had Albert been a setup? Had he been planted at the board parking lot as a pretext for arresting Henry and me? Or was it just coincidence that he was there and that we were immediately followed by a patrol car? But if the police had put Albert up to it, perhaps in exchange for leniency on some previous drug charge, then why had they beaten him so savagely? Was that part of their cynical payoff? I knew that we had been spared a beating because the officer had recognized Henry. Was this part of their plan, to arrest a visible spokesperson for the movement on drug charges? To discredit the movement? My paranoia was working overtime.

In the darkness of our adjacent cells, Henry and I began to talk. We speculated that due to Henry's visibility, and the fact that we were now "officially" in police custody, it was unlikely they would harm us. We wondered, however, about Albert's condition. He was still unconscious in the cell next door, his blood now dried on his face and clothing. I thought of the scores of Mexican youths that had been arrested and beaten during the zoot suit riots and since then in countless jails throughout the Southwest. I realized that however horrific the experience, what Henry and I had just gone through was nothing more than what had been experienced by Chicano youths in this country for decades. At that moment, I hated the United States with all of my heart. Henry and I agreed that as soon as we got out, we would file charges of police brutality against the two officers who had battered Albert.

Henry and I conversed into the early morning. We found comfort and security in each other's voice. Finally, we decided that we should get some sleep.

"Good night," said Henry.

These words had an eerie, unfamiliar ring to them. As I lay in the cell bunk, it hit me: Until this night, I had known Henry as an articulate student, but one who always spoke in English—without an accent. He had told me early on that he had never learned Spanish, but tonight, without even thinking about it, we had carried on our private conversation in adjoining cells entirely in the native tongue of our parents.

A Chicano Initiation

"Are you all right?" Gayla asked anxiously. It was the next morning, and she had finally tracked us to the jail and had been permitted to meet with me briefly.

"Yeah, we're both fine." A guard stood a foot away with his arms crossed—just like TV, I thought. "Tell Raquel that Henry's fine."

"What the hell happened?" She whispered urgently.

"They beat up Henry's friend," I replied in a whisper so the guard could not hear. "He had drugs on him and they arrested all of us. But they beat him up really bad. We're going to charge them with police brutality as soon as we get out."

"They're holding you on charges of possession of drugs and resisting arrest. You didn't resist, did you?"

This was a common ploy: to arrest someone and later charge him or her with resisting arrest or interfering with an officer. In this way, the accused had to undo the charge against them before they could address the fact that a police officer might have abused his power. After the struggle to clear his or her name, most defendants were only too happy to be done with it and would not bring charges against the arresting officers.

"No, of course not. What about the film?" I asked. I was paranoid that perhaps the police might have raided our home the way they had the offices of *La Raza* magazine and the Brown Berets.

"It's fine. I took it into the house."

"Hide it some place, away from the house. Leave it with someone you can trust."

Gayla was more concerned about me. "Don't worry about the bail. Ben and Kay Gurulé have volunteered to put up the money. We'll get you and Henry out of here real soon."

Our conversation was interrupted by the guard. "That's it. You've talked enough."

"I love you," I said as the officer escorted Gayla away.

Henry and I remained at the York Boulevard jail for the rest of the morning. That afternoon they moved us to the Lincoln Heights precinct. Eventually, we were arraigned, but only on possession of drug charges. Inexplicably, the resisting arrest charges had been dropped. In the afternoon, they moved us to the Los Angeles county jail downtown, where we were processed into the main jail population. We were stripped of our clothes, made to shower, then they told us to bend over and they sprayed us with delousing powder.

Several guards patrolled the roomful of naked prisoners. They wore black plastic gloves. If someone didn't move fast enough or spoke out of turn, a guard would slap him across the face or on his genitals. The black gloves assured no marks were left. After delousing, we were issued prison uniforms.

Somewhere along the line, Henry and I were separated. I eventually wound up in a cell with two other Chicanos. One was about my age, the other a few years older. I could tell from their tattoos and demeanor that both came from gang backgrounds. I spoke briefly with them and was surprised by their cavalier attitude regarding imprisonment. For them, it was the natural order of things. I realized how privileged I had been. This was the norm for many of my people throughout the Southwest. Society had determined that people living in a culture of poverty were destined to a life of going in and out of prison.

I began to wonder if Ben and Kay Gurulé would be able to secure our release. I had visions of staying in jail for weeks awaiting trial. This happened to a lot of people, I had heard. And what if the cops decided to come back and attack me, now that I was totally in their hands?

The logical part of me fought these fears: You're overreacting, everything's going to turn out fine, don't panic. I had heard of people being so frightened by encounters with police that they automatically ran when they saw a police officer. Before witnessing the beating, I had always considered this an exaggeration, but now I understood how police terror could leave a lasting mark on one's psyche.

Finally, late that afternoon, both Henry and I were released from jail. The bond had been posted by our friends, the Gurulés.

The first thing I did when I got home was to make sure that my film and audio tapes were still intact. Ironically, the people whose arrest I had filmed had spent little time in jail. Since attorney Oscar Zeta Acosta knew who was going to be arrested, their bond had been paid. They went in, were booked, and were then released within two hours of their arrest.

A Homeboy Returns

The next morning, I returned to New Communicators. Between the sit-in and my arrest, it had been almost two weeks since I had seen my fellow classmates. As I related my experiences at the sit-in, with the two violent officers and at the jail, I saw that my classmates viewed me differently than before. This was particularly true of the Chicanos. Many of them had come from street backgrounds. When we began at the school, they had viewed me as somewhat aloof. Although we were all Chicanos, my college education was evident, and my discourse on *el movimiento*—always cast in lofty words and philosophical concepts—set me apart from them. I had friends like Martín Quiroz, John Parsons, and Frank Vega because we had common roots and because I helped them with their films. Now that my fellow students heard of my real street experiences, however, the other students embraced me fully as a brother in the struggle.

After only three months into the New Communicators semester, quite a number of us had been arrested. During the nine months that the school was in existence, all but two or three of the eighteen New Communicator students were arrested at one time or another. One Black student, Alvin "Ojenke" Saxon, had been filming police officers as they beat up a Black man in one of the South Central projects, when the police attacked and arrested Ojenke and his wife. In the struggle, Ojenke's wife was strangled by a police choke hold and killed. This event, together with our individual experiences, created a strong atmosphere of solidarity at the New Communicators school.

In retrospect, many of these individuals—because of their street-wise backgrounds—would never be able to utilize fully the New Communicators opportunity to its fullest. After the demise of New Communicators, most dropped out of filmmaking. Martín Quiroz and Esperanza Vásquez, however, went on to careers in the media. Martín became a television station executive, and Esperanza went on to win an Emmy award for her documentary film work.

The afternoon after my release, I took my Super 8 camera and returned to school headquarters on Grand Avenue. The board was to meet once more to consider the Sal Castro case. I entered the room and started filming.

Within only a few minutes, the board took a vote on the reinstatement of Sal Castro. This time, Rev. James Jones voted along with Georgiana Hardy, Julián Nava, and Arthur Gardner to allow Castro to return to teaching. We finally had the majority we needed. When the news of the vote sank in, the crowd in the packed room erupted with applause and screams of victory.

Several young men raised Sal Castro onto their shoulders and paraded him through the board room. After two weeks of picket lines and a seven-day sit-in, we had finally won one of the first urban victories of the Chicano struggle!

Chapter Six

Denver Youth Conference

Before the world, before all of North America, before all of our brothers on the bronze continent, we are a nation and are a union of free pueblos; we are Aztlán.

—Alurista

A week after my arrest, I received a letter from my Oxy roommate, Jim Miller, telling me that his petition for C.O. had been denied by the Salinas Draft Board. In an article he wrote for the Occidental College paper, he expressed my own fears:

> Okay, so now I am in the position of having been denied C.O. alternative service by my draft board, a very hostile group of men. My quarrel is hardly with them. They could have done better by me, but they didn't have it in them. Now I am appealing to the State Board of Appeals. I have no great hopes. So it looks like in maybe six months I'll be in jail. I am not a nut. I will be getting something out of this: a clear conscience.

Would a clear conscience be sufficient to make jail worthwhile? I had already seen the inside of a jail cell and knew there was nothing romantic about it.

A few days after Jim's letter, I received a phone call from my friend Dan Rubin. He was calling from Vancouver, British Columbia.

"Vancouver, *Canada?*" I asked incredulously.

"Yeah."

"You did it?!"

"Had to."

Like me, Dan had been reclassified 1-A and had applied for C.O. status at a Portland, Oregon, draft board. His request was flatly denied. Now he and his wife, Stephanie, were struggling to make a living in a foreign country. He wished me the best on my C.O. application, but I could tell he held little hope of its approval.

On October 8, 1968, I decided to act preemptively. I sent my draft board a list of tasks I could perform to fulfill my C.O. obligation. I did this on the advice of the draft counselor at the American Friends Service Committee.

A Victory and a Defeat

It was a smoggy day in November when Henry and I went to trial. As we somberly waited for the doors of the courtroom to open, we speculated on whether we would go home that night or be incarcerated. Ralph Segura, an attorney from the Western Center on Law and Poverty, who had volunteered to take our case *pro bono*, tried to be reassuring.

Segura had recently contacted Albert García—the man that had been brutalized by the two officers that night—and he agreed to testify on our behalf. García had been out on parole when the police pulled us over. Since our arrest, García had recovered from his beating and had been set free on bail, but had been arrested a third time on another charge.

"He's a loser," Segura told us. "Any charge you may try to bring against the police isn't going to hold water against his kind of record."

After waiting for what seemed like an eternity, the courtroom doors yawned open. We filed in with the other defendants awaiting trial and took our seats. Our case was called quickly, and soon Henry and I stood before the judge.

Ralph Segura was brief. He explained that Albert García was present to testify that Henry and I had known nothing about the drugs that the police had found on him the night of the arrests. Segura went on at length about how Henry and I were Occidental College graduates without a record, and that we were actively involved in positive community affairs.

Albert García was brought into the courtroom and took the stand. He was wearing the orange overalls of the county jail from which he had been taken a few hours earlier.

"This case doesn't need to go any further," Segura said to the judge. He nodded at Albert.

"Nah, they didn't know nothing. They were just giving me a ride home."

The judge reviewed the legal brief for only a few minutes before arriving at her decision. The charges against us were dropped on grounds of insufficient evidence.

We celebrated that evening with a dinner at Ben and Kay Gurulé's home. It didn't take long, however, before we focused our attention on another issue. Now that we were free, should we file police brutality charges against the two officers who had arrested us?

Both of us were weary from our recent legal hassles. We wanted to have nothing more to do with the police. Adding to our reluctance was the fact that, since our arrest, the two officers had waged an aggressive campaign of intimidation again us in an effort to keep us quiet.

On several occasions, I looked outside the window of our house to see the two men sitting in a patrol car across the street. They visited one of our neighbors and questioned him about me. Did I smoke pot? Did I throw wild parties? Was I a drug dealer? They were searching for anything they could use that would undermine my credibility as a witness.

A few days after our hearing, Segura called and informed us that the two officers had contacted him. They reminded him that Albert García had been found with two twelve-inch knives. The implication was that the police could still file concealed weapon charges against us if we decided to file brutality charges.

Henry and I discussed the new information. To put ourselves at risk over a case that had little chance of success would be reckless and futile. Plus, we could not afford to be taken out of the struggle. We had work to do. The officers would have to go unpunished.

Back to Film School

Licking my wounds, I jumped back into the film on Eastside educational neglect with renewed vigor. The documentary would include the story of the walkouts, the arrest of the L.A. 13, and conclude with the Sal Castro sit-in. I decided to call it *La Raza Nueva* (The New People), which I felt embodied the vital spirit of my generation. Bill Kerby, one of the instructors at New Communicators, agreed to narrate the documentary, and I decided on guitar music for the background. The twenty-minute Super 8 film was completed in early December. I arranged for a special screening at one of the weekly meetings of the Educational Issues Coordinating Committee meeting.

I had butterflies in my stomach the night of the screening. The house lights dimmed. I flipped the projector and the reel-to-reel tape recorder on simultaneously so that the soundtrack would match the film. A hush fell over the ordinarily raucous gathering.

Bill Kerby's voice was deep and commanding: "A school can be an exciting and motivating experience. But for the student of Mexican-American descent, the present system of education has failed. In Eastside high schools, Mexican Americans drop out at a rate of 50 percent."

"Can't hear it!" someone shouted. I turned up the volume on the tape player. As the film progressed, I periodically had to stop and start the tape recorder because it was out of sync with the projector. But the glitches were soon forgotten as the audience began to see themselves and each other on the screen.

"Look, there I am!"

"Hey, there's Vahac."

"It's Henry. Talking to the press, of course!"

"Do I really look that fat?"

Although the room was dark, I could still see the enthusiasm on people's faces. The film went from the picket line at Lincoln to the sit-in at the Board of Education. Over images of EICC members sitting in at the board room, Kirby's voice-over declared: "This is *la raza nueva*, a new breed of Mexican American." Towards the end of the film, over images of Sal Castro being carried victoriously out of the board room on the backs of his supporters, the narration concluded: "Through the unity and strength of a community, a point has been made—the system is not invincible. United *la raza nueva* can bring respect, dignity, and justice for the Mexican American."

The lights came up, and the crowd rose to their feet amid their own applause. Someone started the *Raza* handclap, and soon everyone was stomping their feet, shouting "*¡Viva la Raza!*"

I was astounded by the response. I had set out to use my filmmaking skills to advance our cause. But I never expected the documentary to have the kind of impact it had, even on this admittedly partisan audience. Here is how media should be used, I thought, to validate the legitimate struggle of my people. The experience of writing, directing, shooting, and editing this short film convinced me that cinema was the career for which I was destined. It married my ambition to be a public voice for my people with my desire to express myself artistically.

A few weeks later, I screened *La Raza Nueva* to a largely Anglo Westside Los Angeles audience at Ed Pearl's folk-and blues-nightclub, The Ashgrove. Although its normal fare was the likes of Doc Watson and Lightin' Hopkins, the film screening was received with enthusiasm. I was hooked. I knew then that I would be a filmmaker for the rest of my life.

Canada

In early December, amid the euphoria of my first documentary film, I took leave from New Communicators, and Gayla and I headed for Canada to visit Dan Rubin. It had been three months since my last letter to the draft board, but they still hadn't responded. What was going on? Draft boards were notoriously prompt. Were they actually considering my C.O. application? It seemed unlikely. Perhaps the letter ordering me to report for military duty was lost in the mail. Might there already be a warrant out for my arrest? Should I contact them?

I decided to wait it out. Maybe they had forgotten about me. If so, I figured, that was their problem.

Dan and Stephanie welcomed us to Vancouver with open arms. We spent a day touring the city. I especially enjoyed the old Gastown section, where Dan performed with a musical group. While Dan and Stephanie were friendly, the strain of their new lives was evident. We stayed only two days, but it was enough to convince me that Canada was not a suitable place for me. Throughout our stay, I kept thinking of the movement and the work to be done.

A Changing of the Guard

When I returned to New Communicators, change was afoot. During the time that I was caught up with filming and editing of *La Raza Nueva*, Tut Hayes and Tommy Scott, the other two student representatives on the board of New Communicators, had been pushing the issue of minority staffing for the school. The continued complaints about the lack of minority teachers, and the ongoing interviews with prospective black or Chicano candidates, had alienated many of our white instructors. Some were seeking employment elsewhere. Others were simply fed up with the no-win situation; it seemed impossible to please all three of the power groups: militant students, harried administrators, and an indecisive board of directors.

Matters came to a head at the beginning of the year. Jack Dunbar and his assistant, Bobbi Ragan, both African American, were terminated by the board on January 31, 1969. Dunbar was replaced by Jim Tartan, a sensitive and accessible man who had worked for the motion picture department at the County of Los Angeles. There was only one problem: Tartan was white. Instead of hiring minority instructors, the two blacks had been fired and replaced with a white. The board had opted to put ethnic politics on a back burner and to hire a film professional. The fallout of this decision, which was vehemently opposed by the other two student representatives and me, would continue for months. I was particularly concerned for Jack Dunbar because of the support he had shown me during the sit-in and because of his even-handed approach. But despite my early opposition to Tartan, we would later become lifelong friends and collaborate on several films together.

When Jim Tartan came on the scene, he saw that, despite the fact that we had been dabbling in film for six months, there was still no real film instruction going on. We had been taught to use the Konica Super 8 camera, the Sony TC-400 tape recorder, and had been given basic editing theory, which we applied using 16mm workprints of the *Gunsmoke* television series. But we had no working knowledge of professional 16-mm film equipment, such as Eclair cameras and the Nagra tape recorder. Ours had been a hit-and-miss kind of training.

Tartan was determined to change all this. He revamped the training program to include hands-on seminars that covered the operation of 16-mm Eclair and Arriflex cameras, the Nagra sound recorder, and the stand-up Moviola editing machine. He instructed us in the transfer of audio tape to magnetic stripe and taught us about the principles of film editing, screen writing, and documentary proposals.

Teaching assistants were assigned a core group of four to five students, and had to deliver daily reports on each student's progress. Tartan arranged for us to visit film production houses and studios to observe film professionals at work. New Communicators was finally on track. The students welcomed the shift from the unfocused manner we had experienced to this thoroughly professional approach. I was among those who welcomed the change.

The only two students who seemed standoffish about what was going on were Tut Hayes and Tommy Scott. They were disgruntled by the selection of Tartan and continued to spend much of their time plotting to persuade African-American board members to fire Tartan. I was puzzled by their efforts and refused to take part in their agenda.

Jim Tartan did his best to shelter the program from board politics. He was acutely aware of the scheming and of the criticism that was leveled at him for being white, but he refused to allow it to interfere with our training.

"Look," he told me shortly after he had come on board. "Whether or not New Communicators survives, I want to make sure that, while I'm here, each and every one of you gets the best film education possible. I want you to walk away from this place knowing how to be filmmakers."

During this turbulent time, we had our first student open house, at which we screened our films to an audience that included friends, families, and professionals from the film industry. It was a resounding success. The audience was impressed with the level of work that we were producing. This added greatly to our optimism about the school and its future.

In the two months that followed, we moved quickly from Super 8 to 16-mm filmmaking. By February, I was ready to plan my first 16-mm double-system film production. I chose the same script that I had used for my first Super 8 film, *"Ya Basta,"* but decided that instead of making the story entirely narrative, I would interweave footage from my documentary *"La Raza Nueva."*

By now, the theme of high school dropouts had become a bit of an obsession with me. For ten months, I had been immersed in the work of the Educational Issues Coordinating Committee and had seen up close the damage done to our children by the inadequate education they were receiving. At Eastside high schools, Mexican-American students were dropping out at a rate greater than 50 percent. And for kids with an incomplete education, it was a short step to a life of gangs, drugs, and crime. The only alternative for a high school dropout was to go into the army, and Chicanos had the highest mortality rate per ethnic group in Vietnam. An entire generation of Chicanos was being offered just two options—crime or death—because our schools were not doing their job.

I read extensively in educational theory—Paul Goodman, Jonathan Kozol, John Holt, and others. I knew that American education was not just failing Chicanos, but all of America's children, and I was convinced that conditions would only change if we, the community, took action. To do this required educating people, Chicanos and Anglos alike, about the intolerable conditions and standards of our schools. I wrote a series of articles on this topic for one of the local community newspapers, the *Eastside Sun.* In one article I wrote:

> The kind of things education should be about can't be packaged. It's about a process of self-discovery motivated by self-interest—not a matter of facts and information. A recent

"reading program" adopted in Los Angeles is based on quantifying education. Behavioral objectives are established that, step by step, are supposed to teach a child to read . . . All these teach a child to do is to perform well on I.Q. tests, fill out IBM cards, and fill out applications to work in a factory. It's the start of a horrible process of becoming a full-fledged, nonthinking and soulless member of our society. And real education, thinking and wanting to learn, being free, that's forgotten.

Now I hoped that my film could help in this regard.

Our first day of filming was on February 20, 1969. I knew little of the casting process and had no monetary resources to attract professional actors. As a result, I had to cast amateurs. For the role of the boy, I selected a young man I had met who was playing baseball outside the Euclid Center. My mother stepped in to act as his mother. My friend Ben Gurulé, played the boy's father. I included my sister and cousins in the ensemble scenes. The home-life scenes were shot at my aunt's home in Boyle Heights, and the school scenes at classrooms at Occidental College.

My rushes (unedited film rolls) were received with interest and support from the instructors at the school. I couldn't help being impressed, myself—the acting was good, the scenes dramatic. I felt I had footage that might grow into something truly worthwhile. But in early March, in the middle of filming what I now called *"The Dropout!"* I received news that put my production on hold.

A Call to Activists

At an EICC meeting in early March, I learned that a community activist named "Corky" Gonzales, who was well-known for an epic poem he had written titled "I Am Joaquín," was convening a National Chicano Youth Liberation Conference in Denver, Colorado. The buzz was that it would be quite an important meeting. Already, many EICC members and other community activists were planning to attend. Although I was deeply involved with my film *"The Dropout!"* I knew that I could not miss the opportunity to chronicle this event.

The next day I spoke to Martín Quiroz about the conference. We went to Jim Tartan and convinced him that this was going to be a landmark event for Chicanos, and that he should let us take a film crew to document it. The next day, he authorized us to take the school's Eclair camera, Nagra tape recorder, and a small Mole-Richardson lighting kit to shoot the Denver Youth Conference. This was quite a commitment, since it meant that for the week of the conference, no one else at the school would be able to film.

The film crew would consist of me as producer-director, Martín Quiroz as cameraman—he had taken to the camera instantly and was considered one of the best and most meticulous cinematographers at the school—and Bobby Romero as sound man. I knew that once we were in Denver, we wouldn't be able to send back for film, so, I managed to convince Tartan to advance us five thousand feet of black-and-white 16-mm film—more film than had been allocated to any single student project to date.

On March 21, we crammed the Eclair, the Nagra, the light kit, the film, the sound stock, and our three bodies into Bobby Romero's VW bug and headed for Denver. Our spirits were high about the adventure ahead.

As we were crossing the Rockies, we encountered a blizzard. None of us had experience with driving through snow, so we were oblivious to the possible dangers. As the snow mounted, we noticed that there was less and less traffic on the winding mountain highway. The VW had neither snow tires nor chains, but we didn't know enough to turn back. All we knew was that it was getting harder and harder to drive. To complicate matters, the VW's tires were bald.

As we proceeded, we realized that the tires were no longer in direct contact with the pavement; we were skidding over a layer of pure ice.

"Slow down, Bobby!" I shouted.

"I'm doing the best I can!"

Martín grabbed Bobby's shoulder in fear as the VW began to slide sideways. "Pull over, man! Get off the road!"

As Bobby cranked the wheel to comply, the back end of the car lost all traction, and the vehicle spun out of control towards the cliff. The chasm below was a sheer drop of several thousand feet.

"Watch out! Watch out!" I cried.

Bobby struggled with the steering wheel. The car skated across the opposing lane. With a final effort, Bobby turned the wheel in the other direction, which reversed the direction of our spin. The VW spun around completely, and we ended up back on our side of the road.

We plowed into the snowy mountain and came to a dead stop. The impact caused a small avalanche, which fell upon the car and covered the front end.

We sat in silence for a long while before anyone spoke.

"Hey, that was close," Martín finally said.

"Lucky for us, nobody was coming the other way," I added.

We managed to open the doors, then faced the freezing winds to dig the VW out of the snowbank with our hands.

After the vehicle was clear, we crept across the icy road to the edge of the cliff and peered into the abyss that had nearly been our graves. We were speechless. All we could do for several minutes was stare into the chasm, transfixed, shaking our heads in disbelief.

A truck approached. It was a road maintenance vehicle that was spreading salt over the road to melt the ice. We got behind the truck and followed it slowly to the nearest town, where we stayed for several hours until the blizzard subsided.

I have often thought about that event. But for that little turn in the wheel, a lifetime of film work would never have happened.

A Crusade for Justice

We drove the rest of the night and arrived in Denver at the Crusade for Justice headquarters early the next morning. The Crusade was housed in an enormous church that had been converted into a community center. It was four stories high and was divided into offices and meeting rooms, with one enormous auditorium that seated several hundred people.

I went to a side door and knocked, with Martín and Bobby close behind. At first there was no response, then I heard some movement behind the door. Finally, the door was cracked open and the barrel of a rifle was thrust into my face.

"Who are you and what do you want?" the gunman demanded.

My eyes focused on the rifle barrel two inches from my nose. I replied as calmly as I could. "We're here for the Youth Conference. We came from Los Angeles."

The rifle barrel disappeared and the door slammed shut. A muffled discussion raged within. Then the door opened up again, and several Brown Berets emerged and frisked us for weapons. All the while, one of the men covered us with a rifle. I thought to myself, "Yesterday I nearly got killed for this kind of welcome? What am I getting myself into?"

We were ushered inside, and I told one of the Brown Berets I wanted to speak to Corky Gonzales. Corky was unavailable. He was still asleep. Instead, they called one of the conference organizers, a young Chicano in his early twenties. I explained to him that we were here to film the conference. He brightened up immediately and gave me the Chicano handshake.

As my hands performed the familiar gestures, the ice was broken. This was the cue for us all to shake hands. Now we were brethren.

The conference organizer took us downstairs to the kitchen, where a group of women was preparing breakfast for the conference participants. We got in line with some of the younger people, who were still rubbing sleep from their eyes. A few minutes later, we were having *chorizo con huevos* breakfast at one of several crowded tables in the basement commissary.

We spent the next few hours getting our bearings and chatting with conference participants. I was struck by the diversity of our people. There were Chicanos with sharp *indio* features, others were light-skinned and could have passed as Anglos, and still others evidenced unmistakable African-American lineage. I later learned that the group had come from all over the States: Chicago, San Antonio, El Paso, Tucson, Albuquerque, Berkeley.

After several hours, a tight-lipped Brown Beret escorted us into Corky Gonzales's office. Corky sat at a desk, dressed in black pants and a tight-fitting black T-shirt that revealed the muscular body of an ex-boxer, for Corky had begun his rise to fame as a middle-weight contender.

Seated nearby were two grim-faced men I took to be his assistants. One was a wire-haired man in his forties with a receding hair-
line, mustache, and dark prescription glasses. His large pendant bore
the logo of the Crusade for Justice—a three-faced Chicano head sym-
bolizing our Indian, Spanish, and mestizo heritage. The other man,
also in his forties, was pock-faced with salt-and-pepper hair. He had
the muscular build and aggressive cold stare I had come to associate
with ex-*pintos* (prison inmates). I later discovered that these two men
were Corky's bodyguards. In the years that followed, as I interviewed
Corky for my documentaries "*Yo Soy Chicano*" and later "*La Raza
Unida*," I grew to accept Corky's bodyguards as a natural part of
doing business with him.

We explained to Corky that we had come from Los Angeles to
document the conference. "We're from CBS," I joked, "the Chicano
Broadcasting System."

"That's good," Corky smiled back at me. "That's really good!"

I explained that we hoped to finish the film at New Communicators and use it to organize the community. I assured him that we would
give him a copy of the film when we were finished.

"We will help you in whatever way we can," he stated.

"What we need to know first is what exactly is going to take place
and where. We need to see locations to plan our shoot."

At this, the two men stiffened and looked questioningly at Corky.

"I mean our *film* shoot," I quickly added. The two men relaxed.

Corky said that the meetings were going to take place downstairs in
the auditorium. There would be a series of plenary sessions and caucuses held to hammer out a national plan for Chicano liberation. We were
welcome to film all but the private meetings. He then encouraged us to
film the performances by the Crusade's Escuela Tlatelolco singers and
dancers. The Crusade for Justice was a multi-purpose center.

"We started off as a civil rights organization," Corky explained,
"which we feel has now become a human rights organization." He
stressed the importance of culture in our struggle and recommended
that we film the school's *ballet folklórico*.

Just then, a Crusader came into the office and whispered in
Corky's ear.

"I must go," he said. He thanked us again for coming, and then excused himself to attend a private meeting of the conference planning committee. He agreed to meet with us later in the week so we might film an in-depth interview with him.

I asked one of Corky's aides to show us the auditorium. The aide led us downstairs along a corridor and threw open the doors to the big room. My heart sank. Dark wood paneling covered every wall. Over the floor was a deep brown rug. Large stained-glass windows provided only minimal lighting. At the head of the auditorium was an extremely wide stage, where all the speeches and debates would take place. It was a cameraman's nightmare. How were we expected to film in this giant room with our tiny light kit?

In Los Angeles, Martín and I had discussed the possibility that we might encounter unfavorable filming conditions, and had decided to bring a combination of low-light high ASA stock and daylight stock. We had three Mole-Richardson lamps. If we placed one at each side of the stage, we could spread just enough light over a portion of it for our 400 ASA film stock. The third would be our "roaming" light, which we would turn to the audience for reaction and applause shots. It was far from ideal, but it would work.

I budgeted our film stock based on what Corky had told us. The low-light stock would be allocated to the debates and speeches that I expected would make up the bulk of the conference. Half of the daylight stock was set aside for the interview with Corky Gonzales. I figured we could film him outdoors or by a window. The remaining daylight stock I held in reserve—in case something unexpected happened.

People continued to arrive throughout the day. Those from Los Angeles that I recognized were: Guadalupe Saavedra and members of his theater company (Lydia Rodríguez, Sylvia Galán, and Conchita Farrell), Ralph Ramírez, Monte Pérez, Susan Racho, Rev. Horacio Quiñones, René Núñez, Ray Cenicéroz, Moe Aguirre, Luis Pingarón, Moctesuma Esparza, and Pat Borjón.

When Corky Gonzalez had sent out the call for the Youth Conference, he had not expected such a large turnout. Conference planners later told me they had expected, at most, a few hundred. Instead, close to fifteen hundred Mexican-American and Puerto Rican youth attended. Although the call had been for a "Chicano" Youth Liberation Conference, Puerto Rican youth were also invited. Many arrived from New York, Boston, and Chicago, among them members of a militant New York-based organization known as the Young Lords. Puerto Ricans from Chicago and other cities would return home and create chapters of the Young Lords after the conference.

In the afternoon, the first plenary session was under way. Hundreds of excited young people were crammed inside the auditorium. The balcony and the aisles were overflowing.

The program began with students from the Crusade's Escuela Tlatelolco. Our lights came up and Martín started filming as the children began their song:

Yo Soy Chicano, tengo color.
Americano, pero con honor.
Cuando me dicen que hay revolución,
defeniendo a mi raza con mucho valor!

Someone in the Crusade had adapted new lyrics to the music of the traditional Mexican *corrido* "La Rielera," the saga of an *adelita* who follows her soldier husband through the Mexican Revolution. The catchy new song "*Yo Soy Chicano*" was quickly becoming the Chicano national anthem:

I am Chicano, I'm of color.
An American, but with honor.
When they call me to the revolution,
I defend my people with great valor!

Bobby Romero recorded the whole day on audio tape, but we decided to conserve our film stock, and shot montages of the performances and portions of speeches. Martín got so excited at times that he started filming without letting me get a head slate to match picture with sound.

Corky's opening address stressed the need for a national program for Chicano liberation. He described the way in which the *gabacho* system had divested Chicanos of our land, property and power:

> We can no longer rely on the *gabacho* system. We must create our own schools so that our children can be educated with knowledge of the contributions of their own people. We must create community control in the barrio*s*, taking over control of schools, civic resources, and churches. We must have self-determination. We can and must determine our own destiny as a nation of people.

Corky called for national unity to bring about change in our lives. It was a spirited call to arms. On more than one occasion, the audience punctuated Corky's speech with shouts of *"Viva la Raza!"* or with the Chicano hand-clap. Martín and I swung the roaming light back across the audience at those moments to capture the crowd's reactions.

The next day focused on what ideological framework we should adopt for our national liberation. One vocal contingent, mainly Chicanos from Berkeley and the San Francisco Bay Area, argued from a Marxist perspective. The Chicano struggle, they said, was part of a larger struggle of oppressed people in the United States that included blacks, Native Americans, and poor whites. They believed we had to unite with other groups to overthrow the present system.

This approach was soundly rejected. Marx was just another *gabacho*. And, after all, it was *gabachos* who had stolen our land from Mexico more than one hundred years ago. It was *gabachos* who ran the United States, who arrested us in our barrio*s*, who locked us up in jails, who sent us off to fight their wars, and who kept us as an oppressed labor force. True liberation for our people could only come about if we joined together as a nation of Chicanos, united by language, culture, and race.

As the discussions continued, a clear consensus emerged: the ideology of cultural nationalism. A caucus was convened to hammer out the specifics of a national plan of liberation that would become known as the *Plan de Aztlán*.

The following day, the session was opened with a reading of the Preamble to the *Plan de Aztlán*, penned by a diminutive young poet from San Diego, whose goatee and black beret were reminiscent of beat generation poets. He went by the single name of Alurista:

With our hearts in our hands, and our hands in the earth, we declare before the world, before all of North America, before all of our brothers on the bronze continent, we are a nation and are a union of free pueblos, we are Aztlán.

Aztlán: the mythical home of the Nahua Indians. I had read about it as I prepared my Chicano history class the summer before. According to the Códice Borturini, one of the pictograph parchments made by the Aztecs, prior to the year 1325, the seven Nahua tribes of Nahuatl-speaking Indians had lived somewhere to the north and west of what is today Mexico City. They lived on an island they called Chicomoztóc, the island of seven caves, in a marshy land of "reeds and herons"—*Aztlán*. When a natural catastrophe destroyed their island home, they moved south to seek a new beginning. It was on Lake Texcoco that they found the sign they were searching for: an eagle perched on a cactus eating a snake. They built their new home in the middle of the lake. After a hundred years, it would become Tenochtitlán, the capital of the vast Aztec empire.

Alurista's preamble struck a chord in all of us. We had come to the conference as an amalgam of disparate individuals in search of a common identity, a unity that might propel our liberation from the discrimination, abuses, and oppression we experienced as second-class citizens in the United States of America. *Aztlán* was this unifying identity. We were united by the ancient history of our people. It was our ancestors who had once lived in the Southwest, where the majority of Chicanos reside today. Now we declared that we were no longer outsiders in a foreign land, but a prodigal people returning to the ancient homeland of our ancestors, a home that had existed long before there was a United States of America. The *Plan de Aztlán* called for a whole generation of Chicano youth to take control of their lives. We would rise up to reclaim our ancient homeland.

I lay awake in my sleeping bag that night, thinking about the *Plan de Aztlán*. There were fifteen million Mexican Americans in the United States. Some Latin American countries had smaller populations: Cuba had only nine million, El Salvador five million, Nicaragua four million, Bolivia six million, Chile thirteen million. We *were* a nation of people, a nation within a nation. True, we did not possess a territory that we might some day leverage into secession, as could our Puerto Rican brothers and sisters. The battle for landed sovereignty had been lost over a hundred years ago. But we were still a nation of Chicanos. We were united by race, culture, and language in a country that despised us. Working together, we might create a parallel government within the United States. Perhaps, some day, we could forge a political unity that would deliver us cities or states where Chicanos could live, work, and prosper.

I'd never felt this kind of *carnalismo* (brotherhood) before, and certainly not with so many people. I met Chicanos from many different walks of life. Most were high school or college students. But there were also street Chicanos, ex-gang members, and *pintos,* as well as religious leaders, community activists, and educators. I began to appreciate how vast the Chicano movement could be.

As the conference continued, so did the ideological debates in both the plenary sessions and the caucuses. One caucus discussed the role of the Chicana. Some Chicanas wanted to be liberated from the male oppression they saw in the *movimiento*—they pointed to the labor intensive work women undertook, and the fact that the men often took this for granted. They also criticized the men for not allowing full participation of women in leadership roles. Others felt these criticisms were divisive, that for the sake of unity, women should "stand by our men against the *gabacho* system." We filmed what we could of this and other debates, but tried to ration the stock so we'd have enough for the days that followed.

Conserving film proved wise. On the third day, we heard about a rally for the Farm Workers' Union at the state capitol building in Denver, which was only a few blocks away from the Crusade headquarters. When Corky announced that we should attend this rally at a plenary session, everyone jumped to his feet and marched through the streets of Denver towards the capitol.

The spontaneous announcement caught us unprepared; we had already put our film equipment away for that day. We scrambled after the marchers and caught up with them on Colfax Street, several blocks from the capitol. Passersby gaped in astonishment at the spectacle of several hundred Chicano youths walking down the street chanting "Chicano Power!" and *"Viva la Raza!"* with fists raised and clenched. It was a sight that would be repeated in many cities throughout the United States in the years to come.

We assembled on the steps of the capitol's west entrance. Facing the capitol was a grassy mall and another government building. To the right was downtown Denver. The air was brisk and clear, the trees leafless. The afternoon sun hit the capitol steps full on. It was perfect: we would be able to use our abundant supply of daylight stock!

From the top of the steps, Corky prepared to address the large gathering. "Form a ring, form a ring," someone shouted. Chicanos from Texas, California, New Mexico, Arizona, and Colorado—and Boricuas (Puerto Ricans) from New York, New Jersey, and Chicago, locked arms and formed a large semicircle that encompassed Corky, the small farmworkers' rally that was already assembled, and the capitol steps.

"Let's film the faces," I said to Martín. We quickly rehearsed a crab-walk pan of the human ring. I walked ahead of Martín, clearing traffic and guiding his body as he recorded the proud faces. The young men stood their ground proudly, as if defying American society to challenge our charismatic leader.

The Colorado flag was being flown at half-mast, mourning the death of former President Dwight D. Eisenhower. When the news of his death had broken earlier, back at Crusade headquarters, the conference audience cheered. It had been a victory—the death of an enemy.

As Corky spoke on the capitol steps, someone took down the state flag and hoisted up a large Mexican flag in its place.

By now Martín, Bobby and I had moved back up the steps to get a panoramic view of the flag raising. A cheer filled the air when the Mexican flag reached the very top of the mast. For a moment, the theory and rhetoric of the *Plan de Aztlán* were a reality. Here were the young faces of the future *movimiento*, the young soldiers of the future, men and women that, in the years to come, would be our lawyers, doctors, educators, and community activists.

By raising the Mexican flag over the Colorado state capitol, we had reclaimed Colorado—land taken from our forefathers in the imperialist war of 1848—as *territorio liberado de Aztlán*, reconquered territory of *Aztlán*. The young soldiers of our nation stood with arms joined, ready to defend our new nation state.

The air was electric with emotion. It was all we could do to make sure we slated the camera correctly and set the proper exposure setting. Alurista's words kept echoing in my mind: "We are *Aztlán*."

A group of about a dozen police officers stood by parked motorcycles and squad cars. They had monitored our activities all afternoon. I half-expected that they might call for reinforcements, but they kept their distance, more concerned with the considerable mass of onlookers that slowed traffic on Lincoln Avenue.

The demonstration by a small group of clergy in support of the farm workers and their nonviolent movement was now totally overshadowed by our presence. Corky spoke on the issue of the farm workers, pledging the support of the Crusade for Justice and of the Youth Conference. Corky made it plain, however, that while he respected César Chávez and his nonviolent approach, the conditions of oppression under which Chicanos lived might, some day, require more drastic measures.

When the speeches were finally over, we returned to the Crusade building for dinner. Hundreds of jubilant Chicanos and Chicanas passed through the citizenry of Denver on the way; they had never witnessed anything like us before.

Although I was personally troubled by Corky's allusion to violence, I felt we had won a victory that afternoon. All of us had participated in an action of self-determination. The Youth Conference planted the seeds for the militancy and cultural nationalist fervor that would sweep the Southwest in the years to come.

For *el movimiento,* it was an ideological beginning. For me, it was an epiphany. The filming of the Mexican flag going up over the state capitol made me realize that my role in the movement could not be limited to educational issues alone. I would document the struggles of *Aztlán* in all its aspects.

Upon returning to Los Angeles, I was convinced that media could and should be used to advance our political struggle. At New Communicators, we were finally getting the kind of film training we needed to achieve this, but there was still a vocal group of students who demanded minority faculty members.

As the weeks passed, I became increasingly impatient with the overriding ethnic politics at New Communicators. By April of 1969, I was emotionally ready to leave the school. Fortunately for me, it was at this time when I heard of a job opportunity at the local public broadcast televison station KCET.

Chapter Seven

Ahora!

Mexican Americans, though indigenous to the Southwest, are on the lowest rung scholastically, economically, socially, and politically. Chicanos feel cheated. They want to effect change. Now.

—Rubén Salazar

In the last week of April 1969, I phoned KCET to inquire about a new Chicano series being planned for broadcast in the fall. I was routed to a man named Eduardo Moreno, whom I had met briefly at a town meeting a few weeks earlier.

"How much do you know about what we're planning?" Eduardo Moreno asked.

"Nothing," I replied. "Just that KCET might be looking for Mexican Americans."

"Let me give you some background."

Eduardo proceeded to explain that in 1968, under a grant from the Ford Foundation, KCET had produced sixty-five episodes of a Mexican-American soap opera entitled *Canción de la Raza* (Song of the People). The soap was unique in that it took place in East Los Angeles, addressed current issues of the day, and involved a cast of local Mexican-American actors. I recalled having seen a couple of the episodes and was impressed by its topical nature.

Ed Moreno had been hired away from his job as news director of Spanish-language radio station KALI to anchor a weekly television phone-in show at KCET called "Línea Abierta" ("Open Line"). "Línea Abierta" was an adjunct to the weekly drama series, and was an opportunity for the community to respond to the social and political issues raised in the series. Ed Moreno had stayed on at KCET after "Línea Abierta" was completed and was now in charge of the Ford Foundation's next step in its ongoing commitment to the Mexican-American community: the production of a nightly talk show originating in East Los Angeles.

I told him I was interested, and he invited me to come by the station. The next day, I visited the KCET studios at the corner of Vine and Fountain. I later learned that this large three-story structure was the home of the original Steve Allen Show. Now, half of the building was occupied by KCET, and the other half by Mark Goodson and Bill Todman Productions, producers of "What's My Line," "To Tell the Truth," and "I've Got a Secret."

Moreno greeted me in the reception lobby and escorted me to his office. "KCET will create a satellite studio in the heart of East Los Angeles. It'll be the first public affairs television show for the Mexican-American community in history." Moreno was looking for Latino talent in a variety of occupations. They hoped to go on the air in the fall.

I knew that KMEX—the flagship of a monopoly of Spanish-language television stations in the United States known as Televisa—and KXLA were the only other stations that addressed the Mexican-American community. But the programming of both UHF stations consisted of *telenovelas* (soap operas) imported from Mexico. Both stations recycled news from Mexico, but neither had local coverage that pertained directly to the 1.5 million Mexican Americans in Los Angeles. But now, here at KCET, there was a chance to do something real for the community.

Ed Moreno took a liking to me from the start, but didn't really know how I would fit in. "I'm not sure what we have for you," he told me. "But I'll see what I can do. Why don't you come back tomorrow?"

The next day, I returned, hoping there would be a job offer. Instead, Moreno reiterated that he was not sure what he could offer me, but that, as long as I was there, I might as well meet the station's programming director.

Moreno led me down to the office of Chuck Allen, a softspoken young man in his mid-twenties.

"Sit down," Allen offered. "Tell me about Occidental College."

I noticed he had my résumé before him. Was this a job interview? I hadn't prepared. What should I say?

I told him about the estrangement I had felt at Occidental College and about my disenchantment with higher education, in general. To make my point, I related the story of a prank I had pulled at Oxy in my junior year.

The art department held a student exhibition in Throne Hall each year in preparation for the school convocation. I had walked through a preview of the exhibit, filled with many modernistic student works. I shook my head in dismay. If this was art, I thought to myself, *anything* could be art! An idea struck me. I mounted two pairs of white socks, which had been soiled rust-red from a summer trip to the Grand Canyon, onto a piece of painted plywood. I sprinkled my "art" with watermelon seeds, then signed it "Arnolfini" (a reference to a famous portrait of the *Marriage of the Arnolfini* by the Dutch master Van Eyk). Then, with the help of some friends, I broke into Throne Hall one night and rehung a wall of paintings to make room for my socks. Not only was the new addition not noticed, but on Convocation Day, I took great delight in hearing students and faculty alike comment on the deep meaning behind my red socks masterpiece.

Allen was delighted with the story. "What do you read?"

I told him of my fascination with Latin American authors that I had recently discovered—Carlos Fuentes, Octavio Paz, Jorge Luis Borges, and Pablo Neruda. Then I described my film work at New Communicators and explained how I thought media could play a role in addressing the social concerns of Chicanos in East Los Angeles. Allen nodded politely. I was about to go into detail about my current film project "*The Dropout*," when he abruptly cut me off.

"Well, thank you for coming in." He stood up, shook my hand, and escorted me to the door. The meeting was over.

Moreno was caught as off guard as I was. He asked me to wait outside, as he had some further business with Allen. As I left Chuck Allen's office, I wondered what I'd done wrong. I had expected a much longer meeting. Is this the way they did things in Hollywood? Should I have asked *him* questions?

After a moment, Moreno joined me. His face was beaming. "He likes you," he said. "You can start work next week!" I suddenly realized that our casual meeting had, in fact, been a job interview, and I had passed it with flying colors.

A Chicano in Hollywood

It was a warm June morning, and I was bursting with anticipation as I walked along Vine Street in Hollywood. At my feet were the names of celebrities embedded on the stars of the famous Walk of Fame: Lionel Barrymore, Red Skelton, Henry Fonda. I played a game trying to find the names of Latino stars. Surprisingly, there actually *were* a few: Pérez Prado, Leo Carillo, Xavier Cugat, Rita Hayworth (Rita Cansino was Argentine). Renee Adoree—was that a Spanish surname? Who was Renee Adoree, anyway?

I was in the best of spirits, relieved that I no longer had to depend on the erratic politics at New Communicators to sustain my livelihood. My spirits were also buoyed by news that in the previous month, Chicano activists had organized a conference on Chicano higher education at the University of California at Santa Barbara. The conference participants, inspired by "El Plan de Aztlán," had hammered out "El Plan de Santa Bárbara," calling for all Mexican-American campus organizations to henceforth be organized as chapters of El Movimiento Estudiantil Chicano de Aztlán (the Chicano Student Movement of Aztlán), more commonly known by its anagram "MEChA," which in Spanish means "match" or fuse. Aztlán was in my blood and I was giddy with anticipation. I couldn't wait to get on with the new adventure at KCET.

When I got to the station, I went to Ed Moreno's office. He took me to a sound stage, where he introduced me to a production manager. On stage, a crew was preparing to tape one of the station's weekly talk shows. There was a bustle about the room as technicians set up lights, laid cable, and checked the large RCA pedestal cameras. I was in awe—this was a real television studio!

"I leave you in good hands, Hessie," Moreno said, and he was gone. From my first day of work, Moreno called me "Hessie," a portmanteau word that combined "Jesús" and "Jess."

The production manager walked me to his office, which was adjacent to the sound stage, and had me wait as he attended his chores. He returned in a short time with a set of headphones.

"Ever do any stage managing?" He asked.

"No," I said.

"Follow me." He took me back to the stage and handed me the headphones. "Just wait here."

I walked nervously onto the stage. I had no experience in stage managing and presumed that I would be getting some kind of on-the-job training.

I fumbled with the headphones and tried to figure out how they worked. I clicked buttons on and off, but nothing happened. The other technicians on the stage ignored me as they went about their business. I tried to catch someone's eye to get me some direction or advice, but everybody was absorbed in their duties. I didn't want to look stupid, so I donned the headphones and pretended that I knew how they worked.

I felt like a fish out of water. Pretty soon, I noticed that the camera and lighting technicians were snickering about something. Then they burst out in laughter. They were all wearing headphones, so I concluded that they were laughing at a joke told by someone in the control booth. It wasn't until I noticed them looking in my direction that I guessed they might be laughing at me. I flipped the headphones control on and off several times, but still got nothing.

My morning optimism evaporated. I stood there, utterly humiliated. The crew went about their business, but occasionally glanced towards me and laughed anew. I endured the embarrassment for a good part of an hour before I began to consider whether or not I should seek out Moreno. But before I took that step, the torment climaxed.

Another crew member appeared on the set wearing headphones

that were identical to mine. He noticed me and did a double-take. The crew almost suffocated themselves with laughter at his surprised reaction. He turned to the others and said flatly, "Very funny, guys."

My face grew red with fury as I realized what had happened. I had been handed a set of headphones that didn't work and was made to stand on stage in confusion until the real stage manager—the latecomer—had arrived. I was the butt of a joke.

"Better watch out," someone said, confirming my suspicions. "He'll have your job before you know it!"

I was infuriated. How could I—a Chicano militant—allow myself to be humiliated by a bunch of racist "*gabachos!*" Flushed and irate, I stomped off the set and I went to Ed Moreno. I told him in no uncertain terms that I was quitting, but was too embarrassed to tell him why.

Moreno saw how upset I was. He genuinely liked me, and had hoped I could be an integral part of the new television program he was preparing. After coaxing me into confessing what had transpired, it was his turn to be angry.

"Well, we'll see about that!" he said. "Hessie, you go home and come back tomorrow. I'll have something for you then."

As I made my way out of the office, still fuming, he called after me. "Don't make any rash decisions," he said. "You have my apologies. This won't happen again."

The next day, Moreno made me production assistant for the forthcoming television series. I never found out what Moreno had told the KCET technicians, but from then on, they treated me with distanced cordiality. Nothing more was ever said about the incident. Only later would I learn that my treatment was part of the backlash by station staff that resented minorities being "forced" on them as KCET management tried to integrate its staff.

Planning a Television First

For the next several weeks, I helped Ed Moreno as he went about the business of staffing the program. Coming onto the project early allowed me to learn firsthand from Moreno and actually to help him shape the series. I became Moreno's right hand.

The first task was to hire as many Latinos onto the show as possible. This had been a mandate from Chuck Allen. I was startled to find such a progressive attitude coming from KCET's programming manager. Moreno filled me in on some history.

In 1967, Chuck Allen had been hired as KCET's programming manager at a time when the station was near collapse. Chuck later confided to me that the week he arrived at the station, he found the telephone bill had gone unpaid and the phones were being turned off. The station had just enough money to meet the payroll and pay either the power bill or the phone bill.

What had rescued KCET from its financial woes was Chuck Allen's master's thesis from the University of Denver entitled "Feedback from Advancement," a forward-looking idea to create a Latino ensemble of actors, directors and producers for a Spanish-language soap opera. This was *Canción de La Raza,* the half-hour drama that I'd seen before. Moreno had been hired for the phone-in segment after each episode. Allen submitted the idea to the Ford Foundation, and it was funded, giving KCET its badly needed cash cow. A major goal of the "Feedback for Advancement" was to offer Mexican Americans opportunities in the television industry. *Canción de La Raza* had done this, and now our new series would do the same.

At the time, Latinos were virtually nonexistent in the motion picture and television industries. I was impressed that Chuck Allen understood this and was prepared to do something about it.

Moreno selected a veteran movie actor, Victor Millán, to be the television director of our series. Millán had starred in several films, notably "The Ring" (1952) and Orson Welles's "Touch of Evil" (1958). He gave a memorable performance in "Giant" (1956) as the Mexican ranch hand whose son (Sal Mineo) dies in battle during World War II. Millán had never worked as a television director before, but his natural talent and willingness to understudy experienced KCET directors quickly made him an excellent choice. Years later, I would put his practiced voice to work as the narrator in my films *América Tropical* and *Yo Soy Chicano.*

The interviews continued. Moreno hired Claudio Fenner López, a communications specialist from a local college, whose salt-and-pepper hair, friendly smile, and loquacious demeanor made him a natural as the show's line producer. As production manager for the series, he hired another young Mexican American with Super 8 film experience, Jimmy Val. Esther Hansen and Armando Sánchez were hired as the show's associate producers.

To do research, and eventually to write on the series as well, Moreno took my suggestion of a young writer fresh out of high school, Luis R. Torres. I had first met Luis Torres during a pilot Upward Bound program at Occidental College in the summer of 1967. He was a high school junior, and I was a college sophomore. We found that we had both grown up in the Lincoln Heights barrio of Los Angeles, and we soon became friends. When the *Ahora!* program started, Torres had just graduated. I recruited him to help me co-write the "La Raza History" series, which he did for several months before enrolling at the University of California at Santa Barbara. A brilliant writer with a rapier-sharp wit and an unwavering social conscience, Torres would become a close friend, collaborator, and intellectual sparring partner for the rest of my life.

As editorial assistant for the series, Moreno hired a young graduate from UCLA—who was also destined to become a lifelong friend—Terri Payne Francis. Francis would go on to become one of KCET's most successful news producers and would eventually produce the national children's series *ZOOM* and *Captain Kangaroo*.

As for my own involvement, my job description quickly changed. In the few short weeks prior to production, I demonstrated to Ed Moreno that my skills lay in writing and in conceptualizing the show, and not in clerical work. I was also strongly linked to the community. Moreno saw me as the voice of activism that was going on in East Los Angeles. I was soon promoted from production assistant to associate producer. I was given writing responsibilities and was asked to be the on-camera co-host. Eventually, I would have a hand in writing all or part of 150 of the 175 half-hour shows we produced.

By July, we had converted a bank on Beverly Boulevard—in the heart of L.A.—into a studio. KCET technicians constructed lighting grids in the ceiling, installed three RCA pedestal television cameras, and linked the feed from the makeshift control booth (what had been the bank vault) to a mini-microwave transmitter located on the roof. Our signal was then transmitted from East Los Angeles to the much larger KCET transmitter atop Mount Wilson. Soon, our staff came on board as full-time employees of KCET, and we began to make plans for the premiere broadcast of our show.

Moreno convened daily staff meetings at which we addressed all the key questions necessary to put a television show on the air. Who was the intended audience? Should it be exclusively for Mexican Americans? Should the show reach out to educate the non-Latino viewer? What kind of format should we use? News? Talk? Remote? Who would write the show? Who would host it? What should we call the series? What issues should we tackle?

Moreno's approach was democratic to a fault. He asked for input from all staffers, regardless of their positions. Within a short time, it became evident that opinions on most matters were polarized. Ed Moreno and I were usually the spokesmen for these opposing positions. Moreno, born in Mexico, had learned English as a second language, had served in the U.S. Army as a nurse, and was devotedly Catholic. He wore large baggy pants and neatly pressed white shirts. All in all, he was a traditionalist. On the other hand, I had been born in the United States and was most comfortable in English. I was vehemently anti-war and, at best, was a religious agnostic. I wore jeans and madras shirts, and was brash and militant in my outlook. Ed and the *Ahora!* staff soon dubbed me "El Chamaco" (The Kid). Though we often argued, Ed and I shared the common vision of wanting to create something bigger than all of us, something that would make our community proud. That we eventually succeeded was, in no small part, due to our ability to compromise and then put all our energies and talents behind a common goal.

Compromise played a key role when it came to naming the show. The name debate started in our first staff meeting and raged until well into the show's planning stages. Lists of names were drafted, but we could not settle on one. To his credit, Moreno wanted unanimity. He had no intention of "forcing" his ideas on us. The debate, which threatened to go on for weeks, reflected the generational differences within the staff.

One contingent, led by Moreno, wanted a title that would give dignity to the series and that would show respect for the traditions of Mexican-American culture. Ed also wanted the title to be in Spanish, to reinforce pride in our native tongue.

Another contingent, which I led, wanted the title to suggest a new generation of Mexican Americans, a generation of youthful Chicanos who wanted change. I wanted a title that would break stereotypes and portray the Mexican-American community as militant and contemporary. And I wanted it to be in English.

We settled on a compromise: *Ahora!* (*Now!*)

Having the title in Spanish made it easier for the community to identify with, as Moreno wanted. I felt that the immediacy of the name conveyed the contemporary flavor I was looking for.

We decided that we should not limit *Ahora!* to a strict, traditional programming approach. While we agreed we would initially start the show in a "talk" format, we decided to be open to remote telecasts, drama skits, musical performances, and showcasing barrio artists, poets, and actors. We would try it all in an effort to remain vital and up-to-date. While we agreed we should reflect the full spectrum of community concerns, we also placed a priority on being on top of community events, personalities, and issues. We would be the pulse of the community.

We decided to bring an attractive Chicana drama student, Rita Saenz, on board to co-host with Ed Moreno and Esther Hansen. To balance the gender mix, and because of my growing importance in the show, I was also asked to be a regular co-host.

I convinced Moreno that we needed a snappy beginning, and he allowed me to design and produce a thirty-second logo opening. I had been impressed by the work of Chuck Braverman, who had produced an animated review of American history in two minutes using hundreds of American paintings and photographs for the CBS *Smothers Brothers Show*. The technique involved exposing only two or three frames of an image before moving on to then next. The result was a kaleidoscopic montage that left the viewer abuzz with images. I decided to use this technique (called kinestasis) and worked with one of the New Communicators instructors, Jim O'Neill, to produce a thirty-second montage of Chicano history from the arrival of Cortez to the present. This became the *Ahora!* logo.

As the *Ahora!* staff met daily to nail down the first few weeks of the show, we were unaware that elsewhere in the barrio there were efforts afoot to block the broadcast of our show.

¡Raza, Sí, Ahora, No!

Opposition to *Ahora!* was not surprising, given the history of how media had ignored the Mexican-American community up to this time. In particular, KMEX had been singled out by community activists as an example of a station that only "took from the community" and that "never gave back." KMEX was principally owned and controlled by Emilio Ascárraga, the Mexican media magnate whose holdings included the Televisa chain of television stations in Mexico City as well as radio stations and newspapers. The monopoly, often criticized by Mexican Americans for violating FCC regulations, was eventually broken up by the FCC in the 1980s.

It had now been a year since the walkouts, and during this time the momentum and activism within the Chicano community had grown. Public protests, picket lines, and other political activities had been ignored by KMEX, and were only occasionally covered by the news departments at the mainstream CBS, ABC, and NBC stations.

When word filtered through the community that there was going to be yet another Mexican-American-oriented television program on the air—this time on KCET—community leaders began to organize. This must not be a replica of what had happened with KMEX, some argued. This time, the community would not be ignored. With rumors circulating that *Ahora!* would whitewash the authentic voice of the Chicano community, activists launched a concerted effort to keep us off the air, sight unseen. The campaign started with anonymous phone calls threatening violence to the *Ahora!* staff. Red paint was splashed on the *Ahora!* building. Moreno advised the staff to take precautions going to and from work. A memo was circulated outlining steps that should be taken if a takeover of the studio was attempted during a broadcast.

We were both startled and disheartened by the community reaction. The opposition was not coming from Anglo racists—who did later attack the show—but from our own community.

The campaign against us came to a head during a series of open debates on *Ahora!* at meetings of the EICC in July and August of 1969. By this time, the regular weekly meetings of the Educational Issues Coordinating Committee had moved to the Euclid Center, an old church located at the corner of Euclid Street and Whittier Boulevard, where Lupe Saavedra's Teatro Chicano rehearsed. In the wake of the walkouts, the EICC had quickly become the community clearinghouse for many issues and debates affecting Mexican Americans. It was not uncommon for meetings to range from a case of police brutality to that of a school principal mistreating a child, to a complaint about welfare rights. In many ways, the EICC was the voice of the community.

Spearheading the drive against *Ahora!* was Raúl Ruiz, the editor of the leading militant movement magazine, *La Raza.* Until this time, my encounters with Raúl were tangential. Both Raúl and I were ubiquitous at community meetings, rallies, and picket lines—he with a 35 mm still camera reporting for *La Raza* magazine, and I with my Super 8 camera. We had both participated in the Board of Education sit-in. Raúl, other student members of the EICC board, and I were viewed, in the words of Rev. Vahac Mardirosian, as the "young Turks." We represented the student generation. As such, we often stood against the opinion of oldsters at the EICC. But other than these brief alliances, we had little to do with one another.

During August of 1969, however, Raúl made it his personal agenda to keep *Ahora!* off the air, and that meant taking me on. Soon, we were arguing and shouting at one another across the EICC meeting room.

At one of the EICC meetings at the International Institute on Boyle Street, I entered the room to find it packed with people. I had placed EICC endorsement of the show as an agenda item for discussion that night, and had expected some resistance, but was surprised at the turnout. Most of the people were there to veto my request. Raúl had made it clear to his supporters and friends that this was the night that the *Ahora!* program was going to be stopped cold.

The EICC endorsement, of course, had little to do with whether or not we would go on the air. The premiere broadcast was already set for September 1, and nothing short of a complete power failure at KCET or sabotage at our satellite station was going to stop its broadcast.

But the EICC endorsement had important symbolic meaning. Unlike programming at KMEX, which was consistently criticized by community activists, the staff at *Ahora!* wanted our show to be of, by, and for the Chicano community. The endorsement was also a particularly important issue for me. I felt *Ahora!* was to be the successor to the media activism I had committed myself to at the Denver Youth Conference, and that it was in the spirit of the *Plan de Aztlán.*

Raúl Ruiz and his supporters saw it differently. Dozens of speakers came to the lectern to speak against my proposal for EICC endorsement. Of perhaps two hundred and fifty people who were there that night, there were only three that spoke on behalf of the program: my friends Ben Gurulé, Henry Gutiérrez, and Rev. Horacio Quiñonez. I was in anguish. Here I was being condemned by the very community I sought to represent. And they had never even seen the program!

Finally, the time came for the community to vote on whether the EICC should endorse or condemn *Ahora!* More than two hundred people voted against endorsement, with just six voting in favor.

I rose to the floor and made an angry speech, in which I compared them to people who condemn books they've never read.

"How can you judge something before it's even on the air?" I asked. "Fine, don't give us your damn support! But I challenge you to watch the first ten shows. Watch the first two weeks of programming and you'll see that you are wrong. You'll be surprised. And I will be back here after those two weeks to ask for your endorsement again!"

Still fuming, I made my way through the crowd to exit the building. Suddenly, I felt someone tug at my arm. I turned to find a group of young men by my side. They grabbed me by the arm and guided me quickly out of the building. Outside, in the shadows of the International Institute, one of the men pulled a gun from under his jacket and pointed it at me. "Just keep it up. Just keep it up and see what you get."

There was a long pause. I turned from Chicano face to Chicano face and saw that they meant business. I was still more angry over the vote than I was frightened. All I could think about was the stupidity demonstrated by my own people. The gun was put away and the young men walked off.

Gayla emerged from the crowd inside the building and joined me, unaware of what had just transpired. She could tell something was wrong, however.

"What happened?"

"Nothing that's going to stop me!"

The threat only served to heighten my resolve. Damn it, we were going on the air, come hell or high water!

A Television First

The *Ahora!* program had its premiere at seven on the evening of September 1, 1969. The first night included a discussion with Henry Gutiérrez, Rev. Vahac Mardirosian, and Rev. Horacio Quiñonez of the EICC, on the aftermath of the high school walkouts. Children sang movement songs from a Mexican-American Head Start program. The artwork of a talented Chicano artist, Gilbert "Magú" Luján, was showcased. We also featured speakers from the League of Mexican-American Women. And all in thirty minutes! If there was one thing that *Ahora!* could legitimately be criticized for, it was that we were overly ambitious with our programming.

For the first time in history, Mexican Americans were on the air—writing, producing, directing, and hosting a live broadcast that addressed their concerns and issues. The community was speaking for itself.

I was awash with pride that night. This was what I was destined to do! After the show, we celebrated into the night, not just for the small victory we had won over the community dissidents, but, more importantly, for accomplishing a milestone in the history of our people.

I was especially gratified a couple of weeks later, when I returned to the EICC to ask anew for their endorsement and got a standing ovation as a response. Even Raúl Ruiz came to me a few weeks later and admitted that he had been wrong. The animosity between us ended a couple of years later when I produced *Yo Soy Chicano*. He granted me an interview for the film, we made up, and from then on we frequently found ourselves as comrades on the same side of community causes.

The experience of confronting popular opinion freed me from the awe in which I held movement leaders and the community in general. If they could be wrong once, they could be wrong twice. I began to scrutinize more closely the issues and debates that surfaced at the EICC. So many positions that on the surface seemed to serve the good of the community, were often, in fact, key to the self-serving agendas of their advocates. I started to trust my instincts with more certainty.

In the next dozen programs of *Ahora!*, we featured organizations such as the Joaquín Murieta College Center, the East Los Angeles Health Task Force, the Comité Cívico Patriótico, the Committee for the Rights of the Imprisoned, the East Los Angeles Service Center, the Neighborhood Youth Corps, and the East Los Angeles Free Clinic. We interviewed Rosalío Muñoz of the Chicano anti-war movement, high school walkout leaders from Roosevelt High, and David Sánchez, prime minister of the militant Brown Berets. We featured the work of Chicano artists Judy Hernández, Frank Martínez, Roberto Chávez, and Raúl Garduño. The writings of the *Con Safos* literary group, whose membership included Frank Sifuentes, the man who had introduced me to New Communicators, were also presented. We staged a live drama production by the Mexican-American Theater Company, and televised a live performance of *ballet folklórico* from a local Eastside park. Also in our first dozen shows, we instituted a regular segment on community announcements, introduced my "La Raza History" series, and started an audience participation format allowing people literally to walk in off the street and speak on the air from our cramped studio seating.

Ahora! was on the air.

It was exciting, exhilarating, and wondrous. For the first time in my life, I was getting paid for doing what I loved. Producing a live half-hour show five nights a week left me physically drained, but I didn't mind. I was learning an incredible amount: being a television host, writing scripts, preparing on-screen graphics, editing videotape, and learning to work closely with people.

Ed Moreno was a great captain at the helm of the *Ahora!* ship. He listened to anyone who had show concepts and shaped the best ideas into excellent programs. He intervened whenever arguments among the staff got out of hand, and always managed to keep us clear-headed and on track.

Ed was always open to my suggestions, and often these were incorporated into the show. One of my more successful ideas was the "La Raza History" series—five-to-ten minute history vignettes, which would later play an important role in my own film work. The "La Raza History" series had come from early conversations I had had with Moreno about the need for Chicanos to know about their past. Moreno gave me the go-ahead, and I recruited Luis Torres to help write a series of forty segments that were broadcast once a week. In the course of one year, the series told the history of Mexican Americans from pre-Colombian times to the present.

During the fall, *Ahora!* consumed all my time. But the film that I had started at New Communicators, *The Dropout*, which I had now renamed *Ya Basta!*, was still far from being finished. This taxed me considerably. I knew what I wanted to do with the film, but I couldn't seem to find the time to finish it. Aluminum CFI cans containing the work print and original of the film were stacked in a corner of our living room—a constant reminder of something left undone. Despite the success of *Ahora!*, I questioned whether I would ever have a 16-mm film to my credit.

Equally troublesome to me was my fear of receiving the dreaded letter from my draft board, a letter that was now a year overdue. I suspected that they had forgotten about me. Still, every time I went to the mailbox, my stomach writhed with the possibility that terrible news might lay within.

On one occasion during the course of *Ahora!*, I arrived at eight o'clock one bright and sunny morning in front of Roosevelt High School with the KCET remote truck. We wheeled the three pedestal cameras off the truck, set them up so they pointed across the street, and fired them up. By nine o'clock we had our cameras set, and it was then that the school's principal came out to see what was going on. He could tell I was in charge.

"What are you doing?" He looked at the assemblage of equipment. "Why are these cameras here?" At that moment, the nine o'clock bell rang, signaling the start of classes.

"We're here to film the walkout," I replied, pointing across the street to where hundreds of Chicano high school students began to exit the school.

The principal was flabbergasted. He stood in shock as students streamed from the thresholds of his school shouting "Walkout! Walkout!" He had no clue that this was going to happen, and yet here was a television crew that not only knew about it, but was recording it for broadcast that night!

My contacts at the EICC had alerted me about the impending walkout, kept secret by the students, and I had talked Ed Moreno into letting me "take the car" to the event. We had scooped all of the Los Angeles media on the event! Later that same night on *Ahora!*, we broadcast the walkout and interviewed student leaders, parents, and teachers.

As they had on previous occasions, the local Los Angeles news teams came to our studio to interview our guests for *their* news coverage. We were on the cutting edge of the events in the community and were using the media to voice Chicano concerns. Such was the case on December 15, 1969, when we hosted members of the Jesús Domínguez Defense Committee, an ad-hoc community group created in response to a particularly disturbing case of police brutality.

Police Brutality

Jesús Domínguez, a resident of Lincoln Heights, had received a frantic call from his teenage daughter on the evening of September 1, 1968. She was attending a neighborhood dance when police arrived to break up the party. She was fearful of being arrested and asked for her father to come pick her up. Domínguez and his wife drove to the Italian Hall on Broadway in Lincoln Heights and found the dance hall surrounded by police cars. The police were indiscriminately arresting participants at the dance. Domínguez identified himself as a parent and asked the police for permission to seek out his daughter and take her home. The police reply was, "We're not talking to any more dumb Mexicans." When he insisted, Domínguez was beaten, arrested, and taken away in a patrol car. But the assault did not stop there.

The two officers who arrested Domínguez took him to a nearby empty lot, where another patrol car with two more officers joined them. The four police proceeded to beat Domínguez mercilessly. In spite of his wounds and appeals for help, Domínguez was jailed for seventy-two hours without any medical attention. On his release, Domínguez's family immediately took him to the hospital, where he underwent four hours of brain surgery.

As in countless cases before, Domínguez was charged with assault on a police officer. Domínguez was tried twice, each trial resulting in a hung jury.

Our *Ahora!* program centered on the fact that despite the hung juries, the office of district attorney Evelle Younger was seeking to try Domínguez for assaulting a police officer for a third time. Remembering my arrest, I raised the issue of police brutality on the program and asked whether the district attorney was singling out Domínguez for a third trial because the district attorney was trying to defend the officers that had allegedly beaten Domínguez.

The Domínguez story had been completely overlooked by the major news teams in Los Angeles. Following that night's show, reporters from rival stations called up to ask for interviews with Jesús Domínguez. Once again, our show was using media in the fullest sense to represent the concerns and the issues of the Chicano community.

The Letter

In one of our early shows, I interviewed a young Chicano who had refused to be inducted into the military the day before our interview, on September 16, Mexican Independence Day. Rosalío Muñoz had recently graduated from UCLA, where he had been the first Chicano to be elected student body president. My interview with Rosalío brought out the somber issue of Chicanos dying in disproportionate numbers in Vietnam. A report had been recently published in *La Raza* magazine citing statistics of Spanish-surnamed casualties in the war: in 1969, 19 percent of U.S. casualties in the Marine Corps originating from southwestern states were Spanish-surnamed! As Rosalío and I spoke of how Chicanos were being used as cannon fodder, I was reminded of the long struggle for equality that my people had waged for generations. It angered me and renewed my hatred for the United States. It also underscored the importance of my role as a media activist for my community: It was my people and I against the United States of America. If that was a separatist position, then so be it!

The Rosalío Muñoz program was one our most poignant shows. I had done my homework, and we ended the show by running an end-credit crawl of the names of Spanish-surnamed Americans who had already died in Vietnam. Single-spaced names moved down the screen, accompanied by dead silence. It lasted three full minutes. The phones lit up as friends and relatives of Chicanos in Vietnam called to congratulate us on the show.

In the weeks that followed the Muñoz interview, my concern over my own draft status intensified. I was now in the public eye. If I had been overlooked, all it would take would be for one draft board member to tune in and wonder "Hey, what about THAT guy?" Was I prepared to go the route Rosalío had chosen? Was I prepared to go to jail?

On November 20, 1969, I received a letter from the San Gabriel Valley Draft Board. More than a year had passed. "This will acknowledge receipt of your SSS form 152 (Special Report for Class C.O. registrants)" the letter began. "We regret the long delay in answering; however, it was unavoidable."

The letter went on to explain that the three choices I had submitted to work out my C.O. were unacceptable. Instead, I was offered a fourth option for my two years of alternate service. *They had approved my C.O. application!*

Suddenly, the worrying about Canada and jail was over. But I was not out of the woods yet. The choices they gave me to work out my alternative service included working at Goodwill Industries, the Los Angeles County/U.S.C. General Hospital in Los Angeles, a hospital in Oklahoma City, or a hospital in Cleveland, Ohio.

What was to become of my grandiose plans to document the struggles of the Chicano Movement? How could I continue with my political activism? What would happen to my career as a filmmaker? The news set me to problem solving. There had to be a way to continue my work for *el movimiento*.

A Community Speaks Out

Meanwhile, work at *Ahora!* continued at a grueling pace. In January, we learned that Rosalío Muñoz had organized a march to protest the war in Vietnam. The staff of *Ahora!* discussed the march, and we all agreed that we should cover it. But rather than use our pedestal video cameras, we decided that, because of its importance, we should commit to 16-mm film. By now, Ed Moreno had given me the green light to start prepping a three-part documentary series on Latinos in the motion picture industry. Claudio Fenner López, the line producer for our show, was the logical person to produce the film, and Ed Moreno agreed to co-produce. This episode of *Ahora!* demonstrated that, in addition to a nightly video program, we could also produce our own independent films.

The film turned out to be a remarkable half-hour black-and-white film chronicling the so-called "Moratorium in the Rain," an East Los Angeles anti-war demonstration that had been scheduled for January 31, 1970. Despite pouring rain, hundreds of people had turned up for the event. The march soon became a statement in itself. What did a little rain matter when so many of our youth were being needlessly killed in Vietnam?

I tagged along on the shoot, although the primary responsibility for the film fell on Claudio and Ed. I was impressed by the image of young Brown Berets—men and women—marching down Whittier Boulevard, their fists held skyward as they chanted "*Raza Sí, Vietnam, No!*"

I cursed the war and our racist nation that had conspired to send a whole generation of Chicano youths to their deaths. And now, here was my generation of Chicano activists standing together, rebelling against what others saw as predetermined destiny.

We undertook several such *Ahora!* specials during the year, programs that were so elaborate that they required several weeks of preparation. Typically, one or two people would be pulled out of their regular assignments to work exclusively on a special while the other staffers covered for them.

The Latino Image in Film

One such special that I wrote, produced, and hosted at *Ahora!* was a trilogy of half-hour programs entitled *Image—The Mexican American in Motion Pictures and Television.*

I had become quite aware of both the negative stereotypes of Latinos that permeated films and television and of the lack of our participation in Hollywood. I knew that mine was the first generation of Latinos to break into any role other than acting. But how and when would we be able to penetrate the nepotism of Hollywood?

The first show focused on the false portrayal of Mexican Americans and Latinos in Hollywood motion pictures. This was largely an historical overview of actors and films that highlighted the extent of racism at the time the films were made.

The second program dealt with the dismal situation of employment for Spanish-surnamed people in the industry. In 1969, the U.S. Commission on Civil Rights hearings addressed employment practices of minorities in the motion picture industry. I utilized the Commission's statistics to show that the employment of Spanish-surnamed people in film studios and television station was less than 3 percent, despite the fact that, at the time, we represented 15 percent of the population of Los Angeles County. This would be the first of many campaigns that spanned three decades, in which I either originated or took part in challenging negative portrayals of Latinos in films and television, and pushed for more employment opportunities for Latinos.

The last program dealt with what I hoped would be the "changing" image of Latino access to the industry. I invited Ricardo Montalbán and Rodolfo Hoyos, two highly respected veteran actors, to talk about their industry experiences.

At that time, the Frito Lay Company had invoked the wrath of the Mexican-American community with its depiction of a Mexican border bandit as the "Frito Bandito," who waylaid travelers to obtain the product of the company, corn chips. I persuaded my good friend from the EICC, the Rev. Horacio Quiñones, to pose for a photo. Being rather heavyset with a roundish face, Horacio was ideal. With him dressed in a big Mexican sombrero with cartridge belts and a fake mustache, I took a black-and-white high contrast photo and blew it up. He was the spitting image of the Frito Bandito. This huge photo became the backdrop for our set.

I ended the final program of the trilogy by highlighting a new training program at the Directors Guild of America, which provided entry-level opportunities for minorities and women. For this, I elicited the opinion of Walter Domínguez, a recent graduate of the program, concerning the prospects for changing the image of the Mexican American in motion pictures and television.

In our conversation, we concluded that no true change could possibly come about until Latinos were employed behind the scenes—as writers, producers, and directors. At the time, I felt the change was right around the corner and that my trilogy would usher in an era of opportunity for Mexican Americans and other Latinos in the television and motion picture industries. The three programs were later reedited into a one-hour special. Of the three episodes and the one-hour special, only the first episode remains extant in black-and-white video format. For economic reasons, KCET, in later years, opted to erase most of the 174 *Ahora!* programs produced and to recycle the video stock. Only a dozen episodes survived.

During the course of the year that I helped produce *Ahora!*, I quickly became a spokesman for the community. Being on the air every night gave me a visibility and a credibility that I had never had before. People looked upon me as an expert, someone whose opinion mattered.

With the new visibility, and my own tendency to be outspoken, I began to make myself heard on key issues that affected not just the EICC, but larger community issues as well.

When *Time* and *Newsweek* magazine reporters came to East Los Angeles to chronicle the emerging Chicano Movement, it was I who gave the reporters a guided tour of the barrio and its personalities.

However, producing a nightly show pulled me away from the community events that I had attended previously. It was all I could do to make the one weekly meeting of the EICC.

By April of 1970, as we prepared to wind down the show, I was anxious for it to end. This stemmed not just from my exhaustion, but from my desire to get back to *Ya Basta!* I was determined to finish this film. The *Ahora!* experience had also shown me that there were some issues that I wanted to treat as film or television that required more resources than were at our disposal at the show. I longed to pursue larger projects and felt that finishing *Ya Basta!* was a necessary step in that direction.

As the end of the *Ahora!* program neared, the staff began to wonder if we could keep the show on the air. But despite the huge success of our program, KCET did not have the budget to continue operating our "remote" studio. If *Ahora!* was to continue, we'd need additional funding. We went directly to the Ford Foundation to see if it could provide more money to keep us on the air.

Community leaders and heads of organizations wrote letters and made phone calls, but to no avail. Ford had always seen *Ahora!* as a pilot program, something to prod the established media into action. In 1970—no doubt prompted by the success of our show—KMEX began its first regular news coverage of the Mexican-American community in Los Angeles. In this way, *Ahora!* had accomplished what it had set out to do. It was never intended to be an ongoing project of the Ford Foundation. Since KCET was unable to interest other sponsors, *Ahora!* went off the air on June 1, 1970, with a compilation show highlighting the programs we had broadcast over the year.

I planned to spend June and July finishing *Ya Basta!* and then begin a project that had been in the back of my mind for some time: writing a Chicano novel.

During the previous year, I had read and reread Gabriel García Márquez's *One Hundred Years of Solitude,* and I was infatuated with the idea of writing a similar epic about the Chicano experience, something that would tie together generations of Chicanos from the time of the Mexican-American War to the present, a novel that would also place us accurately in the framework of American history.

Overriding these tentative plans, however, was the new challenge posed by my military reclassification as C.O. I consulted once again with my draft counselor at the American Friends Services Committee, and he advised that I needn't respond immediately to the draft board letter. Now that I was reclassified, he explained, I was low priority. I had time to plan where and when I might perform my alternate duty. This gave me some breathing room.

A week before *Ahora!* ended, Chuck Allen at KCET wanted to take me to lunch. By now, Chuck and I had become friends, drawn together by a similar sense of humor and literary interests. He was also just as interested in Latino culture as I was. Though my work at *Ahora!* didn't allow me much time to socialize, when Chuck came to the satellite studio in East Los Angeles, it was always I who greeted him and told him of our latest projects.

We arranged the luncheon for a day that I had to go into Hollywood. Chuck picked me up in his 1969 gold Corvette and took me to the renowned Musso Frank Restaurant. I was struck by the elegant, dark wood decor, the lavishly padded seats, and the smartly dressed waiters. This was the first time that I had ever been in such a fine restaurant. Chuck told me that writers such as William Faulkner, Raymond Chandler, Dorothy Parker, and others had lunched there, and that this was one of the chief venues for "business luncheons" of the Hollywood community. We sat down, and I scanned the menu.

I tried my best to be suave. "I think I'll have something light."

I finally ordered the lasagna.

Chuck raised an eyebrow. "Something light?" he muttered under his breath.

My face reddened. I felt like a country hick!

Then Allen got down to business. He wanted to offer me a permanent job at KCET. Chuck knew that he would have to cut loose most of the staff at *Ahora!*, but he had decided that the station could afford to retain a handful of employees from the project. They were to be Ed Moreno, Jimmy Val, Terri Francis, and me.

Without a second thought, I thanked him for the offer, but told him I couldn't accept. I explained to him that I really didn't have time for television now. I had put off finishing *Ya Basta!* for far too long. Then I related my plans for writing the great Chicano novel and told him that I also had to figure out how to deal with my draft status.

Chuck waited patiently as I rambled on about my film and the novel. Finally, he said to me, "Well, why don't you just try the job I'm offering for a few weeks, and if you don't like it, you can always quit."

Now that made sense. What did I have to lose? I told him I would consider his offer.

The next day, after talking it over with Gayla, I agreed to begin working at KCET, but only if I could have May and June to finish *Ya Basta!*

Chuck agreed.

Chapter Eight

Chicano Moratorium

*I accuse the draft, the entire social, political, and economic
system of the United States of America, of creating a funnel
which shoots Mexican youth into Vietnam to be killed and to
kill innocent men, women, and children.*

—*Rosalío Muñoz*

I unpacked another box of books and photos and arranged them
on the shelf next to my desk. It was the first week of July and the second day of my employment in my new capacity as associate producer at KCET. My completion of *Ya Basta!* had gone as planned, taking
up all May and June. Black-and-white, twenty minutes in length, my
first 16-mm film was at long last finished. I could now properly call
myself a filmmaker! Now I was settling into a small, windowless
cubicle located next to the mail room in the basement of the KCET
building on Vine Street.

The phone rang.

"Jesús, got a minute?" It was Chuck Allen.

"Sure."

"Come on up. There's someone I'd like you to meet."

I went to Chuck Allen's office and was introduced to a tall, elegant African-American woman with an impressive Afro.

"This is Sue Booker."

I shook her hand and sat down next to her on the couch.

"You'll both be part of the new department I'm creating," Chuck continued. "The Department of Human Affairs. Sue won't be coming on board for another week, but I thought it'd be nice for you two to meet."

Chuck explained that Sue Booker had just come from Nebraska, where she had co-produced a four-part PBS docudrama entitled "The Black Frontier" for the local public broadcasting station, KUON. He told her about my work on *Ahora!* I could tell from the careful way that he introduced us, stressing our community involvement and our mutual interest in philosophy and civil rights, that he was anxious that the two of us hit it off.

Later in the day, I ran into Sue in the hallway. We quickly discovered we had much in common: we were each twenty-two years of age, had a similar sense of humor, shared a distrust of the established media, and wanted to put our skills to work for our respective communities. We had time on our hands, so we talked into the afternoon.

If ever two people were spiritual twins, it was Sue Booker and me. We left the station together that afternoon.

"Is your car this way?" she asked.

"Yeah, it's over there."

We came to the middle of the block where two tan 1969 VW bugs were parked alongside one another—one was hers, the other mine.

"When were you born?" she asked.

"March 26."

"My birthday's March 25," she said. "What hour?"

I told her the date and time of my birth, and we figured out that we were only a few hours apart. At that moment, we both sensed that our relationship would be special.

Sue Booker would produce at KCET from 1970 to 1973. Later, she left television production to pursue a doctorate in theology. In 1984, she had a remarkable meeting with Archbishop Desmond Tutu in which he bestowed a new name upon her, Thandeka, which in Xhosa means "lovable," and is part of an expression that means "one who is loved by God." Although this is her legal name today, I will refer to her as Sue Booker, since that was her identity during the time of these events.

Sue chose to focus on the life and times of Black Americans as her assignment in the new Human Affairs Department. I opted to cover the Chicano community. There were three others in the department: Anita Solderberg; Dr. Richard Scott, who headed the department; and his secretary, Marjory Cross. Scott had graduated from USC as an MD, but had become disenchanted with how medicine was practiced. He had come to Chuck Allen, looking for an opportunity to "do something."

The mandate for all of us was simple—to produce quality programming. Period.

"I don't care how many shows you do," Chuck Allen told us. "And I don't care what they are about. But they have to grab people's attention."

Chuck had called us together a day or two after the Department of Human Affairs had been created. We were gathered in Dick Scott's office to discuss the programming for the year.

"Most of all," Allen went on, "I want the shows to be good. Good shows that win awards."

The five of us were unclear. "Is this to be a weekly show?" one of us asked.

"Absolutely not. You can't do quality work if you start cranking out a weekly show. Not the kind of quality I want."

"Well, what then? Monthly?"

"That's up to you." He replied.

Part of Chuck's genius at managing people was knowing how to light a fire under someone, and when to retreat, so the person could grapple with an idea and eventually express his passion. He wanted us to have an environment of freedom, one that would nurture and support us as we produced our programs.

Chuck Allen had a knack for identifying talent and nurturing it. It is a tribute to his judgment that the alumni of KCET's "golden era"— all of whom, I later discovered, had passed Chuck's "What books do you read?" test—include such distinguished producers and filmmakers as Terri Francis Butler (*Zoom, Captain Kangaroo*), Lynn Littman (*Number Our Years, Testament*), Barry Nye (*National Geographic*

Specials), Taylor Hackford (*Officer and A Gentleman, Delores Claiborne*), as well as noted film critic Charles Champlin.

"Let me know when you have something." With that, Chuck left the room.

The message couldn't be clearer. There was no pressure to go up to bat, but when we did, we had to hit home runs. Though I feigned nonchalance at the challenge, I was petrified. Could I pull it off? Could any of us pull this off?

From the onset, working in the Human Affairs Department meant working closely with Booker—Solderberg and Scott, though technically in our department, had interests that diverged from ours. It was assumed that Anita's programming would involve feminist issues and that Dick's role was more managerial and editorial. Sue and I, on the other hand, shared a common vision for our communities. Our agenda was to do black and brown programming.

There was a favorite sidewalk cafe just a block down the street where Sue and I would often meet for a leisurely lunch, often staying until two or three o'clock in the afternoon. Lunch was a pretext for talking and sharing ideas. Our conversations sizzled. We talked about who we were as people, about love, the movement, politics, racism, oppression, and heroism. We spent many hours discussing and arguing, which honed our intellectual and spiritual selves. Most of all, we philosophized about our roles as media activists.

We became inseparable.

Occasionally, Chuck Allen would join us for lunch. Because of his iconoclastic style and his abhorrence of pretense and bureaucracy, I saw him as a free spirit, ready to challenge the system or poke fun at bureaucracy whenever the opportunity afforded itself. Chuck was eager to learn. We had long discussions about the works of black and Latino writers, about liberation theology, the civil rights movement, and current films.

Sue had already coauthored an anthology of writings by African-American youth entitled *Cry at Birth*. I had aspirations of writing the great Chicano novel. I thought Chuck Allen was about as erudite and articulate a man as one might find. It was a rich tapestry of ideas that we wove together, and, indeed, a stimulating and rewarding time of dialogue and growth for all of us.

Soon, it was time to put our ideas to work. Sue was interested in doing a documentary on the work of an ex-convict named Cleophus Adair, who was working to rid the black community of drug dealers. My opportunity came unexpectedly, when I decided to film an anti-war march of several thousand people scheduled for August 29, 1970.

A Moratorium March

Earlier that summer, I had become aware that Rosalío Muñoz— the young Chicano whom I had interviewed on *Ahora!* and who had organized the "Moratorium in the Rain"—was convening a much larger national march in Los Angeles, scheduled for August 29. The march was to call for a moratorium on the war.

In March of 1970, Rosalio, along with his co-organizer Bob Elías, attended the Second Denver Youth Conference. While there, they discussed with Corky Gonzales the need to convene a national gathering of Chicanos. At the conference, they hoped to put into effect the idea of a third political party that had been talked about at the first Denver Youth Conference. Rosalío had worked for months to enlist the attendance of Chicanos from throughout the nation to once and for all denounce the Vietnam War, particularly the high rate of Latino casualties. The plan was to convene a mass gathering of Chicanos from throughout *Aztlán* to protest the war, and then to hold an organizing conference the subsequent week in Los Angeles to form the new political party.

Chuck Allen asked Ed Moreno, who was now a producer for the station's Current Events news department, to report on the event. Moreno enlisted Jerry Hughes as cameraman and director.

At the time, I was beginning preliminary research on a program I hoped to produce on free schools, an idea that had grown out of my involvement with the EICC. Although I was not officially part of the KCET crew, I decided that I would attend the moratorium. I spoke with Chuck, and he agreed to pay for an additional camera and Nagra sound recorder so that I could film the event as well. My film crew was made up of one of the KCET stage hands, Henry Rangel, my wife Gayla, and me.

As I made plans to film the event, I got a call from an artist friend who lived in San Francisco, Francisco Camplís. Francisco had decided to attend with his wife, Lencha, and their two children, Marina and Carlos. I invited the Camplíses to stay with us for the weekend. They arrived the night before the march, and we all went out to dinner and got caught up on each other's lives. The kids were particularly excited by the trip to Los Angeles because it would be their first opportunity to visit Disneyland, which they planned to do on Sunday, the day after the march.

The next morning, we all set out to the march. Gayla and I followed Henry's Dodge Dart to the ending site of the march, Laguna Park, where we dropped off his car and then drove back to the starting area at Belvedere Park in our VW bug. By having Henry's car at the end of the march, we'd have a way to get back to our own vehicle without having to retrace our steps (a good four miles) on foot. We parked the VW right next to the East Los Angeles Sheriff's substation, adjacent to Belvedere Park. A sizeable, festive crowd was already gathering.

After much delay, the march began. Throngs of people walked down Atlantic Boulevard. Rangel, the sound man, and I filmed and recorded the entire march starting at the park, moving south along Atlantic Boulevard, and then west along Whittier to the end of the route, at Laguna Park.

It was exhilarating to see so many people out to protest the war, carrying banners of their home states: Texas, Arizona, New Mexico. Police halted the march to let cross traffic along Whittier pass, but otherwise kept a low profile, parking their patrol cars on side streets away from the march route.

We finally arrived at the park after one o'clock. At the route's end, people moved through barriers and around a large flatbed truck, which had been set up as a makeshift stage. The truck was parked along a fence on the eastern side of the park, making entry into the park difficult. People filtered in as best they could and congregated in front of the stage.

I took my camera into the main area and got a shot of the stage and of the people coming into the park. By then, the grassy area was filled with tired marchers settling down on the grass to await the program of speakers and entertainment.

As I looked out across the park, I saw many friends and movement activists. I made out the faces of people I hadn't seen in weeks or, in some cases, years. I chatted with folks in the park area for a while, but Henry Rangel was anxious to get back to his car because he had an afternoon errand to run. I was very grateful for his help, so I agreed that we should leave as soon as possible.

"Okay," I said, "let's get the equipment into your car and you can drop Gayla and me off at my car." Gayla and I planned to return to the park and catch up with our friends, the Camplíses, after we got our VW.

A sea of marchers was still streaming into the park when we reached Henry's car, located a block away. We loaded up our equipment, and Henry drove back to where our VW was parked. We had arrived at our car, and I was in the process of unloading the equipment into the trunk of the VW when we heard the first police sirens wail.

Coming at us from the sheriff's substation, doing at least fifty miles an hour, were dozens of sheriff cars. Each one had five or six sheriff officers, all dressed in riot gear and armed with shotguns and clubs.

As the cars sped by erratically on the narrow street, Gayla, Henry, and I had to press ourselves against the door of the VW in order to avoid being struck. I counted more than thirty squad cars.

Something terrible was happening.

Gayla and I said goodbye to Henry, jumped into the VW, and raced back toward Laguna Park. Gayla drove so I could load another roll of film into the camera.

We slowed down near the intersection of Indiana and Whittier Boulevard. Squad cars were everywhere. I didn't yet know what had happened, so we drove by scores of police and sheriff cars to get a closer look.

Suddenly, a young Chicano on the sidewalk called out to us, "Turn around! Go back!"

I began to get frightened. What was going on? We drove the block from Indiana to Alma Street, passing numerous police and sheriff officers on foot, dressed in riot gear. As we approached Laguna Park, we could see clouds of tear gas hanging in the air. Here and there, policemen charged into what was left of the crowd, brandishing riot batons.

More deputies and police officers lobbed tear gas canisters toward Chicanos congregated around the flatbed truck stage. Other Chicanos fled the park toward Whittier Boulevard.

A group of young men, many without shirts, had formed a cordon in front of the truck. They seemed to be holding off the police so the crowd could escape the park. I heard people screaming and the occasional "thump" of a tear-gas canister being fired.

Ahead of us, a station wagon was pulling out of a space in front of the park. Gayla slid the VW in.

I noticed that the station wagon belonged to Spanish television station KMEX and that two men had just gotten out of the car. I recognized one of the men. It was *L.A. Times* reporter Rubén Salazar, a fact that would become significant later in the day.

I put the camera on my shoulder and headed east along the perimeter of the park to the corner of Whittier Boulevard and Ditman. People continued to dash out of the park, around the corner of Whittier and Ditman, and then they ran east on Whittier.

Three police officers converged on a young Chicano and began to beat him to the ground with their clubs. I became concerned for our safety, so we moved across Whittier, away from the park. I filmed what I could see as I walked along the sidewalk. Then we came across several young Chicanos that were looting a small grocery.

"Watch out!" one of them shouted as he noticed me with the camera. "He's a cop!"

"He's not a cop!" Gayla yelled. Later she told me she was afraid they would try to break the camera, fearing my footage would incriminate them.

By now, my attention was wholly absorbed with the sight of a phalanx of police officers working their way down Whittier Boulevard. I steadied my camera on a light post to film the melee that was raging down the street. There were still a lot of policemen around me, and suddenly I felt a jab at my side.

I took my eye off the camera just as a man dressed in a gray suit came by and shoved me hard into the light post. He gave me another hard elbow in my side, knocking me off my feet.

I nearly lost my grip of the camera as I sprawled out on the sidewalk. I regained my footing and began filming again. The same person that had hit me charged past on his way across the street. As he ran by, I could see that he was wearing a badge.

Meanwhile, a uniformed officer started toward me. I immediately backed off.

"What are you doing?" I demanded.

"Get out of here!" the officer shouted. "Get out of here now!"

I retreated from the officer, whose attention was now diverted by a scuffle across the street. But I didn't leave. The plainclothes officer was now fighting with a young shirtless Chicano. I approached to get a better shot of the action. By this time, the crowd had moved out of the park, and the police were following them along Whittier Boulevard. Gayla called repeatedly for me to get back.

The police began arresting any stragglers they could get their hands on. Between me and the fleeing crowd was a wall of policemen, so I knew I wouldn't be able to get close enough to film anything.

"Okay, let's get out of here." Being hit by the cop had sunk in, and I was getting nervous.

I rejoined Gayla, and we made our way back to the car. Gayla made a U-turn and we took off. We passed a group of people gathered in front of the Green Mill Liquor Store. I didn't think much of it at the time. Later, I learned that it was a disturbance at the liquor store that had sparked the police attack.

Gayla drove us north on First Street and along side streets going east until we finally got back onto Whittier Boulevard. We found ourselves driving through the devastation left by the fleeing crowd. Storefront and car windows had been smashed. Fires blazed in the street. Large plumes of black smoke billowed up to the sky several blocks ahead. The marchers were venting their anger.

"My god," I said as I looked at the black smoke. "This is like what happened in Watts!"

As we drove along Whittier, we could see bands of people ahead, some still running, others stopping to throw rocks through windows. We made our way to the corner of Downey and Whittier, only to find the street barricaded. The police were trying to block off all of Whittier Boulevard to contain the fleeing Chicanos that still were trying to escape from roving gangs of police and sheriff officers. Traffic was being rerouted back along Downey toward Brooklyn Avenue. I still had film in the camera and wanted to document the destruction, so we drove along Brooklyn to Atlantic Boulevard, and then south back to Whittier.

We arrived near the corner of Atlantic and Whittier and found police barricades blocking entrance to Whittier. We parked the VW, got the camera out, and walked to the corner. As I looked west along Whittier, I saw a most incredible sight: the huge plumes of black smoke had increased, filling the sky. There was smoke as far as the eye could see, and flames crackled in nearly all the buildings within view. This was the scene later depicted by Chicano artists Willie Heron and Gronk in a famous mural in the Estrada Courts housing project.

People moved around me, cursing the police and making threats to avenge the attack on the park. It was then that I pieced together what had happened.

A disturbance had broken out at the Green Mill Liquor Store, and the owner had called for police. Laguna Park was situated only a block from the city/county line. Since it was so close to the jurisdictional boundary, both law enforcement agencies had responded in force. Arriving at the park, they had indiscriminately waded into the crowd, swinging batons and shooting tear gas into the crowd. The people responded by defending themselves from the police attack as best they could.

All the onlookers were in disbelief. Why had the police attacked women and children? Why had they attacked families who were guilty of nothing more than sitting in the park? I was overcome by a feeling of despair. How could this be happening in East Los Angeles? A graphic depiction of this violence would later be chronicled in David García and Moctesuma Esparza's film *Requiem-29*, which was compiled from footage donated by all the Chicano filmmakers at the march that day.

A block down the street, I saw sheriff officers arresting more Chicanos. One tried to argue with an officer, protesting his innocence, and was beaten to the ground. The Gestapo had arrived in the United States of America, I thought.

I captured the events until I ran out of film. Then Gayla and I decided to leave. By now, we had heard on the radio that hundreds of Chicanos had already been arrested by the police. We began to worry about our friends, the Camplíses. What might have happened to them? We returned to the house as quickly as we could.

When we arrived home, Francisco and Lencha Camplís and their two children were outside, washing their eyes out with the garden hose. They had been gassed during the police attack, but had managed to escape the park without being arrested.

We immediately turned on the television to listen to the news reports. It was about six o'clock in the evening, and we were all in shock. None of us had ever experienced anything like this before. Carlos and Marina, with their innocent priorities, wanted to know if this meant they wouldn't be able to go to Disneyland the next day.

I decided to call Chuck Allen to let him know I was all right. He told me that Ed Moreno and Jerry Hughes had returned to the station with footage of the march and the police attack. He was mobilizing the station to do a special report for the weekly news program, *Current Events*. I told him I'd help in whatever way possible, and that I'd get my footage processed the next day.

Francisco and Lencha were trying to decide whether to stay another night with us or to start back to San Francisco that evening. What if the riot continued tomorrow? Or spread to Highland Park?

Some time later, I was in the kitchen, replenishing our drinks, when a news update came on the television. There was mention of a bar on Whittier Boulevard called the Silver Dollar in which one or more people had reportedly been killed. From the kitchen, I could make out a few key words: ". . . Mexican-American reporter . . . the *Los Angeles Times*."

I rushed back to the living room in time for the report's conclusion. It appeared that one man killed was Rubén Salazar. A call had been placed to the East Los Angeles Sheriff's office claiming that an armed gunman had been inside the bar. Sheriff's deputies had responded to the call and had fired tear gas into the bar. Later, they went into the bar and found Salazar dead. Elsewhere in East L.A., another man, whose identity was yet unknown, had also been killed.

I was dumbstruck. The moment froze in unreality as we all sat staring into our tiny Sony television. Rubén Salazar? It couldn't be. He was probably the best known Mexican-American reporter we had. I had just seen him alive hours earlier, and now he was dead? The seriousness of the afternoon slammed into me. Not only was it about a riot, fires, and arrests. Now there was a body count.

Chapter Nine

The Salazar Inquest

This inquest has ceased to function as an investigative body to find out the facts of Rubén Salazar's death. Right now they are simply trying to deviate attention from the real question at hand: Who killed Rubén Salazar?

—Raúl Ruiz

On Monday, the station was abuzz with news of the riot and of the death of Rubén Salazar. The news department was piecing together a report for *Current Events*. At KMEX—the station where Rubén Salazar had been news director—general manager Danny Villanueva called a news conference for 10 a.m. I hurried to the Los Angeles Press Club on Vermont Avenue, set up my tape recorder, and waited for the conference to begin.

Soon, Danny Villanueva entered the room, flanked by several men in suits. One of the men was Manuel Ruiz, a recent appointee to the U.S. Commission on Civil Rights. Villanueva approached the microphone.

"The tragic events of Saturday have left our Latin community shocked and paralyzed," he said gravely. "Shocked in disbelief that a peacefully planned demonstration to dramatize the disproportionate number of Spanish-surnamed casualties in Vietnam has resulted in destruction in our community, which is now paralyzed by doubt and concern over the reports of a shooting resulting in the death of our beloved friend and co-worker Rubén Salazar. Our community will be rebuilt, gentlemen, because we will rebuild it. Our pride restored because we thrive on honor."

Villanueva reviewed Rubén Salazar's many concerns about the plight of Mexican Americans and the nonviolent way in which he felt societal change might be brought about. Villanueva urged peace in the community and an end to the violence that had marked Saturday's riot.

Villanueva shuffled through his notes before continuing. "William Restrepo, a reporter on Channel 34's news staff, was with Salazar at the Silver Dollar Cafe on Whittier Boulevard when the tragedy occurred. Also with Salazar was Mr. Hector Franco and Mr. Gustavo García, friends of Restrepo, who had accompanied him on the Moratorium Day March. In addition, Mr. George Muñoz has contacted KMEX to inform us that he, too, was in the cafe at the time. Their accounts of the incident vary substantially from various and conflicting reports by the Sheriff's Department.

"[These accounts] indicate that they did not observe anyone entering the cafe with a gun. They report that the door to the cafe was not locked. They report that no warning to clear the cafe was ever given. They report that people attempting to leave were forced back inside. They report that they insisted to sheriff's officers on the scene at the time of the shooting that Salazar was injured and still inside the cafe, that they were denied re-entrance and were told to clear the area immediately.

"Station executives contacted the East Los Angeles sheriff's station at 5:45 p.m. to notify them of our newsman's account of that incident. We insisted at that time that the report be verified. In spite of our frantic attempts to direct aid to Mr. Salazar, it was not until 10:45 p.m., five hours later, that his death was confirmed."

An uncomfortable murmur rose from the audience as the implications sank in. Villanueva went on.

"These men are ready to give their stories, and KMEX-TV is prepared to turn over all information—which we have available and which, in the future, may come to our attention—to all authorities. To the Los Angeles County sheriffs, to the district attorney, and to the United States Department of Justice. The testimony of these men, because it is in conflict with various versions released by the Sheriff's

Department, makes, in KMEX-TV's opinion, a federal grand jury investigation imperative. We call on Martín Castillo, chairman of the President's Inter-Agency Committee for the Spanish-Speaking, to bring the full resources of the federal government, including the Justice Department, to this investigation to insure that the true facts are determined."

During the question-and-answer period, Villanueva was asked if he recalled how many times from 5:45 to 10:45 p.m. he had tried to reach the Sheriff's Department for information on Salazar's condition.

"We made attempts that were in excess of a dozen."

"Do you recall the replies of the Sheriff's Department?" a reporter asked.

"They replied that they could not confirm [what his condition was], that they had an investigation going on, and that, due to procedural matters, they could not confirm. I even resorted to going to the Police Department to see if they could confirm for me. I told them at that time that my man was in there, and that I wanted him out, and I wanted to know if it was him."

"How many phone calls did you personally make in that five-hour period?"

"I'd say ten," Villanueva replied. ". . . The sheriffs, the police, anyone I could get hold of who might be able to help me. They were all going to look into it. They were all going to call me back, and I continued to make phone calls. It wasn't until we heard on another television station at 10:45 p.m. that we knew he was dead. Suffice it to say that I knew my man was in there and I wanted him out."

Later, Manuel Ruiz spoke, in English and in Spanish, once again stressing the need for calm in the community and promising that the United States Commission on Civil Rights would do all in its power to find out what had happened at the Silver Dollar Cafe.

The five-hour hushup by the Sheriff's Department was extremely suspicious, and the fact that someone as "establishment" as Danny Villanueva requested a federal investigation indicated to me that there, indeed, was something suspicious about Salazar's death.

In the afternoon, Chuck Allen called me into his office. He explained that there was going to be a coroner's inquest into the death of Rubén Salazar. He had been in touch with the news directors of the other Los Angeles television stations, particularly KABC, KNBC, and KNXT (the CBS affiliate). They had agreed to pool coverage of the televised inquest. Each day a different station's cameras and crew would transmit the proceedings of the inquest live; all the other stations in the L.A. area could carry the coverage if they chose. Because of the controversy over Salazar's death, it was expected that most stations would preempt scheduled programming and carry the daily live coverage.

"We're certainly going to feed it live every day," he explained. "I'd like you to help out on our coverage of the inquest."

"Of course," I replied.

The next day, Chuck introduced me to a USC law professor named Howard Miller. Miller was a regular on-camera host for a national PBS weekly series, *The Advocates*, which was produced on alternate weeks at KCET in Los Angeles and at WGBH in Boston. Because of his visibility and legal expertise, Chuck Allen thought he'd make an ideal host for KCET's coverage of the inquest.

Bill Donnelly, who ran the news department at KCET, would be the executive producer. I had met Donnelly some time before, but we had never worked together—he struck me as a bit aloof.

In addition to the video feed, we'd need someone to be at the inquest on a daily basis to take notes and summarize the day's events. Howard Miller's busy teaching schedule exempted him from this task. Donnelly was also too busy—involved with the day-to-day operation of the station's news department. We agreed that I would take on this responsibility of taking notes and writing the copy for the evening broadcast. Because of my contacts, we agreed that I would also be responsible for coordinating interviews with spokespersons from the Chicano community.

That night, KCET broadcasted the riot report that Ed Moreno had produced for *Current Affairs*. Gayla and I watched it at home, transfixed by the sight of police attacking the crowd during the moments when we had been driving from Laguna Park to the East Los Angeles

Sheriff's substation. Ed Moreno and Jerry Hughes had been posi-
tioned near the stage platform, where they captured the horrific police
attack on the crowd.

The footage was frightening: men, women, and children running
to escape the police as officers beat people at random. It reminded me
of the massive attacks on young Chicanos during the zoot suit riots
that Ben Carmona had told me about. By the end of the broadcast, I
was more motivated than ever to cover the inquest.

The next morning, I learned that KCET had received a call from
the Sheriff's Department asking the station to turn in its footage of the
riot so that they might use it to identify lawbreakers.

I thought of my own footage. It clearly showed Chicanos setting
fires and throwing rocks through storefront windows as they took out
their anger over the police attack. When I heard about the sheriff's
request, I was determined that my footage would not be made available to the police.

I went into Chuck Allen's office the next morning to try to convince him not to release the riot footage to the Sheriff's Department.

"I'd like a word with you," I started as I caught him on his way
out of the office.

"Know what you're going to say," Allen said. "Don't need to say
it. Station's attorneys are stonewalling it even as we speak."

Inquest

The Salazar inquest began ten days after Salazar's death, on September 10, 1970, in the Old Hall of Records building in downtown
Los Angeles. I sat in the second row of a crowded courtroom in room
803. Los Angeles County district attorney Evelle Younger had named
a representative Mexican-American "Blue-Ribbon Commission" to
sit in on the non-legally binding coroner's inquest and hear the facts
surrounding Salazar's death. The Commission was made up of members of the Congress of Mexican-American Unity, whose president,
Esteban Torres, also acted as the Commission's chairman. Included in
the ranks of the commission were Irene Tovar, Abe Tapia, Julia
Mount, and Jacobo Rodríguez. Sitting near me were other familiar

faces from the movement: the Rev. Horario Quiñones, Vahac Mardirosian, co-editors of *La Raza* Magazine Raúl Ruiz and Joe Razo, attorneys Joe Ortíz and Oscar Zeta Acosta, and community activitists Mangas Coloradas, Luis Pingaton, Ben and Kay Gurulé.

"Ladies and gentlemen of the jury," hearing officer Norman Pittluck began, "you have been summoned and sworn as jurors to inquire into the cause of death of one Mr. Rubén Salazar."

People in the audience stopped talking and focused on the stuffy, hawk-nosed magistrate who seemed better suited for a courtroom in a Charles Dickens novel.

"We believe the testimony today will show that the deceased person died on August 29, 1970, in the vicinity of or at the Silver Dollar Bar at 4945 Whittier Boulevard, Los Angeles, California."

Pittluck spent the first few minutes of the inquest explaining the parameters to the jury and the television audience. "Because of its public character, the inquest makes available to the family of the deceased and the general public the facts and circumstances under which the deceased died."

"Yeah," I whispered to Horacio Quiñonez seated next to me. "So there won't be any more rioting in East Los Angeles." There had been much talk about the community erupting into violence again if something wasn't done about bringing the killer or killers of Rubén Salazar to justice.

"The inquest, being a preliminary proceeding, should not be confused with a regular court proceeding," Pittluck continued. "No one stands trial at the inquest. No one is determined guilty or innocent as a result of these proceedings."

"So then, why the hell are we conducting them?" I whispered again to Horacio. "Why not conduct a real trial?"

He turned to me with an isn't-it-obvious look. "So the murderers of Salazar can get away with it, of course."

Pittluck explained that only he could ask questions of the witnesses brought to the courtroom to testify. "If either the district attorney or the attorney for the next of kin desires to submit any written questions to me, if they are in order, I will ask those questions of witnesses."

"Great!" I said under my breath. "Not even a chance for cross-examination in this setup." What questions would or would not be asked were at the total discretion of the hearing officer! I wondered who had been behind selecting Pittluck to oversee the inquest.

Pittluck went on to explain that at the end of the inquest, the jurors would be asked to determine how Salazar had died. Their options were: death due to natural causes, death by suicide, death by accident, or death at the hands of another. The morning inched forward with all the pace of a herd of stampeding snails.

Pittluck called the county's deputy coroner David Katsuyama to the stand. Katsuyama explained that he had conducted an autopsy on Rubén Salazar and had determined his death to be due to "a projectile wound to the left side of the head causing a skull fracture and massive cerebral destruction. The wound itself was a gaping, tearing of the skin surface." A projectile had entered Salazar's left side and exited the right side of his head. Pittluck then showed Katsuyama a "flight rite" tear-gas projectile. Katsuyama measured this large bullet-shaped missile and found it to be one and a half inches in diameter and approximately nine and half inches long. He concurred that a missile of this type had caused Salazar's death at about 6:30 p.m. The image of the damage done by such a projectile was stomach-churning.

Next up was Deputy Sheriff Daniel Castrellón, the sheriff's public relations liaison officer who had been sent to the Silver Dollar after Salazar's death to officially confirm Salazar's identity. He had found Salazar lying on the floor of the bar about twenty feet from the front door at about 7:15 p.m. on the evening of the 29th. But instead of elaborating about the circumstances immediately surrounding Salazar's death, or what he found at the site, Castrellón's testimony, instead, focused on recounting purported acts of violence by marchers recorded at sheriff's headquarters throughout the early part of the day.

Methodically, Castrellón related the time and location of each of the reported incidents of rock throwing, bottle throwing, and threats against police officers along the parade route. It was true that I had seen one or two hot-headed Chicanos throw a bottle or rock at a passing patrol car, but these incidents had been minor, and were quickly contained by the moratorium's own security. To hear Castrellón report it now, one would think that the riot had started from the onset of the march. Not once did Pittluck ask about how Salazar had been killed.

Next, Captain Tom Pinkston, the sheriff's operations commander, was sworn in. His testimony elaborated on Castrellón's, enumerating each police call they received before the call from the Green Mill Liquor Store that had instigated the riot.

It soon became evident that the questions Pittluck was asking of sheriff's witnesses, questions given to him by the Deputy District Attorney Ralph Mayer, had little to do with finding out who killed Rubén Salazar, the ostensive purpose of the inquest. Rather, the questions were setting up evidence to justify the police attack on the crowd—the attack that had initiated the riot.

When this became evident, attorney Oscar Zeta Acosta rose to his feet and interrupted Pittluck. "Ask the captain if he authorized anybody to fire that missile, Mr. Pittluck."

Pittluck asked Acosta to sit down or he'd be removed.

Then Raúl Ruiz got up, "When Danny Castrellón was up there, the main question you should have asked him was how did he know to go directly to the Silver Dollar Bar to identify Salazar?"

The same thought had struck me. It seemed all too convenient that Castrellón, the head flak for the department, someone who knew Salazar personally, should be called in to identify his body. What about the sheriff's deputies who had shot the tear-gas projectiles into the Silver Dollar Bar? Who were they? Had they knowingly shot at Salazar? Had they gone into the bar after shooting in the tear gas? What had transpired between the time Salazar was killed and the time Castrellón had "discovered" the body? And wasn't it just a little too convenient that the sheriff's public relations officer, someone expert at dealing with the news media, should be the person that discovered Salazar's body and therefore be the person who would field questions about Salazar's death?

Pittluck ignored the questions from the audience and proceeded with his questioning. After a brief luncheon recess, the inquest resumed with the testimony of more sheriff's deputies: Richard Wallace and Joseph Van Meter. The afternoon session was a repeat of the tone and approach used in the morning.

This time, the seven-member jury was shown photos and a video-tape that Van Meter, the sheriff's photographer, had shot during the day in question. Carefully edited, the video portrayed several instances of people throwing rocks at the police.

By late afternoon, Chicanos in the audience had had enough. When Pittluck asked the deputy district attorney if he had any more questions, Oscar Zeta Acosta angrily rose to his feet and said that *he* did. Pittluck asked him to sit down.

"You're a member of the bar, Mr. Acosta. You should know better."

"Yes, and you're a member of the bar," Acosta replied, "and a disgrace to your profession. You and the other attorneys seated at that desk are prejudicing the jury by showing these tapes."

"Mr. Acosta, will you please be seated," Pittluck insisted.

"We will not be seated! We're leaving. We're walking out. We'll have nothing to do with the Salazar case. It's bullshit!"

With that, Acosta, Raúl Ruiz, and the entire "Blue Ribbon Commission" stormed out of the hearing room. Local TV reporter Bob Abernathy, covering the inquest, asked Esteban Torres to explain the reason for the walkout. Torres responded, "We are participating in a sham." A short time later, Pittluck adjourned the inquest for the day.

I worked for three hours in telecine with a tape editor to pull clips from the day's proceedings. I strung them together on a roll-in reel and wrote transitional narrative to set up each clip. Next, I put together the reel, wrote an opening and closing narrative for Howard Miller, and delivered a copy to him and to my executive producer, Bill Donnelly. Howard Miller sat down to watch the clips I had put together and took his own notes, which he incorporated into the opening introduction I had written.

Fighting for Editorial Control

That evening, the first of what would be sixteen days of live nightly half-hour inquest coverage was broadcast on KCET. I watched from the control booth with great anticipation, but soon grew alarmed as the program unfolded. I had written an opening and closing narrative that pointed out the fact that the inquest was trying to set up an atmosphere of community violence and was avoiding the issue of who killed Rubén Salazar. But instead of hearing this, I heard Howard Miller's rewritten account of the day's events, a narrative that reinforced Pittluck's approach. There was no mention made of how police photos and video were being used to set up a sense of impending community violence. The question of who killed Rubén Salazar was overlooked entirely. To add insult to injury, when my name rolled by on the credits at the close of the broadcast, I was listed not as producer, as I had expected, but as associate producer. Bill Donnelly, who had done little to produce the show, was getting both executive producer and producer credit. My ideas were being ignored, the community was being vilified, and I wasn't even getting credit for my hard work!

I stomped out of the control booth and went directly into Chuck Allen's office, brushing by his secretary as I announced that I needed to speak to him. Chuck was just turning off his office monitor as I stormed in.

"I'm going to quit," I announced before he could say anything. "This coverage of the inquest is bullshit, and I'm not going to be a part of it!"

My fists were clenched; the veins on my neck were bulging.

Chuck Allen was stunned—he had never seen me so upset. "Sit down. Tell me what the problem is."

I tried to control my rage so I could speak. "We're not presenting my community's point of view, and I'm not going to be used to endorse the whitewash that the police are putting out."

"What do you mean?" he asked.

"The hearing officer, Norman Pittluck, is trying to blame the community for what was a police riot instead of getting at who killed Rubén Salazar."

I explained to him that I was taking the notes and compiling the material, but once Donnelly and Miller got through with my copy, the community's point of view was lost.

"Look at what our audience is seeing," I argued. "The report is coming out of Howard Miller's mouth. Howard Miller is a USC law professor, a member of the establishment. What the viewing public is getting is this authoritative point of view that supports the police version of what happened. Howard wasn't there, and neither was Pitt-

luck. I was! On top of all of this, I'm doing all the legwork, and Bill
Donnelly's getting the credit!"

"So," he said to me. "What do you propose I do?"

"Well, if the Chicano community is concerned enough to be in
that courtroom every day, then I feel we should have two points of
view presented on every broadcast. We should have the legal point of
view, and I think Miller does a fine job of that, but we should also
have a community point of view of the day's events. We should have
someone from the Chicano community giving our side of the story."

"What if we make you a co-host for the inquest?" he said abruptly.

I was taken aback by the suggestion. I'd never really thought
about being the on-camera host for the inquest and was, quite frankly,
intimidated by the idea. Miller was much more articulate than I was
and had much more on-camera experience. But if that's what it would
take to make sure our side of the story was told, then I would do it.

"That's fine with me," I told him flatly. Just then, Bill Donnelly
came into the office; my shouting had carried down the hallway.
Chuck told him that there would be some changes: I would henceforth
co-host the show and receive producer credit instead of being listed as
associate producer. Donnelly's visceral response surprised me.

"I am the executive producer of this show, and I will decide what
credit he gets and who is going to be on-camera."

Chuck pretended he didn't hear. "As I was saying, Mr. Treviño
here will get producer credit and will be co-hosting the inquest along
with Mr. Miller."

Bill Donnelly bristled. "Look, Chuck, you're going to have to
decide who's producing this show. It's either me or Treviño. Either I
call the shots or I quit."

I couldn't believe what I was hearing. It was one thing for me to
threaten to quit—I had just been on board for a few weeks. But Bill
Donnelly had been running the station's news department for some
time. To hear him threaten to quit struck me as foolhardy. I was even
more dumbfounded by Chuck's response.

"You make Treviño co-host or you can find yourself another job.
There's the door. You decide." A stony silence enveloped the room as
Donnelly considered Chuck's ultimatum. It was a showdown between

a department head and the station's general manager.

After a moment, Donnelly relented. "All right. He'll co-host the show." Donnelly got up and left the room.

Chuck turned to me. "I look forward to seeing tomorrow night's program."

And so, beginning with the second day of the inquest, I produced and co-hosted with Howard Miller the daily coverage of the Salazar inquest. I soon developed a daily routine. I would arrive at the courthouse before the inquest started and would touch base with community members waiting to be let into the limited seating. I took my notes and, usually by three or four in the afternoon when the inquest closed for the day, I would race back to the station in time to do the edits of the videotape and to write the copy.

By seven in the evening, Howard and I were ready for broadcast. As KCET's "court reporter," I would narrate the unfolding of the day's events, using video clips to highlight what had happened. After this, Howard would come on-camera and give an analysis of the legal implications of the day's events. At the end of the broadcast, we would either discuss what we might expect the next day, or I would interview a community spokesperson for his or her insight into the inquest. For the next sixteen nights, we produced a daily analysis and summary of the proceedings. Coverage on the other stations involved complete reports of the daily inquest proceedings for the first few days, but by the end of the inquest, it had dwindled to a brief summary on the evening news.

During the course of the inquest, I grew to respect Howard Miller. He was knowledgeable about the inquest process, would explain the legal intricacies of which I was very naive, and suggested ways in which we could improve our coverage. To my surprise, we became a solid team.

Framing the Community

From the onset, it became clear that the questions fed to Pittluck by the assistant district attorney were intent on making the case for a justifiable police response provoked in an atmosphere of community violence. The first three days were filled with examination of photos and accounts of violence against deputies by members of the Chicano community.

Several witnesses, including optometrist Albert Forbes, recreation leader Julián Casas, and Sheriff Deputy Raymond Baytos, brought in Communist propaganda they had collected on the march. These pamphlets were filled with inflammatory statements, such as, "People of the World Unite Against U.S. Aggressors" and "How to Make a Revolution in the United States." They were all entered as evidence; the implication was that they had set the stage for the violence that followed.

On the fourth day, Raúl Ruiz was called to the witness stand. By coincidence, he and Joe Razo had been outside the Silver Dollar Bar when sheriff's deputies arrived and surrounded the building. In a series of stunning photographs, they had captured the moments just prior to Salazar's death. These included photos of several deputy sheriffs gathering in front of the bar, after which two of them fired tear gas inside.

But before any of the photos pertinent to the Silver Dollar Bar incident were exhibited, Pittluck showed a series of crowd shots that Raúl had photographed earlier in the day. Once again, the questions sought to highlight moments of Chicano rock throwing and violence, painting a picture of a community on the verge of rioting.

In one photo, Pittluck singled out a sign that read "Viva Che." He questioned Ruiz about the identity of Che Guevara.

"Isn't he Mr. Castro's man?" Pittluck asked.

Raúl was dumbfounded by the bias of the question. "Ernesto 'Che' Guevara fought against oppression in Latin America," Ruiz rejoined. "And he died fighting oppression. He died fighting a very similar type of oppression, which we people in the barrios are suffering daily on the part of the police—on the part of educators, on the part of most of the establishment in this society!"

Pittluck then asked if Ruiz could deliver the rest of the photos he had taken on the 29th to the court, presumably so that lawbreakers in the photos could be identified. Ruiz replied he could not.

"Is that because you can't get your hands on them?" Pittluck asked.

"Most of them are negatives. We believed the sheriffs were going to raid us. Since the day before *La Raza* was published, sheriffs were all over our office. We could not take that chance of having the sheriffs come in and steal our property, so it was removed from the area."

The Ruiz testimony ended dramatically. Ruiz objected to questions that Pittluck asked him about people attacking sheriff officers. "You don't ask me questions like, 'Did you see sheriffs attacking people?'"

At this point, Oscar Acosta chimed in from the audience: "He's right! You didn't ask the sheriffs these questions."

By now Pittluck had had enough of Acosta's interventions. He motioned to one of the bailiffs in the back of the door. "Will you remove Mr. Acosta."

Three deputies approached Acosta.

Someone shouted, "Hey, how many guys does it take to remove a lawyer, man?" One of the bailiffs grabbed Acosta by the arm.

"Take your hands off me!" Acosta resisted. "I can walk by myself!"

Now there were two bailiffs on Acosta, and a struggle broke out. Some community activists restrained others coming to Acosta's defense as Acosta sat back in his chair. Then the bailiffs started to hit Acosta.

Ruiz turned to Pittluck. "Look, these deputies are beating up on a man who is sitting down. This is exactly what we're protesting about!"

Finally, the three deputies forcibly dragged Acosta up the aisle and out of the courtroom. He shouted and struggled all the way.

On day seven of the inquest, George Muñoz, Hector Franco, Guillermo Restrepo, and other people that had been in the bar with Salazar when he was killed, were called to the stand. For the first time, we began to get a glimpse of what had transpired inside. On days eight and nine, more eyewitnesses inside the bar testified: Gustavo García, Tony Angel, Jimmy James Flores, Nicolás Klimenko, and Mrs. Junsil Rhee.

Two Versions

By the tenth day of the inquest, it was clear that two different, conflictive versions were emerging of the grisly series of events surrounding Salazar's death. According to one version, Salazar's death was the outcome of a tragic accident. He was a man killed inadvertently when sheriff's deputies were trying to carry out their duties; he was at the wrong place at the wrong time.

Manuel López, a local citizen who was identified throughout the inquest as "the man in the red vest," was key to this version. López testified that he saw three armed men enter the Silver Dollar Bar as he helped sheriffs direct street traffic at the corner of La Verne and Whittier Boulevard. López reported this to Deputy Sheriff George Grasser, who had been called into the area to safeguard firemen working on a blaze nearby. Deputy Grasser called for reinforcements on his patrol car radio.

Grasser and his partner, Deputy James Dawes, then went to the front of the Silver Dollar Bar, where they were joined by deputies Thomas Wilson, James Lambert, Louis Brown and Charles Brown. A short time later, another patrol car rolled onto the scene with four deputies inside. They parked across the street and helped to cover their colleagues. According to Manuel López and all the sheriff's deputies present, Deputy Louis Brown called out several times for anyone in the Silver Dollar to come out with his hands up.

When no one emerged, Deputy Thomas Wilson shot two rounds of tear gas through the front door of the bar from a standing position on the sidewalk in front of the entrance. Shortly thereafter, Sgt. Laughlin, one of the four deputies in the car parked across the street, fired two more rounds into the bar from behind his patrol car.

After the tear gas was fired, all the deputies responded to an urgent call for police backup at McDonnell and Whittier. They returned forty-five minutes later and continued to safeguard firefighters near Laverne and Whittier.

At 6:30, Julián García entered the back door of the Silver Dollar, thinking the bar was open for business. Instead, he found a room full of smoke and a body lying on the floor. He reported the body to sheriff's deputies, and only then did they call Deputy Castrellón to identify the body as that of Rubén Salazar.

Of more than thirty civilian witnesses who testified during the inquest, only Manuel López and James García, a clerk at the record shop across the street, subscribed to this version of events. García seemed less sure of seeing the men with guns than did López.

The other version of what happened was more sinister in its implications. This scenario was substantiated by the photos taken by Raúl Ruiz and Joe Razo. All of the twelve eyewitnesses who were actually in the Silver Dollar (and more than a dozen eyewitnesses outside the bar) testified that no men with guns had ever entered the bar. Furthermore, they testified that four men and two women were standing in front of the bar when two deputies came down the sidewalk and forced them into the bar at gunpoint.

Gustavo García, a KMEX employee who was one of three men who entered the bar with Salazar, recalled standing at the doorway when one of the deputies told him, "Get into the bar or you're going to get killed." Once the people were inside the bar, one of the deputies, Thomas Wilson, fired two tear-gas missiles inside. None of the other twenty-eight civilian witnesses heard any warnings before the tear gas was fired.

Witnesses from across the street recalled that the order to "come out with your hands up" was given only after all the tear gas had been shot. Once the tear gas was loosed, the people within immediately fled out the back door.

As I sat in the audience and heard the same series of events recounted by sheriff's deputies and then by civilian eyewitnesses, it brought to mind Akira Kurasawa's motion picture *Rashomon*, in which the same event is told from the point of view of several people, each telling a different version. But unlike this Japanese masterpiece of ambiguity, the inquest had concrete photographic evidence clearly substantiating at least one version of the events.

Key to understanding the sequence of events was one of Raúl Ruiz's photos. It clearly showed a deputy pointing a shotgun at four men by the entrance to the Silver Dollar Bar. One of the men had his hands in the air. Two women and another deputy were standing on the sidewalk nearby; one of the women appeared to be in motion.

Witnesses Jimmy Flores, Tony García, Nicolás Klimenko, Gustavo García, and Junsil Rhee all identified themselves as the bystanders in the photograph and reiterated the claim that they had been forced into the bar at gunpoint, as the photo suggested. But when deputies Thomas Wilson and Deputy George Grasser were shown this photo, they boldly denied that these events had ever taken place.

Throughout the first ten days, the assistant district attorney had Pittluck ask every witness pointedly about the "man in the red vest." Had they seen him talking to the deputies? All the civilian witnesses recalled the man directing traffic at the corner of Laverne and Whittier Boulevard, but none could say if he had talked to deputies or not.

Why was the man in the red vest so crucial to the assistant district attorney, I wondered? Then it hit me. The entire siege of the Silver Dollar Bar was justifiable from a police point of view only if the report of an armed man or men inside the bar was verifiable. In the end, the pretext for all the actions undertaken by the sheriff's deputies rested on the testimony of one man.

Perhaps the most chilling testimony was that of newsman Guillermo Restrepo, Rubén Salazar's close friend and one of three KMEX employees who had walked along Whittier Boulevard with Salazar for more than a dozen blocks before entering the bar. Prior to entering, Restrepo recalled Salazar looking behind and around as they walked along the boulevard—he was acting as if he thought he was being followed.

"Mr. Salazar was looking back like this almost every minute." Restrepo reenacted Salazar's motions. "When we were getting very close to the bar, I found that [there] was something funny going on, and I asked him, 'What's the matter?' And he says to me, 'I think I'm stupid.' About a block before we get to the Silver Dollar . . . , he says to me, 'Guillermo, I'm getting very scared.'"

They had decided at that point to return to the KMEX studios in Hollywood, but Salazar needed to use the bathroom and decided they'd stop in the Silver Dollar before going back to their station wagon.

Restrepo confirmed what others had already testified to: No one had heard any warning or call to come out. It was quiet until the tear gas was shot into the bar, forcing everyone to run out the back entrance.

Gustavo García was one of the last to exit. He saw Salazar hit by the flite-rite, spin around on the bar stool, and fall to the ground. Once outside the bar, García told Guillermo Restrepo what he had seen, and Restrepo then approached a deputy standing guard in the back alley. He told the deputy of his injured friend inside the bar, but was denied entry back inside. Over the next few minutes, Restrepo showed his press credentials to two other deputies and repeated his plea to enter the bar and get his injured friend out. In each instance, he was told to move away, and was denied entry. Finally, Restrepo called KMEX and was told to return to the studio.

Restrepo's testimony brought into full light rumors that had been circulating in the community for weeks that Salazar's death had not been accidental, but rather an assassination. Information from Daniel Villanueva and from Salazar's wife revealed that at the time of his death, Salazar had been working on an exposé of the Los Angeles Police Department.

In July, Salazar had reported the accidental killing of two Mexican immigrant brothers, Guillermo and Beltrán Sánchez, during a police raid at a downtown flophouse. Five Los Angeles police officers, along with two detectives from the northern California city of San Leandro, had targeted the wrong apartment in the cheap hotel, while looking for a murder suspect. The police had broken down the door and opened fired on several undocumented Mexican workers who shared the apartment. Two innocent men had been killed.

This incident had been highly visible in both Spanish and English television, and in the print media. KMEX had carried extensive reports of the story. As a result, Salazar began to investigate police policies toward Mexicans and other minorities. He had obtained confidential documents on the police from attorney Manuel Ruiz, then a member of the U.S. Civil Rights Commission.

The extent of his investigations soon brought Salazar to the attention of the Los Angeles Police Department and Los Angeles County

Sheriff's Office. At one point, Salazar told a friend that he had been threatened by the sheriff's office. Police Chief Ed Davis had placed a call to Bill Thomas, Salazar's editor at the *Los Angeles Times*, asking that Salazar be fired.

Although much of this was common knowledge in the community, this was the first time it had been mentioned at the inquest. Community activists were now asking the obvious question: Had Salazar's death been a planned assassination?

Testimony by the sheriff's deputies on the last four days of the inquest added credence to the idea that some sort of coverup was in progress.

Deputy Grasser claimed to have called for reinforcements because there were men with guns in the Silver Dollar Bar. He had used Frequency 1 of his car's radio. Unlike calls from the central sheriff's dispatch made on Frequency 2, which were logged, calls on Frequency 1 were not logged. There was no way to substantiate the testimonies of the deputies and of Manuel López that the call about an armed man inside the Silver Dollar had ever been made. It was also impossible to verify that the call had not been made.

Deputies Wilson and Grasser claimed they could not see into the bar because it was dark and because two curtains obstructed the doorway. If this was true, then it was likely that the tear-gas missile hitting and killing Salazar had been an accident. Witnesses gathered in front of the record shop across the street, however, claimed they could see reflections off chrome in the bar shining through the front entrance. Witnesses inside the bar claimed that they could clearly see Deputy Grasser moving the curtains open as Deputy Wilson prepared to shoot tear gas into the bar from the sidewalk outside.

The sheriff's crime lab compared the remnants of the four missiles found inside the Silver Dollar Bar. Two were blue in color and came from Sgt. Laughlin's tear-gas gun. Two were red in color: a duster canister and a "flite-rite," the latter of which is a bullet-like missile capable of penetrating one-inch pine wood. Although the flite-rite was only supposed to be used in barricade situations, it had been shot point blank into the bar.

The crime lab determined that the red flite-rite missile was the one that had killed Salazar, and that Thomas Wilson had been the deputy who had fired it. Why had Wilson used a deadly flite-rite missile? Could Thomas Wilson have identified Salazar sitting at the bar and purposefully fired upon him with a lethal projectile?

Once the tear gas had been shot into the bar, Deputy Wilson fired another round into the crowd assembled across the street at LaVerne and Whittier, and dispersed it. According to him, the crowd was pelting the deputies with rocks. Civilian eyewitnesses, however, denied that the crowd was throwing anything. Other deputies then told bystanders at the record shop across the street to go inside the store and stay there. This cleared the area of Whittier Boulevard in front of the Silver Dollar of potential witnesses. At this point, all the sheriff's deputies left to answer an urgent request for officer assistance at McDonnell and Whittier. According to the deputies, when they arrived at the intersection, the situation was reported to be under control, and they then returned to LaVerne and Whittier. Throughout it all, no deputies had entered the Silver Dollar Bar.

Witness to Murder?

The testimonies of the final civilian witnesses were riveting. What they saw made the possibility of a police coverup a viable version of the truth.

Larry James Chávez, an eyewitness standing across the street, testified that when Deputy Wilson dispersed the people in his midst, he hid between two cars to see what would happen. Contrary to what had been said by all the deputies, he testified that one of the deputies did, indeed, enter the Silver Dollar, and he came out ten seconds later with his eyes burning. He then pointed back to the bar, indicating to two deputies a location on the floor to the left of the entrance. The three deputies then entered the bar, stayed for a while, and then came out, again overcome by tear gas. An argument ensued between the first deputy and the other two. The duo kept shaking their heads. Finally, one of the duo said "okay," and slammed the front door to the bar shut. Then they all moved away from the bar.

Another witness, Margarita Martínez, testified that she saw an ambulance pull up in front of the Silver Dollar at about twenty minutes till six. One of the three deputies who had entered the bar spoke briefly with the ambulance driver and sent the ambulance away.

Why had all the officers left the scene so suddenly? The tear gas was shot into the bar about 5 p.m. The coroner had cited Salazar's death at 6:30 p.m. Was it to allow time for Salazar to die? If he was already dead when the three deputies went into the bar, did they go somewhere to get their stories straight? Conveniently, the urgent call for assistance at McDonnell and Whittier was also heard on Frequency 1—because of this, there was no record of it other than the word of the deputies.

And what of the ambulance that Margarita Martínez saw? Could Restrepo or someone else have phoned for an ambulance only to have it turned away by one of the deputies? None of these questions was ever pursued by Pittluck or others at the inquest.

Perhaps the most outrageous moment came when Sheriff Thomas Wilson was shown photograph 53 taken by Raúl Ruiz. In the photograph, Wilson can clearly be seen leveling a tear-gas gun toward the entrance to the Silver Dollar Bar. The photo was taken just a few seconds before Wilson fired the deadly projectile that killed Salazar.

Wilson examined the photograph at length before replying to hearing officer Pittluck's question of whether that was he in the photograph. Television cameras in the courtroom showed that the man in the photo was unmistakably Wilson.

"Will you tell us if you ever saw the events depicted in photograph 53?" Pittluck pressed.

The reply, when it finally came, was brazen: "No, I did not!"

When Pittluck asked what Deputy Wilson had been aiming at before he fired into the bar, the courtroom erupted in turmoil. Attorney Oscar Acosta, back for more of the inquest, once more rose to his feet and shouted, "Rubén Salazar! That's who he was aiming at. There's an obscenity in this room that we're tired of, Mr. Pittluck. This room is polluted with perjury and you know it!"

Pittluck advised Acosta to leave the room in an orderly fashion. As Acosta made his way to the door, he shouted once more to Wilson on the witness stand, "So long, Chicano killer!"

On the sixteenth day of the hearing, officer Norman Pittluck instructed the jury that they were to determine the cause of Salazar's death.

Natural causes and suicide were absurd alternatives. Death by accident, when it involves a human agency, meant "unintended or unexpected death as a result of human conduct." Any other situation would automatically be "death at the hands of another." The jury deliberated from 9:30 in the morning until 4:00 p.m. They returned with a split decision.

Four jurors concluded that Rubén Salazar had been killed "at the hands of another," citing the evidence against Thomas Wilson. Three of the jurors, however, concluded that Salazar had been killed "accidentally."

The split decision was confusing. Did a majority vote mean Thomas Wilson had intentionally killed Salazar? Could the community expect that the district attorney would press murder charges against Wilson and perhaps other deputies? The last eyewitness testimonies suggested a sheriff's coverup. Clearly, more questions needed to be asked of civilian and deputy witnesses alike. A bonafide trial or federal grand jury would do just that.

To the shock of community activists and the Los Angeles public alike, District Attorney Evelle Younger announced on television that afternoon that the jury verdicts were legally "meaningless." He said they would review the inquest transcripts carefully but "if the killing constitutes a crime, it would be a crime of involuntary manslaughter." He concluded by saying, "My staff has assured me that there is absolutely no evidence that this . . . was an intentional killing."

The community was outraged. After witnessing the obvious collusion between the district attorney's office and law enforcement, and after hearing the way Pittluck had framed his inquest questions, Evelle Younger's comments smacked of more coverup. Trial or no trial, Wilson was going to get off free!

On the street outside the courthouse, there was talk of another riot. I moved from one group of activists to another, conferring with community leaders, who were eager to find ways of cooling hot tempers. I spoke with Vahac Mardirosian and Esteban Torres, head of the Council of Mexican-American Unity, both of whom agreed to come to KCET that night and participate in a round-table discussion that I had planned as a conclusion to KCET's coverage of the inquest. We hoped this would help put a lid on any rash behavior.

In the days that followed, Evelle Younger opted not to press any charges against anyone involved in the death of Rubén Salazar, citing insufficient evidence to warrant any further legal action. Nor would a grand jury be convened. Community leaders remained outspoken in their view that a travesty of justice had been committed and that Salazar had been assassinated. But no further outbreaks of violence occurred. When all was said and done, it seemed that the Salazar inquest—the costliest in county history and the first to be televised in Los Angeles—had accomplished its unspoken purpose: to vent community anger and quell any further violence. Now that it was over, things in Los Angeles could get back to normal.

Another Tragedy

After the round-table discussion that concluded our coverage of the inquest, I made my way back to the small cubbyhole of an office in the basement of the KCET building. Gayla was waiting for me. Her expression told me something was wrong.

The day prior to the end of the inquest, Eddie, my stepfather, had died of a heart attack while crossing the border from Tijuana to San Diego. I had been so wrapped up in producing daily coverage of the Salazar inquest, that I was sleeping only a few hours each night and was practically living at the station. I rarely saw Gayla. The day that Ed died, my mother informed her of the news. Because of my intense involvement in the inquest and the devastating effect the news would have on me, she decided not to tell me about his death until after the last broadcast.

I was floored by Eddie's death. When was the last time I had seen him? A week, two weeks ago? Three weeks ago? I felt overwhelmed with grief and guilt. The inquest had become so all-consuming that for the past month I had entirely lost touch with my family. And now my stepfather was dead. I sat in my office and cried for a long while, then I went upstairs to Chuck Allen's office and told him that Ed had died and that I had to take time off. He said I should take all the time I needed.

I am grateful that Gayla had withheld the news. I don't think I could have gone on camera that day, had I known about my stepfather's death.

For the next several days, I made funeral arrangements. Compounding my sadness at his death was the knowledge of his state of mind when he died. For several months prior to his passing, my mother and father's marriage had been on the rocks. My mother's, sister's and my own increasing involvement in the Chicano Movement troubled him deeply. He had been out of work for several months with an injury, which served to compound the pain of the estrangement that now existed between him and his family.

In August, when he heard about the impending Chicano Moratorium march, he became very upset and was adamant that no one in his family should participate. He believed in the war and thought the march was un-American.

"Why do you have to call yourselves Chicanos?" he questioned me one afternoon. "Why can't we all just be Americans? That's what we are—we're all Americans."

"We may all be citizens of the same country," I countered, "but some of us are treated more fairly than others. All we want is our due as American citizens, something Chicanos have never had."

Despite my efforts to get him to understand that the Chicano Movement was one of self-affirmation, Eddie remained convinced that the movement was racist and un-American.

But the momentum of the movement was, by now, stronger than anything Eddie could control. My mother spent the day of the march working in the kitchen at St. Bartholomew's Church, preparing food for out-of-town Chicanos who had come to attend the march. My sister Olinda and I ignored his wishes, and we both attended the march. He took our activities as a personal affront.

On the Friday before he died, my stepfather and my mother got into a fight, and she moved out of the house, taking my youngest sister with her. The next day, he drove to San Diego. He was in deep despair. His world was coming apart at the seams. He could neither understand the social changes happening in the world around him, nor could he fathom why his family was participating in protest marches and riots. What about all the years he had sacrificed to keep his family housed, fed, and educated? Why had they turned on him now? He probably longed for that peaceful time of his youth when he had lived in a log cabin in the green hills of West Virginia.

He booked passage on a ship out of San Diego to New Zealand. At age thirty-nine, he had decided to leave the United States and seek a new life elsewhere. The next day, a Sunday, he had crossed the border into Tijuana, Mexico. In my childhood, we had often gone on day trips to Tijuana. He must have thought about these better times with his family as he perused the familiar shops along Avenida Revolución. When he crossed the border back to San Diego late that afternoon, it was to board the ship that would take him to a new life. His heart attack occurred immediately after crossing the border between the United States and Mexico.

The day after the inquest, Gayla and I drove to San Diego to reclaim his body. Two days later, we had an open casket wake, and the next day a simple service. My fifteen-year-old sister, Rosalba, was in denial through it all. After we returned home from the funeral, she pulled me aside and asked, "Jesse, when is Daddy going to be coming home?"

Requiem-29

A few days later, I returned to work. I found that Moctesuma Esparza and David García had been trying to get in touch with me for several days. It seems that many of the Chicano filmmakers who had shot footage on August 29th had pooled their resources. They had agreed that something should come from this footage that would represent the community's point of view. It was decided that two films would be made. One was to be undertaken by David García and Moctesuma Esparza, the other by Francisco Martínez, one of my fellow students at the now-defunct New Communicators.

Moctesuma Esparza told me that, with the help of community leader Esteban Torres, he had already managed to raise several thousand dollars toward producing the film that David García would edit. They had extensive footage of the march and the police attacks, but had nothing from the inquest.

"Can you help us get video clips from KCET's coverage of the inquest for the film?" he asked.

I readily agreed. I knew, however, that we had to act quickly, as many of the tapes that held important information were destined to be erased. The station had invested heavily in tape stock to cover the inquest, but now that it was over, station producers were clamoring for stock. It was just a matter of time before the inquest programs would be degaussed for new programs.

I spent the next weekend with Moctesuma Esparza and David García, poring over my notes and selecting video clips that we transferred onto a dub reel. I had the station pay for the technicians and the tape transfers. When the reel was finally complete, we had it transferred to film format, a kinescope, and it was that format that was later incorporated into the film *Requiem-29,* the first community account of the events of August 29, 1970.

The next week, Chuck Allen called me into his office with another proposition. He wanted me to produce an hour-long summary of the Salazar inquest for national broadcast. In those days "going national" was quite a big thing, and I was excited about the opportunity.

Seeking to distance myself from my guilt over my stepfather's death, I became immersed in producing a one-hour summary of the Salazar inquest, which I entitled *Chicano Moratorium: the Aftermath.*

I found as much information as I could on Salazar and the August 29th riot. This was my first show for national broadcast, so I wanted to take great care in my script so that a mainstream audience, with no knowledge of Chicanos, could easily follow it.

During my research, I found an article Salazar had written in the *Los Angeles Times* on February 6, 1970. In it he addressed the questions "Who is the Chicano? And what is it the Chicanos want?" Salazar explained that "A Chicano is a Mexican American with a non-Anglo image of himself. He resents being told Columbus 'discovered'

America, when the Chicano's ancestors, the Mayans and the Aztecs, founded highly sophisticated civilizations' centuries before Spain financed the Italian explorer's trip to the 'New World.'

"Chicanos resent also Anglo pronouncements that Chicanos are 'culturally deprived,' or that the fact that they speak Spanish is a 'problem.'"

I incorporated Salazar's words into my explanation of the Chicano demonstrators, and as a prelude to the events that led to his own death. I began to see the *Moratorium Aftermath* show as an opportunity to tell all of America about who we were as Chicanos and about the Chicano Movement itself.

Chicano Moratorium: The Aftermath was broadcast nationally as a one-hour PBS special on the evening of October 14, 1970. I began with a concise, hard-hitting report on the riot. In addition to showing riot footage that Jerry Hughes and others had shot on that day, I walked the audience through the sixteen days of the Salazar inquest using video clips from our pool feed. I also recruited Howard Miller to play the same role he had assumed in our daily coverage, that of legal interpreter.

KCET had commissioned Opinion Research of California to take an audience survey on the evening of the inquest verdict. The survey determined that 44.9 percent of the Mexican-American community did not believe a Mexican American could get equal treatment under the law. I included this information in the program's summary and questioned the manner in which the inquest had been designed. I reviewed the fact that, though Thomas Wilson had been the deputy sheriff identified as the man that killed Salazar in the Raúl Ruiz photographs, neither he nor his accomplices had ever been brought to justice.

The *Boston Globe* said of the program: "A dispassionate, dry coroner's inquest that hummed with overtones of bitterness and resentment was turned into a fascinating hour." The *Christian Science Monitor* said, "The program's most creative effect lay in instilling enough knowledge in the viewer's consciousness, and conscience, to enable him to evaluate the facts for himself. The evident Chicano bias seemed more an attempt to give fair representation to an underdog position than a departure from objectivity." A few months later, the program won the San Francisco Broadcast Industry Award for best News Program.

The Salazar inquest confirmed for me the reality of American justice for Chicanos. I had witnessed police brutality personally on two previous occasions, had seen its results when I covered the Jesse Domínguez story for *Ahora!*, and now had witnessed it up close again. But unlike the other instances, which involved individual officers circumventing justice or the law by abusing Chicanos, the Salazar inquest represented a more insidious cancer in the American justice system itself. Here, the entire judicial system had been manipulated to quell community outrage, to give the community a sense of the trappings of justice, while in fact, they defended the possible perpetrators of criminal activity.

Salazar's death may well have been a purposeful assassination committed by rogue elements of the sheriff's and/or police department's. The order to kill him may even have come from the top levels of law enforcement, but even if it had not, I am convinced that the coverup involved law enforcement at the highest levels.

We will never know the truth because of the way in which the inquest was conducted. Abuses were not just at the local precinct, I realized, but institutionalized throughout the system. With countless instances of abuse like this, what was the point in respecting American law?

This question had been driven home to me only a few weeks prior to the moratorium. On August 7, 1970, Jonathan Jackson, the seventeen-year-old brother of outspoken Soledad inmate George Jackson, had walked, armed, into a courthouse in San Raphael, California, to free James McClain, an African American inmate standing trial for the stabbing of a San Quentin prison guard.

After holding everyone in the courtroom hostage for ten minutes, Jackson, McClain and two other African American inmates, made an attempt to escape in a van parked nearby, but were cut down by police fire. Jonathan Jackson, two of the inmates he sought to free and a judge were killed.

At the time, I had thought it a desperate and insane act. What could have driven this young man to such ends? Now, seeing the justice system at work in the Salazar case two months later, I had new insight into what Jonathan Jackson must have been thinking as he attempted to free his friends from the American justice system. The fate of James McClain must have appeared unalterable through legal means. Was it any wonder that an armed escape attempt surfaced as a viable option?

Jackson's death would soon bring me to my next major film project, a documentary on the plight of African-American and Chicano inmates at California's infamous Soledad prison.

Chapter Ten

Soledad

Black men born in the United States and fortunate enough to live past the age of eighteen are conditioned to accept the inevitability of prison. For most of us, it simply looms as the next phase in a sequence of humiliations.

—George Jackson

As I continued my work at KCET in November of 1970, I was haunted by a recurring dream. I would be walking in a park at night. There, I would find my stepfather sleeping on a park bench, his body covered with damp newspapers. As I approached him, he would rise and meet me halfway, newspapers still clinging to his body. My emotion was nothing short of euphoria. He was not dead after all! His death was all a big mistake, a delusion.

Suddenly I was given back the hours and days I felt I had squandered on the movement, hours I should have spent in his company. As my stepfather came closer, I was resolved to devote more time to him. I could now say the words I should have said before. I could teach him the guitar riffs he wanted to learn, write out the chords and words to the original songs that he invented without a trace of musical education—be the son I should have been to him.

But then the wet newspaper pages fell away. From behind his back, he raised an object high above his head and gave me an eerie, ghastly smile. It was the sharp axe of a medieval headsman.

I tried to convince myself that I was not responsible for my step-father's premature death, that my commitment to the movement had not driven him away from me and the rest of the family. But the incessant nightmare would not allow me to believe any of it.

Unable to rid myself of guilt, I threw myself even more vehemently into my work. I needed to affirm my worth to myself in the terms that had come to dominate my life: *el movimiento*.

At KCET, I was moved from my basement office to a larger work space, which I shared with Sue Booker. On the wall behind my desk was a blowup of the photo that Raúl Ruiz had taken depicting Deputy Sheriff Thomas Wilson about to shoot the tear-gas projectile into the door of the Silver Dollar Bar. Behind Sue's desk, on the opposite side of the office, was a large poster of Malcolm X, his finger pointed out like a fiery mandate.

Cleophus Adair

While I was producing the summary of the Salazar inquest, Sue had been deeply involved in chronicling the life of Cleophus Adair—an ex-addict who was battling against the drug addiction that was so prevalent among young African Americans in Watts. He openly challenged the brothers in Watts who dealt drugs, an enterprise that, although brave, was incredibly dangerous.

Sue decided to support Cleophus Adair's cause by featuring his efforts in a Human Affairs special. She had taped several preliminary audio interviews with Adair and was planning a filmed profile. But one night, while Sue was attending a community meeting where he was present, Adair was shotgunned to death as he emerged from the community hall. Following his death, Sue produced a one-hour documentary on Adair's life and work. The program was later nominated for an Emmy.

With both our projects at an end, we were each searching for our next assignment.

Shortly after my return, Sue looked across the office at me. "Jesús, do you have a minute?"

I recognized the tone in her voice. She wanted to talk. This was going to be a thorough debate on a difficult topic. It had become a kind of game with us. We would often end up going on at length and playing devil's advocate in an effort to get to the bottom of an idea, a problem, a theory one or the other was grappling with.

"Jesús," she continued, "why do you suppose some of the most insightful, militant, and revolutionary black men in America have come from prison? Malcolm X, Huey Newton, Bobby Seale?"

"I don't know," I replied. "Prison hardens men, gives them time to think, makes them angry at the oppressor."

She shook her head. "Oh, I think it's more than that. Would you like to help me find out?"

"What, exactly, do you have in mind?" I asked cautiously. I wasn't certain where she was going with this.

"What if we go to Soledad and find out." Suddenly she had my attention.

"You mean, the Soledad Brothers thing?"

She nodded and smiled. "Yes."

I knew immediately what she was talking about. George Jackson, an inmate at California's infamous Soledad Prison, had recently published an autobiography, *Soledad Brother*, in which he claimed that racist prison guards were assisting neo-Nazi inmates in the killing of African-American prisoners.

Along with fellow inmates Fleeta Drumgo and John Cluchette, George Jackson had recently been in the headlines. The three inmates had been charged with throwing a white prison guard to his death over a cell block tier. Since there were no eyewitnesses to the event, the charges were circumstantial, leading many African-American activists to believe that the "Soledad Three" had been framed by prison authorities for their outspoken views on prison conditions. Since the death of the prison guard, the three had been transferred to San Quentin and were awaiting trial.

Three months earlier, George Jackson's younger brother, Jon, had been killed while attempting to free several African-American inmates on a separate trial at the courthouse in San Raphael, California. Ownership of the gun that Jonathan Jackson had used in the attempted jail break had been traced to Angela Davis, a militant University of California instructor and confidante of George Jackson. Angela Davis was now in hiding.

The alleged perpetrators of the crimes against African-American inmates were still at Soledad. Presumably, the same conditions existed. After the travesty of justice I had witnessed with the Salazar inquest, I was ready to expose the American criminal justice system in any way I could.

"You mean investigate the charges of guards allowing the killing of prison inmates?"

"Exactly," she replied.

The idea was growing on me. "Sure, we could focus on the condition of black and Chicano inmates."

"Yes." She was beaming.

"If we can show that the allegations about Soledad are true, that it's still going on, it would vindicate their case."

"But, how do we get in? And once in, will they let us out?" I asked only half-jokingly.

"We can get in," she said thoughtfully. "We're journalists."

That afternoon we called Soledad Prison and were eventually connected to Deputy Warden Jerry Enomoto, who was currently in charge of the prison. We said we were interested in discussing the possibility of filming a documentary inside Soledad. Naturally, the deputy warden was skeptical. But when we explained that we were from KCET, he relented and said we could come up, but only if we first sent him a letter explaining the project.

A week later, Sue and I drove to Soledad in her VW bug. It was a beautiful fall morning when we set out. Sue had never been to Big Sur, so I insisted that we take the coast route along Highway 1, which would take us through Morro Bay, San Simeon, and up through the haunting beauty of Big Sur and Carmel before we headed back down Highway 101 through the Salinas Valley to the city of Soledad. We talked nonstop, shifting freely between political topics to events in our personal lives.

We arrived at the prison and pulled into a parking lot adjacent to a watch tower. Framing a cluster of beige buildings was a tall barbed-wire fence. A guard pointed to the main entrance, and we ventured inside.

We were led past a series of locked doors with plate-glass windows, and were eventually taken to the office of the deputy warden. Jerry Enomoto was a short Japanese American with a ready smile and the self-assured demeanor of a man used to welding power. He was dressed in a brown suit with a yellow shirt and brown tie—the word "dapper" came to mind.

Within moments of meeting him, I could tell he was as astute as they came. He listened quietly as we told him our story of wanting to produce a documentary about Soledad. It would be a PBS first.

"We're interested in showing what life is like here at Soledad," Sue said. "We want to find out the truth."

"For example," I joined in, "most people don't even know what the racial make-up is here at the prison."

Enomoto expounded on details of the prison system. "Here at Soledad, we have about 20 to 25 percent black inmates, 20 to 25 percent Chicano inmates, and I guess 1 or 2 percent would be Asian. The rest are white."

He looked off into the distance, philosophically.

"In America, we have a lot of problems. Why? Because we have limited job opportunities in the ghettos and the barrios. It has been determined by official agencies that racist policies and a lack of opportunities make it more likely that a man will pick up a gun and do harm if he is in the ghetto or the barrio. Doubtless, this has something to do with the disproportionate number of minorities in prison."

We spoke with Enomoto for more than an hour. The more we spoke, the more complex an individual Enomoto revealed himself to be. He had actually been born in Soledad prison in the 1940s, when his parents were interred there during the war. He had spent most of his professional life in some official capacity at correctional institutions and had been assigned to Soledad as deputy warden in July of 1970, following the guard's death in which George Jackson had been implicated. As we got to know each other, a humorous side emerged. I realized that the corrections department could not have selected a more amiable, understanding, and accessible person to represent the prison to the outside world.

We explained to Enomoto our plans for the documentary. We would want to spend several days filming prison life. The deputy warden agreed to our plan and gave us permission to return within a few weeks with a film crew.

Enomoto gave us a brief tour of the facility. He walked us to a small window and showed us the "mainline," a large corridor of white walls and multicolored beams that runs through Soledad Central's prison complex and is the main hangout of the inmates when they are not in their cells. As we walked to the main entrance of the prison, it made me angry to see so many men incarcerated, so many misspent lives, and so many of them victims of a socioeconomic system in which African Americans and Chicanos were at the very bottom. I knew why so many men of color were incarcerated: the cycle of poverty, the subsequent appeal of gangs and crime. At the same time, I also knew that these men had committed heinous crimes—assault, rape, and murder. There was no forgiving these actions, yet I felt profoundly saddened that the culture of poverty had driven so many of my own people to this deadend existence.

Enomoto ushered us through the maze of locked-down doors that led to the outside. We shook hands and departed.

Soledad

In mid-December, we arrived at Soledad Prison with a film crew. KCET did not have a film department, so we hired a freelance cameraman, Robert Maxwell. We were going to be a small crew: Sue, me, Maxwell, a sound man, and a gaffer/camera assistant. Prior to our trip, through our community contacts, we had independently arranged to speak with African-American and Chicano inmates who were willing to discuss the charges raised by George Jackson and others.

Sue, our crew and I were taken to Jerry Enomoto's office.

"We think we can be finished in a day or two," I said. "Of course, it will all depend on how the filming goes. We want to make sure to cover all the aspects of prison life you feel are important."

"Good," Enomoto said, smiling. He explained that he had identified some inmates who had agreed to be interviewed. Earlier, he had made a big point of the fact that he could not force anyone to speak to our cameras, that we would have to approach each person individually. "They're waiting for you now."

We were led to the prison print shop, where inmates were busy at work running off the correctional officer's newsletter. There we were introduced to two inmates, Mordacai Johnson and Richard Van Magnus. We began the first interview by asking general questions about prison life. We found that Enomoto's handpicked inmates—unsurprisingly—had few criticisms of the prison. They seemed happy about prison life and claimed to have been rehabilitated through the acquisition of useful skills in the prison's paper works and furniture mills.

"There are skills to be learned here," Mordacai Johnson told us. "All you have to do is want to learn. I'm learning a few things from the print shop, but I'm really a poet and a musician."

Halfway through the first interview, we found out the reason our inmates were so "cooperative." The two men Enomoto had provided for us were to appear before the parole board in a week. There was no way the pair would jeopardize their chances at parole by bad-mouthing the prison.

Deputy Warden Enomoto assigned Chuck Stowell, the assistant superintendent of the prison, to give us a tour of the facility. We had wanted to be on our own, but understood that for "security reasons" we had to be accompanied. We knew Enomoto was trying to show us only the best face of the prison. We had our own plan as to how to get a balanced picture.

Stowell walked us through the "mainline," and this created quite a stir. Not only were we a film crew from the outside, but this was the first time that a black woman had been allowed in the main population area of the prison. Our guide pointed out some of the day rooms off the mainline and suggested we might want to get some footage of people in there—no doubt people they deemed "safe" for us to interview.

We knew that the prison staff would be monitoring our conversations and that there could be reprisals for inmates who were critical of the prison. The only way we were going to get honest answers was to interview inmates away from the prying eyes of the prison authorities.

As we walked along the mainline, followed by a group of curious inmates, we came to a juncture in the hallway. I put our plan to work. I asked Stowell to show me the opposite end of the hallway. He led me away from the group, and I kept him distracted with questions about the history of the prison. Meanwhile, around the corner and out of earshot, Sue was free to speak candidly with the inmates clustered around the film crew.

"We have heard complaints that there is repression here against black and Chicano inmates. Is there any truth to these allegations?" Sue asked.

"Yes, that's true," said Chris Walker, a tall African-American inmate. "They intimidate a lot of the inmates around here. They threaten you with the hole."

"The hole?" Of course, we had heard about the X and O wings, the infamous maximum security cell blocks in which George Jackson and others had been incarcerated. But Sue wanted to get all of this on film.

"It's the maximum security," Walker continued. "And once they get you down in the hole, they can do what they want with you. They can turn their back, give someone a knife."

"Who gives someone a knife?"

"Officers give certain other inmates knives to get rid of another inmate. This has been done time after time. People have come down from the joint, and the next day he is found dead. You see what I am saying? But now we're watched twenty-four hours a day, close isolation. So how do the knives get in? There is only one way that the knives can get in—the officers bring the knives in and turn their backs."

"What have you personally seen?" Sue pressed.

"Personally, an inmate jumped out of the tier at me with a knife! That was in July when I was down there."

I could stall Stowell no longer. We returned to the film crew as they were ending the interview.

For the rest of the day, Stowell took us around the prison. We filmed the paper works, where inmates worked for four cents an hour making toilet paper for state institutions. Then we went to the furniture warehouse, where inmates made desks and office equipment for the state university system, also for four cents an hour. At each location, Stowell introduced us to an inmate or a member of the prison staff that he thought we should interview. Sue and I took turns distracting Stowell and soliciting interviews with mainstream inmates who were milling about. They were eager to speak to us.

During the course of the day, we heard more and more about the dreaded "hole"—X and O wings in the prison. Several inmates also told us that some white guards were providing "shanks" (makeshift prison knives) to racist white inmates so they could attack outspoken black inmates. This was the same charge George Jackson had made.

The next day, we questioned Enomoto about X and O wings. He referred to the wings as "the adjustment center."

"The inmates call it a hole," he admitted. "That creates the impression that it is some kind of dark hole. But it's not. The adjustment center is the place that's 'hot.' That's where people have been killed. That's where all the publicity has been about. Unfortunately, all that has been depicted about Soledad has been about the violence. Now I don't want to kid anyone. The adjustment center is nothing different than what it is. It is a jail within a jail. What I want to emphasize is that we have dangerous people locked up in X and O wings. The intent of X and O wings is to get the inmate, as quickly as possible, into shape so that he can return to the mainline population. We have very few men who are kept there indefinitely."

"If it is not a hole, then you won't mind if we film inside X or O wings, right?" I asked. "That way we can clear up some of these false impressions and show the public what it really is."

Enomoto smiled. He nodded and reluctantly gave us permission to enter O wing.

The wing was entirely enclosed. There were no windows to the outside. The corridor that faced the wing of barred cells was littered with trash and other debris that the inmates had discarded. Concrete walls amplified the shouts and curses of the inmates, creating a constant, deafening din.

"The most unruly or provocative inmates are kept here," the O wing guard told us, "or inmates who have made enemies on the mainline and whose safety we are protecting."

As we passed by a cell, a white inmate let fly a volley of obscenities and then spat at us through the bars of his cell.

"This is the kind of inmate you'll find down here," the guard said as if his point had been made.

"May we speak with Otis Tugwell?" Sue asked.

"Who?" the guard replied, instantly on alert. I could read what was going through his mind: "How do they know who is and is not down here?" Of course, the reason was that, through Sue's South Central Los Angeles contacts, we had been given a list of African-American and Chicano inmates at Soledad who had been singled out for their outspoken views. We knew that some of them, including Otis Tugwell, had been locked up in O wing for some time.

"Otis Tugwell," Sue said again. "Isn't he one of the inmates down here?"

The guard nodded reluctantly and led us down the corridor to another cell.

Otis Tugwell was a slight African-American inmate who brandished a contraband copy of Huey Newton's *Seize the Time* as a minister might brandish a worn Bible. He had been separated from the main population because of his outspoken political views.

"Black people who are aware of the political conditions and speak out against them," he explained to us, "are taken from the mainline and put into this hole. For the five years that I have been in this joint, I have been without a beef [offense], but they put me down here in O wing anyway. And they constantly tell me that I am a troublemaker because when something happens, I will speak out on behalf of the brothers."

"Has this only happened to you?" Sue asked.

"You have numerous brothers down here in O wing who have been taken from the mainline because they refuse to be passive and go along with the injustices that they perpetrate against you."

"What kind of injustices?" Sue asked.

"If you want to wear your hair in a natural, they'll antagonize you any place you go. They'll use certain terms like, 'Do you consider yourself a Stokely Carmicheal or a Malcolm X?' They do this to antagonize you. And if a brother reacts or explodes, they give you five days in the hole. The next time you look up, you're doing six months in the hole. And in the hole, the only way you can get any attention is with a food strike. We just got off a food strike about three weeks ago, and it was just to get hot soup with our cold sandwiches and a chance to shower. These clothes I'm wearing now—I haven't had a change of clothes in three weeks. These kinds of things antagonize inmates, and when we explode, then they feel justified in using violence against us."

Tugwell was raised in ghetto poverty. He was a man with only a minimal education, and he had been incarcerated at an early age for murder. During his incarceration, he began to understand the politics behind minority presence in the penal system. He had spent the past five years reading, debating with others, educating himself into the articulate, learned, and proud African American before us.

The guard was eager to move us along, but before we left, Otis reached through the bars of his cell and took Sue's hand. "I'm proud of you, sister," he said. "What you and this gentleman are doing is important. We cannot speak for ourselves from this hole. Please, speak for us."

As we continued along the O corridor, we saw an inmate who appeared delusional. This was the kind of inmate, the O Wing guard assured us, for which X and O wing had been designed. But we also encountered African-American and Chicano inmates whose only infraction was to have spoken out against prison policies or actions undertaken by the prison staff. It was no wonder that prison authorities did had not want the public to know about the hole. Here prisoners spent twenty-three and a half hours a day alone, day after day, week after week—in some cases, year after year. The cells measured ten feet by ten feet. Their only respite was a half-hour exercise period once a day.

I looked about the sparsely furnished cell and imagined what it must be like to spend years living there. The cell included a small cot, a tiny shelf that was part of the metal door, and a toilet bowl that was visible from the front of the cell. An area four feet by eight afforded the only place where an inmate might exercise or walk about.

Isolated from the main population, inmates could shout political effusions and protest as much as they liked. They only had each other to listen to. I was struck by what an effective and devastating mechanism it was to quell political dissent.

Given these abject conditions, with the constant blare of voices echoing through the corridor, it was surprising to me that the inmates were so cogent. If ever there was a place to drive someone crazy, this certainly was it.

The idea of the prison staff framing George Jackson, Fletta Drumgo, and John Cluchette now seemed totally plausible. Our visit to O wing, however, had also revealed to the prison authorities our willingness to press for the facts and not be satisfied with the testimony of would-be parolees.

The next day, we arranged for Deputy Warden Enomoto to accompany us to a meeting of the African-American awareness organization, a group that met once a week. At the conclusion of the meeting, Sue turned to Enomoto and asked him on-camera about the charge that white guards were helping white inmates to attack black inmates. Enomoto was taken aback by the question, since he had already denied it in a previous interview we had conducted in his office.

"You tell me that staff are giving inmates weapons," Enomoto replied wearily. "It just doesn't make sense to me."

At this point, Chris Walker, the inmate whom Sue had interviewed on the mainline, stepped forward. Our camera swung over to include him in the shot.

"Mr. Enomoto," Walker said, "let me say this. When an inmate is kidnapped off the mainline and taken down to the hole, he is searched.

He is skin-shaked. He takes off all his clothes. He is spread eagle against the wall. He opens his mouth. He bends over. He lifts up and all of this kind of stuff. You know that an inmate cannot take a shank (knife) in there. We're locked up twenty-three and one-half hours a day. We have no contact with the outside population. There is only one way shanks can get in there."

We had it now. The confrontation between prisoner and prison officials on the issues that Jackson had raised. What made this particularly compelling was that it was not hearsay. Walker claimed to have experienced such an attack firsthand.

"Are you saying that they are brought in by staff?"

"They have to be. How else could they get in there?" Walker replied.

Enomoto maintained his position. "You've been in a lot of these joints like I have," he said. "And you know there isn't a place, even an adjustment center, that is fool-proof, that weapons can't get in. When you tell me it is staff that is doing that, that's where we have to part company."

But Walker persisted. "I know it's hard for staff to stop shanks from coming into the main population. They can come in from the metal shop or be carried in someone's shoe. Now I can understand when an inmate down in the hole has a crude pipe, because he can get on the floor and sharpen that pipe. You can get a bunch of pencils and you can stab. But the inmate that attacked me, that shank that this man had—it came from the metal shop. And it didn't come in by no inmate. There is more killings in that hole than in anywhere else on the mainline. We're watched, supposedly, twenty-four hours a day. But more killings happen down in that hole than anywhere else. You have a man sitting and looking down that tier, and still inmates turn up dead. One just happened three or four weeks ago. And many before that. And all of this under close supervision. Someone has to be turning his head to these attacks."

"This is where we have to part company," Enomoto said. He was standing firm. "We watch our guards, our staff. Staff just doesn't do that kind of thing."

"You know you have guards that don't give a damn about an inmate's life. You have John Birchers on staff, members of the Klu

Klux Klan . . . you can't watch all of your officials twenty-four hours a day."

Enomoto was at a loss. Finally he admitted: "No one can."

Prisoners All

The confrontation between Walker and Enomoto signaled the end of our stay at Soledad. Sue and I pressed Enomoto to allow us to interview two guards. He agreed on the condition that he select the guards. He allowed us to interview Edward Myers and Emilio Carranza.

We began with obvious questions. "Have you ever heard of guards giving knives to inmates to kill other inmates?"

Both guards insisted that they had not.

"Did you know that in November of 1970, two white inmates filed a lawsuit accusing Soledad guards of asking them to kill a black inmate, and they now feared for their own lives because they had refused?"

No, neither had ever heard anything like that.

"Has there ever been any unrest that you could attribute to racism in the prison?"

No.

After a while the questioning assumed a farcical nature. It was clear that the guards would not substantiate anything that we had heard repeatedly from the inmates.

One of the answers we got, however, surprised us.

"What would you like to do if you could have another job?"

"I don't know what I would do," Myers said. "I like this job. I wouldn't want to do any other kind of job."

Carranza's reply was similar. "I don't know how to be anything but a guard. This is all I know how to do."

Later, we asked the same question of some of the prison authorities and received similar replies—none could imagine a job other than the one he had. They were as tied to the prison system as the inmates.

I had heard of some inmates who had become so accustomed to the regimen of prison life that they could not cope in the outside world. When paroled, they would commit a crime just to be returned to the security of the prison. So, too, these prison guards could not imagine life on the outside. They were as much prisoners, in a different but equally permanent way, as the inmates.

We spent a total of four days filming within the walls of Soledad prison. We embarked on an exhaustive editing schedule with a gifted film cameraman and editor who had just joined the KCET staff: Barry Nye.

Soledad had its initial broadcast on the evening of March 19, 1971. In its review of the film, *The Hollywood Reporter* said, "Instead of the usual sympathy pleas that most producers make, this documentary was strong by its absence of such pitches, and was marked by excellent and intelligent writing, fluid camera work and a rare sensibility on the part of the producers." Five months later, *Soledad* won first prize in the documentary category and a Special Festival Juror's Award at the Atlanta International Film Festival.

Model Mexican American, Jess Treviño, serving as Los Angeles City "Councilman for a day" with James Harvey Brown, 1964.

Jesús S. Treviño shooting *Yo Soy Chicano* in Denver, CO., 1971. (Photo courtesy of Martín Quiroz)

Producing the "Image" special for KCET's *Ahora!* Program with Ricardo Montalban and Rodolfo Hoyos, 1970. (Photo courtesy of George Rodríguez)

As a zootsuiter, filming of *Yo Soy Chicano* with Martín Quiroz, 1970. (Photo courtesy of Gayla Treviño)

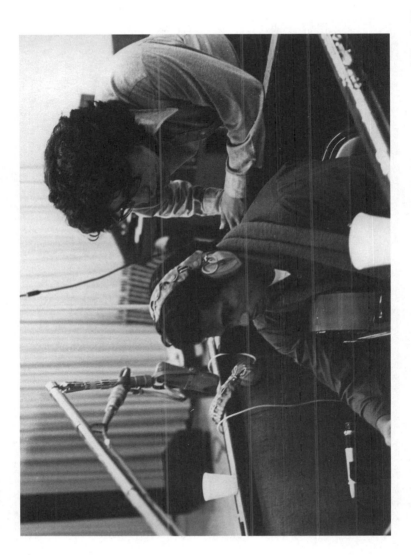

Recording theme music for *Yo Soy Chicano* with Daniel Valdez, 1970. (Photo courtesy of Gayla Treviño)

Directing Teatro Campesino. (Photo courtesy of Gayla Treviño)

Getting a lesson in posture from Mexican muralist, David Alfaro
Siqueiros, 1971. (Photo courtesy of Jaime Mejía)

On the set of *Acción Chicano*, 1972. From left to right; Gilbert Luján, Gloria Osuna, Jesús S. Treviño, Jaime Mejía, and Associate Producer, Antonio Parra. (Photo courtesy of KCET)

With José Angel Gutiérrez, Corky Gonzales, Ramsey Muñíz, and Carlos Muñoz, Jr. at the Raza Unida National Convention in El Paso, Texas, 1972. (Photo courtesy of Oscar Castillo)

Meeting with Rodolfo Echeverría Álvarez to finalize the directing deal for the Mexican feature film "Raíces de sangre" (Roots of Blood), 1975. (Photo courtesy of CONACINE)

Jesús S. Treviño directing "Raíces de sangre". (Photo courtesy of David Sandoval)

With the staff of "El Espejo", 1979. (Photo courtesy of Harry Gamboa, Jr.)

Chapter Eleven

América Tropical

*My mural was the mural of a Mexican painter who had fought
in the Revolution, who knew that his first duty, before aesthetic concerns, was to fulfill the expression of his ideology.*
           —David Alfaro Siqueiros

My firsthand observation of the lives of African-American and
Chicano inmates in Soledad left me profoundly depressed. While I
was free on the outside, many of these young inmates were suffering
inside prison walls throughout the United States. Although, intellectually, I understood the fact that these inmates had been convicted of
crimes and I had not, I could not shake off a sense of responsibility
that years later I would learn to call "survivor guilt."

It came down to a roll of the dice. What might have happened had
I not gotten ill at age nine and learned to read? Would I have joined a
gang from Boyle or Lincoln Heights, breaking into neighborhood
homes instead of going to the library? Might I have been arrested in
one of these encounters, resulting in the first of many offenses on my
own barrio rap sheet? What if I had not decided to renounce my Mexican friends in favor of Anglo friends when I was in junior high? I
might never have gone to college. Perhaps I might have been at the
wrong place at the wrong time and fallen into the barrio crime cycle,
or even killed. An even more profound question loomed: did Chicanos
have to deny their ethnic identity, as I had painfully done in junior

high, in order to avoid America's prisons or to escape being turned into cannon fodder in Vietnam?

I soon realized that I was struggling with something that went beyond the scope of what I had seen at Soledad. It had to do with the nature of American society itself, and how we, as Chicanos, were supposed to fit into it.

In a letter to my friend Jim Miller, I expressed the concerns I faced in reconciling this larger issue of the relationship of my own life to the Chicano Movement:

> If what is being sought is the liberation—personal, spiritual, cultural, physical—of a people, then my involvement in the Chicano Movement has really kind of left me with an impression of utter hopelessness. The history of the Chicano is a history of exploitation and oppression. Why should America go out of its way to secure proper freedoms and rights for a minority, when it is not only easier not to, but economically and socially advantageous to keep the group down? And this is not some Master Plan conspiracy I'm talking about. It's the subtle and perennial conditions that are just easier to maintain than change. It's easier for a cop to kill a Chicano and lie about it than for him not to, and the courts will support and reinforce him. It's easier to put Chicanos in jail or send them off to Vietnam than it is not to. What, then, are the possibilities? If Chicanos work against the system violently, we get even more repression. The final outcome (logically and out of economic and social necessity) of armed struggle will be to lock up Chicanos in concentration camps. If we sit around and do nothing, the results are likely to be the same. We get the continued treatment we have been getting for the past one hundred years. . . . I have really made a case for skirting the issues, for rejecting the Chicano struggle and for "selling out." But I think it is important to assess the situation as I have just done, simply so as not to be misled, so as to be able to see through the system's seductions, so as to be able to under-

stand our "failures" not as catastrophic events, but as natural occurrences. But also to be able to recognize the victories as meaningful and important events that make the struggle worthwhile. As a Chicano, I may not have the luxury of ever ridding the barrio completely of poverty, poor health, drugs, and police brutality, but I do have the power to view my reality as I choose, to determine that my struggle to end these injustices is meaningful, because of my participation in it. If I am not part of fighting against what America is, of changing it, then I am a part of that obscene reality.

After grappling with these issues for several weeks, I returned to KCET, determined that my film work should not stop with denunciations, but perhaps indicate directions for social change. For my next project, I decided to pursue this notion by exploring a lead introduced to me two years before by a friend, art historian Dr. Shifra Goldman.

An Activist Art Historian

I had met Shifra at one of the early meetings of the EICC in 1968. She had been one of the participants in the Sal Castro sit-in at the Board of Education. Several years my senior, Shifra had grown up in a Yiddish-speaking Jewish immigrant family in New York—English was her second language. Inspired by parents who instilled in her a deep respect for civil rights and human justice, she had gone on to become a lifetime social activist. Her brief marriage to a Mexican American had introduced her to Chicano culture, and since that time, she had become a scholar and advocate of Chicano and Mexican art. When the 1968 high school walkouts occurred, she had already earned a master's degree in Mexican art and eventually became an expert on the subject. Her concern for the education of her young son, whom she was raising as a single parent, had drawn her into the Chicano Movement.

During the 1940s, she had worked defending Mexicans from police brutality and deportations through the Los Angeles chapter of the national Civil Rights Congress, a civil rights watchdog organization. As the group's young administrative secretary, she had also coordinated support for striking New Mexico miners in 1952. (The strike would later be chronicled by blacklisted Hollywood filmmakers in the classic film *Salt of the Earth.*) In Los Angeles, Shifra was the representative of the Civil Rights Congress to the Asociación Nacional México Americano (the National Mexican-American Association), an early Chicano civil rights group. These activities resulted in her being called before the House Un-American Activities Committee (HUAC) in 1956. Her refusal to testify before the committee would later cost her a teaching job.

I was impressed by Shifra's no-nonsense approach to the movement. She was logical, tough, outspoken, and she challenged the assumptions that lay beneath people's opinions to ensure they were grounded in fact. While some disparaged her for being confrontational and argumentative, it was these very qualities that I admired most about her. Intellectual sparring was something that had been part of my life as a philosophy major at Oxy, and with Shifra, I was able to enjoy this activity again. I discussed philosophy, justice, civil rights, and politics with her at every available opportunity. Shifra became, for me, as cogent a political mentor as one might want.

In the fall of 1968, while at New Communicators, I had produced a three-minute Super 8 film, *La Historia de México*, telling the history of Mexico through its art. I used the same kinestasis technique that Chuck Braverman had used in his *American History in Two Minutes.* Shifra supplied me with hundreds of images from her vast collection of books, photographs, and slides of Mexican art. During the making of *La Historia de México,* I had learned a great deal about the politically charged work of the Mexican muralists Diego Rivera, José Clemente Orozco, and David Alfaro Siqueiros. These three artists had virtually created the Mexican muralist movement in the aftermath of the Mexican Revolution of 1910. I learned from Shifra that there was no such thing as objective art—that all art was political.

"You cannot separate art from the context in which it was made," she told me, "the economic, social, historical, and political conditions under which the artist worked."

To make her point, Shifra took me to Olvera Street in downtown Los Angeles—the site of the original Spanish settlement in 1781.

A Mexican Mural in Los Angeles

"In 1932, the Mexican muralist David Alfaro Siqueiros was invited to give a series of lectures on murals and to paint a mural at the Chouinard School of Art."

Shifra told me that during Siqueiros's stay in Los Angeles, the owner of a second-story beer garden on Olvera Street, F.K. Ferentz, heard of Siqueiros and asked him if he would paint a mural on the wall of his building. Ferentz's thinking was that Siqueiros would paint something folkloric that his customers might enjoy while quaffing beer. Siqueiros inspected the wall, situated on the second floor of the Old Italian Hall building on Olvera Street, came to terms with Ferentz, and proceeded to paint a mural on the theme of "Tropical America."

Shifra took me to the roof of the Old Italian Hall (the beer garden and steps leading to it were long gone), and I beheld the remnants of a mural that, though deteriorated, still bristled with political imagery. Mr. Ferentz had gotten more than he had bargained for.

Siqueiros's mural depicted the ruins of an Aztec pyramid. In the middle of the debris was an American Indian crucified on a double cross. Atop the cross, perched over the Indian, was the same eagle image that appears on the back of the U.S. quarter. To the right of the dying figure were two guerrillas, their rifles leveled at the eagle.

As I stared at the fading work, which measured eighteen feet high and eighty feet across, the message jumped out at me: this was Siqueiros' denunciation of U.S. imperialism and of the genocide of Native Americans. The presence of the two guerrillas, I surmised, called for revolutionary action against the United States.

Not surprisingly, Siqueiros was asked to leave the country. The mural was later whitewashed. In the years since, the sun and the rain had eaten away at the whitewash, and the image was now beginning to emerge once again.

Shifra explained that she had first heard about the mural in 1965, when she had met Siqueiros in Mexico City. Since that time, she had dreamed of someday getting the mural restored to its original condition. Standing on the roof of the Old Italian Hall, we vowed to make that dream a reality.

A first step to this end might be the production of a film that would tell the history of the mural. We hoped that this might generate enough interest to raise money for the mural's restoration. Although I had often thought of the mural since my first sight of it in 1968, the time had never been right to pursue the project. Now, two years later, I was ready to produce the documentary.

Like the emergence of the whitewashed image of the crucified Indian, Chicano history had been whitewashed by the dominant society and was only now beginning to emerge. The research and writing that Luis R. Torres and I had undertaken for *Ahora's* "La Raza History" series provided a strong foundation for me to link the idea of Chicano activism to the story of the mural. But first, I would have to get KCET to back me on this project. And that, inevitably, meant securing the support and cooperation of Chuck Allen.

A Walk on Olvera Street

By now, Chuck Allen and I were good friends. He was often over to the house for dinner, and just as often he, Gayla, and I would go to the movies together.

One night in February, Gayla and I took Chuck Allen out to eat at our favorite mandarin restaurant in Chinatown, located about a block away from Olvera Street and the mural. We liberally drank wine during dinner and were all in good spirits by the time we were ready to leave the restaurant.

"Chuck," I said. "I've got something for you."

"What is it?"

"It's best if Jesús *shows* you," Gayla replied, with a look in my direction.

I nodded agreement. "This way."

As we escorted Chuck towards Olvera Street, I began to tell him the story of Siqueiros and the mural.

"Imagine this: It's 1932 and a Mexican named David Alfaro Siqueiros has just arrived in L.A. . . . ."

"Siqueiros? The muralist?" Chuck was not only quite literate but was also well versed in Mexican and Latin culture.

"Right!" I continued. "So imagine Siqueiros being here in Los Angeles, here in the downtown area that we're walking in right now."

I recounted the history of the mural without revealing where it had been painted. We ended up at a location on Main Street opposite the building that once housed F. K. Ferentz's beer garden. Although it was evening, the wall of the building was illuminated by street lights.

". . . And that whitewashed mural," I concluded, "is now beginning to reappear." With a flourish of my hand, I revealed the location of the mural across the street.

The combined effects of the wine, the storytelling, and the climactic disclosure of the mural riveted Chuck. As he gazed upon the forgotten work of art, his face glowed with the fascination of a little boy.

He turned to me abruptly. "You've got to do a film about this."

I smiled back. "That's why you're looking at it."

Chuck Allen gave me the green light on the spot. I was to prepare a budget and an outline of what the film might look like. A week later, I began work on the project.

In Search of a Whitewashed Past

My first task was to track down local Los Angeles mural painters who might have worked with Siqueiros in 1932. With the help of Shifra Goldman, I was able to locate Millard Sheets, an accomplished painter in his own right, and John Weiskall, a retired easel artist. (Both men are now deceased.) Sheets was part of the "fresco block painters" who had painted the Chouinard mural. Wieskall had worked with Siqueiros on the Olvera Street mural.

Miraculously, Weiskall still retained two original black-and-white photos taken of the mural at the time. One was an image showing the complete mural before it was whitewashed. The second was a close-up of the crucified Indian with the American eagle perched atop the cross. Shifra Goldman, through her own research, was convinced that these were the only extant photos of the mural in Los Angeles.

Weiskall agreed to loan them to me. The copies I made of the photographs became the basis of much of the film's mural imagery.

Weiskall recounted his experiences working with Siqueiros: "We usually showed up around nine o'clock in the morning, and then we painted till noon. Then we painted in the afternoon . . . It was slow going at first. The first half of the mural we painted in perhaps a week. But then Mr. Siqueiros dug in, and we finished the last half a lot faster."

Millard Sheets, who since 1932 had earned a name for himself designing the mural façades for the Los Angeles Home Savings and Loan buildings, recalled the stir the mural created: "There was great controversy. Some people really liked it, thoroughly, in every possible way. Others were very much against it, feeling it had to do with political controversy or propaganda. I think that very often some of the most potent things that have been done in the history of art over a period of time—all time—produced controversy. I'm sure that Mr. Siqueiros had a very clear picture in mind when he painted the mural, and he expressed it quite well. I don't think he fumbled the ball at all . . . He knew exactly what he was doing."

The interviews with Weiskall and Sheets provided me with great material to tell the story of how the mural had come to be painted. But what I needed was more visuals of the mural itself and of Siqueiros at that time. Shifra helped me scour art books, but we could find very few images of Siqueiros during his stay in Los Angeles. I suspected that such photos must exist and began an extensive search of the *Los Angeles Times* photo archive and of the microfiche collection of *La Opinión*, the Spanish-language daily, during the period of 1931 and 1932, when Siqueiros was in Los Angeles.

After much searching in the *Los Angeles Times* photo archive, I discovered a photograph of Olvera Street that showed the mural partially whitewashed, dated December 11,1934. But I could still find no photos of Siqueiros himself. I reasoned that if photos had been taken but were not part of the archives, the only way to find them would be to see what had been published in the paper itself.

This led me to the *Los Angeles Times* microfiche library at California State University at Los Angeles. Here, I spent a month systematically going through the daily *Los Angeles Times* editions beginning in January of 1932 and ending with December of 1933.

As I read through the newspaper, I could not help but notice other fascinating news items: "The Baby Son of Charles Lindbergh Kidnapped," "Al Capone Enters Atlanta Prison," "Japan Invades China," "Albert Einstein Visits Cal-Tech." Every so often, I would read a small account, often less than a paragraph, of some event related to the Chicano experience: an item about the Mexican farm workers striking in the agricultural fields of California, an item about impending deportation of Mexican nationals, an item about the death of a cousin of Mexico's president Ortiz Rubio at the hands of an Oklahoma deputy sheriff. The more I read, the more apparent it was—Chicanos were exploited then as we were being exploited now—and our exploitation wasn't even newsworthy!

Shifra's words about the context in which artists worked came to mind, and suddenly the opening of the film fell into place. I would visually chronicle instances of Chicano discrimination in 1932—the year in which the mural was painted—and intercut them with events in the present day to link the message of the mural with *el movimiento*.

Though incredibly monotonous, I continued with my daily inspection of the *Times* on microfiche. Eventually, my efforts were rewarded. The *Los Angeles Times* edition for October 9, 1932, had a photograph depicting Siqueiros on a scaffold, still working on the partially completed mural. The caption read "Mural about to be unveiled." I was able to locate two other photographs from the *Los Angeles Times* that we incorporated into the documentary, one taken when Siqueiros was working on the mural he painted at the Chouinard School of Art, entitled *Street Meeting*, and another taken of him upon his arrival in Los Angeles. I spent a week trying to locate the original photographer who had taken the photos of the mural by systematically searching through old telephone directories, but I was unable to locate him.

History as Film Technique

Working on *América Tropical* afforded me the opportunity to work closely with Barry Nye, the very talented filmmaker that Chuck Allen had recently hired, along with his producer wife Linda Reavely, from

PBS station WQED in Hershey, Pennsylvania. Barry had been at KCET only a few weeks and had helped Sue Booker and me edit *Soledad*. Now, *América Tropical* was to be the first film that Barry would completely shoot and edit. I was to be the writer and producer.

Barry Nye approached our collaboration with an open mind. He was an excellent cameraman, director, and editor, and patiently shared his technical knowledge with me on numerous occasions.

Because of the scarcity of historical visuals, Barry and I had to improvise by using "poor man's process photography." First, we took the one photo we had of the completed mural and filmed it. Next, we cut several clear plastic cells to fit over the photo. Then we painted a portion of one of the plastic cells with white typewriter correction fluid, placed the cell over a portion of the mural photo, and captured it on film. We repeated the procedure with each additional cell until the photo was totally obscured by the correction fluid. In a series of dissolves, we were able to show the mural being "whitewashed."

While I did not have many photos of Siqueiros in Los Angeles, I did have access to historical photos of that time period. At *Ahora!*, I had become friends with Bill Mason, the robust and witty curator of the Los Angeles Museum of Natural History. Bill had an encyclopedic knowledge of local history. He could date any photo of downtown Los Angeles by examining key buildings present in the image. Bill had often loaned me historical photos of Los Angeles for *Ahora!*, and he came through for me once again by supplying images for *América Tropical*'s opening narrative.

Still, I needed more authentic voices—people like Sheets and Weiskall, who had actually been there when all of this took place. I called the *Los Angeles Times* on the off chance that I could track down the reporter that had covered the 1932 story on the mural's unveiling. To my surprise, the reporter, Arthur Millier, was still alive and now the *Los Angeles Times* correspondent in Moscow.

I placed a series of phone calls to Moscow, and eventually connected with Millier. He recalled walking from the *Times* building on First Street to Olvera Street, which was just a few blocks away, on the night before the unveiling. He later wrote to me and explained:

At 1:00 a.m. that night in a dead Olvera Street, I found Siqueiros sweating in an undershirt in the cold air, sitting on a scaffold, painting for dear life.

Millier went on to explain that Siqueiros had left the center portion of the mural—the head of the Indian and the Eagle perched above him—till the very end. That is what he was painting so feverishly the night before the unveiling, without the help of his assistants.

Restoring the Past

Having found a way of telling the story of the whitewashing, I next interviewed my friend, artist Gilbert "Magú" Luján on what he thought of the mural. "The whitewashing of the Siqueiros mural is clear evidence of the inability of the racist institutions to allow us to express our experience as we see it," he told us in the interview I staged in front of the Silver Dollar Bar, "allowing our criteria to be used instead of the stereotypes we've had to deal with all these years. Chicano art can only be understood in relation to the people whose experience it reflects."

But could the mural be restored? I decided to address the question and located two Mexican artists who had extensive experience with mural restoration in Mexico City. Although I had already exceeded the budget, Chuck Allen agreed to have the station provide airfare and lodging for the restorers, and, two weeks later, Jaime Mejía and Josefina Quezada arrived in Los Angeles from Mexico City.

Jaime Mejía was to arrive at LAX by himself, and his assistant Josefina Quesada was to come the following day. I took it upon myself to meet Mejía at the airport.

As I watched the passengers disembark at the Mexicana gate, I began to get nervous. I had spoken to him on the phone to make travel arrangements and expected that he would be a somewhat elderly man, particularly because of the long list of restorations on his résumé. No one looked, to me, like an art restorer. My preconception caused me to look for a white-haired gentleman—with horn-rimmed glasses, perhaps. Soon, the plane was empty, and the lobby was clear except for me and a young Mexican in his mid-twenties.

I knew it was a longshot, but I approached the young man and asked if he was Jaime Mejía. He replied, in Spanish, that he was, and then asked, just as incredulously, if I were Jesús Treviño.

"That's me," I replied in his mother tongue.

"You're a Hollywood producer? I thought you would be an old man!"

On the drive to his hotel, Mejía and I instantly hit it off. We were both intellectual, politically progressive, and were both into art. Jaime immediately understood what I was trying to do with the symbol of the mural whitewashing and how it applied to the present-day Chicano Movement. This was to be the beginning of a long friendship.

Over the next few days, Jaime Mejía and the other Mexican restorer, Josefina Quezada, examined the mural and determined that it should be preserved rather than restored. It was a technical distinction, Mejía explained to me, but an important one. To restore the mural would mean painting in the many blank areas of the mural where the paint had faded away, and that would mean that the paint had to match perfectly. Quezada elaborated by saying that Siqueiros had used the experimental technique of mixing paint with Portland cement, which he had then airbrushed onto the wall. The original color had been almost completely lost, and—with no color guide—it would be impossible to replicate all of the original colors.

Barry and I filmed interviews with Jaime and Josefina on the roof of the Italian hall building to include in the documentary.

"The mural should be preserved in the following way," Jaime told us, on camera. "First, we would clean off all the whitewash . . . Next, we would clean off the tar that is covering the lower section. We would then restore color in the blank areas to match those areas where there is color. Lastly we would cover the mural with a plastic coating so that the work can be preserved."

The news of the sad condition of the mural was disappointing. Throughout our work on *América Tropical,* Shifra and I had always hoped the mural could be restored to its original condition. I thanked Jaime and Josefina for their work, and a couple of days later, they returned to Mexico City.

The Mejía and Quesada interviews were the last of the interviews we had planned for the film. The next week, Barry Nye and I began editing the film in a small rented facility on La Brea Avenue. (Now and then, we would run into Sam Peckinpah editing a film called *Straw Dogs* in the room next to ours.) As we pieced together a rough-cut of the film, it became evident that something was missing. We had filmed the mural, we had filmed interviews with artists speaking about the mural, and we had filmed the restorers. But we didn't have the key player in the story—Siqueiros himself. Though this had never been part of our production plan, the film cried out for it.

"Do you think you could talk Chuck into it?" Barry asked me one day as he was splicing the work print.

"The original, above the line budget, for this film was $2,500," I explained. "We've now spent over $5,000."

"So, what can another thousand dollars hurt?" he asked with a grin.

I approached Chuck once more and proposed that KCET pay for my airfare to Mexico City. I could take the station's single system Oricon 16-mm camera and have my friend Jaime Mejía hold the sound mike. I would stay at Jaime's home during my stay, thus saving us lodging costs.

By now, the film was a major station commitment, and Chuck understood the added value that the Siqueiros interview would bring to the project. Two weeks later, I flew to Mexico City to interview one of the most legendary artists on earth.

Return to the Homeland

As the plane circled above Mexico City, I caught my first look at what had once been the capital of the Aztec empire—Tecnochtitlán. I could make out the Latin American tower near downtown, the Juan O'Gorman mosaic on the library, and the adjacent rectory buildings of the Autonomous University of Mexico. These were the only structures I could identify from the photos I had seen in Mexican art books. The rest of the city, stretching out as far as the eye could see, was a smog-covered tapestry of enigmatic buildings and erratic streets.

Jaime had insisted that I arrive several days before our scheduled interview with Siqueiros, and he intended to use this time to introduce me to the city in a way that few people have ever experienced it. Recalling my Super 8 effort to tell Mexican history through its art, Jaime told me, "Now it's my turn to show you Mexican history through its art."

The next morning, we began a four-day tour. Jaime was not only intimately familiar with Mexican art, but he also knew his history. We began with the early pre-Colombian Indian sites of Copilco and Cuicuilco, located near the University of Mexico. We toured the submerged Cuicuilco pyramid, and Jaime explained that this was the location of one of the very earliest Indian civilizations. We then visited Teotihuacan. Located an hour's drive from Mexico City, Teotihuacan was an ancient city that had once been home to 150,000 residents. As we walked the dusty, mile-long Calzada de la Muerte, the Walkway of Death, Jaime pointed out that before us, at the end of the long road, was the renowned Pyramid of the Sun. Smaller and to the right stood the Pyramid of the Moon.

"Both of these pyramids were built as mirror images of two large natural mountain formations located behind each. Now watch what happens as we get closer."

We continued to walk along the dusty avenue. Jaime pointed out the many smaller stone structures, almost house-like in appearance, that lined each side of the path. I noted the intricate designs etched into the walls and the finely crafted heads of the Aztec feathered-serpent god Quetzalcoatl, spectacularly carved out of solid stone blocks. As we approached the pyramids, our perspective began to change. Because we were closer to them, the Pyramid of the Sun and of the Moon soon dwarfed the mountains behind them. By the time we were at the foot of the pyramids, the natural mountains behind them were completely obscured by the manmade versions.

"Imagine the effect this walk must have had on the ancient people," Jaime said. "As they got closer to the pyramids, they saw the manmade mountains designed by their religious leaders overpower those of the natural environment."

We climbed to the very top of the Pyramid of the Sun and looked down upon the entire valley of Teotihuacan. Now, I could see the ingenious vision of these early architects.

The smaller buildings we had passed along the mile-long avenue had been placed to echo the natural hill formations that stretched to the horizon in the valley below. Teotihuacan was an artificial replica of the valley in which it had been built.

Awestruck by the interplay between the structures and the landscape, I was barely able to speak. "How old?" I finally asked.

"The pyramids were built about the time of Christ," he replied. "The Teotihuacan civilization flourished until about the year 650 A.D. There is a saying: 'Before the world began, the gods met in Teotihuacan.'"

Our tour continued with a visit to the ancient site of Tula, with its massive Atlantean stone guardians and distinctive Chamool water deities. On the third and fourth days, we moved on to colonial Mexican history. Near the main cathedral located in the downtown *zócalo* (marketplace) area, we visited several smaller churches in the *pueblitos* (small villages) that ring Mexico City. Jaime pointed out some stone walls that had been originally cut from the Aztec pyramids. Stone figures on the exterior and interior of the church were often disguised Aztec deities that the Indian craftsmen overlaid on the iconography of the Catholic Church. He showed me one massive stone, now part of the wall of a downtown office building, that still bore the same carved head of the Aztec feathered-serpent god Quetzalcoatl that I had seen at Teotihuacan.

After colonial Mexico, we moved onto the Mexican Revolution of 1910 and the renaissance of Mexican art that emerged from it. We visited a crude dingy structure that had once been the storefront studio of the Mexican print-maker José Guadalupe Posada. Then we went to see Orozco's mural "Omniscience," located in the stairwell of the blue-tiled Sanborn's Cafe, where, in 1916, revolutionary leaders Pancho Villa and Emiliano Zapata had dined together after defeating the forces of General Victoriano Huerta. He took me to visit Diego Rivera's "Walk in the Alameda," Diego Rivera's extensive 26-panel mural at the Ministry of Education, and Siqueirios's mural depicting a slain worker at the Escuela Preparatoria Nacional. Then it was on to the Palacio de Bellas Artes, the Fine Arts Palace, to see Siqueiros's "Democracy" mural, with its depiction of democracy as a woman with arms outstretched, breaking her bonds of enslavement. After that, I was shown Diego Rivera's massive mural "Ascent of Mankind."

The experience of seeing these works of art—images I had only beheld in art books—was truly intoxicating. After four days of such sightseeing, traversing hundreds of years of Mexican history, I was overwhelmed by the many proud Indian civilizations that had thrived throughout history. These were my ancient ancestors, the people that had constructed the pyramids, the people that had made Mexico City what it was. This was the pride I should have felt as a child, not the feelings of inferiority and worthlessness that I had been taught by American society to associate with being Mexican.

El Maestro Siqueiros

On the morning of my fifth day in Mexico City, April 4, 1971, Jaime, his wife Leti, and I visited Siqueiros at his studio located near Los Pinos, the historic palace of the Mexican president. A servant led us through a corridor, adorned with oil paintings and photographic reproductions of Siqueiros's murals, and into an office whose walls were covered with historical blowups of the Mexican Revolution. These were primarily scenes of battle: a man standing before a firing squad, the dignified visage of Mexican General Pancho Villa, a group of Mexican revolutionaries preparing for war. I was familiar with many of these photos. They had been taken by a legendary photographer of the Mexican Revolution, Augustín V. Casasola. Many of them had appeared in the book *The Wind That Swept Mexico*.

Within a few minutes, we were joined by a woman, who was, perhaps, sixty years old. She had finely chiseled cheekbones, intensely dark eyes, and striking jet-black hair that was braided down her back. She introduced herself as Angélica, Siqueiros's wife.

"El Maestro llega pronto," she told us in a hoarse, smoker's rasp. Even as she spoke, a tall, ruggedly handsome man of seventy entered the room. His hair—white, long, and curly—framed a face of sharp Indian features. His nose reminded me of Mayan profiles at the Palenque frescoes in Yucatan.

His voice was deep and commanding. "¿Usted es el Señor Treviño?"

"Sí, Maestro," I replied as we shook hands. "Un gran honor en conocerlo."

"Muy bienvenidos." Siqueiros welcomed us. He shook hands all around. I explained to *el maestro* the progress on the film and the role that Jaime had played in assessing the condition of his work. Siqueiros was pleased to hear of the preservation efforts of his mural.

Before he allowed us the interview, Siqueiros insisted on giving us a guided tour of his studio and the works housed therein. He first walked us through the bottom floor of his studio, passing by the photos of the Mexican Revolution.

"Yo fui parte de la Revolución Mexicana." He pointed to an enlargement of a group of Mexican officers. I could see that he had, indeed, been part of the revolution; I could make out the youthful Siqueiros among the officers. The *maestro* went on to explain the importance of the Revolution in ridding Mexico of the corrupt tyranny of Porfirio Díaz. Much of what he told us was history I was already familiar with, but I was hardly going to quell his vibrant storytelling.

Prior to the Revolution, Mexican peasants had been taught that their *mestizaje* (mixed blood) was inferior. Porfirio Díaz and his *científicos* (enlightened advisors) had tried to instill in Mexico and its institutions a European mind-set that negated Mexico's Indian past in favor of Spanish traditions. The Revolution had changed all of that, legitimatizing Mexico's indigenous roots. This, in turn, urged a generation of artists to express their autochthonous identity through their work.

Siqueiros spoke of the Revolution as if it had only recently occurred. I could see how the Revolution had shaped his political commitment and given purpose to his work. His paintings, and those of his famous contemporaries Rivera and Orozco, depicted a national identity for post-Revolution Mexicans to take into their hearts and minds.

This was the same kind of work I wanted to do, myself, by documenting the Chicano Movement. Identity, I felt, was key to it all. The Mexican masters helped to restore their people's mestizo identity. So, too, Chicanos needed to be proud of their own heritage that had been obscured by American history texts, television, and film.

Next, Siqueiros led us upstairs through several rooms, pausing by each painting or photograph to relate some anecdote of why he had painted that particular piece. His studio was a visual autobiography of his life, his achievements, and of his people.

"This one is entitled *Portrait of the Bourgeosie,*" he said as he gestured to a photograph of a large mural depicting a dictator expounding to the masses. The mural had been painted in 1939, at the Electricians' Union, upon his return from fighting in the Spanish Civil War. We moved down the hall to another painting, a color blowup of his *Democracy* mural I had seen the day before at the Bellas Artes. Angélica, his wife, had posed as the model for the image of the unclad democracy. Throughout our tour, I was struck by Siqueiros's deep voice, which still commanded great vitality in spite of his years.

We finished our tour of the second floor, and then went back downstairs to a gallery of enamel-on-Masonite paintings. These were sketches for the most ambitious work he had ever undertaken, a mural purported to be the largest in the world, *The March of Humanity*, located at the Polyforum cultural center adjacent the Hotel Mexico, which was still under construction.

When the tour was concluded, I asked Siqueiros to sit in one of the galleries that was framed on one side by a large photo of the center portion of *América Tropical,* taken from the same photo we had obtained from John Weiskall, and by a large study for a portion of the his *March of Humanity* mural. In a relatively short time, I was interviewing him as Jaime Mejía monitored *el maestro's* responses in the Sennheiser microphone.

Siqueiros recounted his experiences with F.K. Ferentz (el señor Ferentz, as he referred to him), and he recounted the story of how he came to paint the mural. He joked about how surprised Ferentz had been when he finally saw what Siqueiros had painted. The mural was a depiction of a Mexican that had fought in the revolution.

At the end of our interview, Siqueiros asked when I would be returning to Los Angeles. I told him that I was scheduled to leave the next afternoon.

"Then you can visit the Polyforum tomorrow morning," he said with great gusto. I enthusiastically accepted the kind offer.

The March of Humanity

The next morning, Jaime Mejía and I visited the Polyforum. It was located adjacent to the Hotel Mexico, a sprawling twenty-story structure commissioned by Manuel Suárez, a Mexican real estate millionaire, whose dream was to make the hotel and its adjacent cultural center a mecca for American tourists. The hotel was unfinished, but the Polyforum itself, begun in 1967, had just been completed and would open soon.

Siqueiros greeted us at the entrance. He was eager to talk about his work. As we walked to the main entrance of the Polyforum, I surveyed the building's exterior. Twelve large asbestos panels, perhaps twenty feet by forty feet, jutted out of the center of the circular building like mismatched spokes of a giant wheel. Each panel was awash in multiple colors, and each conformed to a specific theme: destiny, ecology, the masses, indigenous peoples, the mingling of the races, Christ, dance, music, acrobats, the atom. Siqueiros led us into a small antechamber that led into the main auditorium of the Polyforum.

The chamber was about forty feet wide and a hundred feet long. We were dwarfed by the vaulted ceiling, which looked like the inside of a giant eggshell. In the center of the room, we had a panoramic view of the entire mural. Surrounding us, figures glazed in heavy enamel reached towards the ceiling. As the bodies stretched upward, they grew in number and became three-dimensional, so that a hand, an arm, or a head would jut out of their previous relief states over the viewer. This forced the eye to be drawn, unavoidably, to the apex of the ceiling. At the top, the march of humanity climaxed in stark, three-dimensional figures that hung precariously over the audience.

"Estoy representando la marcha de la humanidad," he told us.

It was the march of human history.

He pointed out some of the figures at eye level and explained that the floor on which we stood would rotate when the auditorium was filled, thus allowing viewers to remain stationary while beholding the mural in its entirety. Once again, Jaime and I were treated to Siqueiros describing his work, the technique of melding two-dimensional and three-dimensional figures, and his vision of human progress.

All too soon it was time for Jaime to whisk me to the airport for my early afternoon flight. But before I left, Siqueiros took me to a side office and gave me a print reproduction of his oil *Mujeres del Mesquital* (The Women of the *Mesquital*). He signed it: "*Al compañero méxico-americano, Jesús Treviño, con gratitud por su obra fílmica sobre mi trabajo.*"

On the flight back to Los Angeles, I reflected on the experience of meeting Siqueiros. Under the shadow of this great artist and revolutionary, I confirmed the potential of what my own work might someday become. It reminded me of the moment on the steps of the Denver State Capitol, when I had first realized the importance of film as a tool for political and social change. In a certain way, I felt a torch had been handed down from one generation to another, from a Mexican artist to a Chicano artist. I felt honored to be carrying that torch. I returned to Los Angeles with a renewed sense of purpose. It was not only the history and the knowledge of who I was, but also the knowledge that change could be brought about in society, and that art—be it murals or film—could be a part of that change.

A week after my return, Barry Nye and I completed the film by cutting in the Siqueiros interview. *América Tropical* aired on June 22, 1971.

Hell No, We Won't Go!

A few days after my return to Los Angeles, Chuck Allen called me into his office.

"I got a call from your draft board," he said bluntly.

I looked at him, puzzled. "Yeah?"

"What's going on?" he asked.

I explained that I was trying to negotiate a place to work out my C.O. that was not Cleveland, Ohio. I had received a letter from my old roommate Jim Miller, who was now in his second year of working out his C.O. at the University Hospital of Cleveland. I didn't want to give up my work in the movement.

"I suppose there are Chicanos in Ohio," I told him, "but here is where the action is."

Gayla had done some research and had found that the fine print in the state advisory for conscientious objectors included work at an educational television or radio station as an acceptable alternative to working in one of the hospitals where C.O.s were ordinarily assigned. I told Chuck that I had given KCET as a possible place to fulfill my C.O. obligation.

"Well, they want me to go meet with them," he said.

I was astounded. I had convinced myself that my case had fallen through the cracks and was forgotten.

"Are you going?" I asked.

"Of course. We gotta keep you working here."

I looked at him, speechless.

"For the movement," he added.

The next day, Chuck Allen lunched with the draft board. I was on pins and needles all morning. I asked his secretary to inform me the moment Chuck returned. When she called, I sprinted to his office.

"So?" I asked.

"I caught the lunch tab," he replied. A smile crept across his face. "I had more credit cards than they did."

I wasn't interested in who paid the lunch bill. I wanted to know what had happened!

Chuck explained that the meeting had gone quite well. The members of my draft board had asked him about me and my work at the station. Chuck ensured them that I was sincere in my convictions. He told them that I was a valuable person to the Mexican-American community, and that I was an indispensable link to the Chicano community for the station.

"Oh, and they told me about that letter you wrote."

"Why did it take them a year and half to reply?"

"The letter had fallen behind the file cabinet. You were lost to the system until someone finally cleaned behind the cabinet!"

Chuck refused to get to the point. He was killing me with suspense. I think he actually enjoyed watching me squirm.

"So? What did they say?"

"They asked me if I would be willing to supervise your work here at the station for the two years of alternative service. I told them no."

"What?" I asked as the blood drained from my face.

"I told them that you had already been working at the station for one year, and that the past year should be counted towards your two-year obligation. I would be willing to supervise you for the one year that remained." Chuck paused dramatically, milking the moment for all it was worth. "They agreed."

I was elated. My problems were over! Instead of having to worry about leaving Los Angeles and deserting the movement, I could now devote my full attention to it and would have KCET as a base of operations to do my work. How could I possibly thank Chuck?

"Just remember we white power structure *gabachos* are good for something—now and then."

We sat in silence for a moment as I processed the life-changing news. Chuck beamed quietly at me from behind his desk for a while as I took it all in. Finally, he broke the silence.

"I had more credit cards than they did!" he reiterated, quite pleased with himself. "That's what did the trick!"

Chapter Twelve

Yo Soy Chicano

The goal of the Chicano Movement is to coalesce the Chicano people and unify them to the point where we can make our own decisions and determine our own destiny in all aspects.
—*Solomón Baldenegro*

I spent much of the summer of 1971 producing a ninety-minute special for KCET scheduled to coincide with the 16th of September celebration of Mexico's National Day of Independence. The program, entitled *Diez-Y-Seis: The Chicano Movement in Film*, was a look at *el movimiento* through the eyes of its filmmakers. The idea had originated with my experience in the "Image" programs I had produced for *Ahora!* Since that time, I had met several Chicanos, who, like myself, were attempting to forge a career in filmmaking. I thought of *Diez-Y-Seis* as an ideal opportunity to give exposure to emerging Chicano filmmakers while presenting differing views of the Chicano struggle.

In preparation for this program, I met with José Luis Ruiz, an intense young man who had recently graduated from UCLA and had been hired to produce a weekly talk show, *Unidos*, at the local ABC affiliate, and another recent UCLA graduate, Sylvia Morales, whom Ruiz had hired as a camerawoman for the *Unidos* series.

Meeting at my home, we had a warm and lively conversation, punctuated with much humor. Like me, José Luis and Sylvia understood that Latinos had hitherto been depicted in films only by non-Latino filmmakers. We realized that we were the first generation of

225

Mexican Americans that had the potential within our grasp to create films that depicted our people from our vantage point. We talked at length about the concept of Chicano cinema—films that Chicanos would write, produce, and direct. It was, at once, an exhilarating yet daunting challenge.

A few days after our meeting, I arranged to include their films in the *Diez-Y-Seis* anthology: Ruiz's film *An Artist Named Chávez,* profiling Los Angeles Chicano artist Roberto Chávez, and an excerpt from Morales's film *La Gente, La Tierra* (The People, the Earth), a profile of New Mexico land activist Reies López Tijerina. The other films in the program included *Yo Soy Joaquín,* a photo-montage based on Corky Gonzales's epic poem about the Chicano experience, directed by Luis Valdez and George Ballis; *Dying,* a look at Chicano inmates in California prisons, produced by San Francisco's Mission MediArt Collective; and my own film about education in East Los Angeles, *Ya Basta.* Completing the line-up was *Requiem-29,* David García and Moctesuma Esparza's depiction of the brutal attack on Chicanos by police at the August 29th moratorium rally and the subsequent Rubén Salazar inquest. In the publicity for the show, I audaciously noted, "KCET salutes Mexican Independence Day with a look at the contemporary struggle for liberation by Chicanos in the United States."

Diez-y-Seis was treading water. It was the first of what I hoped would be an annual celebration of the 16th of September at KCET, but it involved little production effort—a few stand-up introductions and film-to-tape transfers. After *Diez-y-Seis,* I was anxious to pursue a more ambitious project.

Telling the Story of a People

Ever since the Denver Youth Conference, I had been convinced that to fully tell a comprehensive story of the history and political struggles of Chicanos in the United States, I would need to go all the way back to pre-Colombian civilizations, to Aztlán and our distant indigenous origins. It would also be important to show the Chicano exploration of the American Southwest, our linkage to Mexican history, and, of course, how we as a people had been "created" at the conclusion of the Mexican-American War.

Shortly after *Diez-y-Seis* aired, I talked with Chuck Allen over coffee about my idea for the film.

"I want to do a film that will encompass the entirety of the Chicano experience in America."

Chuck was, understandably, reserved. "Sounds mighty ambitious."

I elaborated on my vision for the film. Finally, he asked me to draft a two-page proposal for the Ford Foundation. "Be careful what you wish for," he said philosophically. "You just might get it."

At the time, Dave Davis was a program officer at the Ford Foundation (years later he would found both *American Playhouse* and *American Documentary* at New York's WNET). I had met Dave Davis when he had come to East Los Angeles in 1969 to visit the *Ahora!* set. I wrote this proposal geared to his ears. To my delight, within only two weeks we received word that the Ford Foundation had granted KCET $35,000 to produce a film that I would write and produce. The film bore the unimaginative title of *La Raza History*. Later, I renamed the project after the song that had become the anthem for the movement: *Yo Soy Chicano* (I Am Chicano).

Once we heard that the project was a go, Chuck called me into his office. He expressed concern that the film, as I had described it in my proposal, sounded too historical. I totally agreed. I told Chuck that in addition to the historical parts of the film, I wanted also to tap into the many events, people, and issues that were going on in the Chicano Movement nationally.

I knew that Reies López Tijerina had made *Time* magazine because of a shootout he had instigated at a courthouse in Tierra Amarilla, New Mexico. Since the Denver Youth Conference, I had followed Corky Gonzales's activities at the Crusade for Justice, and later at the Chicano Moratorium. The year before, there had been a major political victory of a Chicano political party in Crystal City, Texas. In 1971, a national Chicano Movement was under way. National leaders such as César Chávez, Dolores Huerta, José Angel Gutiérrez, Reies

López Tijerina, and Corky Gonzales were emerging.

I explained to Chuck Allen that the film would not only chronicle past "heroes of *La Raza*" but contemporary ones as well. Throughout our discussions, we both understood that my approach would be advocacy journalism—nothing less than an unabashed celebration of the Chicano experience. I wrote about it to Jim Miller:

> *Yo Soy Chicano will be a one-hour color documentary on the Chicano experience in the United States as told through the lives of different Chicanos . . . It will be an inspirational film with emphasis on ways of confronting the realities facing Chicanos today.*

I'd be an upper.

The historical elements of the film prior to the sixties were easy, given my prior research of Chicano history. Far more important was the contemporary activism that was ongoing in the Chicano community. I felt I needed to start with this, since it would dictate the character of the rest of the film.

One day, while sitting in my office working on a draft of the opening of the film, I hit on the idea of telling the historical with the contemporary, in parallel structure, by intercutting the two as I had done in the opening of *América Tropical*. This time, however, I would design the entire structure of the film in parallel.

The Faces of *La Raza*

In early October of 1970, I set out on a preliminary location scout, which took me to various Southwestern cities to identify people and issues to include in the film. Gayla and I had been in need of a vacation for some time, and we decided to combine business with pleasure.

Our first stop was in Tucson, Arizona, where I met Solomón Baldanegro, a longtime activist who had attended the Denver Youth Conference and was running for office under the Raza Unida Party banner. Dark-haired, with intense probing eyes and Indian features, Solomón spoke vehemently about bringing change to the barrios of

Aztlán. He was the personification of the *movimiento*.

"I'm running for councilman of Tucson under Raza Unida because I am convinced that the *Mexicano* here in Tucson has no representation," Baldanegro told me. "Locally or nationally, wherever in Aztlán, we're trying to achieve political self-determination for our people. I think that the movement is going to mushroom in the years to come into something really big."

My initial impulse was to profile only three individuals for *Yo Soy Chicano*. But this would not do. There were many more people—like Baldanegro—with important stories that had to be included. I began to alter my view of the film. It would be a montage of personality profiles—the many faces of *La Raza*.

The next day, Gayla and I traveled to my birthplace, El Paso, Texas. We spent the evening in Juárez visiting my maternal grandmother, aunts, and cousins. The next day, I met with Dr. Phillip D. Ortego, a professor of literature at the University of Texas at El Paso (UTEP), who introduced me to three Chicano poets at UTEP: Abelardo Delgado, Ricardo Sánchez, and a young Chicano studies major named Antonio Parra. I described my documentary to the four of them, and they agreed to help in whatever way they could. Noon approached, and Ortego and Abelardo Delgado had to be off to a faculty luncheon. I invited Ricardo Sánchez and Antonio Parra to lunch in order to continue our discussion.

A Poet of the People

We ate at a small Mexican restaurant not far from UTEP. Ricardo—a heavyset man in his mid-twenties with a mustache, an unruly beard, and a black beret—ordered beers for all of us. I turned on the portable tape recorder. Antonio—goateed and rife with effusion—explained that Chicanos in El Paso had recently won a civil suit against one of the local television stations.

"We're the majority here, and yet we don't have any presence on television. We're invisible. But we're going to change that."

I was delighted to find someone else who understood the importance of media for our people.

Shortly thereafter, Antonio excused himself to attend a class. Before departing, he nodded Ricardo with a gesture of deference and a smile. "Aquí lo dejo con el gran poeta de Aztlán."

Ricardo relished being called "the great poet of Aztlán." He had grown up in the streets of El Paso's Eastside Barrio del Diablo (the devil's barrio). Life on the streets had been tough, and Ricardo had turned to crime. He had recently been released from Huntsville Prison, where he had served out a sentence of several years at hard labor.

"When you get sentenced, they send you to a work farm, where you do hard time." His voice was filled with the pride of someone that had survived a terrible ordeal. "I was sent to the Ramsey One farm near Houston. About 35 percent of the inmates in the Texas system are Chicano, about the same are black, the rest are *gabachos*. A typical day for me would begin at five in the morning with a hurried breakfast in the mess hall. Then I would go back to my *tanque* (cell), and at about 6 a.m. they march you out to the wagons. There are about fifteen wagons pulled by a tractor, and each wagon holds about twenty to twenty-five convicts. All around the wagons there will be guards on horseback, a pistol at their side, a rifle in their scabbard—and a whip. One guard per work squad. There will be a sergeant, a lieutenant, a rifleman, and a dog man; he takes care of the dogs that go with you, and the dogs are trained to tear people apart. They take you about fifteen miles into the field."

"Is this on prison property?" I asked.

"Yes, this is on prison property. So you work until noon. You have one short break to drink water in the morning. How long does it take to drink water? You just grab the cup, gulp it, and then you grab your hoe or your cotton sack, and you go back to work. You work at a very fast pace. During the cotton season, you have a quota. You have to pick four or five hundred pounds of cotton a day. If you don't pick it, you get beat up by the guards."

Recalling the Chicano self-help group I had met at Soledad, I asked if there was anyone doing prison reform in Texas.

"Prison reform is a meaningless thing in Texas," he said bitterly. "They work you all day long. You don't stop for anything. They bring you in at noon to eat. Then you go out and work in the sun for the rest of the afternoon. If you don't work the way they want, you get the hell beat out of you, or they send you to the hole."

"So they have maximum security cells on the farms?" I asked.

"Yeah," Ricardo replied. "When they put you in the hole or the pisser—the *meadera* is what we call it—they take all your clothes off. You have nothing, not even a pair of shorts. It's dark inside. There is nothing but cement. There are no electrical outlets. There is no heating of any kind. You are there completely naked. It is full of animals. It's got a hole in the back of the cell on the floor. You use this as a urinal, a toilet, and a water fountain, when you are thirsty enough. In the summer it is very hot in there. At night it gets very cold. There are all kinds of animals that crawl in there: everything from scorpions, to black widows, tarantulas, ants. They crawl all over you and you get bit a lot."

It was in prison that Ricardo Sánchez had become politicized to the Chicano struggle. I told him about the documentary on the conditions at Soledad Prison in California that Sue and I had produced the year before. He stopped in mid-drink and looked at me as if I were his long lost brother.

"Soledad," he intoned. "My soul bleats lonely, lonely, lonely."

"My god," I thought. "He's going to recite a poem?"

"Nasty wires . . . barbed and piqued," Ricardo continued, without missing a beat. "Fences so celestially high, one can't return, run, oh *mi* barrio Chicano, my other life show me, tell me once more of my peasant origins, give me a happy, canorous *grito,* damn—make these chains break!"

I nodded, not knowing what to say.

He shot me a deadly serious look over his beer mug. "I spent three years at Soledad prison."

Looking into his puffy, bearded face, I saw the many inmates I had met during *Soledad.* Looking at me, I think he saw a filmmaker who was committed to the same struggle that encompassed the life he knew.

I spent the rest of the afternoon with Ricardo. He read more of his poems, and we talked at length about *el movimiento*, the plight of our people, and the need for *liberación*.

Speaking with Ricardo made it evident that I needed to weave poetry and music into the film somehow.

The next day, Gayla and I drove to Albuquerque, New Mexico, to meet the legendary Reies López Tijerina, the man whom New Mexican media had dubbed "King Tiger" in an erroneous but catchy translation of his name. Prior to the trip, I read that, in 1967, Tijerina had been involved in the armed takeover of a national park in the northern part of the state, at the Echo Amphitheater. It was there that Tijerina and others had burned forestry signs. For this he had been convicted and sentenced to two years in prison, which he began serving on September 28, 1969. He was released that summer, on July 26, 1971.

When we arrived in Albuquerque, I left Gayla at the hotel and drove to the address I had for Tijerina. It was a stifling, hot summer afternoon when I pulled up in front of the cinder-block building that was the headquarters for the Alianza Federal de Pueblos Libres (the Aliaza Federal de las Mercedes), Tijerina's land grant organization. I noticed that there was a driveway, but no cars. The reason was soon evident. An enormous hole, perhaps five feet by six, lay in the middle of the driveway. Nearby, huge chunks of concrete were stacked that, formerly, had been part of the driveway.

A young woman with jet-black hair and sharp Latin features answered the door. It was Rosa, one of Tijerina's daughters. She led me through a large meeting hall and up the back stairs to a second story complex of rooms where Tijerina and his family lived. I introduced myself to a rugged-looking man of about six feet who was snappily dressed in a shirt and tie: Reies López Tijerina.

He greeted me very warmly. I explained to him the details of the documentary I was preparing on the Chicano Movement, and he was immediately attentive.

"The Chicano Movement," he said, interrupting me and nodding as if confirming something vitally urgent. "Let me show you what the Chicano Movement is about."

He took me back outside to the concrete driveway, and he showed me the hole I had seen as I came in. "This is what the Chicano Movement, the Indo-Hispanic Movement, the La Raza Movement is about," he said as he pointed to the crater.

A few days earlier, someone had planted a bomb beneath his car. The car was completely destroyed. The bomber's hand had been nearly blown off, and he was, therefore, easily apprehended. The man was released for "lack of evidence."

"This is the kind of justice we get here in New Mexico," López Tijerina said angrily as he pointed at the hole.

We went back inside and I conducted a preliminary interview with him on quarter-inch audio tape. I would later use this interview to formulate questions for the film. He seemed more comfortable speaking in Spanish; next to his eloquent replies, my questions sounded as if they had been framed by a first-year high school Spanish student.

He told me that he had been drawn to New Mexico in the early sixties by a vision he had seen of frozen horses melting in the sun. He interpreted the horses to be the ancient land grants deeded to New Mexicans by the Spanish crown in the 1700s. Although the Treaty of Guadalupe Hidalgo had guaranteed the original New Mexicans' titles to vast areas of the state, after the Mexican-American War, the claims were up for grabs. The U.S. government had confiscated much of the land and converted it to federal parks, leaving many of the original land-owning families penniless. But the land grants were not dead, he told me. They were just frozen, and he was determined to bring them back to life.

I asked him about the now famous raid that he and several members of the Alianza had conducted on the courthouse in the town of Tierra Amarilla.

"It all started with a land grants convention that was to be held in Coyote, New Mexico," he explained. "The convention had been planned for months and had been publicized by the news media— radio and TV—and people from all over the U.S. were coming to Coyote. But it was in the jurisdiction of the district attorney of Sante Fe and Rio Arriba Counties, Alfonso Sánchez. He used the excuse that we were Communists trying to take over the land. He confiscated our files and blocked the roads and threatened people. Anybody going to that convention would be arrested. Now these people in the Alianza, they knew their laws and rights. They were angry because their right of freedom of assembly had been violated. It was an outright crime. So, they went to the courthouse in Tierra Amarilla to make a citizen's arrest of the district attorney."

He went on to tell me about the raid he and other members of the Alianza had conducted at the courthouse and about the long-term goal of the Alianza to win back land for Hispanos in New Mexico. The more he spoke, the more his charisma shined.

"We are the bridge between North and South America," he told me. "In the future, we will play a crucial role in this country. We can be masters of our own future."

I thought to myself, "Another one for the camera." His energy was infectious, his effusions against the United States government convincing.

I wanted to spend a considerable number of days filming him in and around the tiny towns of northern New Mexico that I felt were crucial to the story behind Tijerina's land grant movement. He told me he had been invited to speak at New Mexico Highlands University in Las Vegas, New Mexico, on October 13. He brought out a calendar, and we began to shape a week of filming around a projected itinerary that would set him traveling all over the state. We would start filming Tijerina beginning with his speech at Highlands University on October 13, 1971.

I returned to Los Angeles, eager to plan for the actual production. The cameraman would be Barry Nye. By now, he and I had developed a tight friendship, and after the success of *América Tropical,* he had agreed to be the cameraman for *Yo Soy Chicano.* The sound man would be my loyal friend from New Communicators, Martín Quiroz.

Journey through Aztlán

Our plan was to head out directly to Phoenix along Interstate 10. We had rented a Hertz van and had packed it with KCET's newly acquired film equipment: a 16-mm Eclair camera, Nagra tape recorder, and a minimal Mole Richardson lighting kit. We set out early on the morning of October 11. We spent the night in Phoenix, filming shots of the Chicano barrios there, and arrived in Albuquerque the next day, October 12, 1971. Immediately, we conducted a sit-down interview with Tijerina in his office at the Alianza headquarters.

On-camera, Tijerina explained the background of the Tierra Amarilla raid and the rationale behind the forming of the Alianza. After the interview, he was anxious to begin his speaking tour. There were several carloads of people traveling with him, including his older brother Anselmo, his daughter Rosa, and his son Reies, Jr. Also a part of Tijerina's contingent were his close Alianza friends: grizzly-faced Wilfredo Sedillo, vice-chairman of the Alianza; a skinny, hawk-nosed old man named Juan Roybal who was, improbably, Tijerina's body-guard (he reminded me of an old western prospector); and Tijerina's beefy, loquacious, and ever-present attorney Bill Higgs. Higgs had represented civil rights activists in Mississippi before coming to New Mexico.

Barry, Martín, and I left Albuquerque and drove north, stopping now and then to get scenic shots that I hoped to incorporate into the film. This was the land that people were fighting for, the land that had once been ours—Aztlán.

The next day, we prepared to film Tijerina at New Mexico High-lands University in Las Vegas, New Mexico. There was a reception for Tijerina in the early afternoon, and I was quite surprised by the turn-out. This was his first appearance in this part of the state since he had been released from jail. Tijerina's presence stirred contagious emotions of celebration. He was a conquering hero.

In the evening, Tijerina gave a rousing speech. There were hundreds of people packed into the university gymnasium-turned-auditorium. People crowded together on the floor, stood shoulder-to-shoulder in back; they crammed into whatever space they could find.

As he had in our one-on-one interview, Tijerina spoke eloquently (albeit nebulously) about his plans to bring about reform in New Mexico. It had to start, he said, with the United States government honoring the original Spanish land grants as called for in the Treaty of Guadalupe Hidalgo.

"If we concentrate, if we dedicate energy, money, and manpower to develop and stimulate and revolutionize justice, I daresay that history will record that the spot on this planet where justice played its greatest . . . role was in New Mexico!"

Amid the deafening applause, I was struck by Tijerina's uncanny appeal. It seemed that no matter what he spoke about, he could get an audience to follow him.

The Cricket and the Lion

The next day, Tijerina was invited to speak at West Las Vegas High School, where he was greeted by Hispano students demanding his autograph as if he were a Hollywood celebrity. We set up our camera and lights in a classroom where three groups of students had been combined to hear the great leader speak. It was here that Tijerina told the students his parable of the cricket and the lion, a tale that he had honed over many retellings and that had become emblematic of the Alianza's struggle with the federal government to reclaim their land.

"So there was once this cricket who ran into a lion. Now the lion, naturally, is the king of all the beasts—tigers, elephants, giraffes—king of all the larger animals with claws and horns. So the lion says to the cricket, 'Hey, why are you making such a noise? Aren't you ashamed? I'd be embarrassed to make such a puny noise. You are, after all, such a tiny thing. You're not even important.' So the cricket says to the lion, 'Hey, why do you ridicule me? Why do you mistreat me? What is it that you see in me that makes you want to humiliate me? If you want to test or prove our strength, then I'm ready to fight you whenever you want.'"

Tijerina gestured with his hands for emphasis and imitated the angry lion to the students. "And the lion said, 'What? You fight with me?'" An enormous peal of laughter erupted from the students.

"That's what often times the establishment says to us," he continued, his face suddenly serious for a moment. "The government, the bankers, the rich. '*You*, fight with *me*?' That's what the lion said to the cricket. But when they began to fight, the cricket jumped into the lion's ear and buried himself real deep inside, and he began to tickle the lion deep in his ear. And the lion began to use his mighty claws to get the cricket out of his ear and he began to scratch at himself. Well, soon the lion felt his strength fading. He was becoming debilitated from the loss of blood. And the cricket, meanwhile, with his legs crossed sitting inside the lion's ear, sang his cricket song. And the lion got madder and madder and clawed at himself even more. He was so angry that he couldn't feel the pain, until at last he felt he couldn't claw anymore and he bled to death."

Tijerina stopped for a moment, looking out at the rapt faces of the young high school students before him. "My young brothers and sisters," he continued, "this is what happened in Tierra Amarilla, New Mexico."

Tijerina had told me the parable when I had met with him on the location scout. Now I was delighted that we had captured the parable on film. I knew I would use it in the documentary. This was symbolic of the entire story of how Chicanos had struggled for decades for social justice in America.

Over the course of the next few days, Tijerina warmed to me and the film crew. Soon, Tijerina was playing to the camera and even altering his agenda to make sure we would have the time we needed to set up for filming. For several days, we filmed Tijerina as he met with supporters in Mora and Espanola. We filmed him meeting people, giving speeches, and conducting radio call-in interviews.

Then we parted company, thanking Tijerina for his cooperation. We headed north to Tierra Amarilla to film the site of the famous events that had catapulted Tijerina to national fame.

El Grito del Norte

On our way up to Tierra Amarilla, we stopped at the headquarters of the leading New Mexican movement newspaper *El Grito del Norte*. I had not made any advance contact at *El Grito* when we rolled up in front of the office, a converted house adjacent to a Dairy Queen off Highway 285. I asked to the see the editor, a woman I knew only as Betita (the listing of staff on the *El Grito* masthead was first names only, for security reasons). I had become familiar with *El Grito del Norte* in Los Angeles. I told Betita—whose last name, I discovered, was Martínez—who I was, and that my crew and I were making a documentary about the Chicano experience. I explained that the film would be a series of vignettes highlighting the lives of prominent Chicanos and that, together, their lives would underscore the theme *Yo Soy Chicano*. We were welcomed with great enthusiasm—*carnalismo* (brotherhood) that we would encounter throughout our trip.

I decided that we would do a film profile of the *El Grito* staff preparing an edition of the paper. We quickly set up lights and filmed the cadre of women volunteers who set type, designed layouts, and did paste-ups. I was introduced to Adelita Medina, Betita's daughter Tessa Martínez, and several other women I only knew as Kathy and Betsy. The only male working on the paper that day was a young photographer named Antonio Córdova. He was mightily impressed with our 16-mm camera, asking technical questions as he helped us set up shots. I felt a great affinity with Córdova, and we spent a lot of time exchanging views about the need for our people to have filmmakers and photographers chronicle the movement.

Later in the afternoon, when Betita learned that we were operating on a shoestring budget and were planning to sleep in the van, she invited us to sleep on the floor of the *El Grito* office, an offer we readily accepted. We left the next morning amid hugs and promises to return.

Next, we traveled to Tierra Amarilla, where we filmed shots of the Echo Amphitheater, the national park that Tijerina and his Alianza members had occupied in 1967. At that time, they had "arrested" two park rangers and had tried them for trespassing on land that had once been the San Joaquín del Río de Chama land grant.

Then we drove into the sleepy town of Tierra Amarilla itself. I knew that I would need footage of the courthouse for the sequence in the film that explained the courthouse raid of June 5, 1967. Tijerina and his raiders had gone into the courthouse searching for the state district attorney, whom they intended to "arrest." Once inside, they took over the courthouse and held hostages. When they found out the district attorney was not there, they fled, taking with them two hostages: a UPI reporter named Larry Calloway and a deputy named Pete Jaramillo, who were both eventually released. In the course of the raid, they had wounded two courthouse deputies, Nick Sainz and Eligio Salazar.

I decided that we would recreate the raid on the Tierra Amarilla courthouse. I went into the building and told the clerks I was doing a documentary on scenic New Mexico architecture and that I wanted to get some shots of the building's interior. No one seemed to care about what we did. Martín and I doubled as two of Tijerina's "raiders." With Barry running close behind us, hand-holding the camera, we ran up and down the stairs of the courthouse, in and out of offices, pretending to be holding guns and "raiding" the place.

I knew all I would need would be a few shots that would link together some of the still photos of the raid I had already researched. By shooting close angles and silhouettes, we were able to achieve the moody shots I needed. Clerks and secretaries peered, openmouthed, out of office doorways, wondering at our preposterous antics. As we left the building, we thanked them all for their cooperation.

The following day, we set out for our next stop: my birthplace of El Paso, Texas.

Production Setbacks

On the drive to El Paso, we encountered a glorious sunset and decided to film it. We pulled over and made our way to a hill to optimize the shot. In order to reach the high ground, we had to go over a barbed-wire fence. I jumped over first, and Barry and Martín handed the equipment to me before they crossed. After we captured the scene on film, we started back to the car. While recrossing the barbed wire, the fencepost Martín was using for support gave way, and he fell, twisting his ankle. By the time we arrived in El Paso two hours later, his foot was very swollen, and we realized that he had broken his ankle.

As luck would have it, I had made arrangements to do a profile of a Chicano doctor, Dr. Raymundo Gardea, in El Paso. We immediately went to his office, and I explained that we had an injured person with us.

Gardea immediately attended to Martín, but made it clear that

Martín had to be off of his ankle for at least a week. We had planned to be in El Paso for only a day to film Gardea and student activists at UTEP before heading east to rendezvous with José Angel Gutiérrez in San Antonio in order to get the story of the founding of the Raza Unida political party.

That night, we were all depressed as we sat down to dinner at a cheap downtown cafe. I was dismayed that my carefully laid plans were suddenly shattered. After some discussion, we agreed that the best thing to do was to leave Martín in El Paso. He had cousins there who could watch over him while he convalesced.

I had relatives in Juárez, and I wanted to spend at least one night with them there, but we changed our plans and decided that Barry and I would take the van and head out across the desert early the next day. In Martín's absence, I would do sound for the next leg of our trip. We arrived in San Antonio late the following night and sacked out at a Travel Lodge motel in the downtown area.

The next day, I called José Angel Gutiérrez, but there was no answer. I had been trying to reach him for several days by this time, so I became worried. I decided we should go directly to his home to see if we could locate him.

A woman answered the door. It was Luz Gutiérrez, his wife. She informed us that her husband was in Washington, D.C., attending a unity conference called by New Mexico Senator Joseph Montoya. He would not be back for four or five days.

What were we to do? It seemed senseless to drive back to El Paso and stay a day or two only to undertake the long drive back to San Antonio. We spent the rest of the day in a downtown air-conditioned theater to escape the intense heat and humidity, and to regroup. Barry and I watched George Romero's *Night of the Living Dead*—its first national release—five times that afternoon. That alone convinced us that we could not continue in this way for another four or five days. We'd go nuts! Barry's parents lived in Houston, so we decided that he would rent a car and visit his parents for a few days. I would stay in San Antonio until Gutiérrez returned.

Barry left the next day, leaving me to follow up on something that had been in the back of my mind ever since I knew we would be going to San Antonio: I would call on my biological father, Jesús Vásquez Treviño.

An Estranged Son Returns

My father left when I was three. My only impression of him was what my mother had told me as a child. She never spoke maliciously of him; it was simply a relationship that had "not worked out."

All morning long, I agonized over whether or not I should call him. What would he be like? Would he want to see me? Would he hang up the phone? If he did agree to see me, would I disrupt his family life? Did I have the right to intrude?

I decided to bite the bullet and make the call. My mother had given me the name of a paternal aunt, and I looked her up in the directory. She was shocked to learn who was calling, but immediately spoke to me in a familiar tone, calling me "Jessie." She said she babysat me when I was just a one-year-old. When I told her about my uncertainties as to whether or not I should contact my father, she said that I should and gave me his number.

I called as soon as I hung up the phone with my aunt, so I wouldn't lose my nerve.

"May I speak to Jesús Treviño?" I asked, my voice trembling with nervousness.

"This is Jesús Treviño," came the coarse response.

"Well, this is Jesús Treviño, too. I'm your son."

At that moment, I experienced the longest pause I had ever had on the telephone.

"Hello?" I asked. After an eternity, he finally answered.

"Where are you?" His voice had lost its strength.

"Here, in San Antonio." Another long pause. "I'd like to meet you if I can."

"Yes," he replied hesitantly, then, with more certainty, "Yes, sure. Let me give you directions to the house."

I showered and dressed. Over a late breakfast at the motel cafe, I kept second-guessing my decision. But by then it was already too late.

I had made contact. There was nothing to do but meet him and see where all of this would lead.

I drove from my motel in north San Antonio to the Chicano barrio on the west side. I was unfamiliar with the city, so it took me a while to find the neighborhood. Eventually, I found myself driving through the barrio on Greenway Street, looking for the house.

As I drove along, I saw a middle-aged Mexican man mowing his lawn. I thought to myself, *could this be him?* Then I saw another man working on his car. Perhaps this was him? And then I saw another Mexican man coming out of his house. This guy? At that moment, it struck me that any of these men could be my father. My link to all of these working-class Chicanos overwhelmed me. No matter what image I held of myself—the model Mexican American that had made it to Occidental College, the intellectual, the activist, or even the filmmaker that was now making documentaries at KCET—all these images seemed to pale in comparison to the reality that I saw all around me. When all was said and done, I was, at the core, a Chicano, like any of the men on this block. I felt humbled, inextricably linked to the strangers around me. I was one of them.

I drove around the neighborhood for a few minutes more, part of me not wanting to find the address. Finally, however, I pulled the van up in front of a modest wood-frame house surrounded by a chain-link fence.

As I flipped the latch on the gate, I looked up to see a man emerge from the house. The next thing I remember was stepping back from my father's embrace. Tears were streaming down his face, and I could feel wetness on my own cheeks. I don't remember walking to him, nor do I remember him hugging me. All I remember is the moment when we came apart. I was so profoundly moved that I couldn't articulate words. We stood for a long while, just staring at one another.

This was more than just the meeting of my blood father. It was a confrontation with the reality of who I was. I was not only embracing my father; I was embracing who I was as a Chicano. I was acknowledging that I had come home in a profound way.

My father invited me into the house, and I met my half-brothers David, Peter, and Michael, and my half-sister Elizabeth. I also met my father's wife. Everyone was confused by my arrival. My father and his wife had never told their children of my existence. My presence in their living room was as big a shock to them as meeting my father was to me.

I spent several hours with my father's family that afternoon. Then, for several hours, he drove me from one barrio house to another, where I was introduced to this aunt, to that uncle, to these nephews. At each home, I heard anecdotes and remembrances of me as a small child; they were delighted to see me after all these years. When we returned to his home, my father invited me to spend the night with the family, but I declined, saying that I had to get back to my film crew. The truth was that I was overwhelmed by the experience. I was grappling with deep emotions that I had difficulty understanding. We parted company early in the evening, and I returned to my motel room.

The next day my father called and asked to see me again. I told him that I was here on business, and that I really couldn't afford the time. In truth, the impact of the experience was simply too much for me to bear. I decided to drive to Crystal City and do some preliminary scouting, so that when Barry returned from Houston, I would know exactly what we would be filming there.

I called La Raza Unida headquarters in Crystal City, spoke with a young woman about the film project, and arranged to meet her later in the day.

Crystal City, Aztlán

I drove south from San Antonio along Interstate 35, took a side road through the town of Uvalde, Texas, and proceeded along Highway 83, approaching Crystal City from the north. As I entered the town, I was immediately struck by how small and plain it was. Having grown up in Los Angeles, I was accustomed to large populations when one spoke of a "city." I had imagined Crystal City to be a fairly large community, perhaps something the size of El Paso or Albuquerque or Phoenix. These were the cities of the Southwest with which I was familiar.

The town was made up of dilapidated housing with one main street that contained a handful of shops. I was disappointed and shocked that such a small town could be the center of a movement as important as La Raza Unida.

After driving around Crystal City for a while, I arrived at La Raza Unida headquarters. It turned out to be a residence, the home of José Angel Gutiérrez's mother. There I met the young, attractive, and articulate Raza Unida activist with whom I had spoken on the phone, Viviana Santiago.

I introduced myself, and Viviana agreed to show me around the town. I spent the day with her, taking in the sites where history had been made. Crystal City also held a personal significance for me, since my mother had told me about it when she, my father, and I had lived here. I was an estranged son that had returned to embrace my roots anew. It went beyond symbolism. I was revisiting the site where I had been physically nurtured as a very young child.

Viviana explained that on December 9, 1969, Chicanos at Crystal City High School had staged a walkout to protest discrimination in—of all things—the selection of the homecoming football sweetheart, a process that favored Anglo candidates over candidates of Mexican descent. The walkout had continued for weeks, forcing the schools to shut down. Eventually, the school board conceded to the demands of the parents and students. It was on the heels of this success that a group called Ciudadanos Unidos (United Citizens) had formed La Raza Unida political party.

The more she spoke of the walkout and subsequent events, the more I realized that I would need photos. Viviana agreed to help me locate families and activists in *Cristal* (pronouncing it in English was considered a faux pas) who might have photos of the events.

At the end of the day, I drove back to San Antonio, at once exhausted and exhilarated from the discovery of my roots and of my connection to this place and its people.

Two days later, Barry Nye returned to San Antonio, and we drove to Crystal City to film the town and its inhabitants. When we met up with Viviana, she surprised me with a stack of photos she had collected from local Raza Unida activists. Upon our return to San Antonio, we learned that José Angel Gutiérrez had, at last, returned from Washington, D.C.

El Jefe

My first impression of José Angel was that he was extremely young. Was this the man who had organized the student walkout? The man vilified by Texas Democrats and Republicans alike for creating a "little Havana" (after a trip to Cuba) in the Winter Garden Valley? He was supposed to be twenty-seven years of age, but looked much younger—hell, he was my age.

José Angel ushered us into one of the bedrooms of his apartment that he had converted into an office. Barry and I set up our lights and began the interview.

"Tell me how La Raza Unida got started?" I asked as I adjusted the volume on the Nagra sound recorder.

"Well," he replied, "to understand our party and our success, you have to understand *Cristal* and the area of South Texas known as the Winter Garden. *Cristal* is very typical of the towns of South Texas. It's a small rural community. It has about ten thousand people. It's about 85 percent *mexicano*. The economy is controlled by whites, the small percentage. They own the banks, the drugstore; they are the only lawyers, the doctors. This is typical of South Texas. With one exception: the extreme lower Rio Grande Valley where *mexicanos,* over the years, have been able to win elected office."

I squelched a desire to interrupt, remembering that I needed long interview bytes to weave into the film, possibly as narration.

"After college, when I came back to my community as part of the Mexican-American Youth Organization's Winter Garden project, I had to deal with a lot of the myths and realities of the self-fulfilling prophecy. That *mexicanos* had tried. They had failed, and therefore they were doomed to failure forever. The students at the high school by this time had been grossly hurt in that they were punished for speaking Spanish. They were expelled from school for speaking Spanish. At the school, there was no counseling to speak of; they were all tracked into vocational programs. We had an exorbitant push-out rate. Over 85 percent of our *mexicano* students were being pushed out of the schools. So they were ready to take on the school system, and they decided to walk out.

"The first day of the walkouts we had approximately 100 students. We escalated every day after that until the point where we reached 1,700 students. The strategy here was that we would have large community meetings. We would work with the parents at each grade level—starting with the seniors, moving down to the juniors, down to junior high, down to grammar school—so that we had 1,700 students by the end of the school walkout. By then, the school board decided to negotiate."

"How did that lead to the creation of La Raza Unida?" I asked.

"After we negotiated the settlement of the walkouts, it became evident to us that we must take the school board, the city council, and the positions of power in the county . . . We realized that we had to do it through an alternative method to the Democratic Party. The Democratic Party was too costly for us in terms of filing fees. We could not afford to campaign for office. The political dates were at the wrong time. So we looked to an alternative of a third party . . . and we called it La Raza Unida Party."

I asked him about the reaction from the Democrats and Republicans.

"In November, the white community had to divide itself into two factions, partisan Democrats and partisan Republicans with the block of *mexicano* voters being together under La Raza Unida—so that the tables were turned completely around. We were successful in the spring elections of 1970, when we filed 16 candidates in three communities in the area of the Winter Garden, which is Southwest Texas. We won fifteen of those sixteen seats, thereby winning control of several city councils and school boards in the area. When we began the La Raza Unida Party and were successful in April of 1970, almost immediately the idea caught on throughout the Southwest, the Midwest—anywhere there was a Chicano who heard of our efforts and our success."

"Why is La Raza Unida a viable option for our people?"

"The argument has been that we can only win in rural areas. That is not true. We can win in San Antonio, in El Paso, in Victoria, Brownsville, Houston, Waco, Austin. Many communities that are not rural settings in Texas. Likewise in Albuquerque, Denver, certain parts, almost all of Southern Colorado. The southern part of the state of Washington, places in Wisconsin, numerous communities in Michigan, almost one-third of California in rural and urban cities."

"What about coalitions?" I asked.

"If we establish coalitions with other Spanish-speaking groups, such as *puertorriqueños, boricuas,* from the East," he continued, "we think we can have a very viable political force in this country, a *raza* party made up of all the Spanish-speaking components of *La Raza, la familia de la Raza.*"

Of all the movement leaders I had met to date, this man was the only one for whom I would consider working. He was, above all, a pragmatist, interested less in poetry and more in how things were going to get done. A welcomed departure from the asceticism of César Chávez and the charismatic demagoguery of Tijerina. José Angel understood that it wasn't only about winning victories and creating a mass movement, but also about bringing social change at the grassroots level. He knew this required the full participation of Mexican Americans across the board. His vision went even beyond Mexican Americans, to include Latinos throughout the nation. The resulting unified political clout, I felt, could bring about real change at the national level.

At the time, I was unaware of the fact that José Angel had previous experience with political organizing in Crystal City. In 1963, he had been part of a campaign that had helped to elect Los Cinco (The Five), a group of five Mexican Americans who were voted into political power as members of the Crystal City Council. Their tenure was short-lived because of the enormous reaction from white Americans in the town. This event taught him that you have to do more than merely gain power—you have to keep it.

After the Gutiérrez interview, we returned to El Paso to pick up Martín and film the profile footage of Dr. Gardea. I had planned on profiling the poet Ricardo Sánchez as well, but learned that he had moved to Colorado, where he had secured a university teaching assignment. With the help of Antonio Parra, we finished our film schedule with activists from the student organization Movimiento Estudiantil Chicano de Aztlán (MEChA) at the university. The next day we drove to Tucson, Arizona, to cover another part of the Raza Unida story, the candidacy of activist Solomón Baldenegro for the Ward One City Council.

El Río Park

Solomón Baldenegro was now working out of a modest home in Tucson's Barrio Hollywood, not far from a park that had been the center of controversy just a few months earlier. He told us about the recent victory for the community, something that had come about only after more than a hundred people had occupied a local golf course in an act of civil disobedience.

"We were trying to convert a golf course that was used exclusively by Anglos and people outside the community—tourists and other people," he explained. "Our children had no parks at all in the city. We wanted to convert this golf course into a park for our *Mexicano* children. And in dealing with city hall, we saw that we had no friends over there whatsoever. They didn't care about us. They didn't respect our people."

After they had staged the one-day sit-in at the golf course, they had decided to take the matter to the Tucson City Council and present a petition with several hundred signatures.

"They say that petitioning is the democratic way. Well, 2,300 Mexicans presented a petition. They were ignored and just shoved aside. And their attitude—they treated us very patronizingly, very negative."

It was the El Río Park controversy and the realization that Chicanos had no representation in city hall that had provoked Baldenegro to run for office under the Raza Unida banner. He explained that two of the city council seats, Ward One and Ward Five, were in neighbor-hoods with a Mexican majority, but that these wards had never had Mexican-American representatives. He hoped his campaign would change this.

Like José Angel Gutiérrez, Sal was affable, friendly, and down to earth. We filmed him at this office, and then got B-roll shots of his campaign signs and of the El Río Golf Course.

Finally, it was time to return to Los Angeles. We had been on the road for more than three weeks and were delighted to be going home. On our return, I slept for an entire day, exhausted but relieved that the bulk of principal photography for the film was completed. Only two major persons remained to be interviewed: Corky Gonzales of the Crusade for Justice and César Chávez from the United Farm Workers. I had intended to include filming them during our trip through Aztlán, but could not coordinate our schedules with theirs.

The next step was to begin editing. Barry Nye was to continue his assignment on the film and work as editor under my supervision. While we did that, I began to research and write the Chicano history segments of the film. For the early history, I looked back on the film I had made with Dr. Shifra Goldman, *Mexico Through Its History*. I located the reproductions I had used of the murals painted by Diego Rivera, José Clemente Orozco, and David Alfaro Siqueiros, and dug up photos of numerous pre-Colombian archeological sites. Barry and I shot these in a photo lab we set up in the editing room.

In November, we filmed a profile of Sylvia Morales, the Chicana camerawoman I had met through José Luis Ruiz. I asked her about the role of Chicanos in the media.

"We have had a lot of talented actors, but they have always had to play demeaning roles, stereotyped roles, such as the Mexican whore. The men have always been the bandit or the irresponsible Latin lover." She spoke as she edited a piece of film using a moviescope viewer in the makeshift editing room at her apartment. "It's up to us, as Chicanos. It's going to take us to represent us as people, as human beings, with the faults, but with the richness that we have, because we are rich in culture. I get excited thinking of all the things we have to write about, to make motion pictures about. We have a grand history, not just here in the Southwest, but all the way back to Mexico and all the way back to Spain. It's our history, our culture. It's ours, and we need to make these movies."

I wanted to convey the idea that Chicanos were asserting themselves in the media. I took the clue from her own actions while I interviewed her, and built a montage, showing Sylvia engaged in various stages of the editing process: rewinding film, splicing scenes together, viewing the edited piece, syncing up the soundtrack.

But there was another issue I wanted Sylvia to address.

Since the convening of a woman's caucus at the Denver Youth Conference in 1969, the emerging role of the Chicana in the struggle had become one of the hottest issues of the movement. Some women felt their role was to be supportive of Chicano men. This group pointed out that the nuclear family was crucial to traditional Chicano culture. They saw demands for women's equality as imitating the white women's liberation movement, trying to remake the Chicana in a white feminist mold. Other Chicanas were outspoken about doing all the legwork in the movement (as was often the case) while the men took the credit and did all the planning and speech making. These women felt they should be recognized for their efforts and that they had the right to assume leadership roles in the movement. For them, *machismo* was an aspect of traditional Mexican culture that needed drastic revision. I asked Sylvia about her views on the debate.

"Women have been conditioned not to speak out," she told me. "We have been conditioned to let the man take the lead. And in any kind of situation where we want change, this must change. The Chicana needs to speak out, saying what she feels, exploring her own potential . . ."

"What about the role of the Chicano male?" I asked.

"The Chicano, our men, should not fight us about it. They have got to encourage us. They must not hold us back; no change can come about that way. Change happens when everyone gets involved, everybody participating, everybody doing his or her part."

Sylvia's comments haunted me for some time. It was absolutely true: the movement was made by and for men only. If we were to represent all the people, how could we ignore the participation of half our members?

In December, Martín Quiroz and I flew to Denver and spent a snowy day interviewing Corky Gonzalez and securing B-roll footage of the Crusade for Justice. Throughout, Corky was ebullient and cooperative. We filmed the Crusade's art gallery, bookstore, various workshops, and the activities of the staff in the dead of the Colorado winter.

In January, I decided to change our plans radically on how we would tell the story of the United Farm Workers. For months I had been trying to secure a time and place to do an extended interview with César Chávez. Because of the constant demands on Chávez's time, scheduling such an interview had been difficult. Now I began to rethink this approach. Dolores Huerta was the articulate vice-president of the United Farm Workers' Union. As our editing of the film continued, I realized that, so far, all the key spokespeople in the film were men. Recalling Sylvia's words about the need to have Chicanos support outspoken Chicanas, I changed my tact and phoned the Farm Workers' Union once again. This time, I requested an interview with Dolores Huerta. After some scheduling problems, we finally set out to follow Dolores as she attended the dedication of a farm workers' meeting hall in the small Arizona border town of San Luis.

On a bright Saturday morning, we filmed Dolores giving a fiery, uplifting speech on a flat, dusty field adjacent to the newly completed union hall. Four hundred people were in attendance.

"What we are dedicating here today is not merely a building. Because a building without people is nothing. What we are dedicating here is an organization, is unity, to bring about the needed social changes that will make us free men and women."

The crowd stirred with enthusiasm.

"We are a poor people, a humble people, but a people of action. We are the ones who make human history. The history of the world has always been made by mass movements of people like us."

Afterwards, I interviewed her at length. She gave me an extended history of the forming of the union by Chávez in 1963, the strike that had been called in 1965, and the culminating success of a five-year grape boycott, which they had recently won in June of 1970. But the fight was not over.

"The reason for the existence of the union is to try to get power for the powerless. The farm workers don't have any power to solve their social and economic problems. They suffer from poisoning by pesticides. They live in terrible living conditions. They are exploited by the growers. The average life span of a farm worker is only forty-nine years of age. The average income of a farm worker is something like $1,400 a year, which is what most Americans spend on food."

She explained that the national grape boycott had been successful because farm workers had gone forth from Delano to the cities around the country, enlisting the support of all Americans, getting them to put pressure on the large store chains to take grapes off their shelves. "We were successful because we were able to hurt the employers in the pocketbook."

The Final Cut

The Dolores Huerta interview was the final interview for our film. By March of 1972, Barry and I had a rough cut of the documentary that ran well over an hour without any of the historical segments I had planned. Before cutting back any of this footage, I decided we needed to see it with the historical segments, first. I would do a final cut when all the elements—past and present—were in the film.

Throughout the editing process, Barry was a wonderful ally and collaborator, offering suggestions and acting as a sounding board for my own thoughts. We discussed ways that we could make the historical segments come alive and decided that we needed dramatic recreations.

From the time I had shot the dramatic scenes in *Ya Basta!*, I had longed for the opportunity to work with actors. *Yo Soy Chicano* offered me this opportunity. Barry and I felt it was the right approach to take, but feared that Chuck Allen might reject the idea. After all, this was supposed to be a documentary, not a narrative film. I decided that I would go forth and shoot the dramatic recreations and let Chuck see them after the fact, so he could at least have something concrete and real to react to. I would dramatically recreate key moments in Chicano history for which there was little or no historical record. This included profiles of Juan Nepomuceno Cortina and Ricardo Flores Magón, as well as a depiction of the Zoot Suit Riots of the 1940s.

One afternoon in early February, I walked by Chuck Allen's office. He was on the phone when he saw me and the man I was with. He put his hand over the receiver and peered out the window. Chuck was stunned. Walking next to me was a man sporting a handlebar mustache and dressed in a vintage suit from the early part of the century. It was Ricardo Flores Magón, the legendary Mexican revolutionary who had instigated the takeover of Baja California with an army of several hundred from southern California in 1911. Ricardo had come back to life for a day in the person of Ed Moreno, one of the producers at KCET that I had put in period costume and makeup. I had talked Ed into playing the role of Ricardo Flores Magón for one of the recreations in the film.

"*Yo Soy Chicano?*" Chuck asked, incredulously.

"*Yo Soy Chicano*," I replied. A smile slowly crossed his face and he returned to his phone conversation.

That afternoon, I staged a scene between Ricardo Flores Magón and his brother Enrique (played by another friend from *Ahora!*, Claudio Fenner López) on the eve of their attack against the Porfirio Díaz tyranny in Mexico. I invited still photographer George Rodríguez to shoot the scene. I intended to try out a film technique that had been pioneered by French filmmaker Chis Marker in his unique film *La Jette*. Marker had used still photographs to tell a story of a man caught out of time and in love with a woman from another dimension. At one point in the story, the still photo of the woman blinks. Marker had surprised the audience by breaking out of the still photo montage technique with live action footage for this one moment. I thought that this technique, of going from still photo montage to live action, was ideally suited to bringing Ricardo Flores Magón to life. From the onset, I intended for *Yo Soy Chicano* to make a splash, and I was determined to throw everything I could into it.

Over a period of several weeks, I wrote and put together several of these dramatic recreations and wove them into the historical segments of the film. As our editing progressed, it became clear that we had more than enough material to fit into an hour program. We began the necessary but painful job of cutting things out of the film. First to go were the many profiles we had already shot and edited. It became clear that however poetic and diverse the profiles were, they were not central to the larger story of the Chicano Movement. What had emerged was a documentary that would touch on the different fronts of the movement: the farm workers' struggle, the struggle for political empowerment, the urban struggle of the Crusade for Justice, and the land grant struggle in New Mexico.

Rather than lose the profiles entirely, Barry and I decided to incorporate the footage of Chicano doctors, lawyers, activists, and artists into a montage of the many faces of *La Raza* that would open the film. I knew we would need special music to edit together the montage and determined that it should be rock music to establish that Chicanos were contemporary and not old-fashioned. To this end, I secured the services of two Eastside musician brothers, Rudy and Steve Salas (later, they would form the legendary Eastside band, Tierra). For the film's theme music, however, I felt something else was needed. I decided to approach El Teatro Campesino.

It had been more than three years since I had visited Luis Valdez's El Teatro Campesino in Fresno. Since that time, a friend of Valdez's, Manny Santana, had offered the group a fifty-seat theater in the small northern California farming community of San Juan Bautista. The town of 1,100 people was located just off Highway 101, near the city of Monterey. Luis and the members of his theater company accepted the offer, gave the theater the name, La Calavera (The Skeleton), and resettled in San Juan Baustista, intent on developing original Chicano plays. In March, I phoned Luis Valdez, reintroduced myself, and told him about *Yo Soy Chicano* and of my interest in having El Teatro Campesino contribute to the music of the film. He listened with interest and then directed me to his brother, Daniel, who was in charge of music for the group. Gayla and I drove up the coast to meet with Daniel Valdez and discuss the project.

Our meeting took place at Daniel's home on the outskirts of the town, near the cemetery that overlooked the town. A young man with a broad smile emerged from the house and approached us.

"*¡Órale!* I'm Daniel. You can call me Danny. You must be Treviño."

"Right," I said as we shook hands. "This is my wife, Gayla."

Just then, an attractive Chicana with long jet-black hair emerged from the house carrying a three-year-old boy in her arms.

"This is Armida," Daniel said, indicating his wife. "And this is our son, Emiliano—Mino."

We shook hands with Armida. There was an awkward pause for a moment. "Have you had dinner?" he asked. "We're getting set to barbecue."

I looked to Gayla for agreement. "We'd love to."

While Daniel seemed all smiles and acceptance, Armida was quiet and reserved. At first, I assumed she was suspicious of us, or perhaps unfriendly. But suddenly, she smiled and warmed to Gayla.

"Why don't you come in and help me get the food together," she said in a no-nonsense tone. She turned and entered the house. Gayla followed her inside while Danny and I stayed outside to get the charcoals started.

Over beers, I explained the film project to Daniel. I told him I would need theme music for the film as well as music to play under the film's narration. I told him I didn't have a lot of money but would be able to pay him for the original music and get a studio session with musicians of his choice.

As I elaborated on the footage that had already been shot and on the historical aspects of the film, I could see that Daniel was getting excited about the prospect of doing the music. He explained that if he were to undertake the task, it would have to include the participation of other *teatro* members. I nodded. I wanted this to be a thoroughly Chicano project and felt the *teatro* had to be involved.

Throughout our discussion, Daniel was rather silent, as if he was trying to figure out what made me tick. Soon, Armida and Gayla emerged from the house carrying a stack of hamburgers with buns, lettuce, tomatoes, and dressing. I continued my spiel. As I spoke,

Daniel now and then nodded, appearing to be preoccupied with barbecuing the hamburgers as he listened. Finally, he turned to me.

"Why do you want me to do the music? Why not someone more famous—like Carlos Santana?" The rock musician had recently released his *Black Magic Woman* album, which had catapulted him to the status of a national music figure.

"I know that you and Luis started with the United Farm Workers. I think you're about what the film is about, what I'm about—the struggle of our people."

That stopped him for a moment. He looked me up and down again.

"Okay," he said. "*Pues*, let's do it."

We shook hands and agreed that we would work out the money aspects later. Daniel would work on musical ideas for the soundtrack of the film in the next month, and sometime in April, he would come down to Los Angeles to record the music.

In the course of the next several weeks, I visited San Juan Bautista several times. On my second trip, I met Luis Valdez for the second time and was given a tour of the theater and facilities where the company rehearsed. I received the same warm acceptance that I had encountered on my tour of Aztlán. As Daniel and I worked on ideas for the film's music, our friendship grew. Within a short time, we became very close. Part of this was due to our common devotion to the struggle of our people, and part of it to the similarity in our views about artistic expression. We seldom seemed to disagree on what creative direction we should take; we seemed uncannily in sync with one another. For me, this was quite a new feeling. I had never worked with a Chicano so closely before, nor with someone with whom I felt such creative affinity.

As production on the soundtrack ensued, the musical score became a true collaboration. I had previously read a series of musical lectures delivered at Harvard University in the 1950s by the Mexican classical composer Carlos Chávez. I was very impressed with Chávez's ideas of structure and form in music. I shared the book with Danny, and we began to work on an overall musical scheme that would encompass the entire documentary using some of Chávez's ideas on musical themes, reiteration of motifs, and symmetry of structure.

We began with the title song, *Yo Soy Chicano*, which had been adapted from the popular *corrido* (ballad) of the Mexican Revolution, *La Rielera*, by musicians at Corky Gonzales's Crusade for Justice. We took the song, set it in a minor key, and rendered it with guitar and flute. This became the signature theme of any Chicano personality profiled in the film. It was the music you heard whenever the concept of Chicano and *chicanismo* was mentioned. Then, we developed music for the narration track. Since the film underscored the *mestizo* character of Chicano identity—part Indian and part Spanish—we decided that we would incorporate a blend of indigenous instruments—flutes, drums, and pipes—and the Spanish guitar.

As my friendship with Danny grew, so too did Gayla's friendship with Armida. As planned, Daniel came down to Los Angeles to record the music in April. Armida and young Mino came with him, along with several of the *teatro's* musicians. To save money for the production, the entire group slept on the living room floor of the small three-room house that Gayla and I now lived in on Sunset Drive, located within walking distance of KCET.

We recorded the music for the soundtrack in an extended afternoon session in a small studio I had rented in Burbank. It was an exhilarating experience, no doubt enhanced by the fact that I was working with fellow Chicano artists who understood the creative vision that I was striving for in the film. In addition to Yolanda Castillo, Sal and Ernesto Bravo, and Ben Cadena, I joined in as a musician accompanying Daniel on guitar and percussion. At the conclusion of the soundtrack, I could see that Daniel was as moved as I was about our work together.

"Hey, we should do this more often! You need to come up to San Juan and join the group!"

"Sure," I replied, laughing. "Just up and leave everything I got going here at KCET, right?"

"Well, think about it," he said, no longer laughing. At the time, the idea seemed like a fanciful dream: to run away and join the circus, in this case, El Teatro Campesino. What a lark that would be! Little did I know that in a few years, that is exactly what I would do.

A Draft Board Letter

In early June, I received a letter from my draft board dated June 1, 1972. It explained that I had been released from the performance of civilian work contributing to the national health, safety, or interest. I had "completed twenty-four months of alternate civilian work under the conscientious objector work program." I was finally rid of the draft! As I read and reread the letter, it occurred to me that during the last two years I had worked on *Ahora!* and had completed the films *Soledad, América Tropical,* and *Yo Soy Chicano.* As a citizen of Aztlán, I had fought the war at home, a war against a society whose institutions and laws oppressed and discriminated against my people. I felt entirely vindicated.

Chapter Thirteen

New Forms, Old Visions

We no longer accept the fact that we are powerless and need to be complaining about our powerlessness. We know we are powerful. We know we can be organized. We know that we can triumph.

—José Angel Gutiérrez

In early June, as Barry Nye and I were nearing the completion of editing on *Yo Soy Chicano,* I received a phone call from José Angel Gutiérrez. He explained that he had recently met with Corky Gonzales and Reies López Tijerina. With the victories Raza Unida Party had won in South Texas, and the rapid emergence of Raza Unida chapters in Arizona, Colorado, New Mexico, and California, the three Chicano leaders had decided that it was time for the party to go to the next stage.

"I've been put in charge of planning a national convention, which we're setting for Labor Day weekend in El Paso, Texas," he told me. "We're ready to move on a national level."

José Angel's call signaled that an important accord had been reached between three of the movement's most visible leaders. I knew that the dream of a national convention went all the way back to the Denver Youth Conference and the *Plan de Aztlán.* The plan had called for "creation of an independent local, regional, and national political party." Corky Gonzales had hoped to shape this national party in Los Angeles the week following the August 29th Chicano Moratorium against the war in Vietnam. But the riot and his subsequent incarceration had put his efforts on hold. Since that time, José Angel had achieved sizeable political victories in Texas, beating Corky to the punch and elevating José Angel to the status of a national leader.

The other potential rival to Corky's leadership of the party was Reies López Tijerina, whose recent release from prison made him a larger-than-life personality. His fame as an instigator of armed struggle and a national speaking tour following his release from prison had elevated his prestige among Chicanos nationwide.

Corky sensibly accommodated José Angel and Tijerina in the new plans for a national party. Together, the three developed the idea of a *congreso,* a national congress made up of Raza Unida delegates from each state and headed by a national party chairman. Delegates to the *congreso,* as well as the national party chairman, were to be elected at the national convention in El Paso. A party platform of goals and issues would also be hammered out.

"When we have our national convention," José Angel continued, "we're going to need national press. I want to know, will you be the national media coordinator for La Raza Unida Party?"

I was at once flattered and taken aback by the offer. José Angel knew of my television work load and that I might not be available for the convention—his question was not a rhetorical one. But José Angel did not know that in my own mind my response was a given. As documentor of the *movimiento,* how could I refuse? Also shaping my response was the considerable thought I had already given to our national Chicano leaders and the opinion I had formed of each.

The Four Horsemen

Prior to and during the filming of *Yo Soy Chicano,* I had met and gotten to know the four most visible Chicano leaders in the nation, sometimes referred to as the "four horsemen." Because of my intense commitment to the *movimiento,* I was ever eager to lend my skills for any project involving the movement. I was determined to put my media skills to work. The requirement I asked was simple: I was willing to work with anyone on behalf of Chicanos as long as the person wasn't a demagogue, a gangster, or a nut. My opinion of the four horsemen was mixed.

Foremost on the list of Chicano leaders was the venerated César Chávez. This was someone whom I respected, but my efforts to help his struggle and that of the farm workers had been met with rebuff, from which I was still smarting.

During the filming of farm worker pickets in San Diego for *América Tropical,* and later in filming picket lines at Los Angeles supermarkets for KCET's new department, I had been struck by how media-ignorant the Farm Workers' Union appeared to be. In one instance, a picket line planned weeks in advance had received little publicity merely because the news media had not been properly informed of the event. Given my understanding of how the media worked, I felt I might be able to help out and decided to place a call to César Chávez.

After several attempts I was told by one of his lieutenants that Mr. Chávez could not be reached. I would have to speak to someone else. This miffed me. Other Chicano leaders answered my calls, why not Chávez? Finally, I was routed to the legal counsel for the Farm Workers' Union. I told him how much I thought they needed someone with a media sensibility to help engineer a public image of the farm workers and coordinate some of the press events in Los Angeles.

He wanted to know what I meant.

"Look," I replied. "I hear through the grapevine about a farm workers' picket of a supermarket store here in Los Angeles. But I never get a press release. When I do get word of a picket or rally, it's usually the day before. You need to give news media more advance warning if you expect them to cover the events."

The legal counsel explained that the farm workers were engaged in a crucial struggle, and at times press releases were not a high priority. César Chávez felt the union could not allow the media to dictate their actions, he told me.

I explained to him that my work at KCET gave me a visibility that could help the union. I was willing to devote as much of my time to helping them out with Los Angeles media as I could. But the legal counsel was insistent. Chávez only wanted people working for the union to do press. My offer to help out as Los Angeles press liaison was politely turned down.

The response hurt and disappointed me. I took the rejection personally. Here I was offering to put my skills at work for their cause, for our cause, and they were too distrustful to take me seriously. I felt angry that my valuable efforts would be lost. This cooled me on the idea of working for Chávez or the union, at least for the moment. In years later, I did help out in many union activities.

Reies López Tijerina was a different question. After I had passed muster during the filming of *Yo Soy Chicano*, Tijerina viewed me as a valuable instrument for the movement. Toward the end of our stay with him, he took me aside and told me that the movement needed more filmmakers like me. The problem with Tijerina was that any efforts made on behalf of the Alianza, I was convinced, would ultimately be turned into efforts at promoting Tijerina himself.

By now, Tijerina was caught up in a highly inflated sense of himself—he compared himself to Moses, implying that he would lead Chicanos to the promised land. I knew that promoting Tijerina as a messiah for our people was not something I wanted to be part of. Also troubling was Tijerina's extreme male chauvinism and his single-minded commitment to the New Mexico land grant movement to the exclusion of the urban struggle of Chicanos. However undeniably charismatic the man was, I felt that direct work with Tijerina was out of the question.

Corky Gonzales was someone whose efforts and whose charisma I respected. I had been doubly impressed when I had first met him. After just a few minutes of speaking to Corky at the Denver Youth Conference, I could hear his simple grammar and knew this was not a highly educated man. The Mexican revolutionaries Emiliano Zapata and Pancho Villa had also not been highly educated. I saw Corky as an heir to their tradition of courage, intelligence, and leadership.

My problem with Corky, however, had to do with my commitment to nonviolence. I felt uneasy about the armed men who perennially surrounded him. I had first noticed this during the 1969 youth conference: Corky was always followed by bodyguards who packed guns. I had noticed this throughout my stay at the Crusade; every now and then I'd see the handle of a gun poking out of someone's pants or jacket. What I did not know at the time was that the Crusade was being actively monitored by the F.B.I. and that anonymous threats had been made on Corky's life. Although armed bodyguards made sense in this light, it was not the kind of environment I was sure I wanted to live and work in.

The person that most drew my attention and with whom I felt most affinity was José Angel Gutiérrez. Unlike Corky and Tijerina, José Angel Gutiérrez was of my generation. He was unpretentious, someone with whom I could share a beer. His pragmatism appealed to me. He was determined that Raza Unida would make an impact on national U.S. politics.

José Angel did not have the single-minded religious fervor that came with César Chávez. José Angel was also more accessible. In contrast to Tijerina, he was not so focused on one particular issue; he could see that the movement must encompass the rural struggle in which he had been born, but the urban struggle as well. José Angel also understood the role of art, culture, and media in the struggle.

"We need everyone involved in the movement," he once told me. "Artists, musicians, writers, poets, *toda la bola!*"

Although years younger than Corky Gonzales, José Angel had a much more savvy understanding of the political process and of the importance of media. He understood how media could be utilized to the benefit of the Chicano Movement. Of the four leaders of the Chicano Movement, José Angel was the most pragmatic and someone that I felt I could work with.

"Well," José Angel asked over the phone, "what do you say?"

"Yes," I replied. "Of course."

I was pleased that someone had finally understood the importance of media in terms of promoting our cause and that I was the person who could do the job. But, before fully signing on, I had to let José Angel know my conditions.

"Look," I said, "I'll be glad to do this and I'll certainly get the media that you want to come to this event, but let's just be clear that politically I have to be available not only to you, but for Corky Gonzales and for Reies López Tijerina, and for anyone else who comes to the Raza Unida national convention and needs my help. This is about our people, and the only way I can honestly undertake this is if I am allowed to make my skills and talents available to all."

"I don't have any problem with that," José Angel replied. "The main thing is that we get that national coverage. Can you do that?"

"Of course," I said. "You have my word on it."

A week after my telephone call with José Angel, I had second thoughts about my being able to attend the convention. This had less to do with my desire—I was fully committed to going—and more to do with whether I could break away from my work at KCET for the long Labor Day weekend over which the convention was planned. I was feverishly editing *Yo Soy Chicano,* and already involved in planning a concert program with Daniel Valdez, which I hoped to produce for the annual celebration of Mexican Independence Day.

Nonetheless, in a letter to José Angel dated June 16, I outlined my plan for media promotion of the convention:

1) We need a "press kit" put together: two or three articles on the purpose of the convention, background information about the personalities, several 8×10 photos, and an agenda.

2) All national news and political magazines and newspapers should be personally contacted by phone as well as sending each a press kit.

3) Chicano media and film groups should be explored for the possibility of a Chicano film on the convention or at least some kind of documentation.

4) Southwest media should be invited to special "press conferences" at specific dates and times during the convention.

5) Local El Paso television and radio stations should be contacted for talk shows and news coverage.

6) The site of the convention should be cleared prior to the convention events for lighting, sound recording facilities, and for a location to hold the press conferences.

7) On the conference days, the media coordinator should be the person to whom media people can go for information and to set up interviews.

José Angel called me back immediately upon receiving the letter. His reply was brief: "Yes, go ahead and do it!"

Yo Soy Chicano Broadcast

By the end of June, *Yo Soy Chicano* was finally finished and we had sent off the two-inch videotape master to the Public Broadcasting System for national distribution. PBS had set August 8, 1972, as the national air date for *Yo Soy Chicano*. In Los Angeles, I was ready to premiere it for the local Chicano community. It was an exciting time for me, and I wasted no time in trying to publicize the show as much as I could. I called in a longtime friend, Bay-Area artist Malaquías Montoya, to design a poster for the film that would convey the sense of struggle that the film represented. Malaquías, whose poster designs went back to the Cal-Berkeley Free Speech Movement, delivered an astonishingly simple yet powerful image: a Chicano and a Chicana stood back to back, as if fending off common foes, their arms upraised in struggle, showing chains of bondage that had been broken.

The image became the poster for *Yo Soy Chicano*. I reproduced 4,000 copies of the poster and then set about distributing it to PBS stations throughout the country. More importantly, I spent several weekends placing the poster throughout East Los Angeles restaurants, shops, laundromats, and churches—anywhere I felt Chicanos might get the message that an important film was to be broadcast nationally.

The Los Angeles community premiere of *Yo Soy Chicano* was an evening I shall never forget. I had built up for this premiere for some time, determined that I would invite all of the major players in the East Los Angeles activist community. I looked forward to the evening because I knew that it would be an important time for people to assess where we were as a national movement. As a filmmaker, I was proud that at last my film was completed and the people for whom I had intended it were at last going to be able to see it.

On the night of the premiere, I converted KCET's Soundstage A into a reception area, where a couple of hundred community activists gathered and mixed for an hour before I moved them into KCET's Little Theater. There, I screened a virgin 16-mm print of the film. I had arranged for photos throughout the corridors at KCET for the evening, and a group of people arrived that represented a cross section of the activist community of East Los Angeles. I was happy that so many people had turned out and looked forward to the screening, fully expecting a resounding pat on the back from my fellow activists.

I screened the film. Throughout, I was tense and nervous. I don't recall ever being so nervous about a screening. At certain key moments, I could tell that the film had truly reached its audience as people reacted and applauded or were silent, straining to hear the narrator's words. But the biggest disappointment of the evening came after the film was over. The film credits had closed, and the music of Daniel Valdez singing *Yo Soy Chicano* had played. People in the audience stood up and were singing *Yo Soy Chicano* along with the film. When the film was over, the lights in the theater came on and there was thunderous applause. I got up to accept the applause, and I asked the audience if there were any questions.

I fully expected more accolades. Instead, a lone woman raised her hand. I recognized her as a member of the EICC and of the Barrio Defense Committee, a community police-watch organization. I acknowledged her, and she said, "I wanna know why you didn't speak of police brutality against Chicanos in this film? How can you call this a film about the Chicano experience without making any reference to police brutality?"

She spoke for about five minutes, not only criticizing me and the film, but bringing into question my loyalty to the Chicano Movement, my commitment to the struggle, wondering out loud to the public whether I hadn't sold out, whether this film was not a product of my having sold out to the system. I was devastated. Here was an important voice in my community, a woman who daily protested police brutality against Chicanos, a woman whose home was regularly visited by the police and harassed with helicopters that sprayed spotlights into her home. How could she be calling me into question?

I was speechless. At that moment I wanted to sink into the woodwork and disappear. I did not want to be there. I did not want to be a filmmaker. It was too hurtful, too unforgiving.

"How do you answer these questions?" she said, pointing a finger accusingly at me as she turned to face the audience. I had seen this tactic before. I knew that if I did not do something, others would join in the fray. Soon I would be fair game for anyone who wanted to have at me.

Then, suddenly, from the very back of the room, a high-pitched voice cried out, "How dare you? How dare you call this man into question?" Fire in her eyes, Sue Booker strode angrily down the aisle toward the woman. She raised an accusing finger, pointing it right back at the woman. Sue took a position by my side.

"I have worked with this man for two years now," Sue continued. "I have seen him struggle. I have seen him try to change a system that doesn't really care about Chicanos. I have seen him work long hours into the night to create great television for the Chicano people. How dare you bring his integrity into question? You have not been here these long hours! You have not seen this man struggle with the system! You have not seen this man as he put together this film! What do you know what it takes to make a film of this caliber? You ought to be ashamed. How dare you speak out against this man?"

The crowd rustled. It was an awkward moment. To have a Chicana criticize me was bad enough, but now to have a black woman attacking a Chicana woman in defense of me was not good politics by any stretch of the imagination. I dared not speak to take either side, nor to jump into a defense of myself. Any defensive response would be interpreted as weakness, guilty-as-charged. The icy stalemate was broken inadvertently when someone burst into the auditorium and announced in a loud voice, "The refreshments are ready." Heads turned towards the back, eager eyes looking for a way out, people not wanting to be a part of this escalating episode.

I took the opportunity to intervene. "Thank you," I said, "I appreciate your comments, and I'm sorry if I disappointed you. We can talk about it later. I want the people here to enjoy themselves for the rest of the evening. There's refreshments, and I'll be around if people want to raise any further questions. Remember to tell your friends, August 8th on KCET! Thank you." The crowd once again applauded, and we retired to Soundstage A, where I had set up refreshments and snacks.

As the evening progressed, it was clear that the woman's criticism had been the exception to the rule. Most people had loved the film, considered themselves part of it, and were proud to have been invited. *Yo Soy Chicano* aired nationally on the evening of August 8, 1972. KCET received more publicity on this one program than for any program in years. The *Los Angeles Times* called the film "a splendid work of television . . . rarely has this misbegotten medium been so skillfully and so properly used . . . *Yo Soy Chicano* captures the Chicano soul." The *Washington Post* called it "one of the truely provocative programs of the year." Luis Valdez, invited to write a review of the film for KCET's monthly magazine, was so effusive in his review that we had to retitle it "an appreciation." He said of *Yo Soy Chicano*: "It is germinal and prophetic. It is a giant fistful of seeds thrown into the growing field of Chicano filmic art."

América de los Indios

After the broadcast of *Yo Soy Chicano*, I began to prepare the second annual 16th of September special for KCET. It was to be a KCET special event, a live in-concert program featuring the music of Daniel Valdez to be simulcast with the local Pacifica radio station KPFK.

The idea for the program had originated during the production of the music track for *Yo Soy Chicano*. During our collaboration, it became clear to me that Daniel was a gifted performer with a wide repertoire that included not just Mexican classics but his own original works. Daniel and I decided that we would collaborate on a half-hour concert program that would musically do what I had done in *Yo Soy Chicano*—tell the story of the Chicano people in the United States.

During July, Daniel, his wife Armida, and their son Emiliano lived with Gayla and me in our crowded, three-room house on Sunset Drive. Despite the cramped quarters, it was an enormously creative and exhilarating time for all of us. By day and evening we would work on the music and by night we would party and talk politics. Sometimes, our tiny living room would be jammed with Danny's admirers, movement activists, and musicians, and he would give impromptu concerts that would last into the wee hours. Intermittently staying with us were the musicians who would accompany Daniel in the concert: guitarists Yolanda Castillo, Sal and Ernesto Bravo, and bass player Ben Cadena.

For Daniel and me, it was an important time of bonding. We spoke of continuing our collaboration together in the future. Once again, Daniel suggested that I should move from Los Angeles and join him and his brother and become a member of the El Teatro Campesino in San Juan Bautista.

América de los Indios was taped in mid-August with an in-studio audience of friends and admirers. The program began with Danny entoning, "How can we tell the story of the Chicano, of the Mexicano, of the mestizo?" His first song was a plaintive song/poem he had written titled "América," which told of the conquest of the native American population in Mexico by the Spanish. Next, he turned to the *corrido* (ballad) form and sang of the immigrant experience and the settling of the Southwest by Mexican Americans. The high point of the concert was Danny's rendition of José Montoya's poem "El Louie," set to music. The poem, based on the real life of a Korean war veteran who had personified the pachuco lifestyle, was a testament to Chicano urban survival. Interlaced with classic Mexican *boleros* (love songs) of the fifties, it was the hit of the concert. Danny concluded the concert with an original song, "América de los Indios," in which he linked the struggle of Chicanos in the United States to the struggle of other indigenous peoples throughout Latin America:

América de los Indios,
Siglo explosivo llegó,
Ya van bajando los pueblos
Hacia la liberacion

He cited the present as the explosive century in which the Amerindian masses would descend from their mountain homes to take up the armed struggle for their liberation. It was, in song, what Siqueiros's *América Tropical* had been in mural painting: a denunciation of historical atrocities and an affirmation of survival and struggle. The show was a resounding success. After the performance, my friend from the Diez-y-Seis show, José Luis Ruiz, pulled me aside. In the past year, José Luis had moved from KABC to KNBC, where he was now hosting a local weekly talk show, *Impacto*. José Luis was taken by Danny's performance. He told me he would approach KNBC to do a similar kind of show, but he wanted to showcase the entire El Teatro Campesino on national television. I encouraged him: "To get the *teatro* on a major national network would be terrific!"

Planning a Media Campaign

Concurrent with the rehearsals and preparations for the taping of the *América de los Indios* concert, I dedicated myself to making good the promise I had made to José Angel Gutiérrez about handling media for the national convention. I began with the most obvious: compiling mailing lists. I researched lists of major newspapers in the United States and then took these lists and refined them to include the newspapers in the cities that had sizeable numbers of Latino and Mexican American populations. I added to this all major national public affairs and news magazines. At the end of my survey, I had a pretty elaborate listing of every major newspaper and magazine in the United States that was published in cities with a reasonable population of Mexican Americans. This became my print-media mailing list.

I undertook a similar process with respect to television and radio. When I was finished, I had a listing of key television stations with the names of the program managers or news directors, as well as the names of significant radio stations in both English and Spanish languages and the names of the news directors in each one.

I had my target audience. Now I began to work on the press kit that I knew I had to send to them. Although I had never designed a press kit, I had seen many and knew what it should contain: press releases, photos, and background articles.

I asked permission from Dr. Richard Santillán, a party supporter who had recently published three articles on the rise of La Raza Unida Party in *Commonweal* magazine, for permission to reprint the articles in the press kit. He graciously agreed.

I acquired from José Angel articles appearing in the *San Antonio Express,* the *San Antonio Light,* and other Texas newspapers about the party successes in Crystal City. When finished, the prototype of the press kit was a two-sided folder that included reprints of Richard Santillán's three articles, reprints of other articles that appeared in the *Nation* magazine and local Texas newspapers; three press releases profiling the rise of La Raza Unida Party; and profiles on key personalities expected to attend. The bios included José Angel Gutiérrez, Reies López Tijerina, Corky Gonzales, and César Chávez (José Angel had sent out invitations to the three other leaders to attend).

By this time I had become a fixture at KCET and had full access to all station facilities, night and day and on weekends. During the next two months, I began to use station facilities and resources, in my own mind, *for la causa.* As the date of the national convention neared, I found myself spending entire weekends at the station, duplicating copies of the press kit I had designed, using KCET's photocopy machine and paper. It was a massive undertaking. Through it all, Gayla was at my side, copy-editing, duplicating, and helping to collate and staple.

By mid-July, I had compiled upwards of three hundred press kits. Each press kit had the articles, the press releases, and several photos (courtesy of a sympathetic photographer who agreed to mass produce the photos at a cut rate for me).

The next step was a massive mailing. One Saturday, Gayla and I spent the entire day stuffing the press kits into KCET envelopes and addressing them to national newspapers, television and radio stations. The next Monday, I made a deal with friends at KCET's shipping department to mail the articles bulk rate at the station's expense.

Although all of this was done without the overt knowledge of any of the KCET executives, word soon filtered back to the powers that be of Treviño's weekend marathons. One day while having coffee with Chuck Allen, he abruptly asked me, "Are you taking up another profession?"

"Huh?" I replied, not certain what he was getting at.

"I've heard you may wish to work full-time for the Xerox Corporation, and are spending your weekends doing on-the-job training." Suddenly I knew what he was getting at. Chuck spared me the embarrassment of having to explain anything. He simply said, "Are you finished yet?"

"Yep, all done."

That was the end of that.

A National *Congreso*

As the convention approached, I became concerned that I would not be able to deliver the national media I had promised for the convention. My fears centered on the way in which the national media perceived Chicanos and our activities. Unlike African Americans, who were well known as a minority group to key decision-makers in New York or in Washington, D.C., Chicanos were in many ways the "invisible" minority. These decision-makers understood that African Americans were an important minority because they saw them every day—on the street, at the airport, in the subway, in the local news.

Because of the regional concentration of Mexican Americans in the Southwest, however, we were not visible in large numbers in cities like New York or Washington, D.C., where important decisions were made about national programming and government. We were the "invisible minority" as was evident from our lack of presence on television and on the large screen. All of this convinced me that I could not count on the national media to cover the convention unless we had something to draw them in. I felt this national coverage was important in order to reach out to our own people. In July, I called José Angel to discuss the matter.

"We need a hook to make this convention worthy of national attention," I told him.

"Chuy, we're going to have two or three thousand people from all over the United States. What more do they want? Isn't that newsworthy enough?"

"In an ideal world, yes," I replied, "but we're living in the United States of America."

"What do you recommend?"

I knew I was about to step into dangerous territory. Months earlier, José Angel Gutiérrez had penned an open letter to the National Chicano Political Caucus held in San Jose, California, in which he had argued for gaining leverage from the Democratic and Republican parties by negotiating concessions from a position of power. The letter had inspired much controversy, with many Raza Unida activists labeling Gutiérrez an opportunist. Gutiérrez had been trying to live down these accusations by assuring people that he stood for an independent party, much as did Corky Gonzales.

"The Chicano vote did the trick for Kennedy in 1960," I said. I knew that John F. Kennedy's presidential victory could not have happened without his victory in the South, and the South in turn, had been assured by his success in Texas. It was the Mexican-American vote that had made the difference in Texas.

"I think we should leak the idea that the party is going to endorse McGovern for his presidential bid. Now, that would be a national story. What are we, fifteen million? How's this for an evening news headline: Fifteen Million Mexican Americans to Support McGovern."

"But we're not going to do that," he fired back to me instantly.

Unknown to me at the time, José Angel had already convened a meeting with a young McGovern aide, who had spiritedly tried to convince José Angel that La Raza Unida should, indeed, lend its support to the McGovern bid for the presidency. José Angel had flatly told the brash young man with ambitious political aspirations that this was out of the question. Only later would José Angel appreciate the extent of Bill Clinton's ambition.

"I'm not saying we DO IT," I added hastily. "I'm saying we tell the press we MIGHT DO IT. That's all we need to do to get them there."

José Angel was quiet as he considered the idea.

"Corky's not going to like this," he said.

I was aware at the time that there was considerable tension between José Angel and Corky Gonzales. Corky, from the beginning, was an adamant ideologue and felt that La Raza Unida, in keeping with the *Plan de Aztlán,* should be a separatist, independent organization. José Angel also felt the organization should be separatist, but he saw the value in trying to attract mass media attention to our cause. He felt it important to highlight the potential that Latinos might represent as a national power bloc with respect to the upcoming presidential election in November.

Finally, pragmatism won out.

"Let's do it," he said.

I wasted no time in making personal phone calls to the heads of the news departments at the networks, as well as to Associated Press and U.P.I., to let them know that reliable sources had it that the convention would end up endorsing George McGovern for the U.S. presidency.

My calls immediately piqued the interest of the national news media. My office was deluged with calls. I received phone calls from the news departments at ABC, NBC, and CBS, as well as the public affairs series *NPACT*, the National Public Affairs Center for Television, requesting information about the upcoming convention. The calls got to be so much of a problem that when I published the final press release for the convention, I gave the name of Jaime Aguirre, a local El Paso Raza Unida activist, as the contact person.

The matter came to a head two weeks before the national convention as more and more news people decided that they would attend the convention. In addition to reporters from the dozens of movement newspapers, such as *El Grito Del Norte, La Raza, La Nueva Vida,* and others, the *L.A. Times* was sending Frank del Olmo, who had taken Ruben Salazar's place as the Chicano observer on the scene.

I had already gotten commitments from ABC, NBC, and CBS news. Sander Vanocur, who was the anchor for the PBS *NPACT* program, had also committed to come to the convention. I was delighted, of course, because I felt that we were going to get national recognition, and it placed me in a particularly unique position of being able to coordinate it all.

Beyond *Yo Soy Chicano*

In early August of 1972, Chuck Allen prepared to launch a major news department at KCET that would be competitive with the news departments of the local network stations. While KCET did not have the resources to sustain a daily news program, such as the evenings news on the local ABC, NBC, and CBS affiliates, it did have the resources to produce a weekly news show. What Allen envisioned was a weekly news program that would explore in-depth issues that were only covered superficially on the evening news. He saw the show as pulling on the strength of the different interests and talents of the producers at KCET. It was to be eclectic, diverse, and provocative. The program was to be called *The L.A. Collective.*

To accomplish this, he pulled together the producers who had previously worked in the human affairs, cultural affairs, and news departments. He called us together one day in September to explain the new approach and introduce us to the person who would be the new executive producer of the program, Larry Howell. Sue Booker, myself, and the other producers on staff—Taylor Hackford, Lynn Littman, Nancy Salter, Price Hicks, Terri Francis, Ed Moreno, Allan Baker, and Mark Waxman—would henceforth be reporter/producers for the news department. The show would be weekly, and Chuck hoped that our version of the news would be more hardhitting and provocative than the daily news fare seen on the commercial stations. In effect, our competition was to be the local networks in Los Angeles: ABC, NBC, and CBS.

After the meeting, Sue Booker and I went out for coffee. We were troubled by the direction that the meeting had taken. Most of the other producers were excited about this new innovation. Starting a new department, with such an eclectic and diverse approach, was exciting. The producers looked forward to working together and creating something that would put KCET on the evening news map. But Sue Booker and I had other concerns.

During the time I had produced *Yo Soy Chicano*, Sue had sold PBS on the idea of producing a national news and public affairs centered on Black American themes. She had established an office, news bureau, and a remote studio in Central Los Angeles from which she planned to broadcast a weekly program titled *Storefront*. I was taken by her example, and, remembering the *Ahora!* experience, wanted to produce a weekly Chicano show.

Chuck's plan for an innovative news show, of which Sue and I were to be a part, would draw us away from producing programs specifically for our communities. Sue was well on her way to producing her series, but I had just begun to raise the issue of a Chicano series with Chuck, when he announced the formation of *The L.A. Collective.*

The next day I arranged to meet with Chuck Allen. I explained that while I was open to our working as individual producers under Larry Howell, I did not feel that this assignment should be the full extent of my work. Instead, I felt that the station should provide direct programming to the Chicano community in Los Angeles.

"Don't you think Mexican Americans should be part of mainstream America?" Chuck asked pointedly.

"Of course," I replied, "but I also think Chicanos need specific programming to address their specific concerns."

Chuck argued that by including stories about Mexican Americans as part of KCET's weekly news program, the station would, in effect, indicate that these stories were worthy of being known by all Los Angeles, not just minority audiences. "What happens in this city to blacks and Chicanos should be of importance to all Angelenos," he said.

"We need a platform for Latino to speak to Latino," I replied, "a place where we can discuss, debate and explore our issues, our topics, our lives—in house."

"Your suggestion?" he said looking to me.

This was going to be the tricky part.

"I propose a weekly magazine format program directed at the Chicano community of Los Angeles."

"And you would produce this show?"

"Sure, as well as any news segments you may want me to produce for *The L.A. Collective.*"

Chuck was silent. I could tell he didn't like the idea because it undercut something that he had been planning for some time and for which he had great hopes. He may have even been hurt that I was not buying into what he hoped would be the biggest booster the station had ever seen.

"Let me think about it," he finally said.

With that I left.

Two days later, Chuck Allen sent me a memo replying to my request. In terse language, he reiterated his hopes that the new mainstream program would be able to incorporate stories about all the communities in Los Angeles. I was to be a producer/reporter under

Larry Howell's direction and deliver these reports for the new mainstream news program. My request for a separate program directed at
the Chicano community was denied.

I was severely disappointed. I conferred with Ed Moreno, still on
staff at KCET, about what to do next. We both believed that our community needed something more than an occasional story on a weekly
broadcast through KCET. To convince Chuck was the big question.
How could I do this? I had tried a reasoned approach and had failed.
It seemed the only option left was for me to accept his decision or
escalate the discussion to another level. While I did not relish the idea
of making this a *causa célebre,* neither was I willing to accept Chuck
Allen's decision. I knew what the Chicano community needed, and,
like it or not, I felt I had to fight for it.

I asked Moreno if he would support my efforts to fight for a Chicano series. He said he would. I began to speak to other Latino
employees at KCET. By now, three years since I had started at KCET,
the employment of minorities had grown. Instead of Sue being the
only African American, now there were several working in different
departments at the station. Instead of Ed Moreno and me being the
only Latinos, we now had several Latinos working in the mail room,
as technicians and as cameramen. Still reeling from the nationalism I
had absorbed during the production of *Yo Soy Chicano,* I felt I had
nothing to lose and decided to put everything at stake. I asked every
Spanish-surnamed employee at KCET to sign a letter I had written to
Chuck Allen. The letter called for the creation of a weekly magazine
format to address the needs of the Chicano community in Los Angeles. If this request was not honored, the letter affirmed that the under-
signed employees would go on strike and bring Chicano community
organizations to picket the station until such a series was created.

It was a brash, desperate move. To my surprise, every Spanish-
surnamed person at KCET, more than a dozen people, actually signed
the letter—they agreed to quit if the need arose! This was unprecedented. Securing the signatures was a feat in itself, but to get a commitment to quit—that was unheard of. I knew that many of the Latinos in question had families to support, children to get through
school. It was quite astounding and, in retrospect, an incredible

moment of solidarity that the dozen or so Latino employees at KCET would all be willing to give up their jobs in order to prove to the station that what we really wanted was a weekly television show.

I met once again with Chuck Alien. It was an excruciating moment for both of us. In the past three years, we had become good friends. We often lunched together, we joked together. We valued each other's intelligence, wit, and humor. Chuck would often visit my office unannounced and would plop himself down and proceed to talk for an hour or more. Now I was threatening Chuck with a letter and a picket line.

I placed the letter on Chuck's desk. He read the signatures, sat back for a moment, and then a long, painful silence ensued. He was stunned. He looked at me. I was silent, awaiting a reply. He reread the petition. He looked at me again. It was an ugly moment.

Finally, he said, "I don't like being held up."

"I don't like holding you up," I replied.

More silence.

"What are you going to call the show?"

I left the meeting elated. Chuck had agreed to a weekly Chicano series on KCET! In the meantime, August 27 loomed close at hand, and with it, the first national convention of the Raza Unida Party.

Chapter Fourteen

La Raza Unida Party

Political liberation can come only through independent action on our part, since the two-party system is the same animal with two heads that feeds from the same trough.
—El Plan Espiritual de Aztlán

Across the table from me, José Angel Gutiérrez used a key to pop open another bottle of *Carta Blanca*.

"Another beer," he said, making it more of a statement than a question as he slid the beer across the table to me.

"You're out to get me shitfaced," I replied, accepting the brew. This was the fifth beer I had drunk since my arrival in El Paso only a few hours earlier, and I could feel the alcohol getting to me.

Since my interview with him for *Yo Soy Chicano* almost a year earlier, José Angel and I had become friends. We were seated in his spacious suite on the ninth floor of the Paso del Norte Hotel in downtown El Paso, Texas. With us was an old friend of mine from EICC days, Carlos Muñoz. One of the organizers of the 1968 student walkouts and one of those arrested as the "L.A. 13," Carlos was now a professor of political science at the University of California at Irvine and a Raza Unida partisan. Also in the room was Mario Compeán, the handsome, charismatic chair of the Texas La Raza Unida Party and an original founder, along with José Angel, of the Mexican-American Youth Organization (MAYO).

Carlos and I had arrived early for the national convention of La Raza Unida Party, scheduled for the week of August 30 through September 4. The green light given to me on the proposed new Chicano series at KCET had freed me of money worries. I now had a budget to work with. Instead of having to rely on others to pay for my trip to the convention, I was able to pay my way and that of my film crew, made up of the new cinematographer at KCET, Dick Davies (camera), and Martín Quiroz (sound). The filming of the Raza Unida convention was to be one of the first programs in the new series. Although the series would be largely in-studio, I had made a convincing argument for the need to cover the convention in 16-mm film, and had been given the go-ahead to bring a film crew. While at the convention, I would be wearing two hats, that of news reporter for KCET and that of national media coordinator for the *partido*. It did not strike me in the least that these two roles might be a conflict of interest.

The three of us flew to El Paso, loaded down with camera equipment. On arrival at the convention headquarters in the Paso del Norte Hotel, Dick Davies and Martín downloaded the equipment and scouted the hotel lobby for possible filming sites while I joined José Angel in his suite. First up, he informed me about lodging arrangements.

"I reserved a room for you next door," he said, "so that you can be close by. It'll help us coordinate all this media business."

"José Angel," I told him, "we're friends, but I can't really do this. I should remain impartial. My role at the convention should be to be responsive not just to your needs, but also to those of Corky or Reies, or anyone else who feels that there is some media job that needs to be done. My skills are for everyone." I told him that I had already secured rooms for me and my film crew on another floor of the hotel.

"Fine," José Angel agreed reluctantly. "Whatever you want to do, that's fine with me, but I still want you to do the press releases when we need them."

I said, "That's what I'm here for. But, you know, I could do with some help. Do you have anybody on your staff who can work with me as an assistant media coordinator? Preferably someone who knows this city."

"I'll see what I can do," he replied. Then he handed me a list of names. "Take a look at this. These are some of the people who have been invited to speak at the convention."

I scanned the sheet of paper: Dr. Ralph Abernathy, head of the Southern Christian Leadership Conference; Coretta Scott King, the widow of the late Martín Luther King, Jr.; Reies López Tijerina of the Alianza; Ramsey Muñíz, the Raza Unida candidate for governor of Texas; San Antonio Bishop Patricio Flores; and Lt. Governor Robert Mondragón of New Mexico. Conspicuously absent was the name of César Chávez. I asked José Angel about this.

"We sent a letter to Chávez," he explained. "We invited him to speak, but only about the Chicano Movement. We didn't want him stumping for McGovern." I knew that Chávez and the United Farm Workers' Union had already endorsed George McGovern's bid for the presidency. "I guess he didn't like that. He turned down our invitation."

José Angel went on to say that this was probably for the better, since Corky Gonzalez didn't feel someone who had already come out in support of a Democrat should be speaking at the convention. "And I agree with Corky. Chávez has chosen his side."

Just then there was a knock on the door. Since I was the closest to the door, I got up and opened the door. I was shocked by what I saw.

Standing before me was a young Chicana, not more than twenty years old. She was wearing a traditional *india poblana* white dress with colorful red-and-green trim on the shoulders and on the hem. Straight brown hair, dangling to her shoulders and cut in bangs across her forehead, framed a face that was as innocent as it was distressed. The white dress was covered with a large blob of dried blood, an eerie high-relief Rorschach that extended from the neckline to below her waist. As she stood before me, her eyes welled with tears, and she opened her mouth to speak. Her voice was so strained as to be almost inaudible.

"They've just killed my husband," she said in a whisper.

It took a moment for her words to register. I didn't know who she was or what she was talking about, only that the woman before me was clearly in shock. I opened the door wider and pulled her inside. "Come in, come in."

I sat her down in a nearby chair. José Angel, close by, saw she was covered with blood and immediately came over.

"What's happened?" José Angel asked.

"They've just killed my husband, Ricardo," she repeated through sobs. "We're from Colorado. We were coming to the convention. We were coming to the convention."

By now we were all gathered around her. We listened to her story. Her name was Priscilla Falcón. She was part of Corky's delegation from Colorado. She and several other of Corky's people had been traveling together. The car they were driving had overheated, and they had pulled into a gas station in the desert town of Oro Grande, New Mexico, to get water. The gas station owner had told her husband that he could not use the station's water hose unless he bought gas. Ricardo had cooled down his engine with the station's water, anyway. The gas station owner had gone into his office, returned with a hand gun, and shot Ricardo several times, killing him.

These events had transpired not more than an hour earlier, and Priscilla had been driven down to El Paso from Oro Grande to get help.

"You need to see Corky," Mario Compeán said, thoughtful of movimiento protocol. "He'll get you an attorney."

José Angel and Mario ushered the young woman out of the suite and to the bank of elevators down the hallway (Corky and the Colorado delegates were on a different floor of the hotel). Carlos and I stood at the door, still reeling from the sight of this young woman drenched in blood. As she, José Angel, and Mario waited for the elevator, I could hear her repeating softly to herself, "They've killed my husband."

Carlos Muñoz and I exchanged looks. Welcome to El Paso.

That evening, I helped the Colorado delegation prepare a telegram detailing the tragic events at Oro Grande. By then we had learned that the gas station owner, Perry Brunson, had not been held by the police from nearby Alamogordo, New Mexico, but rather had been released on his own recognizance without having to post bond. The telegram was sent to President Richard Nixon at the White House, Attorney General Richard Kleindienst, George McGovern, and Lt. Gov. Robert Mondragón of New Mexico. The statement read in part:

Because Richard Falcón did not buy gas and because Falcón was using the station's water, he was shot twice and killed. This brutal murder is another dark day in the history of White America. Cannot an American citizen obtain emergency services in an American city, American roads, without fear for his life? Cannot a Chicano attend a political convention without fear for his life? The national office of La Raza Unida Party and all the state delegates present hereby demand an immediate federal investigation into this wanton racist murder. The Perry Brunsons of America must be brought to justice.

Death over Water

The next morning, Thursday, Dick, Martín, and I strategized over breakfast. The hotel was astir with news of Ricardo Falcón's death, and I knew that I would need footage of the fateful death scene for the documentary. I thought of the dramatic recreations I had done in *Yo Soy Chicano* and suggested that we go to Oro Grande and recreate, impressionistically, the shooting of Falcón. Dick and Martín instantly agreed. We piled into the station wagon we had rented and drove to Oro Grande. We arrived in less than an hour.

The town of Oro Grande was little more than a cluster of buildings located along two-lane Highway 54 between Alamogordo, New Mexico, and El Paso, Texas. The Chevron gas station was on the main highway, the tall Chevron mast visible for miles. As we approached, we discussed how we might film the station. We didn't know if Perry Brunson would be there. We knew that other news crews had already been there, but they were local news people, doubtless known to Brunson. We, on the other hand, were clearly an all-Chicano crew (physically, Dick Davies passed as a Chicano). Would we be asked to leave, once Brunson saw the camera? I didn't want to risk not getting the footage we needed. We decided to load up the camera and start filming as we drove into the gas station. While Martín would pump gas, Dick and I would film until we were kicked out.

We put our plan into action. We drove into the station with the camera rolling. I opened the door, and Dick walked out with the camera on his shoulder, filming the bullet holes in the shattered window panes of the office. Evidently Brunson had shot at least two rounds through the glass window.

As we filmed, a friendly young man came out of the garage area of the station and went directly to the pump that Martín was using. He greeted Martín with a smile. When he saw that Martín seemed to have things under control, the young man started washing our car windows, quite oblivious to the filming that Dick and I were doing. We filmed shots of the entire gas station, including the dripping water hose that Falcón had been holding when he was shot. When we were finished, we paid the young man and asked if Brunson was about.

"Nah, he's laying low since all that controversy started. I just take care of the station for him."

We thanked him and prepared to leave. As I was getting back into the station wagon, I noticed a brown stain on the cement near my foot. I bent down and examined it. It was dried blood.

Throughout the day, delegates continued to stream into the Paso del Norte Hotel located in the civic center area of El Paso. The lobby of the hotel was converted into an impromptu registration area. I spent much of the afternoon preparing press releases for the next day and welcoming reporters from a variety of national and local newspapers. I noted that the *L.A. Times,* the *Washington Post,* the *Texas Observer,* the *New York Times,* the *Chicago Tribune* had all sent reporters. In addition to Public Broadcasting's National Public Affairs Center for Television (NPACT), CBS, ABC, and NBC had also sent film crews who were busy filming delegates in the hotel lobby.

The Convention Begins

The next morning, Friday, September 1, the first meeting of the convention was convened in the gymnasium of Sacred Heart Church, located in the *Segundo Barrio* (Second Ward) section of El Paso's South Side. I got up early and helped set up the press conference, which we scheduled in a classroom immediately adjacent to the gymnasium. I had already announced to the assembled press that the convention would convene regular press conferences each morning at 10 a.m.—the Falcón press conference turned out to be the first. The morning was electric with energy as convention delegates poured into the gymnasium. Dick placed Mole-Richardson lights along each side of the stage and placed the camera on its tripod right in the middle of the gymnasium floor—from here we could get a good shot of anyone in the room. Martín set up fixed microphones at the speakers' podium and prepared to cover audience sound with the Sennheiser shotgun mike. José Angel, shadowed by Texas Brown Berets, was conferring with state delegates at the front of the room. He looked up, saw that I and the film crew had arrived, and called me to the front of the room.

"You asked for me to get you someone to help out with the media. Well, here he is."

I turned, and to my surprise, he introduced me to a young man of about twenty-three years of age with a familiar goatee, mustache, and a broad smile. It was Antonio Parra, the film studies major I had first met on my location scout in El Paso a year earlier. A Raza Unida activist, he had volunteered to help out at the convention. It was great seeing Antonio again, and we immediately renewed our friendship. I discovered that Antonio had graduated from UTEP in June and was looking for employment in television production.

In a short while, José Angel opened the convention by introducing the El Paso poet whom I had also met on my earlier visit to El Paso: Abelardo Delgado. The beefy poet read a brief, inspiring poem dedicated to La Raza Unida Party and concluded his reading with explosive shouts of "Viva La Raza" and "Que Viva Aztlán!" The audience erupted in shouts and applause. Next, José Angel asked state party delegates to introduce themselves so that the credentials committee could begin its work compiling national party membership. From our vantage point on the gymnasium floor, we were able to film each state delegate as he or she rose to identify himself or herself.

Soon, it was time for the Colorado press conference to begin. We mounted the Eclair in handheld mode on Dick's shoulder and I guided him, walking from the gymnasium into the adjacent room as José Angel announced the beginning of the Colorado press conference on the murder of Ricardo Falcón.

The press conference was packed. I recognized a few of the reporters—Sander Vanocur from NPACT, Frank Del Olmo from the

Los Angeles Times, Sam Kushner of *People's World,* Tony Castro from the *Texas Observer,* as well as several local and national news crews.

Priscilla Falcón sat in the center of a table, flanked by Corky Gonzales, looking grave and harried, and by a diminutive young man with flowing, shoulder-length hair and thick, black-framed glasses. Behind them, two of Corky's bodyguards stood, grim-faced and cross-armed, against the chalkboard. The young man cleared his throat and all eyes focused on him.

"I am Francisco Martínez," he said. "I am an attorney. I am one of a team that has been investigating this matter. At this time we have conducted a preliminary investigation. We have several matters we would like to relate to the public at this time." The bank of reporters jotted down his words. There were several news crews there, and the cameras started rolling. I stood aside, making sure Dick Davies had a good shot of the table and the speakers.

Martínez continued. "I believe everyone has focused on this event at Oro Grande. Our investigation shows that it is a small town. When the incident happened, the authorities failed to act or cooperate in any matter with our people. The facts, as we understand them, are that there was a caravan of a couple of cars that was coming down from Colorado to the convention. The car in which Mr. Falcón was riding was overheating. They arrived at the Chevron station, and they arrived to cool the radiator off. The owner, Mr. Brunson, got very angry at this. There were words between one of the occupants of the car and Mr. Brunson. We do know that there was a struggle. We do know that there were four shots fired from a .38 Chief Special belonging to Mr. Brunson. Two shots hit Mr. Falcón. There is an autopsy report that has not been released yet."

Martínez went on to chastise the lack of cooperation from the Alamogordo police and civic authorities. Then it was time for Priscilla to speak.

A hush fell over the room as Martínez handed Priscilla the table microphone. Dick instinctively moved in closer, positioning the camera lens only inches from Priscilla's tearful face.

"I would like to say that since I have been here on Wednesday and from what I have been able to see, I know, I know in my heart and in my soul that my husband was murdered. The town of Oro Grande and Alamogordo helped Mr. Brunson in every way that they could with the murder because no attempt of any kind of help was given to my husband. Today, we went to Alamogordo to meet with the district attorney, and he implied that I should not ask him any questions about my husband because I did not know the law of the state of New Mexico. I have no right to question him about my husband. He was murdered in Oro Grande over water, and how do I explain this to my son?"

Next, Corky Gonzales spoke. He reiterated the concern of the Colorado delegation that justice be done, that Falcón's murderer be brought to justice. He read a statement from the Colorado delegation that addressed charges made by local radio and television reporters, clearly sympathetic to Brunson, who alleged that the shooting had been instigated by Falcón, that Perry Brunson had fired warning shots, that Falcón had approached him menacingly, that Brunson had shot in self-defense. The Colorado statement read:

> In response to the coverage given by the press, we state:
> 1) Perry Brunson through his actions provoked the incident that led to the death of Ricardo Falcón. Falcón did not attack Brunson.
> 2) No threats of reprisal were made to Brunson by Falcón's group.
> 3) Of the shots fired, all were in rapid succession. Brunson did not fire warning shots.
> 4) Finally, the death of our brother Ricardo Falcón can in no way be justified. It was a racist act of cold-blooded murder and should be known as such.

After the press conference, we returned to the convention plenary in the gymnasium to find that the thousand-plus delegates had split into state delegations to hammer out a variety of positions on issues that would make up the party platform. We filmed the New Mexico, California, and Colorado delegations as they met to discuss a variety of issues that ranged from support of the Farm Workers' Union to land grants, the status of illegal aliens, and others.

Amid Cactus and Mesquite

That afternoon, the convention moved from the Sacred Heart gymnasium to Liberty Hall, a meeting hall located in El Paso's civic center not far from the Paso del Norte Hotel. There, José Angel gave the welcoming speech. He spoke in Spanish, his words passionate, stirring, and electrifying.

"Crystal City began this party without dreams of this day and without visions of seeing so many people—without the hope of finding so much brotherhood and unity," he said, gesturing emphatically with his hands. "We began the party humbly, as a tactic. Out there, among the cactus, under the mesquite trees, where the gringos used to have us cowered, and where now it is *they* who are terrified of us!"

The audience roared with approval.

José Angel now shifted to English. He cautioned convention delegates to act expediently. "We are wasting time if we think we are here to build a national party, if we still have divided state delegations. If we do not have state parties, there is no national party. We must not and cannot afford the luxury of petty bickering on minute rhetorical points in this convention. We must display not who is more of a Chicano but just simply who doesn't have to debate what is a Chicano."

Next, José Angel introduced Corky Gonzales. The head of the Colorado delegation was dressed in black slacks and a red shirt; like the other Colorado delegates, he wore a black arm band in memory of Ricardo Falcón. Corky looked muscular, self-assured, determined. He and José Angel embraced momentarily, then Corky turned to the audience.

"The Chicano Movement some years ago was considered an impossible dream," he said. "La Raza Unida was considered an impossible dream. This is a historic day for everyone who is here. And maybe everybody's name will not go down in the history books, but you've taken part in creating history."

More applause. Corky went on to declare that La Raza Unida Party had to stay clear of both political parties, which had proven themselves incapable of addressing Chicano needs. "So we say, there is a monster with two heads that eats from the same trough." The applause of the convention delegates thundered through the auditorium. They were alive with enthusiasm and ready to get the convention going. José Angel next undertook some housekeeping chores. Explaining that we would move to the El Paso City Coliseum the next day, where the agenda would turn to defining the issues that would make up state party platforms and where elections would be held for national party chairman.

That evening, I conspired to arrange for a three-way private conversation with the three movement leaders in a hotel room I had reserved especially for this purpose. I had previously spoken to José Angel, Corky, and Tijerina separately, and they had each agreed to be part of this unprecedented film event. This is where I intended to scoop the other media. Only my film would contain a behind-the-scenes look at the three party leaders as they conversed and shaped the party's future.

As Dick and Martín set up the camera and sound in the room I had reserved for the interview, I went to José Angel's suite to corral him and the Texas candidate for governor, Ramsey Muñíz. After some stalling, I managed to get them to head down to the hotel room.

Next, I sought out Tijerina's room in the hotel and knocked on the door. Looking preoccupied, he opened the door.

"Reies, I'm ready to film the discussion between you and Corky and José Angel," I said. "They're waiting."

Tijerina shook his head, adamantly. I could see anger in his eyes. "I can't do the interview with them," he said. "I'll be willing to do a interview with you, but it has to be alone. You let me know when you want to do it, and I will be there." With that he closed the door in my face.

I was dumbfounded. I stood in front of the closed door for a moment, trying to figure out why his mood had changed so drastically and in such a short time. Only yesterday, he had assured me he would be available for the film session and had even jotted it down in his pocket calendar. Now, suddenly, he didn't want to speak to me.

I returned to the hotel room and approached José Angel.

"Tijerina's not coming," I told him. "He agreed to do this thing yesterday, and now he's copping out."

"He and Corky got into a fight," he responded.

"What?"

José Angel explained that he and Corky had met with Tijerina in Corky's room earlier in the day, and that a dispute had broken out between Corky and Tijerina over leadership of the party. Originally, the two had agreed that Corky would run for national chairman of the party and that Tijerina would be the presiding chair of the *congreso* de Aztlán, the executive steering council. But now, Tijerina was questioning Corky's leadership, saying that he did not know how to deal with rural people and could not speak proper Spanish. Tijerina should be the one to lead the *partido*. Corky, in turn, told Tijerina that there was no substance to his talks, no plans for the party, and that it was Tijerina who was unqualified to lead. Corky now wanted to be both national chairman of the party *and* presiding chair of the *congreso* de Aztlán, the position originally envisioned for Tijerina. At this point, Tijerina had stomped out of the room, announcing he would return to New Mexico. José Angel had then told Corky that he could not allow Corky to be both head of the party and head of the *congreso* de Aztlán. Although he had not considered it before, José Angel decided on the spot that he would run against Corky for national chairman of the party. It was clear that party chairman and presiding chairman of the *congreso* were, for practical purposes, the same thing.

"You're going to run against Corky?" I asked.

José Angel nodded. "I'm going to ask Raúl Ruiz to chair the convention, since I won't be able to do that and organize a campaign as well."

All of this was sudden, startling news to me.

With José Angel and Corky now squaring off against one another, I wondered how the informal discussion I had planned in the hotel room would proceed. I was surprised they even wanted to go through with it. José Angel seemed to read my mind.

"Corky and I still want to give you the interviews you need," he said. "We appreciate what you're doing here at the convention."

Just then, Corky arrived, looking nervous and uncomfortable. José Angel returned into the room, freeing me to greet Corky and usher him and his bodyguards into the small hotel room. Corky settled onto the one bed in the room; José Angel sat next to him. There was clearly a tension between them, but hell, they were here and still willing to give me my scoop. Across from them, seated in chairs, were Ramsey Muñíz and Carlos Muñoz. Also present was Oscar Castillo, a still photographer for *La Raza* magazine in Los Angeles. I asked him to help document the historic meeting. I sat on the floor, allowing Dick Davies and Martín ample floor space to move the shotgun microphone and to direct the camera either at me, José Angel, Corky, or the other participants in the discussion. Oscar and Corky's bodyguards peered out of the bathroom, trying not to get in the way of the camera.

I first asked about La Raza Unida's relationship with the older Mexican-American political groups, such as the League of United Latino-American Citizens, the G.I. Forum, and the Mexican-American Political Association.

"I have taken the care and want to continue to take the care to try to get at all of these groups," José Angel replied. "The LULACs, those people in the barrios and the students at the universities. La Raza Unida should go after all of them."

Next I asked about coalitions. Should Raza Unida work out coalitions with other ethnic groups?

Ramsey Muñíz answered this one. He was ruggedly handsome, light-skinned, sporting Elvis sideburns and a thick Texas drawl—one could easily have mistaken him for an Anglo. When he jumped from English into Spanish, however, there was no mistaking his distinctive Mexican identity.

"Let me give you an example that occurred recently just about two weeks ago," he said. "Dr. Ralph Abernathy and the widow of Dr. Martín Luther King came down and gave us their endorsement down here in the state of Texas. Now, when I spoke about an endorsement from them, when I spoke about a black and brown coalition on a statewide basis, to our own people, they did not understand it. They would say the blacks are getting everything. Well, the blacks aren't getting any more than we are. So we have to go to that stage, to educate our people, to tell them that we both have a common problem, that we are *all* oppressed."

Next, I asked about the role of the *partido* and Latin America. What was to be the relationship between Chicanos and our brothers and sisters to the south?

"We've met with the president of Mexico," José Angel replied, "from the point of view of Crystal City, one of the communities where we are firmly entrenched. That has been discussed. There has been curiosity in the movement among Chicanos about Cuba. There have been some trips. People have gone to China and so on. There have been cultural exchanges taking place and educational conferences and this sort of thing. I think we all agree." He looked to Corky for confirmation, ". . . that it is a priority because they are brothers, they are Raza. But we must have our own nation here. We have to organize our own backyard before we go trying to organize anyone else's backyard."

Both men were trying hard to put their personal rivalry behind them for the sake of the camera. The appearance was one of comrades working together.

"On top of that," José Angel went on, "we're at such a regional stage that we have to be very sensitive to consequences elsewhere. I'm sure that Corky is held accountable for some of the things that we say and asked to justify things we say. We're always being pitted and divided against one another. There's no division here, and if there are some disagreements, well, we have to have some healthy fights once in a while."

Corky agreed. "We've possibly had some disagreements on some things. This is our family, and family can have their differences. But we have to create a unified direction and philosophy. We had talked about creating a national *congreso*. Texas took the lead and called for the convention. We recognized it and supported it and came here. We want to involve our ideas and our thoughts, and out of this came unity."

The discussion went on for some time. It was the first time that I had seen José Angel and Corky interacting together. Corky seemed intimidated by José Angel's lengthy and erudite answers. In contrast, Corky's responses were characteristically brief, reiterating the same theme of party independence. All too soon it was time to end the interviews, as both men had to attend a rally where Ramsey Muñíz was to speak.

As the men departed the room, I looked over to Dick Davies with a questioning look. Had we gotten what we were after? He instinctively knew what I was asking. He grinned at me and nodded. "We got it—good stuff."

State Platforms

Saturday, the convention was reconvened at the coliseum. Richard, Martín, and I arrived early the next morning at the coliseum, a massive cement structure that seemed to dwarf the two thousand party delegates. Antonio Parra met us in the parking lot, and from then on he was an inseparable addition to our crew, at times helping to film, at other times helping me attend to press activities. Like the day before, we set up our camera near the front stage, which was raised a good six feet off the convention floor.

While Richard and Martín prepared for the day's filming, I circulated among the press, making sure that everyone had a press kit and fielding questions about the day's events. I confirmed with the producer of the NPACT crew that, in exchange for setting up interviews with José Angel and Corky, scheduled for later that afternoon, they would give me access to the out-takes of the footage they shot at the convention.

The afternoon session started late. José Angel read a reply telegram that the convention had received from George McGovern in which the presidential candidate called for a federal investigation into the death of Falcón. The telegram read,

I am shocked at the killing of young Ricardo Falcón. I assure you of my efforts to assure that justice is done in this act of insanity. I am contacting the U.S. Attorney General to see that immediate action be taken to initiate investigative proceedings.

Next, Juan José Peña, the chair of the New Mexico delegation, introduced Reies López Tijerina, who gave the opening day's address. Having learned of the split between Corky and Tijerina, I was surprised that Tijerina had opted to honor his commitment to deliver a keynote address at the convention. Within moments of assuming the podium, Tijerina was at his fiery best, preaching a secular sermon in Spanish to an audience of some two thousand people. At times his rhetoric bordered on pure evangelism.

"What makes the cause of the Chicano, of the Mexican American, a just cause?" he asked. "What makes it a legitimate cause, a sacred cause? It's not the fact that the laws are on our side, that they support our just claims; rather, it's the tears and the grievances of old men, of mothers, of children in New Mexico, in California, Colorado, in Texas. And that is why I am here. Because a new political party has been borne on this planet, and this new party is called La Raza Unida!"

There was sweeping applause from the audience.

"And if this party is to bring us a new hope, real salvation, and direction, then we must open our doors to it, because we desperately need it!"

Suddenly the tenor of his voice took on a high note. "But if this is going to be something else," Tijerina continued, his voice fluctuating higher and higher, "if its representatives and leaders are going to be victims of the same jealousy," he continued, nearly screaming now, "of the same envy, of the same hatred that we see in other parties, then we must put a stop to it right now!"

The audience was mesmerized by the tone of Tijerina's delivery, but I doubt that it understood the meaning of his words. Looking over to where Corky sat in the crowd, surrounded by Colorado delegates, I could see that Corky understood these words to be directed at him. The personal aside lasted only a beat, then Tijerina resumed by calling José Angel and Corky to come up to the podium so that he could present them with a document he had commissioned, attesting to the validity of land grant claims. Corky Gonzales and José Angel joined Tijerina on stage, and together the three men stood with hands locked and upraised in a symbol of unity.

That night, Antonio Parra offered to show Dick, Martín, and me the nightclubs of El Paso. We spent the evening bar-hopping and listening to salsa and norteño bands on both sides of the border. The more I spoke with Antonio, the clearer it became to me that this was the kind of energetic, committed, and creative individual that I needed for the new show I would launch on my return to Los Angeles.

The next morning, Antonio took us to a local Mexican restaurant, where we introduced Dick Davies to *menudo* (tripe soup) as a hangover cure. Over breakfast I proposed to Antonio that he come out to Los Angeles and join me as an associate producer for the new show I was starting. Without a moment's hesitation, he agreed. It would take him a week to wrap up things in El Paso, and then he would drive out to Los Angeles.

The convention reconvened on Saturday afternoon with state caucuses deliberating on the issues that would make up the national party platform. Dick Davies, Martín, Oscar, and I went from caucus to caucus, filming the debates and discussions. Some of the caucuses were held in conference rooms; most were held in different sections of the enormous coliseum.

The heated discussions reflected the range of issues affecting Chicano communities throughout the Southwest. Demands included a guaranteed minimum wage, the right to strike and support of the Farm Workers' Union. In education, the demand for bilingual and bicultural education at all levels of schooling. Free health clinics and health insurance for Chicanos. A redistribution of wealth and the breakup of corporate monopolies. Withdrawal of United States troops from Vietnam and Indochina. Elimination of United States military and covert intervention in Latin America. An end to police brutality. Honoring of original Mexican and Spanish land grants in New Mexico. Responsible support for Latina women in their struggle for equal rights. Community control of all institutions in the barrio.

Many of the platform items appeared unrealistic to me. Did we really think that we could get the U.S. out of Vietnam? Or curtail CIA operations in Latin America? Yet others appeared eminently doable: passage of laws to insure bilingual education, for example, or to guarantee a minimum wage or the creation of barrio free clinics.

What struck me most about these demands was that this was the first time in the history of our people that we had articulated a broad program of social reform that could potentially improve the lives of Chicanos throughout the Southwest.

Party Chairman

On Sunday, the last day of the convention, the plenary started late in the afternoon. State caucuses had compiled lists of issues and had delivered them to Raúl Ruiz, who read them out loud to the assembled audience. Rather than open the floor to debates on each issue, and since there appeared to be unanimous support for all the platform issues as presented to the main assembly, Ruiz asked for a vote to approve all the issues *en toto*. The proposal was seconded. "The motion reads, that the entire body vote for the approval of all the resolutions as written. If you vote for this motion, then all of the resolutions will have passed by acclamation."

The vote was taken. Our camera caught many of the delegates as they announced their vote.

Raúl read the outcome.

"This is, in effect, the national position of the Partido de La Raza Unida from the first national convention. In labor, to support the right to strike and to support the Farm Workers' Union. Number two: parity in employment opportunity and wages for the Chicano in the federal government, unions, etc."

The list went on. "Enforcement of the Tratado de Guadalupe Hidalgo. Politics, complete political independence. Support neither of the two major candidates for president of the United States of America." The crowd erupted and took to its feet with clenched fists.

The plenary voiced their unanimous approval by rising to their feet and applauding in a thundering, enthusiastic roar.

The party platform was approved.

As the convention moved into the evening, it became clear that the major event of the evening and of the convention would be the vote on who would be elected the national chair of the Congreso de Aztlán, in effect, the national chair and spokesperson for the party. Throughout the previous day's proceedings, I had kept tabs on the mood of the delegates. It was clear that while Colorado delegates were squarely behind Corky, and Texas delegates solidified behind José Angel, the rest of the state delegations were in many cases split. Delegates from California, in particular, were split—some backing Corky, others in José Angel's camp. Early in the evening, Raúl Ruiz raised an issue which would have lasting repercussions: it had to do with the way in that convention votes were counted.

Approval of the state party platforms had been unanimous, but voting on the party chairman was another matter. Corky favored the so-called unit vote, whereby all delegates of a state would have to vote for the candidate favored by that state's majority. If the vote was taken on a per-state basis, as a bloc, Corky could well win. He had majority delegates in many states. On the other hand, if the vote were counted on a per-delegate basis, individually, José Angel might have an advantage, since there were some delegates in pro-Corky states who would vote for José Angel. Early in the evening, the Texas delegation proposed that the chairmanship of the party be decided on individual votes and not by unit vote. A heated discussion immediately erupted on the floor, and the proposal was sent to the appeals committee for a decision. Both Corky's and José Angel's delegates knew what was at stake. The tension between the two factions soon became intense.

In an effort to cool things down, Raúl Ruiz asked both candidates to address the assembly.

Corky arose first. Dressed in black, shadowed by his bodyguards, all of whom appeared to be packing guns, he made a menacing and formidable presence. He spoke first.

"First of all, I want to thank the people that nominated me and the people that support them. Rather than talk about personal things, I want to talk about the unity of the *mexicano*. I want to talk about the unity of the *partido*. Colorado came here to take part in unity. We feel that we did our job in presenting our philosophy of no compromise, of setting forth the idea that we are an independent party, that we are not a negotiating or an endorsing party. And whichever way the vote goes, we will be part of La Raza Unida."

Next, José Angel spoke. "For the last three hours or so I have seen the delegates from California and Colorado at their best. I applaud your skill, I respect your discipline, and I am proud to be in this room with you as an opponent. You have also, I hope, seen a capable organizer staying in the fight with you. Corky as chairman of the *congreso* is not the issue. José Angel Gutiérrez as chairman of the *congreso* is not the issue either. The issue to you delegates that I am sure I will abide by and that I am sure Corky will abide by is that you must choose a chairman."

Throughout the evening, I had grown more and more concerned about the direction in which the vote was going. Each of the two delegates had spent the night before lobbying state delegates and campaigning.

As the evening progressed, I could see the potential for things turning ugly. I knew that both Corky and José Angel's bodyguards were packing guns. The tension in the room was palatable; everywhere clusters of people met in muffled conversations, now and then glancing to the stage, where José Angel and his staff sat at a long table, or to the convention floor, where the Colorado delegation had formed a cordon around Corky and his bodyguards.

Further adding to the tension was a new report circulating through the convention floor that one of the New Mexico delegates had been found stabbed to death in an alley in Juárez, across the border. Rumors abounded as to the cause of his death. Was it a simple robbery or had he been killed by rival delegates?

Delegates from both camps continued to filibuster on the convention floor, arguing and counter-arguing about the legitimacy of the proceedings. Soon it was one o'clock, then two o'clock in the morning, and still no vote on the party chairmanship. Some of the reporters from out of state, such as the NPACT and CBS crews, had early flights the next morning back to Washington, D.C. and New York. They were anxious to leave the convention. I knew that before long we would be losing our press coverage of the decisive vote. Evidently, I was not the only person to realize this.

Suddenly, I noticed José Angel motioning to me from the stage. I walked over to the raised platform, and he bent down to speak to me.

"I'm worried," he said without preamble.

"What do you mean?" I asked.

"You've seen Corky's people?" he said. I instantly knew what he meant—the guns.

I nodded. "I've seen your people, too."

"Whether I win this election, or if Corky wins," José Angel continued, "I'm afraid some of our supporters may not be very happy. I'm afraid of someone losing their temper and doing something stupid. If they do, the other side isn't going to take it sitting down—they'll fight back."

The thought of armed intimidation was one thing; the thought of an actual shootout on the convention floor was something that hadn't even occurred to me. But now, with the tension in the room and the agitation I saw in the faces of tired convention delegates, I realized that such an occurrence was suddenly a very real possibility.

"What can we do?" I asked.

"I don't think anybody is going to try anything if all this press is around. Can you make sure that the national news media stays here until the vote is taken?"

"Sure," I said.

José Angel went back to the table on stage, and I began to circulate among the news reporters that I knew in the audience. I spotted Frank Del Olmo from the *Los Angeles Times* and explained to him the situation. He looked around the room and agreed that people were tense and tempers short; anything could happen. He agreed to help. Next I sought out Betita Martínez, the editor of *El Grito del Norte*. I explained the situation to her and she, too, agreed to help. Within moments, the three of us were circulating among the other reporters, talking up the idea that the vote for national chairman of the party was imminent, that to leave now would be foolish.

It was actually another hour and a half before the appeals committee finally returned its verdict: voting by individual vote was to be permitted. With the national news crews watching, Raúl Ruiz finally called for the vote for national chair of the Congreso de Aztlán.

"All those in favor of the candidacy of José Angel Gutiérrez for chairman of the Raza Unida Party signify by raising your right hand."

Then, "Those in favor of Rodolfo 'Corky' Gonzales."

At four o'clock in the morning, after the count, Raúl announced the results: "256 ⅙ votes for José Angel Gutiérrez, 170 and ⅚ votes for Rodolfo Corky Gonzales, one abstention, thirteen no votes. You have a chairman; José Angel is your new chairman."

José Angel was immediately engulfed in embraces by members of the Texas delegation. He stepped up to the stage, as did Corky Gonzales. They had agreed that a show of unity was crucial, regardless who won the election. The two leaders went to the stage and embraced. I could see the hurt in Corky's face. Despite how much the loss meant to him, he was playing by the rules and showing unity with José Angel.

The two men raised hands in a sign of unity.

Aftermath

The next morning, the stabbing death in Juárez of a Raza Unida delegate from Colorado was confirmed; his murderer was never found or brought to justice. This death, along with that of Ricardo Falcón, brought a somber mood to the end of the convention.

Dick Davies, Martín, and I returned to Los Angeles late the next afternoon. I was elated that I had gotten the footage I needed to cut together a good half-hour film. On our return to Los Angeles, I immediately set Dick Davies to begin assembling the footage we had shot. In the meantime, I began to worry about the new series that I had to air in only two weeks. I was happy that Antonio Parra would be joining me, but I needed more production staff. Suddenly I was overwhelmed by the immensity of what lay before me. I was now about to play the role that Ed Moreno had played on *Ahora!* I would be executive producer of a weekly program directed at the Chicano community in Los Angeles. Whether the program would sink or be a success depended on me and the people I pulled together to produce it. I remembered once again Chuck Allen's words: "Be careful what you wish for; you just might get it." Now I understood what he meant.

Chapter Fifteen

Acción Chicano

We've got to take over the media. We have to tell our own stories; we have to produce our own stories, write them, direct them, and act them.

—*Sylvia Morales*

I returned to Los Angeles, inspired by the Raza Unida convention and convinced that the Republican and Democratic parties were a political dead end for Chicanos and other American Latinos. I vowed to finish my documentary on the convention as quickly as possible and to include it in my new KCET Chicano series.

A week after the convention, Antonio Parra arrived from Texas to assume his role as one of the associate producers of the series. The following week, I approached Oscar Castillo, the still photographer I had met at the Raza Unida convention, and found that his job with the *La Raza* magazine was only temporary. I signed him on as production assistant for the series.

Terri Francis, who was one of the KCET producers, was a close friend and a strong feminist, and more than once she had called me on my chauvinism. "All boys, eh?" she quipped when she heard about my new staff.

She was right.

I thought of Sylvia Morales's words about the need for Chicanos to reach out to include Chicanas in the struggle. I put out a job description for another associate producer—a female. In the meantime, I began preliminary planning of the news series.

While I was in Texas, Sue Booker had been preparing her new black series. She had decided to call it the *Storefront*. Recalling Ed Moreno's meticulous efforts at democracy when we had named the *Ahora!* program, I reluctantly put the question out for discussion. Antonio, Oscar, and I easily settled upon the name *Acción Chicano* (Chicano Action).

It was already September, and the fall television season was upon us. In a remarkable frenzy of activity, the three of us mapped out the first programs. I worked with the KCET art department to design an emblem for the series. Borrowing from the design that Malaquías Montoya had developed as a backdrop to the Daniel Valdez concert *América de los Indios*, we settled on a stylized black eagle on a red background. The Montoya design was reminiscent of the Farm Workers' Union symbol, and I felt it suited our show perfectly.

Our vision for the series was ambitious, ranging in format from studio talk shows, to concerts, to our own documentaries. In addition, I designed a regular segment entitled "barrio report," in which we announced community events, rallies, and celebrations.

Throughout October and early November, the three of us worked assiduously at shaping the first half-dozen shows and preparing for the December premiere of the series.

Inspired by the successful media campaign I had devised at the *Raza Unida* convention, I was determined to continue in my efforts to document and promote the Chicano Movement. I recalled the press release I had published in July, prior to the national broadcast of *Yo Soy Chicano*, in which I had articulated my views of the role of Chicanos in the media:

As Chicanos, we cannot indulge in notions of an apolitical art, not while our people continue to suffer discrimination and repressions . . . Chicano filmic art must be outspoken in its indictments against past and present brutalities, and yet reach beyond: to service community needs, to reflect the beauty of our lifestyles, to point out directions for a future, to join in a common struggle. Ours must be an art of advocacy.

Now, with an entire television series at hand, I could express my beliefs on a broader canvas. I felt elated and optimistic about the media's potential for bringing about social change. I was riding on a wave of nationalistic pride for my people, a pride resulting from years of deep anger about the unchecked discrimination against Chicanos in American society and a heartfelt love of our culture and history. I began to plan the topic for our first program.

América Tropical II

Following the broadcast of *América Tropical* in 1971, while I was busy working on *Yo Soy Chicano*, Dr. Shifra Goldman spearheaded efforts to have Siqueiros's downtown mural restored through the "Save the Mural" committee we had created. In the course of her correspondence with Siqueiros, difficulties arose in the preservation of his mural at Olvera Street. The attention to his work that Siqueiros received from Chicano activists touched him deeply, so much so, in fact, that he offered to rework the mural and donate it to the Chicano community of Los Angeles. The new mural, *América Tropical II*, was to be created at his studio in Cuernavaca on 20-by-40 foot Masonite panels and then shipped to the United States. Now all we needed was a suitable environment for his masterpiece.

During the month of October, Shifra and I approached Frank López. Since Frank's appearance on the *Ahora!* program in 1969, he had labored to build a Chicano cultural center called Plaza de la Raza (The People's Plaza) in Lincoln Park out of an abandoned boathouse and a few adjacent buildings. I was not surprised when Frank López told us that Mexican masons from Tijuana had constructed and donated a children's playground using Aztec motifs for Plaza de la Raza. The enthusiasm evidenced by Chicano activists toward Mexico and its people, part of a heartfelt longing to reclaim our roots, was being reciprocated by Mexican national organizations seeking alliances with Chicano groups. Frank didn't need much convincing when we suggested that the new Siqueiros mural belonged at Plaza de la Raza—it was a logical extension of this blossoming Mexican-Chicano connection. With Antonio and Oscar's enthusiastic support, I decided to mark the occasion by kicking off our new series with a show about the creation of Plaza de la Raza and the possibility of housing *America Tropical II* there, permanently.

Los Vendidos

As we prepared for the first *Acción Chicano* broadcast, El Teatro Campesino arrived in Los Angeles to tape a half-hour adaptation of Luis Valdez's play, *Los Vendidos (The Sellouts)*. Making good on his promise, my friend José Luis Ruiz had secured a prime-time spot for the *teatro* on the local NBC affiliate, KNBC.

During rehearsal, Gayla and I spent much time with members of the *teatro*, but particularly with Daniel and Armida Valdez. To save money, the *teatro* members stayed in the homes of friends. We spent many days together in various homes, discussing theater, film, and television, and the possibility of working together on projects away from Hollywood. Luis Valdez abhorred Hollywood, calling it the city of the devil. He felt that if Chicanos worked within Hollywood, *el diablo* (the devil) would grab their souls. He urged José Luis and me to be careful. Towards the end of their stay, the Valdezes invited José Luis Ruiz, his wife Johnna, Gayla, and me to leave Los Angeles and become members of the theater company. Although joining the group, for the moment, was out of the question (it would require our moving to San Juan Bautista, California, and, leaving our television jobs), I felt affirmed by the invitation.

It was during the *teatro*'s rehearsals that I met Rosa María Marqúez, who was then working as a production assistant for *Los Vendidos*. Vivacious, intelligent and sociable, Rosa María was the ideal associate producer and co-host for *Acción Chicano*. I offered her the job.

On The Air

We taped our first *Acción Chicano* program from Plaza de la Raza on Thursday, December 7, 1972, for our weekly time slot that evening at 7 p.m. The nearby lake brimmed with fresh water. A new fountain erupted majestically next to the refurbished red brick buildings of the cultural center. Antonio Parra and I co-hosted an interview with director Frank López and Esteban Torres, who represented The East Los

Angeles Community Union (TELACU), a community development corporation that had helped fund the reconstruction of the Plaza de la Raza center. Torres would later be elected to Congress, where he would serve for more than three decades. Phone calls streamed in, congratulating us on the show. That week was a particularly rich one for Chicano television audiences, since, three days later, *Los Vendidos* hit NBC with a remarkable rating that garnered one-third of that night's national viewing audience.

Rosa María's input on *Acción Chicano* was immediate. Within a week of her arrival, she suggested two programs specifically geared to Chicanas. The first profiled a newly formed Chicana rights organization, Comisión Femenil (The Feminine Commission). She also proposed a program featuring activist Latinas in film and television.

In our second show, we presented several original one-act scenes and renditions of Chicano protest songs by the Teatro de la Tierra (Theater of the Earth), a Chicano theater company under the directorship of Agustín Lira. Lira had been one of the founder's of El Teatro Campesino, but since my first meeting with him in the summer of 1968, he had broken away to create his own group. His pieces placed a half-dozen actors on stark black platforms with a cyclorama of constantly changing colors serving as a backdrop.

The third show was Rosa María's Comisión Femenil, which she hosted and produced. In our fourth show, Chicano professors discussed the struggle to establish Chicano Studies as a bonafide discipline within the statewide university system.

By the time we did our fourth show on December 28, 1972, our production team was in sync. Typically, we began with a Monday morning planning session for that week's show. I assigned responsibilities for contacting guests, researching topics, and drafting interview questions. We also discussed graphics, slides, and other visuals. By Wednesday, we had a show outline. Then I wrote the script and finalized the working budget, which had to be approved by the station's production manager.

In addition to my daily work on the *Acción Chicano* series, I was also assigned production tasks for the station's weekly news program, *The L.A. Collective.* I delivered regular reports for the show, despite the mounting pressures of *Acción Chicano.* This meant constantly bouncing from one show to the other. By the end of the week, I was beat. All I could do on weekends was try to rejuvenate my body and mind so I could face the challenges of the upcoming week.

In spite of the physical toll the work was taking on me, I was jubilant about what we were doing. Often, I attended community meetings, where I met with overwhelming support and congratulations. Clearly, people were watching our show. This made all my efforts worthwhile.

By the end of December, the strain of producing a weekly program, even with the capable help I had, began to show. I became argumentative with little provocation. *Acción Chicano* required me to stay late each evening and to work on weekends. This left me little time to spend with Gayla. Not surprisingly, she felt abandoned and alone. When I finally did find time to spend with her, we usually fought over how I had been neglecting her. I began to overeat to deal with the stress. By early December, I realized that for the first time in my life I was overweight. The pressure of the weekly grind at *Acción Chicano* was pushing my endurance to its limit.

In late December, Daniel Valdez invited me to a winter acting workshop. Luis Valdez intended to use the experience to develop his play *La Carpa de los Rasquachis (*The Tent of the Underdogs*).* The idea of working on an artistic project with the *Teatro* felt like the perfect medicine for my frayed nerves. But how could I leave *Acción Chicano* with so many of its programs still on the drawing board? What of my responsibility to the community?

I approached Chuck Allen at the end of the year about taking a leave of absence from KCET. As I settled into the familiar chair across from his desk, I told him about my plan. His jaw dropped in amazement.

"You've just gotten the series off the ground. Are you so ready to abandon it?" Chuck understood my interest in joining with the *teatro*, but I could see he was concerned about the future of *Acción Chicano.*

It was an embarrassing question. I had gone to great lengths to force him into approving *Acción Chicano.* While Antonio, Rosa María and Oscar were all capable people, Chuck did not feel they had the experience necessary to handle the series on their own. If I was to leave, even for the two months of the workshop, I would need to find a producer with considerable experience to replace me. I approached José Luis Ruiz, who, following the success of *Los Vendidos,* had landed a job producing a weekly interview series, *Impacto,* at KNBC. It meant juggling two shows for separate networks, but José Luis jumped at the chance.

Chuck Allen approved of my replacement and even offered to subsidize my income for the two months while I was away at the *teatro* workshop. The circus had come to town, and I wanted to run off with it. Chuck understood this and was willing to support my dream, as long as long as I returned to finish my work in the spring. Elated, Gayla and I made plans to move to San Juan Bautista, California, for the months of February and March.

La Raza Unida Aftermath

In the weeks before our departure, I completed work on La Raza Unida, the fifth show of *Acción Chicano.* This was the documentary that incorporated all the footage that Dick Davies, Martín Quiroz, and I had filmed at the convention, as well as the other footage secured from news crews that had covered the event.

As I prepared the documentary for broadcast, I received a troubling phone call from José Angel Gutiérrez. The first meeting of the national *congreso,* which, in theory, would launch the party's national platform, had been set for October in Albuquerque, New Mexico. But Corky Gonzales had avoided the meeting, choosing instead to send his representatives, who unsuccessfully tried to get Corky elected as vice-chair of the *partido.* The Colorado delegates refused to accept José Angel's leadership, blocking efforts by Gutiérrez to shape a national Congreso de Aztlán. They called for the national site of the *partido* to be moved away from Crystal City. With José Angel unable to function as national party chairman, La Raza Unida Party activism was now relegated to city, county, and state elections only.

As disappointing as the news was, our broadcast of the Raza Unida documentary, bookended by interviews of local southern California Raza Unida candidates Irene Tovar and Rogelio Granados, did help to surface the Raza Unida agenda in southern California.

Despite my enthusiasm for the *partido*, the possibility that Raza Unida would become a viable political alternative for Chicanos dwindled. Although Raza Unida candidates were running, the effect of their candidacy was to prompt the Democratic Party to reach out to Chicanos by running their own Latino candidates.

Thus, in the fall of 1972, in each southern California electoral race with a Raza Unida candidate, there was also a strong Latino candidate running under the banner of the Democratic Party. Latino Democratic candidates had the advantage, for they could direct their campaigns to both Latino and non-Latino voters, while Raza Unida candidates appealed only to the hearts of Latino voters with a strong sense of Chicano identity. The *partido* was doomed.

In the November elections of 1972, the southern California Raza Unida candidates lost every election in which they participated. I later learned that Raza Unida campaigns in New Mexico, Colorado, and Arizona had also met with defeat. Despite my success with *Acción Chicano,* the news of these failures hit me hard. The inability of our two movement leaders to reconcile their differences angered me. While the movement was comprised of activists working on a multiplicity of fronts—education, labor, unions, prison reform, the legal system—politics was the crucial element that would lead to the success or failure of all our other efforts. La Raza Unida was supposed to harness this power. Couldn't our leaders see that with so much at stake they should settle their differences and provide true leadership? This grim situation depressed me and forced me to reevaluate the *partido* and the prospects for its long-term success.

The Winter Workshop

Gayla and I arrived in San Juan Bautista in early February after a heavy rain. The green rolling hills surrounding the hamlet of one thousand people sparkled as the morning sun touched water droplets on the knee-high grass. Because of the limited housing available in San Juan, we moved into an extra bedroom at the home of *teatro* members Félix and Lili Álvarez.

Every morning, after some hurried coffee and toast, Gayla and I would join the group—perhaps twenty in all—at the recreation room of the local community center. We spent mornings either learning traditional acting techniques or working at improvisational exercises. One of my favorite exercises was *la casa de los locos* (the madhouse). In this activity, every actor mimed a different animal or object and interacted with the rest of the group as they encountered them. True to its name, the floor of the recreation room soon became a scene of chaos, with actors crawling, rolling, gyrating, and performing outlandish gestures as we developed our characters.

In the afternoon, each member of the group was assigned tasks to keep the *teatro* functioning, such as touring bookings, equipment repairing, and creating performance masks, costumes, and props. Because of my background in writing and production, I spent most of these afternoons working with Luis and Daniel Valdez on *La Carpa de los Rasquachis*, the play being prepared for the fall tour.

During the fall of 1972, El Teatro Campesino had presented this work-in-progress on several stages, and it had been well received. The play utilized the *corrido* form, which Luis Valdez had pioneered. In this theater style, actors mimed actions described in the lyrics of a *corrido* (ballad) as musicians sang it on stage. The actors slipped dialogue between lines of the lyrics and occasionally even joined in the singing.

La Carpa told the story of a *pelado*, a poor Mexican underdog, named Jesús Rasquachi, who crossed the U.S./Mexico border and struggled to subsist in the United States as a farm worker. Continually set upon, first by the border *coyote* (smuggler), then by immigration authorities, ruthless employers, and eventually even by the Catholic Church, the *pelado* marries and raises a family as best he can, only to find that his children despise him and resent the meager life he has provided for them. The *pelado* is horrified as he realizes that his children have lost all sense of their Mexican roots. His children struggle, in vain, to be accepted in American society by denying their language, family, and culture.

When I had read the rough draft of this play the year before, I had been struck by its honest depiction of Chicano life. Not surprisingly, it addressed the same issues I did through my *Acción Chicano* series.

The work with Luis and Daniel Valdez was challenging, exhilarating, and enormously rewarding. We spent the first couple of weeks

reworking traditional Mexican *corridos* and adding pertinent lyrics to
the *pelado's* story. Luis had a general idea of where he wanted the
story to go, but was open to new plot points. Although the work was
labeled "a play by Luis Valdez," in fact, the piece emerged from the
improvised contributions of all of the actors. Luis observed these
improvisations and jotted down the best motifs, ideas, and dialogue.
These notes became incorporated into the "play" as dialogue and
stage instructions.

At one point, each member of the *teatro* was asked to direct a one-
act play. I selected Bertold Brecht's *The Beggar*, one of his early plays
involving only two actors. One character was an emperor. Elated by a
recent victory, he encounters a beggar at the gate to his kingdom. In
their conversation, it becomes clear that while the emperor feels he
has power over the beggar, the beggar refuses to acknowledge this
power, which effectively disarms the emperor's hold over him. In
working out the visuals of the play, I hit on the idea of using a noose
to show the relationship of psychological bondage between the two
characters. Each time the emperor spoke of his sovereignty over the
beggar, he would place a rope noose around the beggar's neck. But
each time the beggar rejected the emperor's power, he removed the
rope. When it came time for me to present the drama before the group,
Luis was immediately taken by the use of the rope to signal human
bondage. At the next group rehearsal for *La Carpa de los Rasquachis*,
the noose was added as a central image, highlighting the bondage
between the *pelado* and his wife, his children, the Church, and the
patrón (labor boss). Work continued on *La Carpa de los Rasquachis*
long after I returned to Los Angeles, but I noted with satisfaction that
in the final version of the play—as performed on the *teatro's* Southwest tour that fall—the rope noose figured prominently in the play.

In addition to the "work," Gayla and I spent much time making
friends with the other actors. The close-knit community forced us to
rely on one another for favors. Sometimes it was helping someone
move furniture or giving someone a ride to the nearest supermarket in
nearby Watsonville. It was a peaceful, slower existence. This allowed
me time to enjoy the pristine beauty of rural San Juan Baustista. I took
long walks through town. Sometimes I meditated in the gardens of the

nearby Franciscan monastery.

I learned more about the group. It had started with César Chávez's farm union. Luis and Danny Valdez and Augustín Lira had led a ragtag handful of labor activists in performing on the back of flatbed trucks in the fields of Delano. In 1967, they had moved to Fresno, California, to broaden the scope of their work to include urban issues. When a friend, Manny Santana, offered them a fifty-seat theater in San Juan Bautista, they immediately accepted. Their aspiration was to develop a more mature theater style and to write and perform original works. Eventually, Augustín Lira broke away from the group.

Now, Luis Valdez had more ambitious plans. He envisioned an arts center that would work in a variety of disciplines to express Chicano concerns. There would be Chicano poetry, theater, film, music, and Chicano dance. Nothing quite like this had ever been attempted.

Daniel Valdez, the undisputed senior musician of the group, was to be in charge of the musical component. Luis Valdez would remain director of El Teatro Campesino. But the brothers hoped that in some indeterminate future, other noted writers, actors, filmmakers, poets, and painters, would join them and help expand the Centro into other departments. The new organization would be known as the El Centro Campesino Cultural, the Farm Workers' Cultural Center, or simply the Centro. Luis and Daniel's enthusiasm was infectious.

Working with the Valdez brothers on creative projects was an exhilarating experience for me. Gayla was enjoying our stay as well. Though she was an Anglo, she was warmly accepted by the group and cemented a close friendship with Armida Valdez. She also found a niche for herself: coordinating the schedule for the *teatro*'s fall tour. Tensions between us subsided as we each found something in San Juan that had been missing from our lives in Los Angeles. Before long, we were both seriously discussing the idea of leaving Los Angeles permanently, and moving to San Juan to be a part of the expanded Centro.

However much fun I was having, I felt obliged to return and finish out the *Acción Chicano* season. All too soon, the end of March arrived, and with it the end of my stay with the circus. With my soul refreshed and my commitment to the *movimiento* renewed, I left San Juan, eager to get back to *Acción Chicano*.

Return to Los Angeles

When I returned in April of 1973, I discovered that José Luis Ruiz had been busy during my two-month absence. Not only had he won the confidence and support of the *Acción Chicano* staff, but he had planned and executed several original shows for *Acción Chicano*. One such show featured the work by my old friend Ricardo Sánchez—the poet whom I had met in El Paso—and by the San Diego poet Alurista, who had risen to national prominence since the penning of the preamble to the *Plan de Aztlán* in 1969. José Luis produced other programs, including a live broadcast from a local *alteña* (rodeo), featuring the tradition of the Mexican *charro*. Another program showcased their female counterparts, the horse-riding Escaramuzas Charras. Yet another show included music of Con Safos, an Eastside literary and musical group.

I shared the enthusiasm of my two-month experience with José Luis and discovered that he, too, was excited about the prospect of someday leaving Los Angeles and joining El Teatro Campesino. We spoke about the limitations of Hollywood. While we didn't necessarily see Hollywood as "el diablo" the way Luis Valdez did, we did see the need to create an alternative cinema for Chicanos, which perhaps we could do someday in San Juan Baustista.

The spring line-up of *Acción Chicano* included: an interview program with Rosalío Muñoz—who had spearheaded the 1970 Chicano Moratorium—about the Vietnam War and its continuing toll on Latinos; a show about the Chicana-led Farah factory workers' strike in El Paso; and concerts with classical pianist Florencio López and rock groups El Chicano and Yaquí.

Perhaps the most controversial of our shows was a program of choral poetry and revolutionary songs performed by the Teatro los Mascarones (The Masked Ones), a company from Mexico on tour in the Southwest. At San Juan Baustista, Luis Valdez told me of the chance meeting of El Teatro Campesino with the Teatro los Mascarones at the International Drama Festival in Paris, France, at the Sorbonne, in 1970. The two companies were surprised to find they had a lot in common. Teatro los Mascarones used choral poetry and El Teatro Campesino used an exaggerated comedia del'arte style, but both groups featured farm worker themes and used the skeleton imagery of the Mexican printmaker José Guadalupe Posada in their plays. Both also used masks extensively. This meeting marked the beginning of a long association between the groups.

When I heard that the Mascarones were to perform in Los Angeles, I began planning a program for *Acción Chicano* around them. I met with Mariano Leyva, the group's director, and invited him to extend the group's stay in Los Angeles for a week. I knew that their purpose was to raise funds for their work in Mexico and that the meager honorarium from *Acción Chicano* would barely cover their expenses for the week, so, to save them money, I invited them to sleep at my home. For the next week, Gayla and I hosted a company of fifteen actors in our cramped, three-room apartment.

Since the majority of the group's songs dealt with radical political themes that might cause KCET to cancel the broadcast, we decided to open with an ancient Aztec dance in honor of Tlaloc, the deity of rain. The dance featured actors dressed in Aztec ceremonial attire and was, on the whole, folkloric and inoffensive. As the show progressed, however, it became increasingly political. The program included a one-act choral poem entitled "The Birth of Capitalism," which was nothing less than a Marxist call to revolution. Another choral poem, "América Es Una" ("America Is One"), was a bold denunciation of United States intervention in Latin America. We concluded the show with a potpourri of revolutionary songs from Cuba.

On the night of the broadcast, the Mascarones stopped by KCET to watch the show from my office. Afterwards, the KCET switchboard lit up like a Christmas tree. The calls, most of them from disgruntled Cuban Americans living in Los Angeles, were overwhelmingly negative. Callers accused KCET of programming communist propaganda and of harboring revolutionaries. I knew I'd have a lot to answer for on Monday, but it was worth it. We had broadcast a message denouncing U.S. intervention in Latin America and praising the Cuban revolution on American television!

In all, we produced a total of twenty-six shows the first season. *Los Angeles Times* reporter Frank Del Olmo wrote an article about the series stating, "Some radio and most television stations in town have community affairs programs about Chicanos. KCET's contribution, *Acción Chicano*, is one of the few broadcast in prime time. It's also the best . . . They've been on the air less than a year, and despite a limited budget, they've tried more things, in more ways, than any similar program."

Somos Uno

Just prior to the fourth annual National Theater of Aztlán (TENAZ) theater festival, held June 21-28, 1973, I had another opportunity to collaborate with Mascarones. This time, I also included El Teatro Campesino in the production. TENAZ was the national organization made up of about thirty Chicano theater companies, and since Mascarones was going to be in San Jose, California, for this theater festival, I persuaded the company to come to San Juan Bautista beforehand for a four-day exchange with El Teatro Campesino. This coincided with the between-season hiatus for *Acción Chicano*, allowing me freedom to devote several weeks to prepare, film, and edit the hour-long 16-mm documentary, which I called *Somos Uno* (We Are One). It also freed up Rosa María Marqúez, Antonio Parra, and Oscar Castillo, and they, too, joined in the effort, along with my veteran film crew: Richard Davies and José Luis Ruiz (cameramen), and Martín Quiroz (sound).

A brand-new play sprung from our efforts, filmed in a hot old warehouse used by El Teatro Campesino. Act One was a reworking of selected parts of the Mascarones play *Don Cacamáfer,* in which farm workers in Mexico struggled to unionize against Mexican land owners who had cut corrupt trade deals with American markets. Act Two was an adaptation of *La Carpa de los Rasquachis*, which was the *pelado* story I had worked on at the winter workshop. Here, the *pelado* represented Chicano farm workers who organized against exploitation in America. The Third Act, titled *Somos Uno,* was an original work authored by Leyva, Valdez and me, which brought the two stories together. It depicted the creation of an international labor union made up of Mexican nationals and American Chicanos in a campaign against exploitative land owners and transnational American companies. The theme of unity between Chicano and Mexicano workers against a common capitalist adversary used in this collaboration inspired me, later, to write my Mexican feature *Raíces de Sangre* (Roots of Blood).

In addition to the play, we also filmed interviews with Luis Valdez, Mariano Leyba, and actors from both groups. They discussed their collective work, the similarities in their dramatic styles, and the need for international solidarity. The film was broadcast on KCET in September 1973.

Our work on *Somos Uno* brought José Luis Ruiz and me closer together. A month after the Mascarones-Campesino collaboration, a theater company under the direction of renowned British director Peter Brook arrived in San Juan Bautista for a six-week exchange with El Teatro Campesino. When Luis Valdez requested that we document the event, José Luis and I agreed immediately. The film project would mean that I would have to take July and August off from KCET, but since the *Acción Chicano* season was over, this was entirely feasible. José Luis agreed to be cameraman and I would do sound. Gayla and I returned to San Juan Bautista and lived with Daniel and Armida Valdez for the next two months, while José Luis and Johnna joined us on weekends to participate in filming the collaborations.

The premise of the collaboration between the two companies was to adapt the Sufi poem by Farid Ud-Din Attar, "The Conference of the Birds," into a play that could be understood by working-class Chicano audiences. Peter Brook and his company had recently toured Africa with the play and were eager to try it out in the United States. The poem was a series of more than 150 allegorical tales recounted by various birds during a conference. It alluded to the different phases in the human quest for God and for personal enlightenment. The *teatro* had never tried anything this esoteric, and the members of Brook's company had never been exposed to the *teatro's* kind of political theater. The tough task forged a quick bond between the two theater groups. The play relied heavily on improvisations, with minimal dialogue, in order to reach the often non-English-speaking audiences who attended performances at local parks and Chicano community centers in San Juan Bautista, Watsonville, Hollister, other nearby towns.

Observing the exchange between the *teatro* and Peter Brook's international ensemble of actors was as instructive, culturally, as it was artistically. The list of actors included: from Great Britain, Helen Mirren and Natasha Parry; from the Japanese Noh stage, Yoshi Oida; from Mali, West Africa, Malik Bowens; from France, Francois Marthouret; and from America, actor Andreas Katsulas and composer Elizabeth Swados. Because of their backgrounds, the actors communicated in French, English, German, and Spanish, but the common language soon became the art of acting. Through the theater, the combined companies were able to elicit applause, summon up an audience's tears or laughter, with nothing more than gesticulation, grunts, and facial expressions. The process gave me profound insight into how deeply an audience could be affected by fine theater, and it drove me, more than ever, to want to work with actors in a dramatic film setting. This experience intensified a desire that I first felt during the filming of *Yo Soy Chicano*: I wanted to move away from documentaries and enter the realm of narrative filmmaking.

José Luis and I filmed many of the acting workshops and the performances that resulted from the collaboration. One such performance was staged in Keene, California, for César Chávez and the staff of the United Farm Workers of America. Another play, called "The Fatties and the Shrimps," was staged off the back of a flatbed truck, El Teatro Campesino style, for striking farm workers.

The collaboration ended at the end of August, when Peter Brook and his company continued on their tour of the United States. The documentary José Luis and I filmed was called *Encounters*. Although the film was never completed, for lack of funds, the summer experience further convinced me, José Luis, and our spouses that we should join the El Teatro Campesino as soon as possible.

Attack on the Crusade

In September, shortly after returning to Los Angeles to launch another season of *Acción Chicano*, I picked up a copy of *La Raza* magazine that was lying around the office. I was astounded by what I read:

DENVER POLICE BOMB CRUSADE FOR JUSTICE
In the early morning hours of Saturday, March 17, the Denver
Police Department in an apparently planned attack provoked a
violent confrontation with scores of Chicano youth who had
been attending a party at the Downing terrace, property that is
owned by Escuela Tlatelolco and the Crusade for Justice
Organization in Denver. By three-thirty that morning one Chicano youth was murdered, three other Chicanos shot (including a sixteen-year-old girl), thirty-six arrested in mass arrests
in the vicinity, four officers shot, and two units of apartments
almost completely demolished by police explosive charges.

The devastating news sent me into a profound sadness that quickly gave way to anger. Even allowing for the admittedly partisan rendering of the *La Raza* report, the easily discernible pattern of police
abuse was evident. A few days later, I tracked down the incident as
reported in *The Denver Post*, which told a different version of the
story. According to the *Post*, a police officer stopped a Crusade member, Luis "Junior" Martínez, and arrested him for jaywalking.
Martínez fled and was chased down a dark alley by officer Stephen
Snyder. According to Snyder, Martínez pulled a gun and fired. Twen-
ty-year-old Martínez was killed, and officer Snyder was wounded.
Snyder's partner, patrolwoman Carol Hogue, called for backup, and
within moments, more than two hundred Denver police officers converged on the Crusade headquarters. For the next two and a half hours,
sporadic gunfire continued. The incident culminated when a massive
explosion blew out an entire wall of an apartment complex owned by
the Crusade for Justice.

The discrepancy between the police account and that of Chicano
eyewitnesses brought back harsh memories of the Salazar inquest.
Snyder claimed he entered a dark alley and was ambushed by an
armed Martínez. Crusade eyewitnesses said Martínez was unarmed
and that he had backed away from Snyder, pleading with the officer to
leave him alone. Then Snyder opened fire.

Police claimed their swift show-of-force response was standard procedure. Crusaders charged that the two hundred police officers had to have been waiting in the wings to arrive as quickly as they did. They claimed that the police provoked the Martínez incident as a rationalization for the crackdown that promptly followed. Police said they opened fire on the Crusade complex in response to sniper fire. Crusaders flatly denied this allegation, pointing to the lack of bullet holes on any police cars or adjacent buildings as proof. Police claimed that an arsenal had been found in the Crusade headquarters. Crusade officials explained that the guns found were dummy rifles used as props during folkloric dance performances at the Escuela Tlatelolco.

Most controversial was the explosion that nearly destroyed the apartment house. Crusade members insisted that police fired explosives inside. According to police, however, the explosion was the result of more than twenty sticks of dynamite that they alleged were set by Crusade members. In order to determine what had actually caused the explosion, Corky Gonzales hired an independent explosives expert to examine the site. Within days of the assault, before Gonzales could obtain a court order to facilitate this investigation, the police bulldozed the building, destroying any physical evidence that might contradict their version of the story. Now it was just the word of a bunch of radical Chicano militants against the word of the Denver Police Department.

The news of the attack on the Crusade was a bleak reminder to me that, given an opportunity, the police would use any means necessary to destroy our movement. I remembered, anew, the deaths of Antonio Córdova, Rito Canales, Rubén Salazar, and Ricardo Falcón, and the instances of police brutality I had personally witnessed. The attack on the Crusade was just one more blow in an ongoing attack on the Chicano Movement—a movement of American citizens seeking equality and justice.

A Time of Decision

Though I felt rested and geared up to initiate the fall season of *Acción Chicano*, my heart was not entirely in the work. My experiences with El Teatro Campesino, Los Mascarones, and the Peter Brook ensemble had convinced me that I wanted to work with actors and to fashion dramatic works that were more universal and lasting than the immediate, topical nature of the television documentaries I had produced in recent years. I felt torn.

On the one hand, I was committed to *Acción Chicano* and to producing programs for the Los Angeles Mexican-American community. I had seen the impact our show had made in just one season. I knew our show was vital to the community and that there were still so many issues that needed exposure, discussion and solutions. The Chicano activist in me knew that *Acción Chicano* could play a crucial role in social change.

Yet, another side of me was demanding attention—the storyteller and the filmmaker. I longed to work on a full-length dramatic production, to design camera shots, to block scenes, to work with actors. I shared my thoughts with Gayla. Although she had enjoyed our winter stay in San Juan Baustista, she was doubtful about making a permanent move there. "What if things don't work out?" she said to me. "You've got a steady job here and you are doing great work. Do you really want to leave this?"

After several days of agonizing over my inner conflict, I finally came to a decision. I told Gayla and she agreed to go along with my plan. I sought out Chuck Allen to tell him that I would be leaving *Acción Chicano* to join El Teatro Campesino and devote myself to theater and film. Once I made up my mind, telling Chuck—something I dreaded—turned out to be quite anticlimatic. Chuck seemed quite prepared for my announcement.

"When will you be leaving?" he asked after I had broken the news.

"End of the year. I'll see *Acción Chicano* through to the Christmas break. I'll prep Antonio, Rosa María, and Oscar so they can take over without any disruption of the shows." He nodded and then noticed the somber expression on my face—telling him it had not been easy for me.

"It's what you want to do, right?"

"Yes," I replied, as much to myself as to him.

"Then smile. You're going to have fun."

With that, he gave me a firm *abrazo*, the Chicano embrace I had taught him years before.

The Fall Season

I continued to serve as executive producer of *Acción Chicano* during the fall of 1973, although I spent much of my time making preparations for our departure from Los Angeles.

The second season of the series was distinguished by a closer link to community events, as evidenced in our biweekly "Barrio Report."

Our outreach to the community also included inviting guest producers, who were assisted by our staff, for individual episodes. With so few Chicano writers, producers, and directors on television, I felt that *Acción Chicano* had a responsibility to help groom a new generation of media activists, and so I wanted to give qualified Chicanos with no connections a leg up in the industry.

One of the first of these guest producer programs was the touching fifteen-minute film *Carnalitos*, which I co-produced with Bobby Páramo, a young Chicano prison reform activist. While growing up in East L.A., Páramo had been a member of the notorious White Fence Gang and had served time in prison. Hoping to make a difference in the lives of Chicano youths, he wanted to recount his terrible period of incarceration. At a social gathering we had both attended, he introduced himself and told me of his interest in producing a program to deliver his message to young Chicanos. I agreed to help him produce the program as a short film.

Carnalitos was filmed during several visits to the California Youth Authority prison in Chino and Norwalk. It was shot and edited in black and white by Richard Davies, the KCET cinematographer, whose sharp eye and fluid camera work rendered an impressionist, moody portrayal of the desolation and pain of life behind bars. The documentary included interviews with remorseful young offenders, who spoke about the need for their peers "on the outside" to stay off drugs, out of gangs, and out of prison.

As we visited the different prisons, I was overwhelmed by the sheer number of young people we met—many not more than fifteen and sixteen years of age. Many of these juveniles would go directly to adult prison when they turned twenty-one. These were hard-timers, in for life. On the last day of our shoot at the Chino facility, a young man of about sixteen approached us and said he had written a letter to the *carnalitos* (young brothers) back home. He wondered if there was a way we could include his thoughts in our film. When I read the letter, a lump formed in my throat. I decided on the spot to film the young man reading his own words:

> Being in jail isn't what's happening, *carnalitos*. On the outside, that's where it's all happening. Staying in school with a classroom full of beautiful brown Chicanas. Instead of wanting to be in here with the *batos* (dudes). I wish I had never started coming to these jails in the first place. It's a conspiracy by the *gabachos* [gringos] to keep us where we are at. They bring these problems upon us—anxieties, tensions, and hostilities that build up inside us. And then we try to hide from these problems by getting loaded, drinking wine, and dropping reds, but this only adds to all the tensions we have, until we blow up. But we don't take it out on the *gabachos*. Instead, we take it out on our *carnales* across the street. Killing each other. Open your eyes and see what he is doing to us. Don't let the *gabacho* get you down, so you will wind up in these jails. Stay in school and learn all you can. Be brown, think brown, and be proud of it. For you are the future hope of Aztlán, *carnalitos*. *¡Qué viva Aztlán y que viva la Raza!*

Another program in which we offered the *Acción Chicano* resources was a rendering of the works of Chicana poet Dorinda Moreno. This program involved the dramatic staging of several poems using a style reminiscent of Luis Valdez's *Los Corridos*. The works focused on themes of Chicana self-awareness and emancipation from traditional roles.

In September, I was visited at my KCET office by two young political activists who sought a career in film and television production. One of the young men, David Sandoval, had been introduced to me by Gayla a few weeks earlier. He had helped her coordinate a performance of El Teatro Campesino at Cal-State University at Los

Angeles, where he was enrolled. David was heavyset with a beard, prematurely thinning hair, and a round face that had prompted his friends to dub him "Chairman Mao"—a name that would stick with him for years to come. Gifted with an exuberant sense of humor, David had self-effacing shyness that masked the sharp intelligence of a political activist.

David brought with him an aspiring film student in the UCLA film program, Adolfo "Rudy" Vargas. Complementing Chairman Mao's quiet, unrelenting barrio humor was Rudy Vargas' infectious smile and effusive speech. Rudy's good looks endowed him with a bold gregarious nature. A natural leader with an instinct for problem-solving, he easily took command of situations and won people over. In grade school, his friends had compared him to Mugs McGillicutty, a character in the Dead-End Kids motion pictures. Somehow the "Mugs" became "Bugs" and the barrio moniker of "The Bugs" stuck. It was the name by which I would know him from that time forward.

In my office, Chairman Mao and The Bugs told me they wanted to produce a show that would explore the possibilities of the then recent innovation known as cable television.

"This can be a new way to reach the barrio," David told me with authority. He had been part of a preliminary study for a cable television franchise in East Los Angeles and had all the facts and figures.

"Exactly, *carnal*," Rudy added with more gusto. "With cable television, we can get around the racism at the mainstream stations that don't want to do Chicano programming. On cable, we'll be able to deliver programs like the *Ahora!* series, programs directly aimed at Chicanos. We'll be able to do all kinds of programming for *La Raza*." It wasn't till Rudy reminded me that I recalled I had met him years earlier, when he had been a guest on *Ahora!*

I was impressed by the passion in these young men. They possessed exactly the kind of motivation and talent I intended to foster with the guest producer outreach program for *Acción Chicano*.

For the next three weeks, I worked diligently with David and Rudy. I taught them how to research, prepare, and tape their studio talk show about creating an East Los Angeles cable enterprise. I was determined that the two would learn as much from me as possible during their short tenure as adjunct producers at KCET. I teamed Rudy up with Barry Nye, KCET's premier cinematographer, who agreed to film some of the documentary footage for the program. In the process, he gave Rudy hands-on experience with a 16-mm film camera and with film editing.

After three weeks of intensive work, the program was broadcast on October 4, 1973. From that day forward, my life would be inextricably linked to the lives of Chairman Mao and The Bugs. They would inform, help to shape, and participate in many of my film and television projects in the years that followed.

Wrapping It Up

The fall of 1973 was a busy one for Gayla as well. Throughout this period, Gayla worked without pay as coordinator for El Teatro Campesino's tour of Southern California, which featured the finished version of *La Carpa de los Rasquachis*. In addition to handling the bookings, she wrote press releases and made media contacts for the group.

She also had her hands full hosting Daniel and Armida Valdez at our home as Daniel prepared to record his first album. Following the previous year's *America de los Indios* concert, I had introduced Danny Valdez to Taylor Hackford, a friend and producer at KCET. Taylor had recognized Danny's talent and had helped secure him a recording agreement with A & M records. Daniel's first album was to be named after his soon-to-be-born daughter, Primavera (Springtime). Often, friends would drop by the house, and Daniel would entertain with impromptu living-room concerts. Our house was in constant turmoil with guests and visitors at all hours of the day and night. For all intents and purposes, Gayla and I were already members of El Teatro Campesino.

As I prepared for this major change in my life, I reflected on the status of the movement. In one short year I had seen the bold dream of a national La Raza Unida Party crumble into ineffectual local campaigns. José Angel's hold in Crystal City was tenuous, and the police attack on Corky's Crusade had all but destroyed the organization. Reies López Tijerina was noticeably absent from the national agenda—no more courthouse raids, no more speaking tours. He had settled back into relative obscurity as he continued to battle quietly for the land grants in New Mexico.

Only the farm workers' movement continued in its methodical, tenacious manner. But even here, the farm workers had met with serious obstacles. Their efforts to unionize lettuce pickers in the Salinas Valley had been met with organized opposition from the Teamsters. The ensuing conflict over which union would represent them had resulted in the tragic murder of two farm workers during the previous summer.

With the urban movement in disarray, or engaged in internecine fighting, and the rural movement stymied in a jurisdictional impasse with the Teamsters, the move to San Juan Bautista at this point in my life made all the sense in the world. At least in San Juan I could continue to explore the notion of Chicano politics and identity through film and theater, and I could do so with other committed Chicanos.

Chapter Sixteen

El Teatro Campesino

We have discovered Aztlán *in ourselves . . . This knowledge*
provides the dynamic principle upon which to build a deep
unity and brotherhood among Chicanos.
—Armando Rendón

Gayla and I moved to San Juan Bautista on January 20, 1974. Each of us viewed the relocation differently. Gayla still had misgivings, but was resolved to make the best of it. On the positive side, she looked forward to renewing friendships and hoped to work closely with Daniel Valdez as coordinator of his Southwest musical tour. For me, our new life in San Juan Bautista meant the opportunity to work on a day-to-day basis with Luis and Daniel Valdez and with José Luis Ruiz, who arrived in San Juan with his wife, Johnna, the day after we did.

This time, however, Gayla and I did not have the economic cushion of a KCET subsidy that had sustained us the previous year. Instead, we received the standard monthly stipend per couple—$250. Apart from the salary, the Centro Campesino Cultural provided neither room nor board for its members; our income barely covered rent, utilities, and food.

José Luis and I immediately began shaping the new film component of the Centro. In Los Angeles, he and I had never directly collaborated on a project. Now we would not only be working as a team, but we would be peers with all the others in the Centro "collective." The philosophy of the group was not "collective" in a Marxist sense (a Communist study group) but simply in the sense that we all worked, lived, and created together.

Our arrival signaled a new era in the life of El Teatro Campesino. Until this time, the group had derived its livelihood from theatrical performances on a circuit that included colleges, universities, and community centers. Now, with the new film and music components, in theory the *teatro* would be subordinate to the larger concept of the multi-arts Centro. All decisions about how the Centro would operate would be determined by the same board of directors that had made decisions for El Teatro Campesino. The members were Luis and Daniel Valdez, their wives Lupe and Armida, and several members of the theater company who had been with the *teatro* for the longest period of time: Félix and Lili Álvarez, Phil and Roberta Esparza, and Olivia Chumacero.

While it would have made sense to have José Luis and me on the Centro board, some of the Centro members seemed intimidated by our professional experience. Luis Valdez suggested that we wait until trust was established before asking to be on the board. Presumably, we would be invited onto the board when the members felt more comfortable with us.

Luis Valdez's request and the insular make-up of the board should have set off alarms in our heads, but José Luis and I were bending over backwards to fit in. After all, we were the newcomers. If the board felt more comfortable without us at first, we would go along with it.

The extent to which we were willing to acquiesce was made clear when Johnna Ruiz discovered that there was a choice parcel of land, some forty acres, on a hill overlooking the San Juan Valley. She and José Luis wanted to purchase the spread and eventually raise horses; they initiated negotiations with a realtor. When members of the Centro board heard about this, they approached Luis and Johnna and told them they wanted to purchase the land themselves for the proposed Campesino Cultural Center. Luis and Johnna graciously agreed to give up their claim to the land so that the Centro could make a down payment on the property.

Adding to the natural distrust of newcomers was the fact that we were outsiders to what appeared to be common religious beliefs practiced by many of the Centro members. Although I was aware that many of them held spiritual beliefs, it had not occurred to me that their convictions would conflict with my empirical humanism or our collective work. But at the first weekly assembly of the Centro, I was in a for a surprise.

As we sat in a large circle on the floor of the warehouse that served as workshop and meeting place, Luis expounded on the need to bring a spiritual life to Chicanos. I pointed out that in our quest for spirituality, we must not lose sight of the material poverty, police brutality, and political impotence that marked our lives. Luis said that these issues required faith, and that Quetzalcoatl was the true salvation for the Chicano people.

I was baffled by his statement. Was he making a metaphoric reference to the ancient Toltec/Aztec deity? Perhaps he was alluding to the importance of our Indian heritage in our struggle for political equality. Later, I asked Luis directly about what he had meant. He asked me to read a recent tract he had written entitled *Pensamiento Serpentino* (Serpentine Thoughts). I agreed to read the piece in order to understand his views better.

A Neo-Mayan Philosophy

A few days later, I read *Pensamiento Serpentino* and came away dumbfounded. The text was a rambling philosophical discourse that began with Chicano colonization—the oppression and abuses I had first read about in *North from Mexico*. Chicanos must be free of this colonization, Valdez asserted, but our salvation was not to be brought about by American democratic ideals or by Marxist communism. The answer lay in going back to our indigenous roots. This part, at least, I agreed with. But Valdez went further. As I interpreted the tract, written as a free-verse poem, Valdez asserted that salvation for Chicanos lay in returning to Neo-Mayan beliefs linked to Christianity. According to Valdez, following the crucifixion and resurrection, Jesus Christ reappeared in the New World as the leader of the Toltec nation: the religious emperor Quetzalcoatl! I could hardly believe the printed words before me.

I reviewed my research on pre-Colombian history from the making of *Yo Soy Chicano*. According to ancient codices and archeological evidence, the Toltec emperor known as Quetzalcoatl was banished from Tula, the capital of the Toltec empire, sometime in the 13th century by a rival religious order. His entourage traveled to the Atlantic coast, built ships, and sailed away to the East, promising to return. Archeological evidence supports the theory that a real Quetzalcoatl did, in fact, reign in the city of Tula and did travel by water craft to the Yucatan Peninsula. The Mayan Indian architecture in the Yucatan acquired a distinctive Toltecan influence at precisely the time Quetzalcoatl was supposed to have sailed to the East. When the Spanish conquistador Hernán Cortés arrived in Mexico in 1519, the Aztec Emperor Moctezuma II, a believer in the religion based on Quetzalcoatl, had interpreted the arrival of the Spaniards as the return of the legendary Quetzalcoatl. The belief that Cortés was Quetzalcoatl contributed to the destruction of the Aztec civilization.

Luis Valdez appeared to be asserting in *Pensamiento Serpentino* that the second coming of Jesus Christ predicted in the Bible was also the return of Quetzalcoatl—they were one and the same event. As Chicanos, we should put our faith in God, worship Jesus Christ/Quetzalcoatl and await a rapturous return that would deliver us from our earthly travails. It was unabashed Christian fundamentalism in Neo-Mayan garb.

Having left Los Angeles, I was committed to incorporating myself into the group. This meant adapting to the group's way of life and, yes, even its beliefs. But how could I adopt a creed that went against everything I believed in? I had long ago rejected the fundamentalist interpretation of the scriptures. I knew that accepting Christian dogma inevitably led to the "my God is better than your God" syndrome and intolerance for the beliefs of others. One thing I knew for certain: I was not prepared to believe in the divine return of Jesus Christ/Quetzacoatl, even if he wore a headdress made of Quetzal bird feathers and spoke Mayan.

More troubling to me were the political implications of *Pensamiento Serpentino*. If we left our liberation to the distant return of a supernatural being, what then of the struggle here on earth? Were we to give up *la lucha* (the struggle) and the dream of a better life for Chicanos in the here and now for pie in the sky after we died? I interpreted Valdez's manuscript as wanting to define a religious belief that would be uniquely Chicano. After all, the *Plan de Aztlán* had called for a radical restructuring of our lives based on our Chicano heritage. But Luis Valdez had apparently taken the *Plan de Aztlán* to its logical conclusion and had devised a Chicano religion based on Christianity and ancient indigenous mythology. Part of me wanted to help in this effort to build the new Aztlán. But the logical part of me was appalled by the idea of perpetuating Christian dogma with a neo-Mayan veneer. Though I didn't believe in it, I had to respect the fact that they sincerely did.

I decided to put my concerns aside. My own empirical humanism called for tolerance. As long as Luis Valdez did not demand that I adopt his beliefs, I would not ask him or the others to believe as I did. I would continue to integrate into the group while trying to maintain the integrity of my own beliefs.

Creating a Film Company

Meanwhile, José Luis Ruiz and I continued working on the film division of the Centro. Since San Juan had no resources for filmmaking whatsoever, we started from scratch. A film editing table was the first logical step. In a month, we built the finest editing table one could want, complete with film rewinds, opaque light box, storage drawers, and trim bins. Then we drew up plans for an editing and projection room. In order to make our editing table better, we had to listen and concede to one another's ideas. Through this process, we learned to put our egos aside; it was as unselfish and united an enterprise as I had ever undertaken.

The *carnalismo* (brotherhood) that José Luis and I shared in creating our editing table was a goal promoted amongst members of the Centro. One of the precepts that Valdez had culled from his Mayan studies was an indigenous concept of brotherhood expressed in the Mayan phrase *En Lak Ech,* "you are my other self." The logic was incisive: if you were my other self, then it followed that if I did harm to you, I did harm to myself. If, on the other hand, I sought to do good by you, I was doing good to myself. Valdez urged us to put this admirable philosophy to work in our daily lives. I learned about this firsthand when, shortly after our arrival, I came down with the flu. One night, there was a knock at the door. I opened it and found Luis Valdez standing there with a cup of homemade eucalyptus tea he had just brewed for me. Thoughtful gestures like this, not uncommon among members of our group, made our communal life in San Juan Bautista more than merely *carnalismo* rhetoric.

Soon, spring came to San Juan Bautista, and we settled into a regular work pattern. The actors, under Luis Valdez's direction, took workshops similar to the ones I had participated in the previous winter. José Luis and I, with the help of the few Centro members assigned to us, worked on establishing a film production and distribution center. We spent many hours writing proposals for film and television productions and, occasionally, drove to Los Angeles to pitch ideas. Though Luis Valdez still viewed the film and television industry in Hollywood as "el diablo," he reluctantly agreed that we should try to land contracts for productions. Already, José Luis and I had bid with the McGraw-Hill Company to produce documentaries on Chicanos. Now we pitched ideas to KCET and KNBC for co-productions by these television stations and the Centro.

The Individual Versus the Collective

By the time José Luis and I joined the group, equality was an implied, often stated goal of the Centro. It began with every member's $100 a month stipend (slightly more, $250, for couples). We formed a food cooperative and bought food in bulk from the local markets and the town bakery. We divided our staples of meat, rice, beans, cheese, and tortillas into equal shares, and distributed them amongst the Centro members.

Equality was also stressed when it came to determining the work of the group, which was decided by the Centro board.

Although great store was given to what the group founders Luis and Daniel Valdez said, each member had one vote. Our goal was to create a society of peers, in which everyone performed specific tasks that they enjoyed for the betterment of all.

What was not addressed, however, was how to deal with the assets of an individual in a collective setting. Although we were all supposed to be equal, in fact, not everyone was equally skilled nor equally capable of contributing to the group's efforts. Educationally, the make-up of the Centro was extremely diverse. Some young members had never finished high school while others had college degrees. Some had extensive skills and highly disciplined work habits, while others were less gifted and unaccustomed to self-discipline. Despite attempts to regulate and parcel out job assignments and daily chores, the inevitable outcome was that the work load fell disproportionately heavy upon a handful of people. Of course, this generated resentment among the harder-working members (myself included), but because we were supposed to be a collective, many of us bottled up our frustration.

In March, I received a surprise visit from an old friend, artist and sculptor Gilbert Magú Luján who had come up from Los Angeles on his way to San Francisco. I spent the morning showing off San Juan to Magú and his wife, Mardi. Eventually we found ourselves at the top of the forty acres of land that had been staked out by the board for the Campesino Cultural Center.

Below us, we could see busy San Juan Bautista with its inhabitants going about their daily business. To the left, was the town cemetery and the road that led to Highway 101, to the right, the abandoned cement factory that had once been the town's main industry. Behind San Juan were onion and potato fields that stretched to the town of Hollister in the distance.

"The problem we're having with Los Four is how to coalesce our individual efforts into a collective group vision," Magú said as a breeze swayed the tall grass around us. "I'm stressing Aztlán, but not everyone agrees with me."

Los Four was an art collective of four renowned Los Angeles artists that in addition to Magú, included Carlos Almaraz, Roberto de la Rocha, and Frank Romero. Magú had organized a recent joint exhibit of their work at the Los Angeles County Museum of Art—the first time that Chicanos had exhibited in that elite venue.

"I'm facing the same problem here in San Juan," I nodded. "I think we're all agreed we want to affirm our indigenous identity, but everyone has a different idea of how that's to be done."

"So how do you guys decide what projects you're going to work on?"

"Luis Valdez makes the decisions for the *teatro*, Danny for the music department, and José Luis and I decide for the filmmaking. But do we give more resources for *teatro* projects or for music or for filmmaking? We're still hashing that one out."

"We decide things democratically with a vote," Magú chimes in. "But only after a lot of arguing and debate. The other problem we're having is the difference in our artistic aesthetic and work habits. Each of us does it differently."

Below us I could see some of the *teatro* members gathered outside the warehouse—it must have been time for a group workshop.

"This issue of work habits is really driving me nuts," I said. "José Luis and I set really high standards—maybe too high. That's why it took us a month to build that editing table I showed you. But there are some members who do things half-assed. When we call them on it, they laugh it off. They say it's okay because we do things *rasquachi* around here. Like it's something good."

Luis Valdez's play *La Carpa de los Rasquachis*, had popularized the notion of *rascuachismo,* the low taste aesthetic of the underdog, making do with what one had, piecing things hurriedly and sloppily together. A few Centro members, however, used this to excuse their shortcomings.

"Well, just don't let your guard down," Magú cautioned me. "You can compromise so much in trying to work with the collective that eventually all your own contributions are lost."

I vowed to remember Magú's cautionary advice, but at the same time I felt comfortable about Luis Valdez and his quest to define a spiritual dimension to *chicanismo* based on our indigenous roots. In many ways, this sense of purpose helped me to rationalize my continued participation in the Mayan spiritual workshops and in the new activity Valdez instituted among group members: weekly Bible study classes!

The Bible sessions started shortly after our arrival in San Juan. Participation was voluntary but almost everyone attended. Luis Valdez would read passages from the Bible and then interpret them from his neo-Mayan perspective. I hated fundamentalist doctrine and found it hard to keep my mouth shut. At times, this disrupted the meetings. Finally, after several visits, I stopped attending.

A Film Opportunity

The previous year, the Citizens Communications Advocacy Group challenged the sale of five television stations by the Time Life Corporation to the McGraw-Hill conglomerate, charging that the new owners would continue a programming policy of ignoring Mexican Americans, a sizeable part of its broadcast audience. In order for the sale to go through, McGraw-Hill agreed to fund and broadcast ten one-hour documentaries on Mexican Americans in the United States. Three documentaries were produced with poor results, and its advisory board, made up of Mexican-American educators, attorneys, and activists, asked that future films be contracted to Chicano filmmakers.

In early April, José Luis Ruiz and I were informed that we had been selected to direct one film each and that two films had been assigned to our filmmaking competitor Moctesuma Esparza. The filmmaker delivering the best product would be commissioned to produce the remaining three films in the series. Each film was budgeted at seventy thousand dollars, an enormous budget for a documentary at the time.

Thrilled, we immediately informed Luis Valdez. He agreed to convene a meeting of the Centro board, since the contracts, totaling $140,000, was clearly something that would affect all of us. Instead of the enthusiasm we expected from the other Centro members, however, we met with caution and suspicion.

Led by Luis Valdez, the board decided that José Luis and I should not accept the McGraw-Hill contracts as individuals. Instead, Valdez wanted the Centro board to administer the funds and produce the films.

José Luis and I were stunned. We knew that, historically, when members of the group had worked as individuals—for example, when

Luis Valdez gave lectures, or when Daniel Valdez recorded his *Mestizo* album—they had negotiated and retained payment for their work. Now, suddenly, things were to be done differently.

Luis Valdez explained that the issue was not about the money. It centered on whether the individual or the group would have final say in San Juan. According to Valdez, we were asking for special consideration, the right to make a personal film and to administer the funds. In the new San Juan it had to be the group that decided these issues. We argued our case vigorously. At a certain point in the debate, however, José Luis stopped talking and drifted off to watch a football game on television. I was left to fight it out on my own. The meeting ended inconclusively.

Later, I found José Luis at Vincent's, a regular watering hole for those of us in the Centro who drank. Anger reddened my face as I downed a beer.

"So why did you give up and walk away?" I asked.

"I didn't. We just have different ways of confronting the board. You shout at them. My way of reacting is simply to avoid confronting them. I plan to do what I want with my film, anyway."

"What does that mean?" I pressed.

"We give them too much say in our lives. I'm not going to ask the board every time we need to rent equipment, buy film, or hire actors. I'll go to the individual members. And if they don't want to act in the film or the board says they can't, then I'll get somebody outside the group who will. Eventually, the board will have to come to us. After all, we're the ones that got the money, not them."

Neo-Mayan Capitalism

For the next several days, Jack Shafer, a television executive at McGraw-Hill, called regularly to see if we would accept the film assignments. José Luis and I stalled, waiting on another board meeting that had been scheduled to settle the matter.

A few days later, I was asked to meet with the board alone. Phil Esparza, Luis Valdez's second-in-command, spoke for the group. He reiterated their decision: The McGraw-Hill films would be produced by the Centro, with the checks made out directly to the Centro Campesino Cultural. José Luis and I should go to New York and negotiate with McGraw-Hill under these conditions. If they balked, we were to refuse the films entirely. If we chose to do the films as individuals, it would be without the Centro, and we would be asked to leave the group.

I felt insulted and cheated. In spite of the good faith that José Luis, our wives, and I had shown, we were being given ultimatums. There was no middle ground. I loathed the notion of giving in to them, but I still harbored a strong desire to be part of the group. My inner turmoil was fueled further when Luis Valdez tied the McGraw-Hill film contracts to his neo-Mayan spirituality. The board's decision, he explained, was, in fact, the spirit of God working within all of them. Their decision had been divinely guided.

I could understand board members looking after their own interests, but Valdez using God to justify their decision—no matter how much he might believe it—was more than I could bear. I returned home and wept. It was the worst disappointment I had felt since arriving in San Juan.

I was torn. What of the dream that had brought me to San Juan? What of Aztlán? What of the multi-arts center we were building? And what of the work we had ahead of us for our people, for the *movimiento*? Complicating the situation was the fact that Gayla had successfully integrated herself, managing Daniel Valdez's music operations. She found the work challenging and rewarding, and I wanted to safeguard her success. We had found a community that accepted our mixed marriage. Despite the majority of Centro members being Chicanos, they accepted Anglo members of the group with as much respect and love as they did each other.

After much soul-searching with Gayla and discussions with José Luis and Johnna Ruiz, we all decided to give in. Although we were still not allowed to be on the Centro board, we had sacrificed much to come to San Juan and were not ready to throw it out without giving the process a fair shake.

A few days later, José Luis and I traveled to New York and met with the head of McGraw-Hill at its fifty-story office building on the Avenue of the Americas. We met in an opulent, wood-paneled board room, where we proposed that the two film contracts be awarded to the Centro Campesino Cultural. The McGraw-Hill executives agreed to funnel the monies through the Centro on the condition that José Luis and I produce and direct the films.

On our return to San Juan, the board of the Centro reluctantly agreed to the McGraw-Hill conditions. A few weeks later, we hosted the McGraw-Hill chief of operations and several members of the Mexican-American Advisory Committee, who flew to San Juan Baustista to meet Luis Valdez and to sign the final documents. Through it all, I was amazed that we had managed to lure these high-level Manhattan executives to visit us in a hamlet of 1,000 people.

Film Production

In early May, José Luis and I flew to Los Angeles to attend a script meeting of McGraw-Hill's Advisory Committee. The group was made up of a number of distinguished Mexican Americans, including television executive Claudio Gallegos, child psychologist Uvaldo Palomares, attorney Mario Obledo, educators Ted Barros, Armando Rodríguez, and Julián Nava, who was still on the Los Angeles school board.

Julián Nava urged that the documentaries shy away from a sociological approach to our community and, instead, address universal themes such as childhood, tradition, family, and love. We agreed that José Luis would develop a documentary on the theme of "Growing Up Chicano," and that I would devise one with "Chicano Love" as its theme.

After returning to San Juan, I outlined different kinds of love as I saw them: romantic love between a man and woman, maternal love between mother and child, the love of comrades (man to man), the love of an individual for his people, and the love of God. My goal was to show how love in our community also promoted political and cultural empowerment. I would present the entire Chicano family—young people and old, working people, and activists—as I had in *Yo Soy Chicano*. As with this earlier work, I planned to mesh documentary with narrative.

Within a short time, I narrowed the film's concept into four parts. The first piece was a narrative love story involving a young Chicana school teacher and her love interest, a photojournalist for the movement. The conflict centered on issues of identity and self-determination as the young woman struggled with her overly possessive, macho boyfriend. This story would set up three other stories, shot documentary style, which would profile three real individuals as examples of other kinds of love.

As we began pre-production, José Luis and I knew we needed able assistants to work as associate producers. We felt that there was no one in the Centro who had either the experience in film production or the inclination to learn. Therefore, we went outside the group, turning to the two Chicano media activists I had mentored on *Acción Chicano:* Rudy Vargas and David Sandoval. We invited them to live in San Juan Baustista for the duration of the production as associate producers. They agreed, and within a week, Chairman Mao and The Bugs were in town. David was assigned to work with me on "Amor Chicano" and Rudy was assigned to work with José Luis Ruiz on "Growing Up Chicano."

With David on board, the next step for me was to find the real stories that would make up the bulk of the documentary sections of my film. To this end, David and I traveled to Tucson, Arizona, and did three weeks of scouting for locations and individuals.

One of the people we settled upon was an eighty-year-old Yaqui Indian named Manual Álvarez. Through a profile of this soft-spoken and wise man, I intended to explore the concept of man's love of nature and God.

To explore family love, and the social and cultural traditions of the Chicano family, we settled on a seventy-year-old grandmother named Mrs. Josefa Romero. Using old still photos, I proposed to recreate the ups and downs of her fifty-year love affair with her late husband.

The third individual we settled on was a thirty-year-old construction worker and father of four, Joe Cuesta. Featuring Cuesta was an attempt to depict family love and the *compadrazco* (godfather) tradition of extended family.

Meanwhile, José Luis and Rudy traveled to New Mexico for their research. In his film, José Luis proposed to chronicle various aspects of growing up Chicano, also using dramatic and documentary techniques. We were ready to start principal photography in June. To economize, we hired the same camera crew for both films and piggybacked the filming of one film right after the other. Of course, the entire crew was made up of Chicanos we had hired out of Los Angeles. I went first. David Sandoval, Gayla, and I traveled to Tucson with our film crew and spent two weeks filming Señor Álvarez, Señora Romero, and Joe Cuesta. When we returned to San Juan, as José Luis prepared his filming, I worked on the dramatic sequences of the narrative story. I cast members of the *teatro* in the lead roles of the film.

As I finished up principal photography on "Amor Chicano," I received a curious invitation from Mexico City. The Center for University Film Studies at the University of Mexico (in Spanish, the CUEC) was convening an international seminar on Latin American cinema. Key film directors from every Latin American country were invited. I was asked to attend as a representative of Chicano cinema. I was both honored and giddy. I would be in the company of film giants!

New Latin American Cinema

A month later, on August 15, 1974, I found myself in Mexico City at the home of Mexican director Pepe Estrada, one of the leading Mexican film directors to emerge in recent years. His lavish split-level home was in the ritzy neighborhood of San Angel. I surveyed the living room. Expensive paintings and prints—here a Posada, there a Cuevas—graced the walls. Low-hanging chandeliers gave off soft light that was swallowed up in the vastness of the room before it reached the Spanish tile floors. The room bustled with servants dressed in Hollywood black and white. Forty famous Latin American filmmakers sipped cocktails, mingled, and conversed in their mother tongue.

I settled in with the others at a large dinner table, concentrating on my own broken Spanish, hoping I wouldn't let a blunder spill over my lips. I met legendary Cuban film director Julio García Espinosa, alert, looking younger than his fifty years, director of the Cuban feature films *Joven Rebelde* and *Las Adventuras de Juan Quin-Quin.* Nearby, Miguel Littin, writer and director of *El Chacal de Nahueltoro,* in exile from Chile following the fall of the Allende government, was engaged in a serious conversation with Jorge Sanjines, whose film *Blood of the Condor* had exposed the forced sterilization of Bolivian women by the U.S. Peace Corps.

I soon fell into a conversation with Sergio Olhovich, another director of the Mexican new wave. The son of a Russian emigré and Mexican mother, he had studied filmmaking in Moscow. I quickly came to like this bearish, jovial director, who embraced me repeatedly as a "Chicano brother." He told me all about his recent feature film *Encuentro de un Hombre Solo* (Encounter with a Lonely Man). I didn't know it then, but Sergio would become a lifelong friend and collaborator.

As the evening progressed, I felt like an outsider, listening in on this and that conversation but not really being a part of it. Everyone made an effort to make me feel at home, but I was too much in awe of the filmmakers around me to contribute much.

I was honored that Chicanos were recognized as part of the Latin American experience and that I was the representative. Throughout the week, I participated in a number of seminars and round tables, and by the end of it, I began to feel that I did belong in this group of filmmakers. I saw their films and compared them to my own, realizing that we shared common themes: labor struggles, political empowerment, cultural affirmation. At the same time, I recognized how naive my political awareness was compared to that of my Latin American colleagues. While not everyone was a Marxist, everyone I met seemed deeply rooted in his Latin American identity and believed that class struggle was a given for Latinos. In contrast, my films dwelt on Chicano identity and the racism and discrimination we experienced, but overlooked analysis of underlying issues of class in the United States.

This became evident when I screened the four films I had brought to the encounter: *América Tropical, Yo Soy Chicano, Somos Uno,* and *Raza Unida.* While my presentation summarizing the Chicano struggle in the United States was well received, the films caught considerable criticism. Much of this centered on the lack of Spanish in the films. Even more criticism was leveled at the symbols of the Chicano Movement, particularly the use of the Virgin of Guadalupe by the United Farm Workers. Many questioned this icon of our liberation, which for them was a symbol of the Church's oppression in Latin America. I had no answer except to say that as a filmmaker, I was reflecting what was going on in the community.

This response brought on even more criticism. Wasn't the role of the filmmaker to educate the public? To merely reflect the status of a social movement was to fail in my responsibility to use cinema as a weapon of liberation. Why did my films not focus more on the struggle of the urban working class in America? Why were Chicanos so parochial? Why weren't Chicanos working with African Americans and other working-class minorities in the United States? I took all of these criticisms to heart, realizing how primitive my approach to cinema seemed in comparison to that of the sophisticated filmmakers who were creating something they called *El Nuevo Cine Latinoamericano* (the New Latin American Cinema). These were filmmakers who used cinema as a tool for social protest and national liberation for the poor of their countries.

I vowed to examine anew my role as a filmmaker for Chicanos on my return to the United States.

At the end of the week, Julio García Espinosa led a small group of us on a night of club-hopping at Mexico City's famed Garibaldi Square, the plaza that had over decades become the meeting place of mariachi bands. As we listened to *rancheras* and *boleros*, García Espinosa and another Cuban director, Miguel Torres, pumped me for information about Chicanos. I was the first Chicano the Cubans had ever met, and they were exhaustive in questioning me about our social movement. García Espinosa seemed genuinely interested in the phenomenon of Chicanos (it had taken him a moment to get the idea that we were Mexicans *born* in the United States) and wanted to know more about our cinema. We talked about the possibility of mutual Cubano-Chicano exchanges in the future, and agreed that a first step would be to find ways of bringing the Chicano filmmaking community closer to filmmakers of Latin America. I agreed to give him a list of Chicano film-makers, their works, and background articles about the Chicano struggle, and they invited me to visit Cuba at some future date.

A Marxist Meeting

Back in San Juan, amid the scramble to edit my film, I spent the next two months intensely involved in bringing myself up to speed on Marxist theory. I read James Conway's *The Analysis of Marx, Jesus and the Theology of Liberation,* Adolfo Sánchez Vásquez's essays on Marxist aesthetic, and I also read the work of liberation theologist Gustavo Gutiérrez.

It was clear to me that Marxism was no longer the anathema it had been to Chicanos in 1969. In 1972, Carlos Muñoz, Jr. and Mario Barrera had written a seminal study, "The Barrio as Internal Colony," and Dr. Rodolfo Acuña had published his landmark book *Occupied America.* Both works spoke of Chicanos as a colonized people who provided the manual labor necessary for capitalistic expansion in the United States. I had been deeply impressed by both works, but particularly with Acuña's work, which would soon become the standard text for Chicanos Studies.

Now, several Chicano groups with Marxist philosophy had recently come onto the scene. Among them was the Centro de Acción Social Autónoma (CASA), under the direction of veteran labor activist Bert Corona, which published a newspaper, *Sin Fronteras* (Without Borders), linking the struggle of Mexican workers to that of Chicano workers. With another group, the August 29th Movement, Chicano activists who had converted to Marxism sought to organize Chicanos as a "national minority" within the United States. They accentuated the teachings of Mao Zedong.

For months I had been approached by Chicanos in Los Angeles who were members of the Communist Labor Party, an offshoot of the Communist Party of America. At first, I had scoffed at any association with them; I saw them as political extremists, kooks. But after my exposure to Latin American Marxists, I was a bit more open. I agreed to a meeting with Nelson Peery, the secretary general of the Communist Labor Party, on my next trip to Los Angeles. I knew the meeting, arranged by a mutual friend, would be another attempt to recruit me into the CLP. But I was intrigued, and so I went.

Nelson Peery was a fifty-year-old African American with a distinguished gray beard. He dressed in modest work clothes, had a broad smile, and laughed deeply and often. We began the evening with a screening of *América Tropical*. Afterwards, we discussed the film and the political and artistic work of muralist David Alfaro Siqueiros, an avowed Communist. Our conversation soon shifted to Chicanos in the United States. I shared my views with Peery on how the Chicano Movement fit into the larger effort for social change in America.

As I saw it, our activism ought to proceed in three stages. The first stage was to work along cultural nationalist lines, to educate Mexican Americans about our economic and social plight in the United States as a people, and to suggest actions for social change. The next step was for us to link ourselves with other Latinos suffering under similar economic and political repression. A common language and culture were natural links for our unity. Lastly, I saw unifying the Chicano Movement with the social movements of African and Native Americans. I believed Chicanos should form coalitions, but to avoid being overwhelmed by stronger movements, we needed to organize ourselves first. By breaching ethnic and racial boundaries with this third stage, we would be more concerned with unifying the underclass in America around common issues for positive social change.

Peery listened attentively to my ideas and then shared his convictions. He drew the analogy of train tracks that begin at a station and head out along parallel lines, appearing to merge at the horizon. But this was an illusion. The train tracks never do meet at the horizon. Therein lay the danger in using nationalistic or racial strategies toward an eventual unity of the working class in America. The ruling class was famous for using divide-and-conquer tactics, pitting one race against another to the benefit of the employer. He proposed that Mexican Americans be encouraged to unify with other working-class people in America from the onset.

Peery used words I did not often hear: "basic human dignity," "justice and truth," and "common sense." He reflected a profound faith in humankind, believing that all races could pull together for a better world. As we parted, Perry suggested that my film work, grounded in socialism, could be used to advance a class understanding among Chicanos.

I liked Peery, but distrusted the CLP. I was particularly wary of my filmmaking being guided by political activists for their own ends. I recalled having read about James Baldwin's flirtation with the Communist Party in the forties and his disenchantment with their attempts to control his art. I didn't need to repeat his mistake. The meeting with Nelson Peery and my readings only widened the gulf I felt between my ideas and those of Luis Valdez and the other Centro members.

By September, José Luis Ruiz and I had both finished principal photography of our films, "Growing Up Chicano," which he had now retitled *Primavera,* and "Amor Chicano," which became now *In Our Lives.* Next came the editing. We hired Peter Rostin to edit both films in our new Centro editing room. Editing took up all of October and November.

The End of a Dream

One evening in mid-October over drinks at Vincent's, José Luis told me he had asked for a special meeting with the Centro board. "I'm going to be leaving San Juan," he said, trying to sound matter of fact, but unable to mask the emotion in his voice.

For the past month, both of us had openly discussed the possibility of leaving. I was convinced the Centro was off track when it came to its politics. For José Luis, the summer filming had been fraught with creative differences with Luis Valdez and other Centro members. José Luis was not used to having his creative decisions questioned at every turn.

On November 8, with an answer (test) print of *Primavera* delivered to the board, José Luis loaded up the family (including his very pregnant wife) and prepared to drive back to Los Angeles. Just as they were about to leave, Johnna's water burst. With medical arrangements already made at a hospital in Los Angeles, Luis drove Johnna to the

San Jose airport and flew to Los Angeles, where his daughter, Somerset, was born in an ambulance on the way from the Los Angeles International Airport to the hospital.

In mid-November, we screened the answer print of *Primavera* for the group. It was a splendid film, and I was envious of his masterful work. Its documentary and dramatic moments merged beautifully.

Now the pressure was on me to finish up *In Our Lives*. By early December, we had a rough cut ready to show and a more finished answer print of *Primavera*. Representing the Centro, I flew to New York to screen the two films for McGraw-Hill's final approval.

The advisory committee and McGraw-Hill seemed to like *Primavera*, but they found *In Our Lives* unacceptable because, in their opinion, it presented a one-sided view of the struggle of the United Farm Workers' Union. In particular, they objected to scenes in the narrative section in which the Chicana school teacher and her activist boyfriend participated in the lettuce boycott undertaken by the United Farm Workers' Union. I had filmed scenes at a real picket line in Stockton, California, where my actors mingled with union activists. During the filming, the strikers were attacked by the Modesto County Sheriffs, and everyone, including our camera crew and actors, was maced. We narrowly escaped arrest.

As Chicanos, I felt the Mexican-American Advisory Committee would see the honest struggle of farm workers and would be supportive of my film. Instead, the members of the committee saw my film as propaganda for the United Farm Workers' Union. The McGraw-Hill executives explained that there was no way they could show my film on their stations, particularly the Bakersfield station located right in the middle of the grape strike controversy. By association, McGraw-Hill decided that they didn't want to broadcast Luis Ruiz's film, either.

I returned to San Juan Bautista dismayed. I explained to the Centro board that I had gotten no support from the advisory committee and that McGraw-Hill wouldn't complete either film. This decision had serious implications. Throughout production, we had received funding in increments with a major advance upon the signing of the contract. The last payments, about $12,000 per film, were contingent on final approval, which I had just failed to get. The bulk of this $24,000 was to be profit for the Centro.

I called McGraw-Hill, hoping to change their minds, but the company was adamant. Finally, they came to us with two options. If the Centro really wanted the films completed, they could do so on their own. McGraw-Hill would hand over all rights and ask only that they not be credited. But the final payments would not be paid. As for the other contingency, McGraw-Hill would pay the Centro the final $24,000, but only if all film originals and copies were returned to McGraw-Hill. They would then store the films rather than broadcast them. The decision was in the hands of the Centro board.

I was delighted with the proposal. I knew that completing my film only required a few hundreds dollars to cut the negative and get a print out of the lab—something I knew we could easily afford. José Luis's film was already at answer print stage. Within a few weeks, we could have prints of each film and begin to use them for political organizing. I envisioned a national campaign similar to that which I had launched for *Yo Soy Chicano*. It never occurred to me that the Centro Campesino Cultural would seriously entertain the other option that McGraw-Hill offered.

In January of 1975, the board met to decide on the future of the films. At the meeting, Daniel Valdez told me that the board had decided to accept the McGraw-Hill money, give up all the film materials, and relinquish all rights to both films. They would use the $24,000 to make final payment on the forty acres of land overlooking San Juan Baustista. As they saw it, the sacrifice of the films was necessary for the success of the larger concept of the Centro.

I was stunned. What about our lofty discussions on creating Chicano films uncensored by El Diablo in Hollywood? What about our commitment to the farm workers' struggle? Films that could advance the cause of the Farm Workers' Union would now be destroyed or end up on a dusty shelf.

Tears swelled in my eyes. How could this be? Each board member averted his or her gaze as I looked questioningly from face to face. These were the people who had become my closest friends, and now they had turned their backs on me. Finally, Danny Valdez got up and gave me a hug. We both openly wept as the others squirmed in their seats. Daniel and I understood that this was the end. I could no longer be part of the group that had betrayed all the work I had undertaken for the past nine months.

The next day, with Gayla's tight-lipped assent, I announced to the group that we would be leaving San Juan Bautista at the earliest possible moment.

Before I left, I had a private meeting with Luis Valdez. I told him that, in my opinion, he and the others had created a see-no-evil, hear-no-evil utopia in San Juan Bautista, dressed up in a neo-Mayan religious mythology, but had forgotten about the struggle of the common people. Instead of distributing films that would help the farm workers' struggle, which had given birth to their organization, they had opted to acquire land, just like any capitalist grower in the region. In spite of my anger, I had a sense that Luis Valdez was equally disappointed and hurt by the acrimony of our parting. Years later, we would reconcile and join forces to advance opportunities for Latinos in the motion picture and television industry.

Back to Los Angeles

On February 21, 1975, with the help of a few Centro friends, Gayla and I packed up our belongings in a twelve-foot U-haul and drove back to Los Angeles. We arrived broke, without any prospects of a job.

Trying to understand what had gone wrong left me deeply depressed. We had all worked so hard to achieve our ambitious goals at San Juan Bautista, but our idealistic dream had failed. Perhaps José Luis and I were to blame for wanting too desperately to be part of the group, for acting against our own best interests. Perhaps, as Magú had warned, we had given up too much for the collective. Maybe the Centro members could have been more open in their dealings with us. Or maybe the notion of building Aztlán as an indigenous collective society within an America fueled by capitalism was something simply beyond all of us. I recalled the countless gestures of sincere friendship and love shown to Gayla and me throughout our stay. I recalled the honest efforts we had all made to reach out to one another and create a utopian world based on equality, mutual respect, and *carnalismo*. I clung to one thought: that we had all acted in the best of faith. To believe otherwise would be to make villains of all of us and forsake any hope that Chicanos and Chicanas could work together to change American society.

Gayla and I moved into a dilapidated, roach-infested garage that had been converted into a two-room apartment—the only housing we could afford. We immediately started looking for work. I discovered, to my relief, that I was eligible for unemployment compensation due to my work at KCET. At the end of my first week in Los Angeles, I stood in the unemployment line and wondered how such a noble dream had turned into such a nightmare.

Chapter Seventeen

Infinity Factory

The experience of Chicanos in the United States parallels that of other Third World peoples who have suffered under the colonialism of technologically superior nations . . . Chicanos in the United States are a colonized people.
—Rodolfo Acuña

During the month of February and in early March, I spent a great deal of time with my two friends David Sandoval and Rudy Vargas. With no prospects for immediate employment, I planned for future work down the road. The three of us formed a film company, Amanecer (Dawn) Film Associates, and applied for funding from the Corporation for Public Broadcasting's Program Fund. We proposed two film productions, a film about Crystal City, Texas, the last stronghold of the failing La Raza Unida Party, and another film on Mexican immigration to the United States.

Hueristic Devices

In early march, I learned of a job opportunity. An East Coast educational firm, The Education Development Center, was looking for an executive producer for its upcoming national television series. The series would teach mathematics to minority children of the inner city, ages eight to eleven. Representatives of the firm would be in Los Angeles for two days of interviews.

The notion of my working on anything to do with mathematics seemed farfetched. I was terrible at math. How could I possibly produce something I knew so little about? And what did mathematics have to do with the Chicano Movement? I might as well be doing documentaries on semiconductors or food processing. Nonetheless, I was desperate for a job. I arranged to interview for the position.

The interview was conducted in a hotel room at the Holiday Inn on Highland Avenue in Hollywood. I met a 70-year-old, white-haired physicist named Jerrold Zacharias, who was the series creator. He knew nothing about television. With him was an ever-smiling thirty-year-old Jamaican named Evans Wilby, the assistant project director. They explained that the Education Development Center (EDC), with offices in Newton, Massachusetts, a Boston suburb, was a think tank that had been founded by scholars from Harvard and the Massachusetts Institute of Technology in the early sixties. The previous year, it had been awarded a four-million-dollar grant from the U.S. Office of Education to produce sixty-five half-hour programs on television targeting minority youth. The show, whose working title was *Project One*, would teach children mathematics, similar to the way in which *Sesame Street* taught younger children the alphabet.

Zacharias, who did most of the talking, explained that America's children—especially minority children—were failing at math because they were taught mathematical theory at school, instead of being shown how mathematics worked practically in their day-to-day lives. What he proposed was an approach that linked mathematical precepts to the daily activities children enjoyed.

For reasons they didn't elaborate on, the project director and the executive producer they had hired had been unable to get a half-hour pilot produced. They were now looking for a new executive producer for the series, someone with extensive production experience who was also sensitive to the minority experience. They wanted someone to spark new life into the show.

As Zacharias explained the goal of the proposed series, he walked across the room to where I was seated and gave me a white card exactly the size of a business card. Two words were printed at the top of the card: "Heuristic Devices." What the hell was a heuristic device? Beneath the two-word heading was a neat list of words, equally enigmatic: "successive approximation, reiterative estimation, dual approach, extrapolations, mapping, and scaling." I knew some of the words, but what did they have to do with the interview at hand?

Zacharias studied me. "How would you make a television show out of that?"

I sat there for a long while eyeing the card, hoping for sudden inspiration. Nothing came.

"To tell you the truth," I replied, "I'm terrible at math. I would have to understand personally what each one of these concepts meant before I could even attempt to explain it to an eight-year-old. Only then could I tell you how I'd approach this stuff. Right now, I don't have a clue."

A smile spread across Zacharias's face. "You know, everyone else I've asked that question to has immediately launched into a long oration. You're the first person whose been honest enough to explain that you don't know how."

"Well, let's be sure of one thing. If these concepts could be made understandable to me, someone who is terrified of math, then I could certainly translate that into exciting television for children."

"That's a good start."

When I left the interview, I noticed that my old competitor Moctesuma Esparza was waiting in the hallway. I wondered what sense he would make of this peculiar interview.

A week later I received a phone call informing me that I had been selected as a finalist for the job. I was to fly to Boston for a final interview on Friday with the Education Development Center.

In spite of the income from a job Gayla had secured as a high school teaching assistant, we depended heavily on the $90 a week I received every Friday at the unemployment office. If I went to Boston, I wouldn't be able to stand in line and collect my unemployment check. I told them I was busy with important television meetings all week long and that I would not be able to go until after Friday.

Project One

On March 19, I was greeted at Logan Airport by two Chicanos who worked at *Project One*: Bob Carrasco, a math content specialist who was completing his Ph.D. at Harvard, and José Luis Sedano, one of the film producers already on staff. They took me to dinner at Harvard Square.

This was my first time in Cambridge, so I asked them to drive me around famous Harvard Square before we settled on a restaurant, the Blue Parrot.

Over dinner, my two hosts filled me in on the racial politics at *Project One*. It appeared that the political rifts were so intense as to threaten the very future of the series. I learned that although it was funded as a minority project under Title VII of the 1965 Civil Rights Act, the minority staffing was almost entirely black. This included project director Lee Colquitt. Bob and José Luis were the only Latinos on board. My two hosts complained that Latinos had been excluded from meaningful participation. The executive producer of the series, a white man named Chris Sarson, had recently resigned. Their hope was that if I was hired to replace him, I could bring more Latinos on staff.

Racial politics seemed to be the all-encompassing dynamic of the project. No wonder Zacharias and Whilby had been vague about why they had been unable to produce the pilot. I talked late into the night with my hosts before they dropped me off at my hotel, the Ramada Inn on Soldier's Field Road, along the Charles River, within eyesight of the ivy-covered buildings of Harvard University.

The next morning, I ate breakfast with Lee Colquitt. In his early forties, Colquitt was thoughtful, sincere, and committed— a true scientist determined that *Project One* should give minority children a new lease on the future. But Colquitt also seemed to be incapable of dealing with the fierce infighting.

I learned that there was a staff of sixty divided into three conflicting groups. The largest, numbering perhaps twenty-five, were the mathematicians. On the whole, they were white males from either

Harvard or MIT, whose job it was to engineer and oversee series content. Leading this operation was Jerrold Zacharias. Because he had dabbled in television before coming on board, another white mathematician, Mitchell Lazarus, was the acting executive producer. Though they knew their math, their approach to television seemed to be to put a teacher in front of a chalk board and have him lecture to the camera. They didn't have a clue on how to reach out to minority children of the inner city.

Another twelve to fifteen staffers were minority mathematicians, outreach specialists, educators, publicists, and content writers. Only three had any film or television experience. Not only was each minority group resentful of whites, but they pitted themselves against one another: the African Americans against the Puerto Ricans, the Puerto Ricans against the Chicanos, the Chicanos against the African Americans.

The third component of *Project One* was the management team for the Education Development Center. Colquitt was directly answerable to these men for his every action, yet they were inexperienced in dealing with minorities. This left Colquitt on his own. With this tangle of opposing interests, it wasn't surprising that every suggested model for the series had been rejected by one or another of the three groups and that Chris Sarson had chosen to quit.

The series had a recurring ten-minute dramatic segment entitled "Scoop's Place" produced out of a corner drugstore set in Yonkers, New York, by a group of African-American producers. *Project One* had also commissioned the production of a couple of minutes of cartoon animation. In addition, Mitchell Lazarus had rented a studio in Worchester, Massachusetts, to produce a ten-minute segment featuring a kid-friendly math instructor. Lee Colquitt, Evans Whilby, and Jerrold Zacharias drove me to the taping of this piece the following day.

I watched from the control booth in amazement. The instructor mumbled as he worked at lathing a table leg, explaining the mathematical concept of successive approximation as he worked. It was television guaranteed to put anyone, child or adult, to sleep. Evans explained that the segment would be integrated into the fifty minutes that had so far been produced for the series.

I winced, then turned to face Evans, stunned. "You've had four million dollars, and have been in operation for a year, and all you have to show for it is fifty minutes of videotape?"

He nodded gravely. "That's why we need you to take the job. We need someone who knows television, who can get us out of this mess."

That afternoon, I met with the upper management team from the Education Development Center. Bill Dale was a gregarious, outspoken administrator in his early forties. Erik Butler, assistant to the president of the EDC, was an intense, softspoken man with prematurely greying hair. Also present was Joe Stavenhagen, the lean, intellectual vice-president of EDC, an economist, and Ed Campbell, the president of EDC, a tall, gruff man with rugged features.

I was questioned extensively about what I would do, if hired, to get the project back on track. I told them that they had blundered from the start. I pointed to their staffing. They had too many of the wrong kind of people and not one television producer on staff. It was worse than putting the cart before the horse—they had no horse.

I told them they needed to fire people in outreach and publicity and replace them with television producers. "If you are teaching math in a classroom," I told them, "then it's fine for mathematicians to be in charge. But if what you want is a television show, then you need experienced producers to plan it. The best mathematical ideas aren't going to make a difference if no one is watching."

The managers listened attentively to my analysis. While they didn't agree with everything I said, I could tell that they knew that the project needed to be restaffed. By the specific questions they asked about my immediate availability, I had the sense that I was the top contender for the position.

A week later, I received the official offer from the Education Development Center. Because they were under pressure from the U.S. Office of Education to bring someone on board as quickly as possible, they asked if I could make a Thursday-afternoon flight for a meeting to discuss salary and relocation plans at the end of the week? Once again, I told him about a previous appointment in order to make sure I could pick up my unemployment check on Friday.

That weekend, my friends David Sandoval and Rudy Vargas came by the house to help Gayla and me consider our options.

"*Carnal,*" Rudy said, "look at the big picture. Here you have a chance to influence national television for millions of children—not just Chicano kids, but black and Asian and all kids. We talk about how, as Chicanos, we never get a chance to effect real social change, but here is a chance to do just that."

"The Bugs is right," Gayla said. "This job is what you make of it. Who's to say you can't make mathematics socially relevant? I mean, you said yourself you're going to have to hire more producers and writers. Hire people who can get across a Chicano or a black point of view. Here's a chance for minority kids across the United States to see themselves on television and to see themselves doing smart things!"

"How much social change do you really think I can get into mainstream television? I'll be coopted."

"Homie," David replied, "we know who you are. We trust Jesús Treviño."

"What about the documentaries?" I pressed. "What if we get funded?" I looked from Rudy to David.

"We'll do them ourselves," David replied. "We'll make you proud of us, Homie."

"Yeah," Rudy chimed in, "get you out of our way, and we can do those documentaries the way they're supposed to be done."

I turned to Gayla. "You up for spending a year or more in Boston?"

"You go, I go."

A Chicano in Boston

The next Monday, Evans Wilby picked me up at the airport and took me to the Education Development Center. He was delighted that I had been selected and went out of his way to be friendly. It suddenly struck me that I would be his boss and that he was courting my favor. In the afternoon, I met with Erik Butler and Joe Stavenhagen to negotiate my salary. They offered $33,000 a year. I told them I was used to more than that. We finally settled on $36,000, with an increase at the end of the first year. I tried to hide my delight. After surviving on a $90 per week unemployment check, $36,000 a year seemed like a million to me.

The Office of Education had given the EDC an ultimatum: Deliver a half-hour pilot for the series by June 5, only two months away, or they would close down the production. I called Gayla and broke the news that I couldn't go home. She would have to pack our belongings and move us to Boston on her own. "This better be worth it, Treviño," she said.

By day, I worked at my EDC office in Newton, Massachusetts, and by night I worked in my hotel room at the Ramada Inn along the Charles River. My first task was to develop a production schedule and budget for all sixty-five shows we'd have to deliver. With a quarter of the $4 million grant already spent, I had to figure out how to produce them for $3 million. To help me with the budget, I flew David Sandoval out. He became my righthand man in planning the series. Concurrently, I began to scout for key television staff.

I needed people I could count on, so I asked my old friend from KCET, Terri Francis, to apply for one of two producer slots, and she agreed. I also actively interviewed African Americans and Latinos from New York for the television staff we'd need to produce the skits I was planning for our Boston studios.

Among the more unpleasant tasks I had to perform was to work with manager Erik Butler on a timetable for restaffing. This we kept from the *Project One* personnel. I felt terrible and shared my feelings with Erik.

He thought about this for a moment. "Look at it this way. If we don't decide who has to be thrown out of the lifeboat, we'll all sink."

This made me feel better. "I would characterize it slightly different. I feel like we're trying to build a ship while we're trying to steer it out of the harbor."

The more I worked with Erik, the more I liked his straightforward style. He had a quiet way of making sense out of confusion and of deescalating a crisis. We soon became friends. He agreed with me that one of the project's chief liabilities was its creator, Jerrold Zacharias. Though well-meaning, his old-fashioned style and lack of political sense often got him into trouble—such as his attempt to ingratiate himself with the African Americans on staff by telling them anecdotes of the black mammy who had reared him. For the sake of the project, Erik and I agreed to keep him at arm's length from the staff.

After two weeks of hard work, the structure of the pilot emerged. The show would include two ten-minute dramatic segments: "Scoop's Place," which originated from a family-owned drugstore in Yonkers, New York, and "City Flats," which took place at an East Los Angeles family bakery. The remaining ten minutes would be made up of musical and dramatic skits performed by a multi-ethnic group of children at the WGBH studios, the PBS station in Boston. The show would also include two to three minutes of cartoon animation and mini-documentaries showing how math works in the lives of inner-city children.

Although our series was different in concept and in no way comparably funded, I knew that we would inevitably be compared to *Sesame Street*, the premiere children's series on PBS, and I was not bashful about learning from their experience.

By mid-April, I finally completed an extensive production plan, a revised budget, and an outline of the show format. Before any work could actually begin, however, we had to have final approval from our project officer at the Office of Education. We planned a trip to Washington, D.C. Then, out the blue, Lee Colquitt dropped a bombshell: the strain of the racial politics was too great for him to bear. He was resigning immediately as project director.

We postponed our trip to Washington, D.C. for a few days while we regrouped. Knowing that Colquitt's sudden resignation would not reassure the Office of Education, Erik Butler convened a hasty meeting with Joe Stavenhagen, Jerrold Zacharias, and me to discuss strategy. Stavenhagen explained that Colquitt's resignation would convince the Office of Education that the series was doomed. To counter this, he would open the meeting by announcing that a search for Colquitt's replacement was under way. He expected me to convince them I'd be able to produce the series.

"I'm not sure I can do that," I said.

The three managers turned to me with questioning looks. This is what I had been hired to do.

"What do you mean?" Joe asked.

I explained that the underlying problems plaguing the project from the start were still there. At the top were two individuals: the project director, in charge of content, and the executive producer, whose domain was television production. In an ideal world, the two would work together, meshing content and form into good television. But instead, the project director had been constantly undermined by the racial politics of the staff, and, therefore, Chris Sarson, the executive producer, could not get a production plan going because the staff didn't think a white man could program to minority children. It was no wonder Colquitt was quitting.

The fact that I had replaced Mitchell Lazarus as executive producer did not mean these tensions would automatically go away. Since Colquitt was African American, it was a foregone conclusion that racial politics on the project would dictate that the new project director would also have to be black. Instead of a white person pitted for power against an African American, now it would be a Chicano pitted for power against an African American.

"Look," I said, "we have only two months to get this pilot produced. That's tough enough under any circumstances. Add to that negotiating compromises between the mathematicians and the television producers. If, on top of that, I'm locked in a power struggle with the new project director, we're never going to make the June 5th deadline."

"What do you propose?" Erik asked.

"This is going to sound preposterous," I said. "But I propose that I take over Lee's job as project director."

There was silence.

"Who would be the executive producer?" Zacharias asked.

"Me. I'm proposing that I serve as both the executive producer and the project director in charge of content."

"But you're not a mathematician. How can you be in charge of the content?"

"It's the only way we're going to avoid a daily tug of war between content and production. I'll be able to make the necessary decisions to get the show produced. We have more than enough content specialists on board. If we're serious about getting this pilot produced, we're going to have to streamline decision-making and cut to the chase."

Zacharias grinned. "I like it. If that's what it's going to take to get the project done, I say let's do it! At least until we get over the pilot hurdle."

Joe Stavenhagen explained that it wasn't that easy. If we chose to undertake such a daring move, it would have to be with the official approval of the Office of Education. Given the history of the project, he doubted that they would go along with such a plan.

"It won't hurt to try," Erik said. "Let's run it up the flagpole and see what happens."

A few days later, we flew to D.C. and visited the austere offices of the U.S. Office of Education at 400 Maryland Avenue. Present were our project officer, Dorothea Perkins, the Office of Education television advisor, Dave Berkman, and Herman Goldberg, a high-ranking Office of Education official. They made no effort to hide their displeasure over Colquitt's resignation and promptly started quizzing me about the status of the project. Dorothea Perkins, who was African American, was supportive of the project, but she had been disappointed for more than a year by the managers of the EDC. With Colquitt gone, she had little faith that they would be able to save the show.

I laid out my plan for the series and showed them budgets, production schedules, and a list of candidates for the new television staff. When I finished, Joe and Erik advanced the idea of combining the project director position with that of executive producer, at least until the series was under way. They expressed great confidence that I would be able to handle both jobs.

Across the table, the three Office of Education officials bristled at the suggestion. They said it was much too risky to put so much power in the hands of one person, especially someone that was untested. Dorothea Perkins was particularly adamant. The answer was a definite no.

Erik stepped in and tried to clarify the suggestion. He pointed out the advantage of having more time to find a project director while not interrupting the production of the series.

As he made our case in his usual quiet, reasoned manner, my mind was suddenly a million miles away. As I read the grim faces listening impatiently to Erik, I realized that they were not going to agree. It occurred to me that, at this point, I had only one card left to play. Although I had been employed in Massachusetts now for several weeks, Gayla was still living in Los Angeles. It was still not too late to return to Los Angeles and abandon the project altogether. I imagined a year of trying to produce a show and being harassed from below and above. I surprised myself by coming to a hard decision.

"Excuse me," I interrupted, "but it's as simple as this. Either you give me the authority to make the decisions I need to make to get the series produced, or I am not interested in the job. Either I'm the project director *and* the executive producer, or I'm on a plane back to Los Angeles and you can find someone else to produce the series. You decide." I got to my feet and left the room.

As I left, I could see the blood drain out of Erik and Joe's faces. We had never discussed any of this, and they were aghast at my apparently capricious ultimatum. The truth was, I didn't know until that very moment just how prepared I was to reject the job.

I waited outside the meeting room, and after a couple of minutes Erik came out, hopping mad.

"What do you think you're doing?" he demanded. "You're jeopardizing the future of the entire project! Now they can pull the plug whenever they want!"

"Maybe they should," I replied. "Look, I'm not going to waste my time trying to produce a pilot for a show that's doomed. Either they authorize what we need to get the job done or they should close the project down."

"You can't do this!" he said urgently.

"Of course I can," I replied.

"What about the jobs of all those people back in Boston?"

"I'm not responsible for the situation that exists. You guys created it. I have nothing to lose. I can get on a plane right now, fly back to Los Angeles, and I'll be right where I was before I met you two months ago."

Eric returned to the meeting. After about twenty minutes, they called me back in. As I entered the room, Stavenhagen gave me a hostile look. Zacharias had a twinkle in his eyes; he was enjoying the high drama. Dorothea Perkins, our project officer, reluctantly agreed that at least for the next two months I was to act as both project director and executive producer.

Math and Culture

Erik and I completed the staff review and concluded that fifteen individuals had to be fired. This was tremendously stressful. By now, I had become friends with many of the people we had to let go. I was also fearful that we'd be charged with discrimination, given the racially charged atmosphere of the show. Erik and I made sure that the layoffs included all ethnic groups: a third were white, a third African American, and, of course, a third Latino.

In the meantime, Gayla moved to Boston, and we settled in a large house at nearby Watertown, Massachusetts. I started to bring new staff onto the project. Terri Francis moved to Boston in July, and shortly after that I filled the second producer slot with an African American producer from New York, David Roderick. I signed a deal with WGBH to build a "home base" set of a three-story East Coast brownstone apartment complex. We used this for skits that would involve a half dozen multi-ethnic kids, the show's "regulars." I hired an old friend from KCET, Allan Muir, to direct the "Brownstone" skits. As I had planned with David and Rudy, I converted an old garage in East Los Angeles into a bakery set and hired three Mexican-American producers, Rosemary Alderete, Gilbert García, and Deborah Gómez, to work with Rudy in producing the "City Flats" segments. I also contracted the producers of "Scoop's Place" to continue those episodes for each show.

Each show also contained one or two minutes of cartoon animation and a three-to-five-minute documentary, which I commissioned from a variety of independent black and Latino producers across the country. To edit it all, I contracted a postproduction facility in Los Angeles, Compact Video, for Terri Francis and David Roderick.

Project One's content specialists devised a set of mathematical objectives. These included the decimal number system, estimation, approximation, measurement, mapping and scaling, and graphing. Keeping in mind what Gayla had said about empowering minority kids, I felt we had to provide. I knew that part of that was providing them with positive role models. Our multi-ethnic content specialists were only too happy to accommodate me and devise a set of cultural objectives for the series as well. This included profiling important black, Chicano, Puerto Rican, and Asian-American heroes who had contributed to America's history.

Improbably, a series designed to teach mathematics to inner-city children introduced them to such people as César Chávez, Martín Luther King, Jr., Marcus Garvey, Ricardo Flores Magón, Malcolm X, Harriet Tubman, W.E.B. Dubois, Franz Fanon, and Mao Zedong, by showing how these individuals had used mathematics in their lives. The cultural objectives extended to the documentaries, which showed how mathematics were used in cultural celebrations of minority communities in America.

Jerrold Zacharias had offered a bottle of champagne to the individual who came up with the title most favored by the staff. Gayla won with a title that suggested the endless potential of a child's mind: *Infinity Factory.*

On June 5, we screened the pilot for the officials from the Office of Education. After the screening, the education officials congratulated us and—relieved that their $4 million government investment had been salvaged—gave a go-ahead to produce the additional sixty-four shows.

Funds had been so mismanaged in the past, it was clear that I'd have to take some drastic measures if we were going to make it through the season. After several meetings with the Office of Education, we got them to agree to reduce the number of programs from sixty-five to fifty-two. I also devised a way of recycling cartoon, documentary, and other elements to form new episodes without having to produce entirely new programs. Instead of having to produce fifty-two original one-minute cartoons, for example, we would produce a third that number and repeat each cartoon three times.

Throughout this period, the ethnic politics intensified. I was barraged with angry tirades from one group or another about my imagined "favoritism" or "discrimination." African-American producers charged that I gave privilege to Chicano and Puerto Rican producers.

The Latinos were equally convinced of my prejudice: the Puerto Ricans felt that by establishing the "City Flats" operation in Los Angeles, I had favored Chicanos over them, while the Chicanos felt I favored African-American producers over my own people. Whether it was a promotion, a salary raise, or more favorable job perks, everyone on staff played the race card. Before long, the constant pressure began to take its toll. By mid-fall I was experiencing anxiety attacks that awoke me in the middle of the night, when I was drenched in sweat, screaming in despair, and drained of energy. I realized that Lee Colquitt must have gone through this as well. Only the advice and support of Gayla and my close friends kept me sane.

As the shows began to reflect our diverse cultural objectives, however, the tensions between the minority staffers lessened. In spite of the early personal attacks and staff intrigues, the content specialists, writers, and producers, on the whole, had the best interests of the children at heart. Whether black, brown, or white, the staff of *Infinity Factory* had a mission and was working hard for America's children. The tide began to turn, and soon we were all taking enormous pride in the show.

As the year wore on, the sense that we were operating from one crisis to the next began to subside. As the Christmas holidays approached, Gayla and I even got some time to explore the back roads of New England and relax. By the end of the year, I was able to divide my weekends between working on *Infinity Factory* and on a screenplay that had been commissioned by Rodolfo Echeverría, brother to Mexico's president and director of the National Film Bank of Mexico. I presented the completed screenplay, which I had entitled *Raíces de Sangre* (Roots of Blood), to Rodolfo Echeverría at the end of December, and he agreed that I should direct it as well. Filming was set for August of 1976.

The End of an Era

Infinity Factory first premiered on PBS stations in Boston, New York, and Los Angeles on January 31, 1976. Later in the year, it was carried by all national public television stations. I recruited my old friend Luis Torres to plan a nationwide publicity campaign targeted at minority communities and at public schools, which he accomplished with great success. The series was immediately utilized in classrooms across America. Along with *Sesame Street*, the series was presented with the Excellence in Children's Programming Award by Action for Children's Television.

With *Infinity Factory*, I realized that I had come full circle in how I viewed myself and my role in American society. As a young man, ignorant of my own social history, I had learned to hate myself for my Mexican ancestry. I had desperately sought to emulate the American ideal by denying my own heritage and identity.

The Chicano Movement had opened my eyes to the outrageous poverty, discrimination, and social injustice experienced by my people. I had embraced *chicanismo* and had grown to hate America and its educational, penal, legal, and business institutions for discriminating against Mexican Americans. I had been empowered by the *Plan de Aztlán* to fight actively against these abuses and to affirm my identity through the media.

Later, I came to realize that the economic, social, and political issues that affected Mexican Americans also affected African Americans, Native Americans, and other poor people. The presence of a strong political Chicano Movement had dwindled, but I nevertheless wanted to produce programs for all Americans that advanced the same issues of justice, equality, and self-determination that I had learned from *el movimiento*. Indeed, I had internalized the values of the Chicano Movement as I understood them and had put these values to work in *Infinity Factory,* a program seen by millions of American children. To my surprise, I discovered that there were Americans from all races and backgrounds who shared in these same ideals and were willing to work for them.

I no longer hated America and its people. But I continued to despise the injustices perpetrated by American institutions. I accepted the fact that I was an American with the responsibility to make it a better country. The end of discrimination and injustice would not come about on its own, only through a constant campaign of struggle. And media, film, and television were key to this struggle.

Chapter Eighteen

The Road Ahead

The arm of the moral universe is long, but it bends toward justice.

—Martin Luther King, Jr.

The alien soldier was six feet tall. His long black braids hung down the back of his uniform. He spoke with difficulty due to the prosthetic nose and fangs that grew out of his outsized mouth. The make-up around his eyes was so encrusted with latex and hair that he could hardly see. A four-foot sword was strapped to his side, and he brandished a laser weapon in his paw.

"How does it look?"

"Looks great," I replied. "Just hang out, we'll be ready to go in a minute."

I settled back in my director's chair on the set of *Star Trek Voyager*. Actors dressed in a variety of alien costumes, adorned with fantastic facial make-up, milled about the set of a futuristic bazaar complete with weapons shops, spice stores, fabric stalls, and food vendors. The *Voyager* set was abuzz with last-minute preparations: gaffers adjusted lights, grips inserted wooden wedges under a metal track to stabilize the camera dolly, and everywhere, make-up artists applied last-minute touches to the alien horde. As I looked out at the exotic trade center, Robert Beltrán, one of the *Voyager* stars, approached.

"Pretty cool," Beltrán said to me as he surveyed the set with its legion of diverse life forms. Even for *Voyager* this was a rarity. More than twenty different alien species had been created for this one scene alone.

"But where are the Mexicans?" I asked, jokingly. Beltrán, a Chicano actor originally from Bakersfield, California, smiled.

"We're here," he said, indicating me and him.

I nodded, only too aware that he and I were anomalies—two Chicanos working in mainstream American television.

Just then my assistant director, Jerry Fleck, cut in. "We're ready," he said. I indicated for Beltrán to join Robbie McNeill, another of the *Voyager* cast, near the entrance to the futuristic marketplace. In the background, visible through a doorway, a large blue-screen had been hung. I would later electronically superimpose aliens over the blue-screen doorway to give the impression of even more bodies in the crowd. The two *Voyager* actors moved to their positions, and the aliens settled in around them.

"Sound is rolling," Allan Bernard, the sound mixer, called out.

The assistant cameraman slated the scene. "Fair Trade, Scene 13, take one."

"And. . .action!" I shouted.

As we filmed the scene in which the Voyager crew visits a rogue space station in the Delta Quadrant, my mind drifted from the set, aliens, and film crew. I thought of the thirty years that had passed since I had filmed 1,500 Chicanos gathered at the First Denver Youth Conference. In my mind's eye I could still see the young Chicanos raising the Mexican flag over the Colorado state capitol and proclaiming themselves to be citizens of Aztlán. How times had changed.

In 1976, after a successful broadcast season of *Infinity Factory*, I had moved from Boston to Mexico City to direct the feature film I had written, *Raíces de Sangre* (Roots of Blood). The film, which featured Mexican and Chicano actors, was shot on location in Mexico. It was a love story between a Harvard-educated Chicano and a passionate community organizer, set in a Texas border town where Mexican and Chicano workers were organizing an international union.

Described by *Daily Variety* as "a solidly made call to political involvement and activism," the film was nominated for an Ariel, the Mexican equivalent of the Oscar, and years later was singled out as one of the top twenty-five Latin-American Films of all time at the quincentennial celebration of the Valladolid, Spain, International Film Festival. In 1980, I wrote and directed the American Playhouse drama *Seguín*, which told the little-known story of the Tejanos, Texas-born Mexicans, who fought on the Texas side of the Texas revolt against their own Mexican compatriots.

During the early 1980s, I joined forces once again with José Luis Ruiz. We formed a partnership and devoted ourselves to directing and producing documentaries for PBS—mostly on Latino and Chicano themes. In the sixties and early seventies, we were both able to secure financing for films and television programs that directly addressed the issues raised by the Chicano Movement. The United States of the 1980s, however, had turned conservative. Under the Reagan and Bush administrations, funding for PBS documentaries was curtailed. By 1984, it had dried up entirely, and José Luis Ruiz and I were forced to shut down our film company.

Unable to find employment as a documentary filmmakers or to penetrate Hollywood (the exclusionary practices that kept Latinos like myself out of mainstream television and motion pictures continued unabated), I hit the lowest point of my life. After sixteen years of marriage, Gayla and I divorced. After being unemployed for more than a year, and on the verge of bankruptcy, I resolved to give up filmmaking. I moved to Tucson, Arizona, where I studied writing and taught documentary filmmaking at the University of Arizona.

Eventually, I returned to Los Angeles. In 1988, I decided to give filmmaking another try. I interviewed for a job directing a CBS afterschool special titled *Gangs*. Although well-intentioned, the script about Chicano gangs was insensitive to the notion of self-empowerment for Chicanos. I rejected the offer and, instead, delivered five single-spaced pages critiquing the script. To my surprise, the producer of the show called back to offer me the directing job, but also asked me to work with the writer to reshape the script to include my suggestions.

Gangs won the Directors Guild Award for best daytime drama in 1988 and landed me agency representation with International Creative Management, which bumped me up from directing documentaries to directing episodic television.

Since 1988, I have been regularly employed as a director of episodic dramas such as *NYPD Blue, Chicago Hope, Dawson's Creek, The Practice, Nash Bridges, The Pretender, Star Trek,* and others.

Following the success of *Gangs,* and, later, the success of my episodic work, I came to see that if I were to continue in my efforts to advance the ideals of social justice and equality—the values instilled in me by the Chicano Movement—I would need to be clever about doing so. During my time in Arizona, I had learned a bitter lesson: without a presence in the media, I was ineffectual as a social activist. I needed to remain a high-profile player in mainstream media if I was to continue my efforts for social change. I have found that the most effective way to advance my ideals is to make my livelihood directing commercial fare, creating Latino opportunities where and when I can, while producing my own films on the side that more openly express my beliefs.

Thus, during the early 1990s, while I earned a living directing episodes of such mainstream programs as *Seaquest, Hawkeye, New York Undercover, Space Above and Beyond,* and *Babylon 5,* I also helped José Luis Ruiz, my old friend, write proposals and raise funds for an epic project. For six years, we worked to finance and produce what would eventually become the four-part documentary series *Chicano! History of the Mexican American Civil Rights Movement,* a landmark series he and another old friend, Luis Torres, had initiated. I served as one of its executive producers.

Back on the *Voyager* set, as I prepared to shoot close-ups of the bizarre aliens around me, I fleetingly wondered what the real future of space might be like. Would there, someday, really be Chicanos in outer space? Would Chicanos ever overcome the myriad social problems addressed in this book? Would Chicanos and other Latinos ever take their rightful place in American society?

At the beginning of the new millennium, it is appropriate to ask, did the protests and social actions chronicled in this book bring about social change? Are Chicanos and Latinos better off today than in the 1960s? What can we learn from the experience of the Chicano Movement? In what ways can it inform strategies for the challenges facing Latinos in the year 2001 and beyond?

A Legacy of Positive Change

The social protests of the Chicano Movement ushered in a new era of progress for Chicanos and other Latinos in the United States. At its most basic, events like the August 29th Chicano Moratorium added to the national outcry that eventually stopped the war in Vietnam. The conclusion of the war brought with it an end to the disproportionate number of Spanish-surnamed soldiers dying by the thousands in the rice paddies and jungles of Vietnam.

On the educational front, efforts by groups such as the Mexican American Legal Defense and Educational Fund (MALDEF) and the Educational Issues Coordinating Committee (EICC) resulted in programs that better prepared students for higher education. The dropout rate at the four East Los Angeles high schools has been reduced from 50 percent to the less alarming rate of 28 percent at Wilson, 20 percent at Roosevelt, 15 percent at Wilson and 8 percent at Garfield. College enrollment of Latinos went from under 4 percent in 1968 to as high as 10 percent in the 1990s. Programs initiated under the Civil Rights Act of 1965 and the Bilingual Education Acts of 1968 and 1974 resulted in the creation of numerous opportunities that empowered Latino youth at the elementary, secondary, and college levels. They also generated programs to recruit and train more Spanish-surnamed teachers, counselors, and administrators. In 1968, for example, less than 4 percent of the teachers and counselors in the Los Angeles Unified School District were Spanish-surnamed; in the year 2000 that number had risen to 22 percent of the teaching staff.

In the political arena, efforts by groups such as MALDEF and The Southwest Voter Registration and Education Project (SVREP) reversed years of gerrymandering and redefined voting opportunities for Latinos, which have resulted in the registering of millions of hitherto unregistered Latino voters and a corresponding proliferation of Latino-elected officials.

At the time of the La Raza Unida Party convention in El Paso, Texas, there were four Mexican-American representatives in the United States Congress and one member of the U.S. Senate. Combined, there were only a few dozen local and state officials elected in Texas, California, New Mexico, Arizona, and Colorado.

Today, there are nineteen Latinos in the U.S. House of Representatives, but we have no senators. Spanish-surnamed mayors have been elected in San Antonio, Denver, and other Southwest cities, and Latinos have been appointed to the cabinet of the United States as U.S. Treasurer, Secretary of Transportation, Secretary of the Department of Health Education and Welfare, and Secretary of Energy.

At the beginning of the year 2000, there were 1,724 local and state elected officials in Texas, 603 elected officials in New Mexico, 264 in Arizona, and 151 in Colorado. In California, the lieutenant governor is Latino, as is the speaker of the house and the senate majority leader. This makes a grand total of 762 local and state elected officials, including twenty-four state legislators.

While there is a lot for which Chicano activists can claim credit, after all—a whole generation of Mexican Americans were inspired to give back to the barrio as its present-day doctors, lawyers, educators, politicians, artists, writers, and filmmakers—the present condition of Latinos in the United States is by no means a rosy picture.

Passage of legislation, such as California's Proposition 187, which denied educational opportunities to the children of undocumented immigrants in spite of the taxes they pay (most of which was later overturned in court), and passage of Proposition 209, abolishing affirmative action programs at California universities and colleges, are only some of the setbacks facing Latinos today.

Then, Now, Better or Worse?

In 1970, at the height of Chicano Movement activism, Chicanos made up about 4.5 million of America's 9 million Latinos. At 50 percent of the total, Chicanos were the majority, followed by Puerto Ricans (16 percent) and Cuban Americans (about 6 percent). Central and South Americans and other Spanish origin people made up the difference. The Latino immigrant population, largely from Mexico, was estimated at 300,000 a year.

Today, Chicanos and Mexicans make up 63 percent of the Latino population, followed by Puerto Ricans (12 percent) and Cuban Americans (4 percent). Not present in large numbers in 1970, but a sizeable presence today, are immigrants from Central American countries such as Guatemala, Nicaragua, and El Salvador, who account for 14 percent of all U.S. Latinos—a direct result of U.S. foreign policies that contributed to prolonged wars in these countries, resulting in massive dislocations. A total of more than a million immigrants are estimated to enter the United States illegally each year.

In 1970, the majority of Chicanos were trapped in a cycle of poverty. Unemployment for Spanish-surnamed males was at 8.5 percent of the workforce compared to 4.5 percent for Anglos. In some states such as New Mexico and Texas, unemployment was as high as three times the rate for Anglos. Sixty percent of those working were employed in manual labor occupations. Twenty percent of Spanish-surnamed families lived below the poverty line.

Today, unemployment for Spanish-surnamed males is even worse at 9.2 percent compared to 4.3 percent for Anglos. The per-capita income for Latinos is still half that of Anglos, and now 26 percent of the national Latino population lives below the poverty line of $12,000 a year for a family of four. More than before, under-employment in marginal jobs has surfaced as a recurring phenomenon. Often, men and women hold down more than one job to make ends meet.

In 1968, when high school students defiantly walked out of the four East Los Angeles high schools to protest inferior education, the national dropout rate among Spanish-surnamed youth was 30 percent and reached as high as 50 percent in some schools with large Mexican-American populations.

Today, there are more Latino teachers and counselors than ever before and even Latinos on boards of education. But, while the dropout rate at the four East Los Angeles high schools may have diminished, the national Latino dropout rate has remained at about 30 percent for the past three decades. It peaked at 40 percent in 1992 (nationally, 40 percent of the Latino children who entered elementary school dropped out before they could reach the 12th grade in 1992).

In 1967, when Tijerina launched his celebrated courthouse raid to reclaim land originally deeded to Mexican-American families of New Mexico, 30 percent of all Chicano families lived in deteriorated housing and 53 percent of Mexican Americans owned their own homes. Today, the land grants movement, for all practical purposes, is dead.

Nationally, 48 percent of Latinos own their own homes (though a smaller percentage, in actual numbers it is much more than ever before). But a new Latino underclass, made up largely of immigrants, continues to live in dilapidated and overcrowded housing, particularly in urban areas.

In 1969, the U.S. Commission on Civil Rights reported that there were "widespread patterns of police misconduct against Mexican Americans," including police violence, discriminatory law enforcement, and excessive arrests, resulting in a disproportionate number of Chicanos in jails and prisons.

Police brutality against Latinos continues. The Los Angeles Rampart Division Police Station scandal, which compromised dozens of criminal convictions achieved through officers' perjured testimony, underscores continued abuse against Latinos. They are the primary victims of the scandal's verified instances of beatings, illegal shootings, planting of false evidence, and framing of innocent people. Rather than protest these abuses, Latino elected officials have come to the defense of the police, stubbornly clinging to the myth that such cases are isolated.

California's three-strike law, mandating twenty-five-years-to-life sentences for individuals with three felony convictions, has a disproportionate impact on Latino and African-American youth who, because of felonious barrio drug abuse, are most likely to fall under its jurisdiction. This has resulted in what Elizabeth "Betita" Martínez has labeled the "criminalization of Latino youth."

When Ricardo Sánchez sat in his cell at the state correctional facility in Huntsville, Texas, Spanish-surnamed inmates made up 17 percent of the Texas inmate population. Today that number has risen to 26 percent. In 1970, when I filmed inside the walls of Soledad Prison, Chicanos and other Latinos made up approximately 16 percent of the California prison population. Now they make up 34 percent of the statewide prison population. While this increase can be explained, in part, by the boom in the state's Latino population, the numbers are still disproportionately high. In the 1960s and 1970s, Chicano activism was alive and well in the prison system with such self-help groups as the Grupo Educacional Mexicano Americano (GEMA). Now, these self-help groups founded on the *Plan de Aztlán* have been replaced by the pervasive presence of the Mexican Mafia, peddling drugs and promoting violence both inside and outside prison walls.

There are more gangs, gang members, and gang crime in the Southwest barrios than ever before. The severity of violence has also escalated. In the 1960s, gang "warfare" consisted largely of fist fights; when weapons were used, they were usually knives or crudely fashioned zip-guns. Today's gang arsenals include sawed-off shotguns, uzi machine guns, and AK 47 semi-automatic rifles. Drug abuse, always present in the barrio, has become rampant in recent years. Here, too, the stakes have risen. In the 1960s, Chicano youth smoked pot, popped uppers and downers (amphetamine and seconal), and an occasional acid tab. Today's youths are hooked on the more deadly crack cocaine and PCP, and have lifelong addictions to heroin.

The continued second-class citizenship of Latinos is clearly seen in the field of television and film production. In 1970, at the time I produced the three-part *IMAGE* study of Mexican Americans and Latinos in the motion picture industry, there was only one program on the air with a Latino theme, *Chico and the Man*. At the time, less than one half of a percent of television programs and motion pictures were directed by Latinos, less than one half of a percent of the screenplays were written by Latinos, and Latino actors comprised less than 3 percent of screen roles. We were hardly a blip on the radar screen.

At this writing, there are only two Latino-themed programs on American television, *Resurrection Boulevard* and *The Brothers García*, in spite of the fact that Latinos are now 12 percent of the national population and comprise 44 percent of the Los Angeles/Hollywood population, where much of American television is produced. Today, Latinos direct only 2 percent of American films and television, Latino writers pen 1 percent of the screenplays, and Latino actors account for only 3.5 percent of the acting roles. I am one of only a handful of fortunate Latinos who can claim regular employment in the industry. At the start of this new century, network executives have promised improvements, but if history is any judge, these are likely to be empty promises.

In society as a whole, there are some signs that progress has been made. Many of the Chicanos who comprised the underclass at the time of the *movimiento* have taken advantage of enhanced economic opportunities created by that social movement and have become successful in education, politics, business and the law. The so-called "Hispanic Market" has been identified as a booming economic opportunity, not just for mainstream entrepreneurs, but also for the growing number of "Hispanic" business enterprises. Spanish-surnamed Americans spend $383 billion dollars a year. For an emerging class of Latino businessmen, this had been a goldmine.

Better then or now? The report card is mixed. While an emerging Latino middle class of both native-born and immigrant Latinos can be identified with such markers as median incomes of $50,000 or more annually, and increased home ownership, a larger number of Latinos, in both real numbers and percentages, are to be found at subsistence blue collar and poverty levels. Many of these people are immigrants from Mexico and Central America, who now comprise the underclass previously occupied by United States-born Mexican Americans. There continue to be waves of immigrants fueled, in part, by U.S. economic and foreign policies. But it's not just an issue of immigrants. Latino families who have been here for generations are still battling poverty and subjugation.

It would appear that whether one thinks that things have gotten better or worse depends on whether one is part of a small emerging Latino middle class, or part of the much larger population of Latinos who find themselves in abject poverty with its attendant high unemployment, high crime rate, poor housing, poor health care, and institutional discrimination. Sadly, thirty years after the Chicano Movement, the conditions of inequality and discrimination that provoked the movement remain. Is there anything that we can learn from the experience of the Chicano Movement to aid in this continuing struggle?

Identity

When Chicanos embraced the nationalist *Plan de Aztlán,* they did so for a variety of reasons. One of these was the need to feel pride in one's heritage, to reject the notion of Mexican Americans being "culturally disadvantaged." Our *Chicanismo,* rooted in our Indian heritage, was not just a political strategy for group empowerment or a tactic to achieve social justice; it was also a movement of ethnic self-affirmation. *Chicanismo* replaced a sense of inferiority with a sense of empowerment, self-hatred with pride, nihilism with hope, aimlessness with purpose. For many of us, it became a major element in our lives, embodying an entire set of ethical and ideological principles.

In spite of the limitations of cultural nationalism, without a sense of identity, I, and many of my generation, would not have had the sense of purpose and self-worth to compete effectively in American society. *Indigenismo*, the embracing of an indigenous identity, has less to do with any innate merit in being Indian, than with the concept of accepting yourself for who you are. The lesson we learned from *indigenismo* is that all people should be respected for their humanity. All people have something in their heritage of which they can be proud, and this sense of self-worth can be empowering and fulfilling. This is a truth to be learned by Americans of all races.

Today, Mexican-American youth can benefit from the *indigenismo* of the 1960s. Instead of succumbing to vapid seductions of becoming amorphous, media-manipulated, consumer-oriented Hispanics or Latinos, Mexican Americans can claim their Indian heritage and take pride in it. We can link with other native peoples of the Americas to address the pressing social issues in our communities that continue to exist. However, embracing our heritage should be done with caution. We must not repeat the mistake of making a cult of our indigenous identity, or waiting for "pie in the sky" solutions to our earthly problems. Rather, we must use it to empower ourselves to confront the economic, political, and social issues still facing *La Raza*.

We need only look to the experience in the southern Mexican state of Chiapas, to the Ejército Zapatista de Liberación Nacional (EZLN), to see how a sense of indigenous identity can be focused for political and social change. Significantly, the Zapatista movement has also shown us that we must avail ourselves of modern technology. In 1999, the Rand Corporation undertook a study of the Zapatista revolutionary struggle and concluded that without its strategic use of the Internet, the Zapatista revolt might have been easily quashed by the Mexican military. It was the outreach to sympathetic groups via the Internet, what the study called the "War of the Networks," that summoned worldwide attention to the indigenous cause. Today's Chicano and Latino activists can learn from this example. We must not be fearful of utilizing the latest technology to advance the cause of social justice and to affirm our unique identity.

However, to remain fixated on our ethnic identity without any further expansion of our social thinking is to fall into the narcissistic trap of identity politics, a political approach that says, "I got mine, so why should I care about anyone else?" Identity must not become an end. It must be an empowering experience that motivates struggle. We must expand the borders of our thinking and link our social and political efforts to those of other disenfranchised groups in the United States.

The Work Ahead

The demise of La Raza Unida Party confirms the limited nature of the extreme cultural nationalism called for by the *Plan de Aztlán*. This is not because it was unable to attract and mobilize large numbers. It was because of its inability to confront successfully issues of a mixed constituency. Because of the multi-ethnic make-up of the United States, an electoral program geared only to one racial group is doomed in America in all but the most parochial situations. So too, historically, are attempts at third political parties. But this is not to say that the harnessing of America's vast Chicano, Puerto Rican, Cuban American, and Central American populations envisioned by La Raza Unida isn't a possibility. Indeed, in many ways the goals set down by La Raza Unida have been partially accomplished: enormous strides have been made in voter registration and the election of Latino officials at all levels of government.

It can be argued that an increased Latino presence in the educational, political, and criminal justice systems is the lasting legacy of the Chicano Movement. This is, in part, true. Yet this recognition surfaces an apparent contradiction. What are we to make of the fact that we have more Latino teachers, counselors, and principals in many schools with predominant Latino populations, and yet see continued high dropout rates? How do we reconcile the plethora of elected Latino officials at all levels (city, county, state, and national) with the dismal economic, health, and crime conditions that still haunt the barrio? How do we explain the increased numbers of Latino police and law enforcement officers, as in the LAPD Rampart Division, with an increase in Latino prison population and the continued instances of police brutality?

In the early days of the *movimiento*, we held the naive assumption that if we replaced white people in power, many of whom were racist, with Chicanos, this would automatically bring about improved social conditions. What we have learned in the interim is that unless the core social institutions in which these people work are fundamentally changed, conditions will remain the same. This is clearly the reality behind the contradictions we have noted.

Until barrio poverty is eradicated, well-meaning Latino teachers and counselors at our schools will continue to be deluged with problems beyond the scope of their control and will only minimally affect the high dropout rate and the proliferation of gangs, drugs, and crime.

Many Latino politicians have become what Dr. Rodolfo Acuña calls "power brokers," leaders who speak for the community without achieving any significant gains for that community. As long as politicians are not held accountable to their electorates but rather to high-finance campaign contributors, their desire to remain in office will dictate legislative and administrative priorities. Passage of a subsidy for the builders of the new shopping mall, for example, will overshadow passage of a tax to create the new anti-gang after-school program.

Until our law enforcement agencies are overseen by effective civilian review boards, the police will continue to police themselves. Officers like Raphael Pérez, the man who ignited the Rampart police scandal when he agreed to testify against fellow abusive officers as part of a deal to lighten his own sentence, will continue to feel they can break the law as long as they limit their abuses to impoverished Latinos and African Americans.

The lesson of the Chicano Movement for today's generation of activists is, in part, that progress can be achieved, but that merely to get Latinos in positions of power—school teachers, city administrators, state officials, or national politicians—will not guarantee positive social change. Latinos, too, are human—they make mistakes; they forget; they make deals. We must hold our elected officials up to public scrutiny and demand accountability. If necessary, this may mean public protests—whatever it takes to make certain that these elected Latino officials respond to the concerns of our community. On the other hand, those teachers, scholars, politicians, city, state and federal officials who carry on the struggle in a positive way must be rewarded with our support.

In the final analysis, our Latino leaders live and work within a pseudo-democratic political system, whose parameters are defined by a capitalist economy. Until this reality is changed, we cannot expect an equitable, democratic society for all Americans.

Tactics

Without a doubt, elements within the Chicano Movement that espoused violence or were perceived of as a physical threat to the United States and its institutions were met with direct violent persecution. The attacks on the Brown Berets, the 1970 Chicano Moratorium, and the attack on the Crusade for Justice are only three examples of this kind of brutal police repression. In other cases, activism was undermined through political infiltration and agent-provocateurs. One thing we can learn from the experience of the *movimiento* is that public posturing of violence is a sure way to destroy an organization—and any chance at social change.

The verdict is still out on the best way to organize the masses of people required to bring about lasting social change. On the one hand, one might argue that the public call to arms on key social issues can be achieved more effectively by using today's Internet and other modern technologies. On the other hand, it can be argued that there is nothing more inspiring and empowering than to see hundreds of people marching arm in arm with a common vision and a righteous goal.

Prudent tactical planning for effective social change requires that we keep all options open, including street demonstrations and civil disobedience, but certainly that we also utilize all the modern technologies at our disposal. Today's activists must conform their tactics to the new realities and find opportunities to fight for a better, more humane and compassionate world.

In so doing, Latino activists must expand their vision of struggle beyond *La Raza*. We must join with Americans of all races who are committed to transforming this nation into one that will fulfill the American promise of social justice, equality, and prosperity for all of its citizens. Is this possible? I think it is, and I look to recent examples on the American landscape for inspiration.

In 1999, multi-ethnic students at the University of California at Berkeley undertook a hunger strike to protest cutbacks in ethnic studies programs and faculty. This and other protest actions resulted in a new commitment by university officials to increase ethnic studies faculty and courses—one of the hard-fought victories of the sixties. Also in 1999, Americans in the labor, ecology, civil rights, gay, and ethnic movements joined forces to protest the globalization dictates of the World Trade Organization in the historic so-called "Battle in Seattle." Nationally, African-American organizations such as the NAACP and Latino organizations such as National Council for La Raza and the National Hispanic Media Coalition, joined forces to take American television producers to task, demanding more presence of all minorities on American television. In each of these instances, Americans of different races have pulled together in coalitions to affirm the principles of justice and equality and have said "no" to the premise that the present system is cast in stone. As in the 1960s, young people have been in the forefront of these struggles.

American Me

Perhaps the most difficult lesson for me to accept has been that of reconciling myself to being an American citizen, despite my having been born in the United States. In the most strident moments of my activism, I hated the United States with a passion for the crimes perpetrated against my people. I wanted to have nothing to do with this country and everything to do with helping to bring down its racist institutions. Today, I believe that as a Chicano and as an American, I must do more than merely criticize our society. I have a responsibility to work to transform it.

The simplistic perceptions I once held, that the United States was made up of oppressed minorities (the good people) pitted against Anglos with ingrained racism (the bad people), has been replaced by a more mature appreciation of the complex nature of the United States and its institutions.

The American capitalist system, over time, has empowered a small group of wealthy people to benefit from the sweat and labor of the much larger population of poor and working-class people of all races. The system creates enough opportunity for a middle class to emerge, thus safeguarding societal stability, while ultimately serving the ends of a class of wealthy individuals and ignoring the needs of the majority of Americans.

It is a fact; it cannot be rationalized away.

The result has been the creation and perpetuation of governmental, civic, and social institutions that are riddled with racism, discrimination, and injustice. An unavoidable outcome of this economic system has been the creation and maintenance of an underclass of impoverished Americans. But it doesn't have to be that way. I don't think it's pollyannaish to believe that these institutions, and the capitalist infrastructure of which they are a part, can and must ultimately be transformed.

These changes will not happen overnight and will not necessarily be accomplished in the leaps and bounds that characterized the sixties. Chicanos and other Latinos, as American citizens, must be a part of this effort to transform the United States into a better nation. We must do so in spite of media propaganda that would persuade us that we are powerless, in spite of the racism that would pit us against poor whites, African Americans, and other disenfranchised groups, and in spite of popular cynicism that would convince us that the future is foredoomed.

I believe that Latinos can play a major role in this national transformation. I look to our demographics for support. By the year 2005, Spanish-surnamed people will comprise the largest minority in the United States. According to the United States Census, by the year 2050, one in every four Americans will be Spanish-surnamed! The majority of these people will be of Mexican descent.

What we do with this sizeable presence in the United States is what is at stake for the next fifty years. Will we allow ourselves to become the pliable, exploitable workforce for the burgeoning capitalist expansion known as globalization? Will we allow our culture and language to be stripped from us in a vain effort to make us more "American," to accommodate some product merchandiser's idea of what we should buy, wear, and consume? Will we allow fearful, xenophobic Americans to seek passage of English-only laws and create new legislative propositions designed to curtail our freedoms? Or will we, instead, take a stand to affirm our identity as unique Americans with our own distinct culture and language, who demand respect, equality, and justice? One need only look to our northern neighbor, Canada, and the success of the Quebecois movement, to know that in numbers there is strength. By the year 2050, we will certainly have the numbers. But it isn't only about that. It is also about who we are, who we want to be, and about the kind of world we want to live in.

The prospects for the future are, still, very much in our hands. We must look at the glass as half full and not half empty. The society we live in is not cast in stone; it is not immutable. Men and women created the social world we live in, and men and women can also transform and improve that world. All of us must be prepared to struggle to create a better nation.

Perhaps the final lesson to be gleaned from the Chicano Movement is that when masses of people are organized and united, empowered by a passion for justice and social equality, they can transform society and bring about positive change. We can succeed. We've done it before. We can do it again. *Sí, se puede.*